Successful Prevent
Youth Development Programs
Across Borders

Successful Prevention and Youth Development Programs
Across Borders

Laura Ferrer-Wreder
The Pennsylvania State University—Capital College
Middletown, Pennsylvania

Håkan Stattin
Örebro University
Örebro, Sweden

Carolyn Cass Lorente
George Washington University
Washington, D.C.

Jonathan G. Tubman
Florida International University
Miami, Florida

Lena Adamson
Swedish National Board of Health and Welfare
Stockholm, Sweden

Springer-Science+Business Media, LLC

Library of Congress Cataloging-in-Publication Data

ISBN 978-1-4613-4800-9   ISBN 978-1-4419-9120-1 (eBook)
DOI 10.1007/978-1-4419-9120-1

©2004 Springer Science+Business Media New York
Originally published by Kluwer Academic / Plenum Publishers, New York in 2004
Softcover reprint of the hardcover 1st edition 2004

10 9 8 7 6 5 4 3 2 1

A C.I.P. record for this book is available from the Library of Congress

The Swedish National Board of Health and Welfare, Centre for Evaluation of Social Services, and the Swedish National Board of Institutional Care provided the impetus and financial sponsorship for the writing of this book. The authors gratefully acknowledge their contribution.

Preface

From a European Perspective

This book charts territory that is profoundly important, and yet rarely fully understood. The authors have attempted a task that has relevance to the widest possible range of professionals working with children and adolescents. In describing and assessing the fields prevention and promotion they have performed an immense service to researchers in this field, but also to practitioners across the spectrum, from mental health nurses and doctors to teachers and psychologists, from social work professionals to psychiatrists and youth counselors. There are two other key elements that should be emphasized from the outset. The first is that the approach in this book is truly multi-disciplinary, with the authors making a genuine attempt to draw upon knowledge and practice derived from all the relevant disciplines. The second element which makes this book so important is that the authors have worked across countries, to ensure that work in the field of intervention from both North America and from Europe should be included. This is as welcome as it is refreshing. There appear to be so many barriers to true collaboration between the two continents, and so many examples of either North American or European social scientists appearing blind to what is going on "across the border" that the approach taken here should be wholeheartedly commended.

This book is essentially a review, but a rather special review. It takes as its subject programmes of intervention that are aimed at either promoting youth development, or at ameliorating the long-term consequences of problem behaviours in young people. Of course there are many thousands of such programmes across all of North America and Europe, but this book has used two other criteria upon which to base the selection of programmes. First, programmes are only included if they have been scientifically evaluated. A second criterion, although one that is less rigorously adhered to, is that the authors have preferred to include those programmes that have involved the participants in the design, implementation and maintenance of intervention programmes. These organizing principles have produced, after enormous hard work and amazing perseverance by the authors, a book which will undoubtedly prove to be a landmark text in its field.

What of the achievements of the book? To my knowledge no other book has attempted such a complex and difficult task, taking into account prevention and promotion in the widest possible sense. This book includes programmes across the age range, from pre-schoolers to older adolescents. It covers interventions in the family, in the school, and in the community. Not only that, it has excellent chapters to start and end with, both of which serve as models of their kind in providing a synthesis and critical analysis of the design and implementation of intervention programmes in different social and political settings. Finally it also includes a resource guide at the end, making it an invaluable tool for any social scientist or practitioner wishing to undertake interventions with children or adolescents.

I wish this book every success. It should be required reading for anyone concerned with the emotional health and well-being of young people. The authors are to be congratulated on their achievement, and I am proud to have been associated with this endeavour.

John Coleman, OBE, Ph.D., FBPsS
Director, Trust for the Study of Adolescence

From an American Perspective

There has been growing concern in most Western societies as increasing numbers of children and adolescents are having difficulty managing the challenges of development. The rate of societal change, both economic and social, and the rising demands of modern society have created ongoing pressures on families, neighborhoods, schools, communities, and nations. During the past decade researchers across North America and Europe have turned their attention to understanding these changes and developing programs and evaluating policies to both prevent youth problems as well as promoting healthy youth development. As a result, there is now a corpus of research findings indicating that such programs and policies can effectively reduce mental disorders and problem behaviors and promote youth competence.

Successful Prevention and Youth Development Programs: Across Borders is an important compilation of the newest and most exciting work in field of prevention science. Aptly titled, a unique aspect of this volume is its integration of research across trans-Atlantic borders. Written collaboratively by American and Swedish researchers, this volume clearly illustrates the need for more international communication and collaboration in further developing prevention theories, models, programs, and policies. A valuable contribution is made by directly addressing the issues of culture and cultural adaptation of programs as well as the potential benefit of further cross-cultural collaboration. North Americans researchers will find this book especially valuable, as we are often unaware of exciting innovations in European communities. Ferrer-Wreder and her colleagues' *Successful Prevention and*

Youth Development Programs: Across Borders fills a substantial gap for students, researchers, and policy-makers both by providing a timely review of findings in the field, as well as providing a primer in the conceptual foundations and future directions of prevention science.

Mark T. Greenberg Ph.D., Bennett Chair of Prevention Research,
Director of the Prevention Research Center and Associate Director, Child,
Youth and Families Consortium, The Pennsylvania State University

Acknowledgements

We acknowledge the many colleagues who shared their comments, expertise, and time with us. Thanks also go to the Swedish National Board of Health and Welfare, Centre for Evaluation of Social Services and the Swedish National Board of Institutional Care for its sponsorship of this project. We thank Bill Tucker at Kluwer/Plenum for his vision and encouragement. For personal acknowledgements, Laura especially thanks Richard, the Ferrer and Wreder families for their love and support. She also recognizes important financial support from the National Science Foundation (Grant Number INT-9901348) and the U.S. National Institutes of Health Minority Access to Research Careers Program. Carolyn wishes to thank Rafael for his consistent support (and his many edits of this book), her family for their value of love and scholarship, the students and youth who continue to inspire her, and Rebecca and Camille, her young teachers to the world. Jon would like to acknowledge the patient support of his partner Thomas W. Seiler.

Disclaimer

This book was originally commissioned by the Swedish National Board of Health and Welfare, Centre for Evaluation of Social Services and the Swedish National Board of Institutional Care. Opinions stated are the authors and do not necessarily reflect the endorsement or official policy of the Swedish government or any other entity.

Contents

Contents

LIST OF FIGURES

INDEX

Part I
Introduction

Chapter 1
Overview

Purpose

An attempt has been made by the authors to locate[1] American and European **interventions** that have ameliorated youth **problem behaviors** and/or promoted youth development under adequate testing conditions[2]. What follows is a concerted effort to describe a sample of useful programs tested in the United States and Europe. Programs from the member states of the European Union, post-Soviet nations, and countries bordering Europe, as well as the United States and Canada are described. Given that American programs largely characterize the intervention research literature, steps were taken to seek out and consolidate knowledge on empirically strong European programs. Emphasis is also placed on the identification of interventions conducted and/or tested on a **cross-national** scale. The focused and in-depth approach used in this text will hopefully impart useful information to those individuals across the globe who are interested in the interplay between context, culture, and successful prevention and **youth development programs**.

Book Organization

This book is divided into three parts: 1) introduction, 2) review, and 3) resource guide. Part I – Introduction is made of one chapter. In this chapter, an organizational outline of the book is presented. This chapter ends with an analysis of selected topics, principles, and debates within the prevention and youth development literatures. Part II – Review is made up of six chapters. Chapters two through six provide examples of good prevention practice in family, school, and community contexts. Interventions can be accurately described in a number of ways depending on one's aim (c.f. *Relevant Narrative Reviews* – Catalano, et al., 1999; Durlak, 1997; Flay, 2000; Gullotta & Bloom, 2003; Hawkins, Farrington, & Catalano, 1998; Holder, 2000; Schinke, Brounstein, & Gardner, 2002; Sherman, et al., 1997; Weissberg & Greenberg, 1998). Because a central purpose of this review is to provide the reader with clear examples of good prevention practice in family, school, and community contexts, interventions are organized first and foremost by the context of intervention. Other elements that weighed heavily in the organization of programs included the developmental level and risk

1

status of program participants, the nature of the intervention actions taken, and **spreading-specific program effects**. Chapters two through six also contain a **best evidence syntheses** of salient research literatures and a consideration of questions relevant to prevention and promotion work in each setting. Existing narrative and **meta-analytic reviews** of the literature guided the authors' best evidence syntheses of the status of intervention research in selected areas[3]. Because **cross context interventions** frequently embody the state-of-the-science in terms of reducing youth problem behaviors and promoting positive development, a review of these programs is integrated into the chapters. Chapter seven summarizes the findings of an interview study with program developers and implementers who have taken part in cross-national intervention trials. The chapter addresses intervention design and implementation issues across borders – national, cultural, ethnic, disciplinary, and professional. Part III – Resource Guide consists of three chapters: 1) the glossary, 2) program examples, and 3) web resources. Chapter eight – The Glossary contains a description of key terms are **bolded** the first time they appear in the text. The glossary is meant to give an explanation of how the authors thought about and utilized these underlined words. The program summaries contained in chapter nine – Program Examples provide a level of detail not usually possible in traditional reviews of the literature. The summaries also present readers with a road map for the development of intervention programs and policies. Chapter ten – Web Resources is intended to give the reader the tools to explore the most current intervention-related literature. Both chapters nine and ten are designed to help to further independent analysis of the research literature.

Key Ideas in the Prevention and Youth Development Field

Prevention, Promotion, and Youth Development

Prevention is by definition proactive. A central goal of prevention is to act now as a safeguard against undesirable future consequences and to encourage a positive tomorrow. As Bloom and Gullotta (2003) noted, a positive form of the word prevent is to promote. Promotion, which includes efforts to advance positive youth development, implies a positive bent that focuses on wellness and the optimization of developmental assets or strengths. "Promotion is a positive activity in its own right, and is not simply a reduction of risk for illness" (Bloom & Gullotta, 2003, p. 13). The terms prevention and promotion may ultimately involve different processes (Silverman, 2003). Yet, there is evidence to suggest that such processes are not in all instances unrelated (e.g., Leffert, et al. 1998). While prevention has historically done a better job of addressing   disease   and   social   problems   (Bingenheimer,   Repetto,

Zimmerman, & Kelly, 2003), prevention and promotion can both be viewed as opportunities to establish boundaries for change or plasticity across the lifespan, as well as occasions to better understand human development in its positive and negative forms.

Contemporary prevention and promotion work shares the common purpose of generating the theory and methods needed to create change that yields concrete and enduring benefits in the lives of people (Catalano, Berglund, Ryan, Lonczak, & Hawkins, 1999; Coie, et al., 1993; Greenberg, Domitrovich, & Bumbarger, 1999; 2001). Scientists and practitioners from a diversity of perspectives are increasingly finding that a prevention and/or promotion framework provides a useful way to think about and further their own day-to-day work. Theory and evidence from a number of fields have come together to support present-day prevention and promotion efforts. Relevant fields include: Anthropology, clinical psychology, community psychology, criminal justice, economics, education, epidemiology, developmental psychopathology, life span developmental psychology, public health, social work, sociology, and statistics. The scope of this multidisciplinary work is broad, with relevance to the areas of normal and abnormal behavior as well as physical and mental health.

Classification Systems for Prevention, Promotion, and Treatment

An important consideration in intervention research is the amount of protection or risk experienced by a given person or population. The amount of risk and protection usually determines the type of intervention used as well as the outcomes evaluated. There is considerable debate about how to best categorize prevention and promotion programs (c.f. Bloom & Gullotta, 2003; Durlak, 1997; Mrazek & Haggerty, 1994; Silverman, 2003). Until recently, most prevention programs were described with the terms primary, secondary, and tertiary. This terminology is tied to the public health tradition and has at its core the goal of reducing diagnosable physical diseases (Mrazek & Haggerty, 1994). Specifically, these terms have been defined as follows:

> Primary prevention seeks to decrease the number of new cases of a disorder or illness (incidence). Secondary prevention seeks to lower the rate of established cases of the disorder or illness in the population (prevalence). Tertiary prevention seeks to decrease the amount of disability associated with an existing disorder or illness. (Mrazek & Haggerty, 1994, p. 19-20)

In 1994, the Institute of Medicine (IOM) produced a report that was one of several catalysts that prompted a reconsideration of prevention terminology in the United States. The IOM is a part of U.S. National Academy of Sciences. The U.S. government founded the National Academy to serve as a consultant on science and technology. The National Academy and the IOM function as non-government organizations. The IOM is commissioned periodically by U.S. federal government to undertake studies on health matters. The editors of the 1994 IOM report, P. J. Mrazek and R. J. Haggerty, presented an in depth treatment of intervention classification terminology as it related to the prevention of mental health difficulties.

The editors of the IOM report (Mrazek & Haggerty, 1994) supported the adoption of the words **universal, selective, and indicated prevention** in order to clarify the prevention classification system in ways that are consistent with the current state of knowledge on mental health disorders including risk-and-protective-factor models drawn from the field of developmental psychopathology. The universal, selective, and indicated classification system has also been used to describe prevention programs that deal with youth problem behaviors (e.g., Weissberg & Greenberg, 1998) and the promotion of positive youth development (e.g., Catalano, et al., 1999).

In the IOM report (Mrazek & Haggerty, 1994), universal prevention was defined as an intervention that does not emphasize the difference between higher and lower-risk groups. No individual or group is singled out for any reason. The intervention is thought to have a beneficial function for all individuals irregardless of the amount of risk they experience. Thus, one of the main jobs of the universal prevention is to turn away from an exclusive focus on risk and direct the bulk of intervention efforts towards the promotion of positive forms of development. An important outcome in these types of programs includes maximizing a young person's protection against adversity (c.f., *Program Example* – Klepp, Tell, & Vellar, 1993).

In the IOM report (Mrazek & Haggerty, 1994), promotion was separated from prevention. That is, universal prevention, which seeks to decrease risk and increase protection in the service of preventing a mental illness was differentiated from mental health promotion, which aims to promote wellness. In an investigation of the research literature, Catalano and colleagues (1999) found that **youth development programs** could be characterized by their focus on the promotion of the following qualities in youngsters: bonding, **resilience**, a wide range of life competencies, self-determination, spirituality, self-efficacy, a clear and positive identity, belief in the future, recognition for positive behaviors and opportunities for prosocial involvement, and prosocial norms. At present, there seems to be a thin conceptual line between universal prevention and youth development programs (Weissberg & Greenberg, 1998). It can be argued that this definitional obscurity stems from the under investigation of positive forms of development in comparison to maladjustment.

Many social institutions and scientific disciplines are expressly geared towards the resolution of problems. In many cases, this focus is justifiable and certainly necessary. However, risks and protections are often experienced together (Jessor, 1998). Advances in basic and applied research efforts promise to yield a wider range of tools available for the improved description of positive processes and the interaction between risk and protection across the lifespan (Catalano, et al., 1999; Lerner, Anderson, Balsano, Dowling, & Bobek, 2003).

In the IOM report (Mrazek & Haggerty, 1994), selective prevention was defined by its focus on subgroups within the general population that experience known **risk factors**. As in universal prevention, no individual is identified on the basis of risk. In selective prevention, the subgroup is identified as being at-risk not the individual. A main goal of the selective program is to divert individuals within the identified subgroup away from chronic and heightened lives of maladjustment. Key outcomes in this type of program include changes in risk-**protective factors** and early problem behavior patterns (c.f. *Program Example* – Olds, 2002).

In the IOM report (Mrazek & Haggerty, 1994), indicated prevention involves the identification of at-risk individuals. The indicated program makes a further distinction between at-risk subgroups and those who have been individually identified as at-risk for chronic and severe problem behavior. The distinction between universal and selective versus indicated prevention can be described this way:

> A critical component of universal and selective preventive interventions is that although some members of the group may have mental disorders when the intervention begins, this information is not relevant to the choice of the targeted groups. If individuals are chosen for a preventive intervention because of early psychological symptoms, by definition the intervention is an indicated one. (Mrazek & Haggerty, 1994, p. 26)

The goal of indicated prevention, like universal and selective prevention, is still to reduce the incidence or the number of new cases of significant social problems or mental illness[4]. The only difference is that indicated programs are based on the identification of the individual. When the prevention of problem behaviors is the goal, youth in indicated programs often have had some form of social welfare or juvenile justice system contact. In this case, outcomes can be measured in terms of reduced institutional contacts such as lower rates of reoffending (c.f. *Program Example* – Alexander, et. al., 1998).

In the IOM report (Mrazek & Haggerty, 1994), there is a clear distinction between indicated prevention and **treatment**. Treatment is given to those who meet a preset threshold of diagnostic criteria for a known mental disorder. Applying a prevention–treatment diagnostic cut off system with socially defined problem behaviors is admittedly somewhat of a shakier but perhaps still workable proposition. In the prevention of youth problem behaviors, a main idea is to guide **young people** away from life paths that are likely to lead them towards future adjustment difficulties like chronic unemployment, entry into the adult criminal justice system, mental and physical disease. Once the young person has entered into certain social institutions, such as an adult prison, a drug rehabilitation center and/or a recognized disease state, then it seems reasonable to consider that individual as being in need of treatment, with the idea of rehabilitation taking on its traditional meaning and importance.

Why would it be desirable to have an agreed upon intervention classification system? In program evaluation studies, it is not uncommon to find that an intervention's program benefits differ and depend on characteristics of program participants (c.f. *Program Examples* – Loveland-Cherry, et al., 1999; Perry, et al., 1996). So it is a worthwhile endeavor to understand the benefits of programs for various populations, subgroups, and individuals. To do so, we must continue to develop clear methods for selecting and describing program participants[5].

Problem Behaviors

Problem behaviors, for young people, are typically grouped into the following domains: a) violence and criminality, b) substance use and abuse, c) teen pregnancy and risky sexual behaviors, and d) school failure (Jessor, 1998). Links between problem behaviors, mental, and physical disease have been identified by researchers (e.g., Huizinga, Loeber, Thornberry, & Cothern, 2000, November; Schinke et al., 2002). Yet, problem behaviors in and of themselves are not necessarily pathological behaviors that fit neatly within a disease paradigm. Problem behaviors are inherently social in that they have been defined as undesirable by the mainstream culture of a given society (Jessor, 1998). In many cultures, the societal stance taken on problem behaviors among young people is not arbitrary and does have some scientific support. Prevailing evidence on the subject shows that the accumulation of certain youth problem behaviors carries considerable weight in the prediction of adult adjustment (Dryfoos, 1991; Jessor, 1998; Jessor & Jessor, 1977). Problem behaviors are therefore legitimate targets for change not only because they present societies with real time negative consequences but also can cause future harm.

Interventions can be designed to address a single problem behavior such as a drug or violence prevention program. On some occasions, prevention and promotion programs have yielded a wide range of benefits that spill over into different areas of functioning and adjustment (c.f.

Program Example – Olds, 2002). Because problem behaviors tend to co-occur (Jessor, 1998), it is not difficult to imagine that an intervention designed to address a specific problem behavior such as substance use may also have the potential to significantly impact a configuration of problem behaviors in a given sample, even though the intervention was not specifically designed to produce such changes. Contemporary thinking in the prevention and promotion fields is that noncategorical interventions have a stronger scientific footing in the developmental research literature and are a potentially more efficient use of social resources (Catalano, Hawkins, Berglund, Pollard, & Arthur, 2002).

Risk-Protective Factors and Resilience

There is a growing body of scientific evidence that helps to shed light on the different configurations of risk and protection that would make a young person more or less likely to engage in problem behaviors (e.g., Derzon & Lipsey, 1999; Durlak, 1998; Herrenkohl, 2000; Huizinga, et al., 2000, November; Lipsey & Derzon, 1998; Rhodes, et al., 1997; Schinke, et al., 2002; Spooner, 1999). A great deal of attention has been directed towards investigating the risks that can threaten the development of young people. Risk factors can be found within (individual attributes) and outside (environmental contexts) of the individual. The specific risks that can endanger youth development may take a variety of forms including family dysfunction and disempowerment, school and community disorganization, and exposure to pervasive violence and substance abuse within family, school, and community contexts (Hawkins, Herrenkohl, et al., 1998; Jessor, 1998). As these risks accumulate, the individual is placed in increased danger of escalated involvement in problem behaviors and experiencing adjustment difficulties in adulthood.

As we have come to learn more about risk, an emphasis has been placed on better understanding those individuals who thrive in the context of adversity (Catalano, et al., 1999; Davis, 1999). Unlike risk factors, protective factors can bolster the chances that a young person will not experience significant problem behaviors and adult adjustment difficulties. Protective attributes and contexts are thought to act in multiple ways (Coie, et al., 1993; Luthar, 1993; Luthar & Cicchetti, 2000; Rutter, 2000). Greenberg and colleagues (2001) summed it up as follows:

> Coie et al (1993) suggested that protective factors may work in one or more of the following four ways: directly decrease dysfunction; interact with risk factors to buffer their effects; disrupt the mediational chain by which risk leads to disorder; or prevent the initial occurrence of risk factors. (p. 5)

For example, protective factors in their buffering capacity can serve as a shield against the consequences of risk. Improvements in the use of cognitive and social skills do not necessarily take away a child's risky home environment but such protective attributes can help the young person adapt to and capitalize on opportunities within challenging life contexts.

An important and related idea is the concept of resilience. When an individual is able to maintain a normative or high level of functioning when confronted with a developmental challenge or time-limited stressor this ability is often called resilience (Luthar, 1993; Rutter, 1987; 1989; Werner, 2000). Rather than implying a predetermined trait-like invincibility within the individual, the concept of resilience suggests that a subset of young people, in spite of seemingly severe experiences of adversity or high levels of risk, exhibit competent or even exemplary functioning. This positive adaptation or other evidence of high quality developmental outcomes in the presence of ongoing risk is a hallmark of resilience (Luthar & Cicchetti, 2000; Masten & Coatsworth, 1998). It is this reservoir-building capacity that is at the heart of many interventions, in that the aim of a given intervention may be to enhance specific protective factors that permit continued functioning even in the presence of adversity (Rutter, 1987).

Problem behaviors and related risk-protective factors often interact in a dynamic fashion (Rutter, 2000). Many prevention programs have been developed to address youth problem behaviors via reduction of risk and the promotion of protective factors (Jenson & Howard, 1999; Jessor, 1998; Peterson & DiClemente, 2000; Wasserman & Miller, 1998). Other promotion efforts focus solely on strengths or the enhancement of developmental assets (Catalano, et al., 2002; Lerner, et al., 2003). While our understanding of these interactions is by no means complete, the consideration of risk, protection, and resilience forms the conceptual and empirical foundation of contemporary intervention programming.

Developmental Considerations

Researchers have noted that the relevance and potency of some risk and protective factors change across developmental periods (e.g., Reid & Eddy, 1997). Although many risks and protections are consistent in one or more developmental periods, some risk and protective factors maybe salient in only one developmental period. As an illustration, unique and predictive childhood risk factors for delinquency include individual characteristics such as hyperactivity levels and early substance use. In adolescence, the risk configuration changes to emphasize the influence of antisocial peers (Farrington, 1996).

If time specific risks are not addressed, an important opportunity can be missed. For instance, a strong predictor of academic achievement before a child enters school is socioeconomic status. However, once a child enters school, a key predictor of academic success is prior success (Durlak, 1997). In the area of child literacy, Clay (1991) noted that in many countries remedial reading instruction does not begin until after a child's eighth birthday. Interventions that take into account developmental salience emphasize early detection to prevent a child from falling behind. By taking advantage of the developmental opportunity to intervene early, learning problems can be addressed before the child enters school or upon the first years in school.

One also has to be mindful of the normative onset of certain problem behaviors. In some cases, drug prevention programs have shown utility but only before a young person's first experimentation with drugs. Take the Child and Parent Relations Project (CAPR – Loveland-Cherry, Ross, & Kaufman 1999) as a case in point. This intervention is designed to promote family-related protective factors and reduce risks as a means for delaying the initiation of alcohol use of children and preadolescents. Intervention children and adolescents who reported no previous alcohol use at pre testing had smaller increases in the level of alcohol use relative to the increase evidenced by those in the **control group** who had no previous experience with alcohol. In the third and fourth intervention years, the impact of CAPR was most evident. At this time, those in the control group with no-prior drinking experience had a level of alcohol use that was double the level of those with no-prior drinking experience in the **intervention group**. Intervention benefits were not found for those participants who reported drinking at the pre-testing thus emphasizing the importance of the timing of intervention, before onset of first experimentation.

It is widely recognized that interventions should work in concert with and capitalize on the developmental changes that may be taking place. Understanding developmental changes in risk-protective factors and the normative onset of problem behaviors are critical for the timing of intervention efforts. Prevention programs should therefore be designed to target risk and protective factors that are developmentally appropriate and open to change (Catalano, et al., 2002; Sloboda & David, 1997).

The Context of Intervention

The setting in which an intervention is to be implemented is an important issue that merits considerable attention and forethought. In an effort to adequately take into account the unique opportunities presented in certain environments and the potential for synergy between contexts, it is worthwhile to integrate contemporary reconsiderations of the connection between the person and environment into the daily business of prevention and promotion work.

Traditionally, influential developmental theories have viewed the individual and the environment as separate entities. In the last few decades however, prevailing outlooks on the connection between individuals and their physical and societal environments have experienced a conceptual reawakening (Bronfenbrenner, 1979; 2000). Regarding the environment, Bronfenbrenner (2000) conceptualized it to be like a series of interlocking nested structures, with each context embedded in part of the next system (e.g., Family – School – Community – Culture – History). Humans are immersed in these multiple environments and their development is, to differing extents, shaped by this interrelatedness.

Bronfenbrenner (1979; 2000) devised the following concepts to describe the ecology of human development. The microsystem is the innermost layer of the environment that consists of all of the settings or contexts that individuals directly experience (e.g., home, school, and neighborhood). The mesosystem is the next environmental layer where interactions take place between environmental systems. The interface between systems is thought to have consequences for human development. So it is not just a child's experience in a particular environment that is important. It is also the how the many layers of the environment coincide to contribute to the socialization of a child. As an example, intervention activities aimed at increasing parent interaction with teachers and involvement in a child's life at school represent an attempt to harmonize socialization efforts across these two settings, at the level of the mesosystem.

The exosystem makes up a third and even more far removed layer of the environment. In this case, children have little direct contact with this part of the environment but events taking place at the exosystem level still have an impact on their lives. For example, stress at parents' workplace or local school board decisions help to form parenting or teacher practices that will have an impact on the children who are on the receiving end of these adult behaviors. Thus, exosystem changes do have some influence on the individual's experience of the microsystem. The macrosystem is also not highly accessible to individuals but it is still an influential part of their lives. The macrosystem represents the collective knowledge of culture and sub-cultural groups (e.g., codified and informal customs). An example of a macrosystem influence might consist of a particular cultural belief that often holding and bringing newborn infants to work is beneficial to the child and caretaker. This belief might make a parent who identifies with that cultural group more likely to engage in this practice. The child will accordingly be more liable to experience a great deal of physical contact and form certain expectations about the environment and the meaning of relationships on the basis of this care giving experience. The most far removed part of the environment is the chronosystem, which deals primarily with the historical events and conditions that influence individuals and societies. For an illustration of a chronosystem level influence, one can consider the impact that changing technologies has had on childrearing practices and childbirth over the past hundred years.

As a parallel to the changes that have taken place in how the environment is considered, views of the developing person have also been revisited. The holistic perspective, for instance, moves away from viewing the individual in terms of single aspects or variables taken out of context of each other (Magnusson & Stattin, 1998). By reducing the lens of investigation on too narrow a range of behavior or functioning, we risk losing sight of the person in her or his totality. Another key idea regarding the individual is the view of people as producers or contributors to their own development (Brandtstaedter & Lerner, 1999; Lerner & Busch-Rossnagel, 1981). People bring a life history of personal experiences and dispositions to each new experience. They interpret these new circumstances in terms of this history and work out lines of adaptation that maintain or fundamentally alter the direction of their lives (Elder, 1998; Giele & Elder, 1998). From this perspective, it is essential to leave room for the individual's influence on the course of human development and the environment.

When one considers the ecology of human development as well as holistic and active views of the individual, we begin to form a more thorough explanation of our interaction with the many systems of social experience that permeate our lives (Sameroff & Fiese, 2000). This explanation stresses the notion that to truly understand human development one must sincerely look at both the totality of the environment and person. Most importantly, the challenge is to accurately capture what happens when these dynamic systems come together.

Ecological-transactional models have been used as way to capture the ongoing interactions among aspects of contexts and persons (e.g., Cicchetti & Lynch, 1993; Cicchetti & Rogosch, 1996; 1999; Cicchetti & Toth, 1998; Lynch & Cicchetti, 1998). This model assumes that the emergence of any specific developmental outcome is not a certainty but a product of a series of interactions between individuals, the multiple environments they experience, and their prior developmental history (Sameroff & Chandler, 1975; Sameroff & Fiese, 2000; Sroufe, 1997). Development maybe said to be occurring in an ongoing and fluid manner as youth experience these multiple, interlocked social realities all of which influence each other (Belsky, 1993; Bronfenbrenner, 1979).

This way of thinking has direct implications for prevention work (Greenberg, et al., 2001; Weissberg & Greenberg, 1998). From this approach, problem behaviors are thought to have multiple determinants and represent larger or smaller deviations from normal patterns of adaptation. Secondly, there are multiple pathways to a specific problem behavior and that any given starting point, including the onset of a particular problem behavior, will lead to a range of potential outcomes. The former phenomenon is called **equifinality** with the later being termed **multifinality** (Cicchetti & Rogosch, 1996).

An ecological-transactional model provides a rationale for prevention efforts that target multiple risk factors for a specific problem behavior outcome and enhance protective factors predictive of more adaptive outcomes. The ultimate goal of many prevention and promotion efforts is to change the individual's attitudes, motivations, skills, knowledge, and behaviors. It is widely recognized that the family, school, and community are important socialization contexts or microsystems. The main agents of socialization within these settings include parents/caregivers, siblings, peers, teachers, and other significant adults at school and in the broader community (Asher & Parker, 1989; Baumrind, 1971; Hartup, 1983; 1996). Interventions can be designed to work with youth or socialization agents directly, within a particular environment or in multiple socialization contexts.

Recently, there has been an emphasis on developing programs that intervene in multiple settings (Sloboda & David, 1997). Cross context interventions have increasingly become the gold standard of contemporary intervention efforts (Ellis, 1998). These interventions try to promote change both within and across microsystems. For instance, giving an anti-drug message in both the school and in the home is considered to be more likely to produce change than working in either context alone. This premise is founded on the hope that a consistent message across settings will impact multiple risk and protective factors, promote the transfer of prosocial behaviors across contexts, and strengthen supportive links between microsystems.

Despite benefits associated with cross context intervention, some complications have arisen as the technology around these programs has matured. One potential limitation of the cross context program lies in its replication and later dissemination. The consistency of cross context intervention efforts is widely thought to be ideal in terms of fostering long-term healthy development (e.g., Catalano et al., 1999; Sloboda & David, 1997). Yet, when a given cross context intervention is brought beyond its initial efficacy trial, the large commitment of time, resources, and expertise sometimes needed to successfully reproduce a highly successful but elaborate program may become overwhelming. The shortfall of this type of program can be likened to an expanding universe that at a certain point reaches its maximum size and begins to collapse back in on itself.

One way interventionists have come to terms with the possible big bang effect of cross context programs is to develop focused interventions that work extensively within and between two particular settings (e.g., school and family). Another approach has been to dismantle, strip down or decompose successful interventions. The goal of **unpacking or component delivery studies** is to determine which aspects of an intervention are most essential for producing lasting change. Such a focus highlights the continued need to develop useful intervention components and techniques even within a single setting. This need becomes more pronounced in the context of limited or competing resources and in areas of prevention and promotion work where we have less scientific knowledge about successful intervention practices.

Dissemination and Sustainability

Controlled **outcome evaluations** demonstrate what is possible, but what do we do with this knowledge? The answer to this question seems obvious but reality can challenge us in unexpected ways. On a practical level, even the most successful interventions are often difficult to do and are not without critics. Interventions in many cases are designed to promote change in some of the most intimate aspects of our lives. Those who try to implement such interventions often learn that cooperation and trust is not easily won nor sustained. From of a scientific viewpoint, in some cases, we have good evidence to make decisions about 'what works' in prevention and in the promotion of youth development. However, questions still revolve around the problem of how to best integrate useful interventions into everyday life.

Attempts to bring programs to wider audiences as well as efforts to engage difficult to reach populations have shown that **science-based prevention** can run the risk of being overly top-down or expert oriented (McCall, et al., 1998). **Top-down intervention models** place a great deal of confidence in scientific methods and knowledge. Arguably, much of the contemporary advancement in intervention programming can be attributed to an increasing culture of rigor and accountability among interventionists. Despite the advantages of a top-down model, many interventions attempt to engage individuals and communities that have experienced difficulties participating in mainstream social institutions. Top-down intervention models may further marginalize people who already experience various forms of social exclusion. A lack of participant investment in an intervention can have a number of serious consequences (c.f. *Program Example* – Nye, Zucker, & Fitzgerald, 1995). An expert orientation that discourages participant involvement can significantly impair a program's utility as well as handicap efforts to institutionalize an intervention beyond its initial development period. Elmeland (1999) captured this sentiment well when she stated that:

> Local people are simply tired of well-intentioned project initiators invading their local community and initiating activities, just to disappear afterwards and leave it to the people of the local community to keep the projects going, or simply let them sit with a bad conscience thinking 'here was another thing that did not succeed in our community.' (p. 118)

As a means for avoiding this problem, it has been argued that the interventionist's work should not end after a program's utility has been demonstrated (Swisher, 2000). Sustainability should be a principal concern throughout the intervention process.

A **bottom-up intervention model** may encourage greater program durability. This approach emphasizes participants' capacity to affect positive change in their own lives and community. Interventions based on this model often create activities designed to improve participants' sense of mastery and work with program participants in a collaborative way. Participants are thought to become empowered as they experience the possibility of affecting meaningful positive change rather than weathering the next set of circumstances thrown their way (Bloom, 1996). Bottom-up approaches also often attempt to take things a step further by promoting program ownership. Communities who are supposed to profit from prevention or youth development efforts are explicitly encouraged to become involved in the actual process of intervention from the start.

In general, bottom up approaches are designed to yield increased levels of program investment and the reengagement of previously excluded individuals and communities in the broader social system. Further, this approach helps to build a strong foundation for continued intervention activities and program benefits. The increasing number of local communities who are initiating and running interventions as well as the explicit inclusion of collaborative intervention strategies among the most successful interventions attests to the growing acceptance of bottom-up intervention models.

Bottom-up approaches clearly have a number of potential benefits. Yet, this model of intervention can also have serious shortcomings. When grass roots decision-making goes against the scientific knowledge base then a number of difficulties can arise. The complete exclusion of scientific knowledge and methodology has a number of limitations like the possibility of wasting limited resources by developing new programs that already exist, the complete absence of reliable knowledge about a given program's impact, and in the worst case the implementation of policies and services that actually cause harm by unintentionally increasing problems. One way that people have come to terms with the top-down–bottom-up dichotomy is to develop hybrid approaches that combine aspects of both models (c.f. *Program Examples –* Hawkins, Catalano, & Associates, 1992; Holder, et al., 1997).

Prevention and Promotion: Lessons from the Past

Prevention and health promotion have long been integral parts of the public health and mental hygiene movements (Albee & Gullotta, 1997; Bingenheimer, et al., 2003; Cicchetti, 1990; Hosman, 1992; Spaulding & Balch, 1983; Walsh, 1982). Many concepts, techniques, and dilemmas associated with these movements remain with us today. A important lesson from the past with currency for today's interventionist is that our understanding of the phenomena we seek to intervene on often goes through a developmental process. This process moves in jumps and starts depending on the phenomena in question.

Forms of inoculation, for example, existed well before we had insight into the viral mechanisms of certain diseases such as small pox.

> A method of inoculating people against smallpox was developed in Greece and Turkey by the 17th century, and was discussed in British medical journals as early as 1714. This method involved taking pus from someone with active smallpox and inserting it in the arm of a healthy individual. It was used widely in colonial America; in fact, General Washington ordered that all troops in the Continental Army be inoculated against small pox in 1776 (Duffy, 1990). (Bingenheimer, et al., 2003, p. 21)

There are other instances in our history and even today in which our understanding of the processes that cause disease and health lag behind the technology of intervention (e.g., the modern-day use of quarantine and sequestration to stop the spread of communicable diseases like Sudden Acute Respiratory Syndrome – SARS).

Today, ecological models predominate the field of health promotion. These perspectives situate health and disease at the intersection between individuals and the many layers of the environment (Bingenheimer, et al. 2003). As in our past, we do not yet have a complete understanding of how the dynamic interactions between persons and contexts come together to yield disease or health. In a symposium entitled *Prevention research: Progress in the field, gaps in the knowledge base and future research initiatives*, Dr. Nora D. Volkow, Director of the U.S. National Institute on Drug Abuse (2003, June) highlighted a study that demonstrates this point.

This study by Morgan and colleagues (2002) involved 20 male monkeys who took part in a longitudinal experiment. For a year and a half these monkeys were housed separately. Over this time period the monkeys' hormonal levels, behavior, and brains were observed. The monkeys' brains were studied using a brain imaging technique called a PET scan. After this year and half period, the monkeys were placed into social housing units and began to live communally in groups of four. A social dominance hierarchy then took shape in each of the housing groups. Once stable dominance hierarchies were formed, after three months of living in social groups, PET scans were taken again. Compared to a previous PET scan when the monkeys lived on their own, there was an approximately 22% increase in the number of D_2 receptors among socially dominant monkeys. No significant change in D_2 receptors were found in subordinate monkeys. D_2 receptors are an indicator of how dopamine, an important neurotransmitter, is working in the brain. Dopamine functioning has been linked to a person's susceptibility to the addictive properties of drugs such as cocaine (Morgan, et al., 2002). Researchers concluded on the basis of the results of this experimental longitudinal study that, "...rather than a predisposing trait, the changes were a consequence of becoming the dominant monkey in a social group" (Morgan, et al., 2002, p. 170).

The next step in this study involved placing these same monkeys in a situation where they could self administer cocaine. Researchers observed that subordinate monkeys exposed themselves to significantly more cocaine than dominant monkeys. Morgan and colleagues (2002) then concluded that socially dominant monkeys,

> ...ability to control resources may induce neurochemical changes that are reflected in the over 20% increase in D_2 receptor... and a decrease in vulnerability to the reinforcing effects of cocaine...... This latter finding is even more striking when one considers that in non-human primate models, cocaine functions as a reinforcer in nearly all individually housed subjects. (p. 171)

Why is this study relevant? A key finding here was that changes in the living situation of the participant monkeys allowed for changes in social behavior to be expressed. This environmental-behavioral change was then linked to changes in brain functioning. When many of us think about brain functioning, we often place the brain before behavior in a causal chain. Now in light of evidence such as that presented in the Morgan and colleagues (2002) study, as well as by other scientists, we are having to rethink the relations between the brain, behavior, and the environment.

When we talk about person-environment interactions, our understanding of what is taking place undergoes change. Despite our present limitations, there is a strong conviction that science has the potential to generate the knowledge and tools that will help us come to terms with the 'how' and 'why' of preventing youth problem behaviors and advancing the positive development of young people (Coie, et al., 1993; Gullotta, 1994; Schinke, 1994; Spilton-Koretz, 1991). As in the past, today's interventionists retain the humanitarian aim of preventing suffering and promoting wellness. Ironically, also like many early interventionists, we remain in the midst of a struggle to gain greater insight into the workings behind the phenomena we observe and hope to change. This is one of the reasons why prevention and promotion continues to be an exciting field.

Today, is also an exciting time in the history of prevention and promotion. Prevention work with young people has reached an unprecedented level of scientific activity. Durlak and Wells (1997), for example, found that

"...half of all controlled outcome studies have appeared since 1980" (p. 116). It is also a hopeful time because we have had successes in certain problem areas, some of which were once thought to be largely beyond our capacity to change (c.f. *Relevant Narrative Reviews and Meta-Analyses* – Durlak, 1997; Durlak & Wells, 1997; 1998; Franklin, Grant, Corcoran, Miller, & Bultman, 1997; Greenberg, et al., 2001; Gullotta & Bloom, 2003; Mrazek & Haggerty, 1994; Kim, Stanton, Li, Dickersin, & Galbraith, 1997; Kok, Van den Borne, & Mullen, 1997; Lipsey, 1995; 1998; Lipsey & Wilson, 1993; Redondo, Sánchez-Meca, & Garrido, 1999; Schinke, et al., 2002; Sherman, et al., 1997; Tobler, et al., 2000). Further, cost-saving analyses demonstrate that well implemented interventions make financial sense (c.f. *Relevant Cost-Benefit/Saving Analyses* – Bukowski & Evans, 1998; Cohen, 1998; Haveman & Wolfe, 1994; Karoly, et al., 1998; Scott, Knapp, Henderson, & Maughan, 2001). For instance, Karoly and colleagues (1998) explained that even our most precise financial estimates can underestimate the value of intervention:

> ...cost-savings analysis is a useful tool because, when the results are positive, it provides strong support for program worth. That is, it shows that only a portion of the benefits – those easily monetizable – outweigh the program's entire cost. However, because only some of the benefits are taken into account, a negative result does not indicate that a program *shouldn't* be funded. Policymakers must then decide whether nonmonetizable benefits – e.g., gains in IQ, in parent-child relations, in high school diplomas – are worth the net monetary cost... (p. xx).

Based on these and other lines of evidence, the prevailing belief in the prevention and promotion field is that when an intervention is done right it can save money, enhance lives, and reduce a great deal of unnecessary misery.

Chapter Endnotes

---

[1]*Search Procedures:* Two search strategies were used to locate eligible prevention and promotion programs. The first approach involved a traditional review of the research literature. A search was conducted via the PsycINFO® electronic search engine. Lipsey and Wilson (2001) described this database as, "The online version of Psychological Abstracts; indexes published research in psychology and behavioral sciences from approximately 3000 journals and technical reports published throughout the world" (p. 170). The PsycINFO® search yielded information on a number of program evaluation studies and previous reviews of the literature. The reference lists of relevant documents were manually searched for additional studies, reviews, and reports. Selective literature searches were conducted up to June 2003.

The second search strategy consisted of making up to 800 contacts with European and American interventionists. This included individual research scientists, voluntary and paid intervention workers, government officials as well as contacts with universities and organizations like the Society for Prevention Research. Contacts received an explanation of the book project and an invitation to share information on their activities. Primary contact persons helped to generate new contacts. A number of people were responsive to requests for information and while others were more difficult to reach. Therefore, the number of contacts made for this review certainly under represents the total number of people and institutions knowledgeable of or engaged in intervention work with young people.

Because many strong reviews of the American intervention literature exist, a smaller scale investigative search was conducted in the United States. Government entities and agencies that review or sponsor prevention work in the United States, like the White House Council on Youth Violence, the U.S. National Institute of Mental Health, the U.S. National Institute on Drug Abuse, and the U.S. Center for Mental Health Services, were visited and research directors were interviewed. The European search was more fine grained with particular care taken to adequately cover Scandinavian countries.

Language is a historic obstacle to research synthesis (Hosman & Clay, 2001). With few exceptions, reviews of the intervention literature consist primarily of English language program evaluations. Although it was not overcome, several steps were taken in this review to minimize such a language bias. In instances when outcome evaluations were published in a non-English or non-Scandinavian language, attempts were made to contact program developers and enlist their help in summarizing the basic elements of their work. Where relevant, the assistance of program developers is acknowledged in a series of footnotes. In order to further reduce language bias, a systematic review of the European Monitoring Centre for Drugs and Drug Addiction's Exchange on Drug Demand Reduction Action (EDDRA)

---

information system was performed. EDDRA is an internet database that allows European interventionists to enter a description of their intervention in several languages. Descriptions that meet certain criteria are then translated into other languages including English, French, and German. While this approach is also not without limitations, in particular the content of the database deals solely with drug prevention and treatment, the use of EDDRA helped to begin to address the language bias problem.

[2]*Criteria Used for Program Inclusion/Exclusion (Content Area Requirements):*

- The present review is aimed at highlighting and summarizing the research literature on exemplary American and European interventions that successfully ameliorate youth problem behaviors and/or foster positive youth development.

- In this review, we have made an explicit attempt to move away from a categorical view of problem behaviors and prevention programming. As a result, interventions able to produce **spreading effects** across problem areas and those that have some unique proficiency for yielding more specific results in a single problem domain are noted throughout the review. Also, interventions not expressly aimed at changing youth problem behaviors but have nevertheless shown a positive impact on these behaviors and/or associated risk-protective factors are integrated into the review.

Criteria Used for Program Inclusion/Exclusion (Design Requirements):

- Because this review is mainly concerned with the program utility, our primary focus was on the examination of outcome evaluation studies. Interventions that were able to conduct an outcome and **process evaluation** were considered to be of particular value.

- Interventions eligible for inclusion in this review must have had at least a **pre-post test research design**. Prevention programs eligible for inclusion in this review must have successfully improved youth problem behaviors and/or youth development (along with related risk-protective factors) relative to a control, comparison, or alternative intervention group. A qualification to the design criteria was made in order to broaden what is known about European youth intervention work. European interventions were integrated into the present review if the program trial met at least one of the design criterion (i.e., pre-post test research design or control-comparison group). No proscriptive statements about the utility of these initiatives are made unless the program trial is a replication of an already rigorously tested intervention. In all other cases, the design criteria have been applied uniformly.

- The focus of the present review is on interventions that utilize scientific principles and methods, however emphasis is also placed on programs that have successfully involved program participants in the process of intervention.

For a comprehensive review of intervention design options, see Tebes, Kaufman, and Connell (2003).

[3]*Criteria Used to Determine 'Intervention Success':* In the midst of methodical diversity, it is important to be clear about the criteria used to make judgments about intervention success. The number of acceptable program evaluation strategies and statistical metrics are many and ever increasing. The choice of an approach to evaluation depends in part on the particular research questions to be answered, program characteristics, design and practical issues, as well as the program evaluator's expertise. Yet even under ideal testing conditions, conclusions about program utility should be made with care. In some cases, a well evaluated program may have yielded a null or negative result due to improper implementation or a lack of statistical power to detect change (Lipsey & Wilson, 2001). When making a judgment about the merit of a single intervention trial, however, the occurrence of a statistically significant change in the context of a strong evaluation design can provide worthwhile preliminary information about an intervention's ultimate value.

Judgments about utility of *individual interventions* were made by using the following criteria:

- When judgments were made about program utility, an important question was whether the intervention trial met the design requirements. If this was the case, then the occurrence of statistically significant change was further weighed against the following factors: measurement considerations, the procedure used for assignment to condition, group comparability at pre-testing, the number of participants per condition, **program attrition**, the appropriateness of statistical analyses conducted, and the success of replication attempts.

- All well described and appropriately applied statistical metrics were considered when making judgments about program evaluations. Outcome evaluation results were, however, predominately reported in terms of test statistics that yielded **p-values** or **effect sizes**. For p-values, intervention-related increases or decreases described in this document are statistically significant at the .05 or less level. Exact values of marginally significant results are noted where relevant. The meaning of effects size statistics was determined by using Lipsey and Wilson's (2001) distribution of mean effect sizes for intervention studies, with a small effect size described as equal or less than .30
standard deviation units, a medium effect size equal to .50 standard deviation units, and a large effect size as equal or greater than .67 standard deviation units. Lipsey and Wilson's effect size classification system was adopted because of its basis in contemporary meta-analytic research (Lipsey & Wilson, 1993).

- In the present review, interventions with statistically significant and predominately desirable results in at least one empirically sound outcome evaluation are called **promising** and initiatives that have shown their utility under repeated and scientifically strong outcome evaluations and/or have

---

- demonstrated positive long-term program related effects in a single trial are called **well established**.

For a comprehensive review of intervention analysis options, see Tebes, Kaufman, and Connell (2003).

Summative or synthesis statements were constructed using the following method:
- In this review, a synthesis of the research literature is offered in the cases where enough evidence has accumulated. The synthesis technique used here involved equating a qualitative analysis of the exemplary programs described in this review with relevant narrative reviews and meta-analyses that already exist in the research literature. Thus, this book does not aim to provide a meta-analysis nor does it employ a "...vote-counting on statistical significance" system to consolidate knowledge (Lipsey & Wilson, 2001, p. 6). Instead, a variation of a best evidence synthesis of the research literature (Slavin, 1995) is used to make summative statements about particular areas of intervention research.

[4]In the previous classification system (i.e., primary, secondary, tertiary), the definitions of universal, selective and indicated programs would all fall under the rubric of primary prevention (i.e., reducing the incidence of new cases).

[5]*Classification System for Prevention, Promotion, and Treatment Used in This Book:* The term universal prevention, in this document, refers to a prevention program that does not select program participants based on any consideration or assessment of risk. This usage of the term

universal prevention is in agreement with the aforementioned Institute of Medicine report (Mrazek & Haggerty, 1994). Youth development programs are also categorized as universal prevention programs in this document. The placement of youth development programs into a universal prevention framework diverges from the Institute of Medicine classification system. The use of the terms selective and indicated prevention in this book are in line with how these terms were described in the Institute of Medicine report. The term treatment, in this document, is used in relation to socially defined youth problem behaviors and known mental health disorders. In the first case, a young person's entry and exposure to programming in an adult rehabilitative setting, like an adult prison, is considered an instance of treatment. Treatment also retains its traditional meaning in that individuals who meet the diagnostic criteria and receive services to address a mental disorder are viewed as the recipients of treatment. Interventions dealt with in this review were in some instances created as mental health treatments. To be included in this review, the treatment must have also demonstrated utility as prevention program with relevance to amelioration of youth problem behaviors and associated risk-protective factors.

Part II
Review

Section 1
The Family Context

The impact of the family on the development of the individual has been of pervasive interest (Bowlby, 1969; Freud, 1965; Mead 1928). Salvadore Minuchin (1974) and other family researchers have explored basic family systems, along with the impact of alliances, coalitions and subgroups, which make up the structure of family relations and the consequent effects of the family on individual development. There is a growing recognition that young people also have some measure of influence on the nature of family life (Kerr, Stattin, Biesecker, & Ferrer-Wreder, 2003; Reiss, Neiderhiser, Hetherington, & Plomin, 2000). Further, the family and the individual do not exist in a vacuum but are embedded in the values, morals and mores of the surrounding and broader cultural context (Bronfenbrenner, 1986). These external environments such as social networks, parents' workplace, neighborhoods, schools and public policies all influence the functioning of families and the individuals within them. For instance, Youniss and Smollar (1989) described some of the social and historical events associated with transformations in the nature of the family, including the advent of reliable birth control, extended life expectancy of parents, widespread formal education and a change from industrial to information societies. These authors posited that these events not only alter the quality of parent-child relations and the immediate familial experience but may also promote sustained interaction between parents and children well beyond childhood. It is widely recognized that, while familial relationships are molded within a cultural context that will either affirm or reject parental behavior, it is these primary relationships that provide our first model for our sense of the world (Ainsworth, Blehar, Waters & Wall, 1978; Bowlby, 1969). With the family playing such a significant part in individual development, it becomes clear that family life provides an important context for socialization (Kumpfer, Alexander, McDonald, & Olds, 1998).

The nature and effectiveness of socialization efforts within the family can either act as a developmental advantage or liability. There are many conceptualizations of family life (e.g., *Attachment* – Bowlby, 1973; 1982; *Parenting Styles* – Baumrind, 1971; *Social Ecology* – Bronfenbrenner, 1979) and youth problem behaviors (e.g., *Problem Behavior theory* – Gottfredson & Hirschi, 1994; Jessor & Jessor, 1977; *Social Development Model*– Catalano & Hawkins, 1996). There also is a large body of research linking youth problem behaviors to the family (e.g., Gorman-Smith, Tolan, Loeber, & Henry, 1998; Griffin, Botvin, Scheier, Diaz, & Miller, 2000; Hawkins, Catalano, & Miller,

1992; Patterson, Reid, & Dishion, 1992; Taylor & Biglan, 1998). Family risks found to regularly co-occur with youth problem behaviors include: parental addiction and antisocial behavior, the quality of family interactions including the extent of conflict, the effectiveness of parents' management of youth behavior, and the level of involvement and emotional bonds among family members (e.g., Dishion & Kavanagh, 2000; Dusenbury, 2000; Kumpfer & Alvarado, 1998, November; Lipsy & Derzon, 1998). The predictive power of many risk factors is modified by other dynamics taking place within and outside of the home, including the family's structure, social and economic disadvantage, as well as ecological and peer-related risks. The presence of protective factors also weighs into the equation (Adlaf & Ivis, 1996; Griffin et al., 2000; Juby & Farrington, 2001; Sokol-Katz, Dunham, & Zimmerman, 1997). Research suggests that certain experiences within the family, like positive parent-child relations, have protective properties (Biglan, et al., 1997; Kumpfer & Alvarado, 1998, November).

Chapter 2
Early Family Intervention

Introduction

Relationships within the family continue to be the subject of extensive research and theoretical contemplation. Attachment theory (Ainsworth, et al., 1978; Bowlby, 1982)[1] provides a rich account of the inner workings of relationships and relational contexts. Attachment relationships are thought to be evolutionarily important and have resonance across development (Bowlby, 1969; Ainsworth, 1989). "An attachment can be described as an enduring affectional bond that unites two or more people across time and context..." (Thompson, Easterbrooks, Padilla-Walker, 2003, p. 100). Attachment theory particularly explores the issues of emotion and independence within important relationships. Contemporary attachment theory has a widened scope of inquiry, by investigating how multiple attachment relationships, as well as the growing infant's psychobiology and temperamental characteristics influence the nature of attachment (Thompson, et al., 2003).

The actual relational mechanics that make up an early attachment relationship are played out in the myriad of exchanges between infants and key caregivers. An example of one of these occasions is when an infant and caregiver must work out mutually satisfying levels of responsiveness and stimulation during a face to face encounter (Bowlby, 1973; 1982; Thompson, et al., 2003; van Ijzendoorn, Schuengel, & Bakermans-Kranenburg, 1999). Such interactions may involve eye contact, sound, touch, movement, and other types of communication. Another illustration of a common situation in which infants and caregivers must balance emotional and physical closeness with autonomy is the daily separation that happens in the course of a given day. "Putting baby down for a nap or going to the grocery store, to work, for dinner, or to a party are all events that separate parents from children" (Fitzgerald, Mann, Cabrera, & Wong, 2003, p. 150).

If a caregiver and infant's interactions are promotive and in tune with the infant's individual preferences for interaction, then a secure attachment may take shape. On occasions in which infants perceive a threat or find themselves in a strange situation, a history of positive experiences with important caregivers in a variety of situations can provide the reassurance necessary to allow the infant to self-assuredly venture out into the environment. A secure attachment provides a relational context in which infants can develop a sense of trust in the relationships formed with significant others and build confidence in their own ability to affect change (Olds, 2002; Thompson, et al., 2003). Secure attachment relationships early in life may also make it more likely that important basic competencies will take root in infancy and flourish in later developmental periods. Yet, early attachment relationships are contingent. They provide a starting place but individual characteristics, events that transpire during a person's life, environmental conditions, and the nature of later relationships each continue to be influential throughout the life course (Thompson, et al., 2003).

Attachment theory provides a heuristic explanation of relational contexts. Yet, ecological-transactional models of human development (e.g., Sameroff & Fiese, 2000) offer a wider perspective that situates relationships within a dynamic environment. Such models assume that developmental outcomes are a result of multiple interactions or transactions between persons, the many environments they experience, and their developmental history. A focus on relational contexts embedded within the broader ecology of human development translates into early intervention efforts aimed at helping caregivers select or construct environments conducive to positive development. An enriched environment includes access to relational contexts that offer abundant opportunities for youth to experience emotionally warm care giving that is in tune with the youngster's developmental needs and unique characteristics.

From an ecological-transactional perspective, relational contexts also transact with other contexts. Therefore, the ecological context that families find themselves situated in matters. Marital discord, stress due to economic disadvantage, neighborhood disorganization and crime, lack of access to essential services can complicate care givers' efforts to adequately provide for the developmental needs of their charges (Garbarino & Ganzel, 2000; Olds, 2002; Thompson, et al., 2003). Environmental risks compounded with poor birth outcomes and/or poor infant-caregiver interaction can place an infant in danger of significant adjustment problems later in life (e.g., Chapman & Scott, 2001; Joffee, 1982; Piquero & Tibbetts, 1999; Raine, Brennan, Farrington, & Mednick, 1997; Weiss & Seed, 2002). Thus, as Fitzgerald and colleagues (2003) noted,

> All development takes place in a complex environment......
> Contemporary prevention programs designed to enhance child
> development during the early years reflect this thinking. They
> address issues related to child development, parent involvement,
> consistency of care, and networking to the broader community of
> human service agencies and to the schools. (p. 138)

This chapter offers concrete examples of successful early family interventions. Interventions have been organized primarily by programmatic content into two overlapping categories: **home visitation** and **early educational enrichment**. Individually, these interventions draw broadly from many theoretical traditions. Yet as a group, these types of programs deal extensively with the interface between relational and other ecological contexts. Home visitation for expectant and new parents, for example, is particularly marked by a focus on preparation for the experience of parenthood, enriching and protecting the child's prenatal environment, fostering successful births, and the promotion of high quality parent-infant interaction once the child is born. Early educational enrichment provides intellectual and social developmental activities in the child's home and/or early school or daycare environment. Such initiatives work directly with young children and caregivers across settings and are designed to promote broad forms of developmental competence. Early enrichment programs, especially those that involve substantial home components, can be categorized as a cross context intervention (e.g., family + school or family + community). Because the programmatic goals of home visitation and early enrichment are similar, early enrichment interventions are described at this point. Chapter six (Community Intervention and Community Related Cross Context Interventions) has further details on community mobilization efforts linked to early child development initiatives.

Chapter Organization

This chapter deals with interventions designed for infants and children age zero to five and their families. First, exemplary program elements and examples are described. A best evidence synthesis of the early family intervention literature as it relates to the prevention of youth problem behaviors and the advancement of positive youth development then follows. The subsequent *Questions* subsection addresses issues that arise when examining the utility of early family interventions. These subsections are followed by a listing of *Future Directions*.

Exemplary Program Examples

Home Visitation

From the U.S., Nurse-Family Partnership offers an illustration of a well established selective home visitation program. This intervention works from the prenatal through early childhood periods. During home visits nurses encourage mothers to make use of prenatal and well-baby medical services, to improve their lifestyle and life prospects, as well as to become more knowledgeable about their baby's health and development. Visits also consist of instruction in positive care giving techniques, coping through problem solving and goal setting, and parent mobilization of social and material support within the family and community.

The Nurse-Family Partnership's original program trial was conducted in a semi-rural area in upstate New York (Olds, 2002; Olds, Henderson, Tatelbaum, & Chamberlin, 1988). The intervention group that received the complete pre/postnatal protocol had the greatest and most enduring gains, relative to the three other intervention groups[2]. Advantages associated with participation in the complete intervention included better maternal prenatal health, improved knowledge and use of child development services, and fewer low birth-weight and pre-term births. During childhood, demonstrated benefits for the complete intervention group included fewer cases of child abuse, child injuries, emergency-room contacts, and child behavioral and coping problems. In adolescence, this group evidenced fewer juvenile arrests, greater rates of maternal entry into paid work, fewer maternal arrests and substance-use related problems (Olds, 1997; 2002; Olds & Henderson, 1994; Olds, Henderson, Phelps, Kitzman, & Hanks, 1993; Olds, et al., 1988; Olds, et al., 1998).

It should be noted that a criticism of this first trial is that program benefits were primarily demonstrated for European American or White participants (c.f., Olds et al., 1983). Later tests of the Nurse-Family Partnership were explicitly designed to investigate the program's utility with American ethnic minority families in urban settings (Olds, 1997; 2002). The Nurse-Family Partnership has subsequently been refined and tested with ethnic minority families living in Memphis, Tennessee and Denver, Colorado.

Participants in the Memphis trial were predominately disadvantaged African American first-time mothers. The Memphis visitation protocol[3] was similar to the original protocol tested in upstate New York with greater articulation and action on the program's theoretical foundations, such as increased emphasis on **parent capacitation** and mastery activities. Home visitors also used a survey to explore parents' health attitudes as a starting point for parent education. As in the original intervention trial, the complete intervention group in Memphis evidenced pre- to post- test (at the child's age of two) program associated benefits on indices of child abuse as measured by the number of hospitalizations for accidents.

Four and half years after the birth of their first child, mothers in the complete intervention group had fewer later pregnancies and less utilization of social welfare programs. All program related benefits were found in comparison to a minimal intervention group (Olds, 1997; 2002; Olds, et al., 1999). Outcome results for the Denver trial were still forthcoming at the time this book was written (Olds, 2002).

An attachment-based intervention developed by Van den Boom (1994; 1995) in the Netherlands provides an example of a selective post-natal visitation protocol. The intervention began when the infant was six months old and spanned a three-month period. This initiative was designed to improve caregivers' emotional availability and responsiveness to their temperamentally difficult infant. An attempt was also made to alter the child's conceptualization of the primary caretaker–infant relationship for the better (van Ijzendoorn, Juffer, & Duyvesteyn, 1995). Intervention sessions took place in the home. A home visitor observed parent – infant interactions and offered education and skills training to the caretaker. The intervention focused on raising the caregivers' skills, especially in relation to developing greater sensitivity and an ability to respond appropriately to infant cues or signaling behaviors (Van den Boom, 1994).

A **random**ized efficacy trial demonstrated pre- to post- test intervention gains for maternal care giving skills and decreased infant irritability. Other demonstrated advantages connected with this program included more enduring positive changes, at 12- and 42-months, in the quality of the child's attachment style, caregiver responsiveness, and child cooperation. See Hanrahan and Prinsen (1997; 1998) and Riksen-Walraven, Meij, Hubbard, and Zevalkink (1996) as examples of other Dutch home visitation programs.

The visitation programs developed by Olds (2002) and Van den Boom (1994; 1995) represent a sampling of a number of valuable selective interventions that provide pre- and/or post-natal services to expectant and new parents (c.f. *Relevant Narrative Reviews* – Gomby, Culross, & Behrman, 1999; Olds, Robinson, Song, Little, & Hill, 1999; Tableman, 2001). In America, the Community Infant Project (Huxley & Warner, 1993) and the Norfolk Resource Mothers Program (Julnes, Konefal, Pindur, & Kim, 1994) are examples of visitation protocols with a track record of significant accomplishment. Illustrations of other promising European home visitation interventions, at the universal-selective level, include the Child Development Program (Barker & Anderson, 1988), Mothers Inform Mothers (Hanrahan & Prinsen, 1997), and the EU/WHO Multi-Center Psychosocial Promotion Project (Tsiantis, et al., 1996). European program examples at the selective level are the Parent Advisor Service (Davis & Rushton, 1991) and Wilstaar (Ward, 1999). We will come back to many of these programs in greater detail in the *Questions* subsection.

Home Visitation and Parental Substance Abuse. The effects of parental maladjustment can be profound. Maternal addiction, in particular, is associated with low birth-weight, premature birth, infant substance addiction, poor parent-infant interaction, and child neglect and abuse (e.g., Ondersma, Simpson, Brestan, & Ward, 2000). Young people need basics like food, shelter, clothing, and protection from physical harm. But they also require stability from their parents along with emotional honesty and a warm, welcoming response to their physical and emotional needs. These are precisely the functions that are likely to break down under the pressure of parental drug addiction (Drummond & Fitzpatrick, 2000; Steinhausen, 1995).

Because home visitation is able to enter the very private world of families, this approach affords an opportunity to recognize family distress. By providing quick assessment and referral or direct intervention, visitation has the potential to deal with problems before they have a chance to accelerate. A small number of specialized home visitation interventions are designed to work with expectant and new mothers who have chronic and severe drug abuse problems (Olds, et al., 1999).

A small-scale, home visitation trial by Black and colleagues (1994) offers an American pre- and post-natal intervention example. This collaborative visitation protocol, facilitated by nurses, made use of traditional visitation components often used to improve the quality of care giving, like social support, education, and training for mothers. In a randomized controlled efficacy trial with a total of forty-three infant-mother pairs, significant pre- to 18-month **follow up** gains were found in positive care giving practices like emotional and verbal responsiveness. Statistically significant short-term (at six months) improvements were also found for intervention children's cognitive development. However, the positive changes in cognitive development were not evident at later assessment points (at 12- and 18-months). Finally, marginally significant trends were found for reduced self-reported drug use among intervention mothers, greater use of medical services, and improved care giving environment. A few other small-scale American initiatives have also demonstrated at least short-term promise working with new mothers who have addiction problems (e.g., Carroll, Chang, Behr, Clinton, & Kosten, 1995; Marcenko & Spence, 1994).

Home Visitation and Early Educational Enrichment

As infants make the transition into childhood, the enrichment of early educational experiences in daycare centers and preschools represents a natural progression of the home visitation approach. The visitation components of strong early enrichment programs are often overlooked (Weikart & Schweinhart, 1997). However, visitation is an important way to not only reinforce center-based activities but also to support parents in their role as caregivers. Visitation protocols implemented as part of educational enrichment initiatives often retain many traditional visitation elements like advocacy for medical and social services, encouraging positive parent lifestyle changes, and promoting responsive, warm care giving.

The Infant Health and Development Program (IHDP) offers an illustration of a home visitation/center-based early educational, enrichment approach. IHDP was a large-scale clinical trial conducted in multiple regions of the United States (Brooks-Gunn, et al., 1994; Ramey, et al., 1992). The IHDP was a selective intervention aimed at preventing developmental delays associated with low birth weight (LBW) and premature birth. Families with low birth weight (less than or equal to 2500g) and premature infants (less than 37 gestational weeks) were asked to participate in this study. The families that agreed to take part were matched by location and birth weight group, heavier LBW and lighter LBW, then randomly placed into an intervention- or control-condition.

After hospital discharge, intervention parents were visited in their homes and offered education on child development and training in problem solving. From their children's age of one to three, intervention parents were given access to bimonthly parent education and support groups. During the same time period, children attended a daycare center where they were exposed to a developmentally promotive curriculum. Two years after intervention activities ceased, children in the heavy LBW intervention group evidenced the greatest program related-benefits with significantly higher scores on indices of cognitive development relative to a comparable control group[4].

The High/Scope Perry Preschool Project represents another well-established, selective visitation and enrichment program example from the United States. The High/Scope Perry Preschool intervention materials now go by the title Educating Young Children (EYC). In its efficacy trial, EYC demonstrated impressive long-term benefits (Weikart & Schweinhart, 1997). EYC's programmatic components contained parent-, child-, and preschool-focused activities aimed at fostering better parent practices and involvement, and providing an intellectually stimulating preschool experience. The early education component emphasized a child-centered pedagogy. Intervention children were encouraged to create and complete educational activities within a standardized daily routine (e.g., planning time, clean-up time, recall time, small- and large-group time). Preschool teachers attempted to identify and capitalize on everyday opportunities to raise the child's level of functioning. Teachers also regularly visited the child's parents to provide informal social support and training in the preschool curriculum. Long-term program benefits in adolescence and adulthood were shown in terms of less delinquent behavior and fewer lifetime arrests, fewer repeated crimes in adulthood, superior educational attainment and employment, and reduced social welfare system contacts. These program-associated gains were made in comparison to a no-intervention condition (Schweinhart, et al., 1993; Schweinhart & Weikart, 1989; Weikart & Schweinhart, 1997).

Today, High/Scope Institutes distribute and provide support for EYC program activities. There are several Institutes active in various parts of the world. Program materials have also been translated into a variety of languages. EYC is offered as part of the ongoing Communities that Care Initiatives in the United Kingdom, Ireland, and the Netherlands. The United Kingdom's National Plan for the promotion of child development, Sure Start, also recommends the use of EYC. No controlled European outcome evaluations were available when this review was written. With such a broad dissemination network, controlled replications of High/Scope programs in Europe and elsewhere in the world, should hopefully be imminent.

The Mother Child Education Program (M-C/EP), formally known as the Turkish Early Enrichment Research Project, offers an example of a well established, European, center-based enrichment initiative. M-C/EP does most of its work with children, ages three- to five-years, who are at risk due to their exposure to social and economic disadvantage (Bekman, 1998; Kagitcibasi, 1995). To date, M-C/EP has been used as a selective intervention in 58 Turkish provinces and communities within Belgium, France, and Germany. Two trials of the program in Turkey provide an evidence base for the program's dissemination.

In the M-C/EP, participating mothers are offered training in child development, reproductive health and family planning, and how to promote positive parent-child interactions. Intellectual simulation is a cornerstone of this intervention with instruction to mothers in the use of a cognitive development program. This cognitive enrichment component focuses on the promotion of pre-literacy and numeracy skills. Mothers receive center-based training through weekly or bi-weekly discussion groups. Besides direct training, the groups are also used as an occasion for mothers to talk about their own development and relationships.

In the first trial, the intervention was conducted for two years with follow up testing until the children were 13- to15-years old (Kagitcibasi, 1995). This controlled efficacy trial indicated significant pre- to post-test intervention associated gains on indices of cognitive development and school achievement/attachment. Intervention children also evidenced significantly less aggressiveness and negative emotions. Intervention mothers showed benefits such as a more positive parenting orientation, improvements in the quality of observed mother-child interactions, higher satisfaction and educational aspirations for their children, as well as higher status within their families.

The M-C/EP also evidenced enduring significant program effects. The intervention group maintained previous gains relative to the control group on a standardized intelligence test (WISC-R, see Sattler, 1992). Intervention youth also remained in school significantly longer with higher grades, more positive school attachment, higher academic aspirations, more positive self-concepts, and retrospectively reported more positive family environments and parent-child relations. Interviews with mothers also indicated the maintenance of positive parenting and family status benefits.

In a second trial, the intervention was conducted for 25 weeks with a one-year follow up (Bekman, 1998). Follow up in this evaluation was much shorter than in the efficacy trial. However, a similar pattern of program-related benefits was evident. Intervention children showed significant gains in pre-literacy and numeracy skills relative to a comparison group. Teacher ratings of children's cognitive- and social-development, and overall grade point averages provided corroborating evidence. Intervention mothers were significantly more likely to report the use of positive parenting practices, to have a more positive view of themselves, and were more involved in their child's schooling than comparison mothers.

The visitation-enrichment and center-based enrichment initiatives described are just a few of the many interventions that have shown promise (c.f. *Relevant Narrative Reviews* – Fitzgerald, et al., 2003; Karoly et al. 1998; Olds et al., 1999; Yoshikawa, 1994). Other successful American enrichment programs include the Carolina Abecedarian Project (Ramey & Campbell, 1991), the Chicago Parent–Child Center (Reynolds & Temple, 1998), Early Head Start (Commissioner's Office of Research and Evaluation, Head Start Bureau, Administration on Children, Youth, and Families, and the Department of Health and Human Services, 2001, December-January), Parent Child Development Center Programs (Johnson & Walker, 1987), Syracuse Family Development Research Program (Lally, Mangione, & Honig, 1988; Lally, Mangione, Honig, & Wittner, 1988), and the Yale Child Welfare Project (Seitz & Apfel, 1994; Seitz, Rosenbaum, & Apfel, 1985). For rigorous examinations of variations in child care see the NICHD Study of Early Child Care (NICHD Early Child Care Research Network, 2000) and the Göteborg Child Care Study (Campbell, Lang, & Hwang, 2000).

Synthesis

Program Utility by Risk

Visitation and enrichment initiatives have been for the most part tested as selective prevention programs and have demonstrated success with families who experience moderate risk. Preliminary evidence does exist on how home visitation fairs when implemented at the universal to selective and indicated to treatment levels. A small number of visitation protocols that work with first-time and at-risk parents have undergone controlled evaluation (c.f. *Program Examples* – Barker & Anderson, 1988; Hanrahan & Prinsen, 1997; Tsiantis, et al., 1996). While still tentative, these mostly European trials are of considerable importance because they add to the emergent knowledge base on the cost, practicality, and utility of delivering home visitation on a more universal basis. At the indicated-treatment level, research has been conducted in order to test the utility of home visitation with expectant and new mothers who experience substantial multiple risks due to drug addiction. To date, these visitation initiatives most often yield short-term improvements in mothers' well being, parenting practices, home environment, and the use of medical-social services (c.f. *Program Examples* – Black, et al., 1994; Carroll, et al., 1995; Marcenko & Spence, 1994 – *Relevant Narrative Review* – Olds, et al., 1999). Yet, breaking parental addiction, preventing the separation of families, and improving child outcomes in high-risk families through home visitation alone is not a commonly achieved intervention result. Large-scale early interventions expressly designed to work with parents who have serious substance abuse problems are of critical importance (SOU, 2000; U.S. Department of Health and Human Services, 1999) and clearly warrant vigorous development and testing.

Core Early Family Intervention Components

Returning back to successful visitation and enrichment interventions implemented at the selective and in some cases universal-selective intervention levels, the programmatic components of such initiatives are regularly theory-based and draw upon the pre-natal and early childhood risk and protective factors research literature. Home visitation, for example, helps families avoid hazards associated with poor pregnancy outcomes, a risky care giving environment, and negative parent-child interactions. By bringing services to parents, visitation breaks down barriers that block access to prenatal care, which is vital to ensuring healthy infant development. Visitation at this early point not only bolsters the physical development of infants but also aids in the identification of family distress and helps overcome the isolation that parents with infants and young children may feel by providing social support (Olds & Kitzman, 1993; Sherman, et al., 1997). The available research literature indicates that successful home visitation includes combinations of the following program components: offering parents accurate information about the principles of infant and child development so they can form accurate expectations about care giving and their child's behavior; providing easily accessible prenatal care and well-baby visits; parent training and practice in warm and responsive care giving that is balanced with the infant's emerging attempts to act on and control the environment; and parent training and practice in child management techniques that preclude the use of inconsistent and/or harsh reinforcement/punishment (c.f. *Program Examples* – Barker & Anderson, 1988; Davis & Rushton, 1991; Heins, et al., 1987; Olds, 2002 – *Relevant Narrative Reviews* – Berlin, O'Neal, & Brooks-Gunn, 1998; Broberg, 2000; Eckenrode, 2000; Gomby, et al., 1999; Kamerman, 2000; Karoly, et al., 1998; Lagerberg, 2000; Olds & Kitzman, 1993; Olds, et al., 1999; Roditti, 2000, Sherman, et al., 1997; Tableman, 2001; Wasik &

Karweit, 1994; Yoshikawa, 1994 – *Relevant Meta-Analysis* – MacLeod & Nelson, 2000).

Successful early educational enrichment initiatives have some of the same programmatic features as home visitation, with a particular stress on providing children with linguistic, cognitive, and socially promotive experiences in their home and/or early educational environment (c.f. *Program Examples* – Johnson & Walker, 1987; Lally, et al., 1988; Seitz, et al., 1985; Weikart & Schweinhart, 1997 – *Relevant Narrative Reviews* – Durlak, 1997; Fitzgerald, et al., 2003; Karoly, et al., 1998; Olds, et al., 1999; Sherman, et al., 1997; Wasik & Karweit, 1994; Yoshikawa, 1994). Moreover, there are indications in the research literature that children and parents in visitation-enrichment programs may benefit from methods and strategies that have collaborative or bottom-up features (c.f. *Relevant Meta-analysis* – Bremberg & Karlsson, 2001 – *Program Examples* – Barker & Anderson, 1988; Barker, et al., 1992; Day, et al., 1998; Weikart & Schweinhart, 1997). Enrichment programs have demonstrated utility both with and without home visitation (c.f. *Program Examples* – Bekman, 1998; Brooks-Gunn, et al., 1994; Kagitcibasi, 1995). The same goes for home visitation, which has also shown significant long-term, intervention-related benefits without center-based programming (c.f. *Relevant Narrative Review* – Sherman, et al., 1997 – *Program Example* – Olds, 2002). Meta-analyses and controlled trials are needed to compare the relative utility of the different early family interventions: home visitation, center-based early enrichment on its own, combined visitation plus center-based programs, versus no intervention.

Specific vs. Spreading and the Duration of Effects

Successful home visitation and early enrichment initiatives have been associated with both problem specific and spreading program effects. Outcome evaluations of well-formulated and implemented home visitation initiatives indicate that families who participate in such interventions evidence fewer low birth weight and premature births, higher immunization rates, fewer cases of child abuse, fewer child injuries, less infant irritability, and fewer child behavior problems. In a meta-analysis of controlled visitation trials, for example, a medium total effect size (ES= .41) was found on indices of family well-being and child maltreatment across post-intervention and follow-up assessment points (MacLeod & Nelson, 2000). In a comprehensive narrative review of the early intervention literature, Olds and colleagues (1999) identified 23 interventions that positively impacted risk and protective factors related to child behavioral- and emotional-adjustment. Of the 23 interventions, 17 used home visitation as a form of intervention.

Exemplary visitation protocols can also have a wide-ranging effect on participating families. In some instances, immediate improvements have been found for the quality of the home environment (c.f. *Program Examples*– Barker & Anderson, 1988; Davis & Spurr, 1998; Hanrahan & Prinsen, 1998; Huxley & Warner, 1993; Olds, 1997; 2002 – *Relevant Narrative Review* – Olds, et al., 1999 – *Relevant Meta-analyses* – MacLeod & Nelson, 2000; van IJzendoorn et al., 1995). Visited parents have shown more sensitive and promotive care giving, improved well being, and educational competence. Parents who take part in model visitation initiatives have also benefited in terms of greater participation in the paid work force and decreased problem behaviors (c.f. *Program Example* – Olds, 2002).

For early educational enrichment initiatives, immediate and enduring program-related impacts on child cognitive development and educational success have been observed with some regularity in exemplary programs with components that specifically emphasize early learning (c.f. *Program Examples* – Brooks-Gunn, et al., 1994; Kagitcibasi, 1995; Weikart & Schweinhart, 1997 – *Relevant Narrative Reviews* – Durlak, 1997; Fitzgerald, et al., 2003; Karoly, et al., 1998; Olds, et al., 1999; Yoshikawa, 1994). Model enrichment initiatives have also shown spreading program effects, with positive changes noted for parent-child relations, as well as the long-term amelioration of child (e.g., Kagitcibasi, 1995) and adult antisocial behavior (e.g., Weikart & Schweinhart, 1997).

Future work should center on establishing the extent of long-term outcomes. Model enrichment-visitation programs have shown maintenance of program benefits into adolescence (c.f. *Program Example* – Kagitcibasi, 1995) and adulthood (c.f. *Program Example* – Weikart & Schweinhart, 1997). Yet, much still remains to be learned about the long-term benefits of the majority of early intervention programs (Olds, et al., 1999). Replicating and **disaggregating** model interventions as well as a greater investment in documenting possible long-term program effects are needed in order to advance both the visitation and early enrichment fields.

Unresolved Questions about Program Utility

Other factors that possibly relate to the utility of visitation and enrichment initiatives revolve around: program duration and timing of intervention actions. From the field of home visitation, evidence exists in favor of the idea that intensive visitation over a longer period of time yields greater benefits than shorter initiatives (c.f. *Relevant Narrative Reviews* – Olds & Kitzman, 1993; Yoshikawa, 1994 – *Relevant Meta-analysis* – MacLeod & Nelson, 2000). The majority of exemplary early educational enrichment programs commonly last more than one year. Durlak (1997), for instance, concluded after a narrative review of the early enrichment literature that, "…at least 1 year and preferably 2 or more years of a half-day or full-day program is usually necessary to produce the best results" (p. 62).

What about the timing of programs? There is little empirical guidance on this point, but a preliminary conclusion based on the available evidence is that comprehensive visitation should ensure sound prenatal development, work with new parents as they are just beginning to actually become parents, and provide continued services during infancy (c.f. *Program Example* – Olds, 2002). In terms of the timing of enrichment efforts, current research indicates that a young person's readiness to participate in formal education is multi-determined (Blair, 2002). By positively impacting parents' views on learning-education and strengthening a range of basic skills and competencies in young children, model enrichment programs can play an important role in bolstering school readiness and ultimately improving the chances of later educational and social success. In sum, more systematic research is needed to determine the optimal dosage and timing of early intervention programs in general (Sherman, et al., 1997).

Questions

Key points of debate within the home visitation and early educational enrichment fields include some of the following questions: Is it better to use professional or non-professional home visitors? Should parents be told how to properly raise their children or should interventions strengthen parents' and children's own capacity for decision-making and action? Is it feasible or desirable to disseminate useful visitation and/or enrichment initiatives more broadly? Some of these issues are unique to the visitation and enrichment programs, while others have implications for family interventions across developmental periods.

Expert vs. Non-Expert Implementation

As mentioned in *Chapter 1*, top-down intervention models tend to place more program control in the hands of experts. Bottom-up approaches often focus on sharing control between program initiators and participants. The top-down/bottom-up controversy has possible implications for home visitor qualifications. While there is evidence in support of childcare workers' and preschool teachers' formal education and/or specialized training (c.f. *Relevant Narrative Review* – Durlak, 1997; Fitzgerald, et al., 2003 – *Relevant Meta-analysis* – Bremberg & Karlsson, 2001), unanswered questions still remain about the relationship between home visitor qualifications and intervention success.

It is sometimes thought that using non-professional, resource parents as facilitators will increase the program involvement of difficult-to-reach families (e.g., Johnson, Howell, & Molloy, 1993). Resource parents are typically experienced caregivers, who are demographically similar to program participants, and are drawn from the community in which the intervention is being implemented. There are home visitation trials in the United States that show the potential benefits and limits of using non-professional resource parents (c.f. *Program Examples* – Heins, et al., 1987; Huxley & Warner, 1993; Jacobson & Frye, 1991; Julnes, Konefal, Pindur, & Kim, 1994; Rogers & Peoples-Sheps, 1995).

In Europe, the Dutch Mothers Inform Mothers (MIM, Hanrahan & Prinsen, 1997; 1998) offers an example of a visitation protocol that utilizes resource parents. MIM is aimed at empowering new and at-risk parents. Experienced mothers work with intervention parents to improve their knowledge of child health- development and to provide social support for parent-initiated changes in care giving practices. A checklist and series of care giving-child development cartoons provide a starting point for the discussion between the more- and less-experienced parent. MIM underwent a quasi-experimental outcome evaluation in 1998-1999. In this efficacy trial, intervention mothers showed pre- to post-test gains in self-confidence, social participation and educational competence relative to a comparison group of mothers (Hanrahan, & Prinsen, 1997; 1998; Turner & Shepherd, 1999).

An evaluation conducted by Heins and colleagues (1987) of a pre-natal visitation program in the United States provides clues as to the conditions that may help resource mothers be more successful in their work. This selective pre-natal visitation program was conducted in the Southeastern United States. It was designed to improve pregnancy outcomes for first-time adolescent mothers and their infants. Mothers were provided health information, such as education on health risk behaviors, and advocacy for medical and social services. Home visits were made approximately once a month during the entire pregnancy. Registry information showed that intervention mothers had better prenatal care, as measured by more clinical visits, and fewer low birth-weight infants relative to a matched comparison group.

After this first trial was conducted, the original visitation protocol that served 1,140 mothers was revised and implemented as Large Scale Service Program (LS-SP) serving over 6,500 mothers (Rogers & Peoples-Sheps, 1995). Like the original intervention, the LS-SP was designed to improve pregnancy outcomes through pre-natal health and social service provision. In the original program trial, each resource mother was trained for over a month, supervised by professionals, and visited 30-35 intervention mothers. In the LS-SP, each resource mother received three weeks of training, was supervised by professionals, and visited 50-65 intervention mothers. Although program benefits were associated with the LS-SP, the original intervention was considered to be the more potent of the two intervention trials due in part to the effectiveness trial's ambition to serve more mothers which yielded heavier visiting caseloads.

A preliminary conclusion can be drawn from the resource mother studies just described: If visitation protocols have sound program elements and implementation practices (e.g., a good evidence-base, comprehensive training, moderate case loads, and multidisciplinary professional supervision), then there should be little reason not to utilize non-professionals. While this proposition seems reasonable, the relative utility, ease of dissemination, and cost-effectiveness of visitation initiatives implemented by experts versus non-experts has rarely been directly tested (McCurdy, 2000; Musick & Stott, 2000). Expert home visitors may have certain advantages that are difficult to match, such an ability to deal with the medical questions of new parents, as well as social creditability and respect (Olds, 2002). These advantages may translate into better access and improved retention of families. An ongoing trial of the Nurse-Family Partnership in Denver, Colorado promises to yield a direct test of this question (Olds, 2002).

Parent and Child Capacitation

The top-down/bottom-up distinction also has potential consequences for the way in which program facilitators interact with parents and children. Intervention involvement and program-related benefits maybe improved by working with parents in a respectful partnership (e.g., Barnard, et al., 1988). Scott (in press) offered a series of concrete examples of how respect can be nurtured in a family intervention:

> Features of a collaborative approach include asking about child strengths as well as difficulties, praising parents for good aspects of parenting, respecting them as the expert on the individual characteristics of their child, listening carefully to, and showing understanding of their beliefs about their child's behaviour, working on solutions parents generate themselves... (p. 9)

The Parent Advisor Service (PAS) provides an illustration of a collaborative intervention approach that focuses on parent capacitation. PAS is a British visitation protocol designed to foster parents' sense of their own problem solving and coping capacity. Parents and home visitors explore a variety of topics related to childrearing. This parent-lead talk forms the foundation for the intervention actions. These actions include problem solving and planning activities, information giving, clarification of parenting and child development beliefs, skills training, social support for positive parenting practices and, in cases of need, advocacy for social, medical, and psychiatric services.

PAS was originally aimed at families who have an infant with a developmental delay (Davis & Rushton, 1991). It was later tested with families who have preschool children with social and emotional problems (Davis & Spurr, 1998). Controlled efficacy trials of the PAS have indicated the program's utility in terms of pre- to post-test improvements in environmental conditions within the home, mothers' well being, and child's development and behavior as measured by an independent observer and parent ratings. PAS has been further refined and implemented as a multi-tiered, mental health service model in the United Kingdom (Day, Davis, & Hind, 1998).

At least one visitation intervention study (Barnard, et al., 1988) has directly compared a top-down versus collaborative method of intervention (Olds, et al., 1999). In the top-down program variation, disadvantaged mothers received home visits from a nurse who provided health- and development-education and services. In the collaborative version, intervention mothers and nurses worked explicitly on forming a mutually respectful and supportive relationship. The parent–visitor relationship was thought to provide mothers with a model for positive interactions with their infants. The intervention was conducted during the pre- and post-natal periods for approximately a year and a half until the intervention child was one year old.

In this controlled efficacy trial (Barnard, et al., 1988), mothers in the collaborative model were rated as showing greater caregiving competence and sensitivity compared to mothers in the top-down variation. Subgroup analyses indicated that the collaborative approach may have been more appropriate for higher risk mothers and the top-down model was more useful with lower risk mothers. Because families who experience high levels of risk are often difficult to engage in intervention efforts (Nye, Zucker, & Fitzgerald, 1995; Szapocznik & Williams, 2000; Taylor & Biglan, 1998; Tolan & Guerra, 1994), collaborative intervention strategies may represent a promising way to address the challenge of intervention disengagement in these populations (Dusenbury, 2000).

When one looks to the early educational enrichment field parallel issues emerge, particularly in the form of how parents, teachers, and caregivers interact with children. There is some debate as to whether or not children in enrichment programs benefit more from a child- or adult/teacher-centered pedagogy (Bremberg & Karlsson, 2001). In the child-focused system, there is an emphasis on tailoring the learning process to the child's own initiatives and performance. In an adult-teacher centered pedagogy, there is little room for the child's own initiative, teachers provide the structure and content of learning, and instruction is more uniformly administered.

Many of the most successful early, educational, enrichment programs explicitly adopt more collaborative forms of teacher/child interaction (Roditti, 2000). A meta-analysis of 52 studies, for instance, examined the impact of preschool and daycare experiences on child problem behaviors and cognitive development (Bremberg & Karlsson, 2001). The authors of this meta-analysis concluded that the use of child-centered instruction methods, as well as formal education for preschool teachers, was associated with a significant lessening of externalizing and internalizing behaviors in children. Increases in cognitive development were also evident. The success of visitation and enrichment initiatives that assume a collaborative tenor with parents and children also provide evidence in support of this approach.

Dissemination Research

Is it possible and beneficial to take dissemination efforts one-step further by implementing strong early family interventions on a large scale basis? There is a movement in the United States and Europe to more widely disseminate successful visitation and early enrichment protocols. Two approaches seem to be evident. In the U.S., dissemination models for successful, selective, early interventions have been developed and are being made more accessible to greater numbers of at-risk families. In Europe, a two-pronged approach has been taken in which selective visitation protocols are made more available to at-risk families and similar programming is increasingly extended to families that are not a part of a high-risk group.

From the U.S., the Nurse-Family Partnership provides an example of how a selective home visitation program can begin to move into the mainstream of practice and service. The Nurse-Family Partnership's dissemination can, in part, be credited to the impressive long-term benefits the intervention demonstrated in its initial efficacy trial (Olds, et al., 1988). Another ingredient is the National Center for Children, Families and Communities at the University of Colorado Health Sciences Center, which was created to provide organizational support for the program's dissemination (Olds, 2002). The U.S. Department of Justice has also included the Nurse-Family Partnership in its Weed and Seed initiative (Olds, 1997). This multi-agency plan is designed to bring evidence-based interventions to inner-city areas by weeding, removing community risks, and seeding, supporting positive community development. The Nurse-Family Partnership is also included in the Center for the Study and Prevention of Violence's and the U.S. Office of Juvenile Justice and Delinquency Prevention's Blue Prints web site and book[5]. The Blue Prints series provides practical information on eleven well-established interventions that have been shown to reduce violence and its precursors. The U.S. Office of Justice Programs and the U.S. Department of Justice have jointly supported effectiveness trials of the ten Blue Print model programs in implementation sites across the United States. In the context of nationwide dissemination mechanisms like the National Center, Weed and Seed, and Blue Prints, the Nurse-Family Partnership should continue to bring much needed insights and advancements to the home visitation field.

European initiatives have tested the feasibility and utility of bringing visitation programs to a broader cross-section of expectant parents (Aronen, 1993; Puura, et al., 2002; Tsiantis, et al., 1996). The history of the Child Development Program (CDP) provides an illustration of how a promising universal-selective visitation protocol has managed to receive exposure in the general population. The CDP has been widely disseminated in the United Kingdom and the Republic of Ireland (Barker, 1992), with over 100,000 families having participated. A variation of the CDP that uses non-professional resource mothers has also influenced the development of a similar intervention in the Netherlands.

In the CDP, professional home visitors work with first-time and at-risk parents to set goals related to the child's health and development. These goals include teaching play activities to promote language or cognitive development, providing nutritious recipes, encouraging positive parenting practices, and promoting utilization of health services. The implementation and readjustment of these plans is regularly tracked during monthly home visits. While its long-term impact is yet to be assessed, an efficacy trial has indicated immediate and important program benefits[6].

After its initial efficacy trial, the dissemination of the CDP began in 1984. Variations of the CDP were subsequently developed: An Urban and Rural Model, the Irish Community Mothers Program, and an Asian Parent Program. Health visitors from 20 to 30 health authorities have regularly implemented CDP, or one of its variations, through monthly home visits to all first-time and at-risk mothers in their respective service areas. In all, approximately 20,000 families participate annually. All CDP variations provide at least one prenatal visit and eight, one-hour visits through the first year of life. Evaluation is done using the Health Visitor Survey. The survey is accompanied by a software package that helps service providers make use of information derived from the evaluation. An effectiveness trial of CDP yielded positive results. One hundred and fifty professional health visitors participated in a cross-sectional follow-up evaluation of 31,791 CDP intervention children. These intervention children were compared to a matched sample of non-intervention children from the same health authority. Relative to the comparison group, intervention children were 41% less likely to be on child-abuse registers and 50% less likely to experience physical abuse (Barker, Anderson, & Chalmers, 1992).

There have also been multi-national attempts in Europe to implement and test universal-selected visitation programs. The European Union/World Health Organization Multi-Center Psychosocial Promotion Project was a cross-national home visitation initiative (Tsiantis, et al., 1996). Primary health care workers in Cyprus, Greece, the Federal Republic of Yugoslavia,

Portugal, Slovenia, and Turkey served as home visitors in this effort. As in other European visitation initiatives, the EU/WHO Multi-Center Project focused on helping first- time and at-risk parents recognize and develop their own capacity as care givers. Families were visited from the pre-natal period until the beginning of the third year of life. Intervention activities were guided by a collaborative intervention protocol that conceptualizes visitor–parent interaction as an intimate and respectful relationship. Visitors used a semi-structured interview to explore with parents a variety of topics related to parenting and childrearing. This discussion provided a foundation for intervention activities such as information sharing and support for positive forms of care giving. In a controlled efficacy trial, intervention mothers evidenced a number of benefits relative to a control group of mothers who received standard health/welfare services. Benefits associated with program participation included increased self-reported comfort in care giving and the caregiver role, improved mother well-being and promotive parenting practices.

The European Early Promotion Project (EEPP) represents another major European cross- national, home visitation effort (Puura, et al., 2002). Program development began in 1992 and implementation is currently underway in health-care centers located in Cyprus, Greece, the Federal Republic of Yugoslavia, the United Kingdom, and Finland. The outcome evaluation for this initiative includes pre-, post-, and follow-up testing with intervention and comparison health-care centers. One hundred families from each participating country are scheduled to receive EEPP visits and 100 families are to receive services as usual. As in the EU/WHO Multi-Center Project, primary health-care workers are trained to conduct home visits to new and at-risk parents using collaborative intervention strategies. The ultimate goal of this program is to improve the quality of parent-child interactions as a way to promote the infant/child's physical, social, and emotional development. EEPP represents one of the most ambitious controlled trials of a universal-selective visitation initiative to date. A complete outcome evaluation was still pending at the time this review was written.

In the U.S., the home visitation-enrichment field is largely characterized by a number of rigorously tested programs for at-risk families. These are families who maybe poor, young, of ethnic minority status, or they may be families that have children with a developmental challenge or adjustment difficulties (Olds, et al., 1999; Sherman, et al., 1997). Although the empirical research literature on European home visitation-enrichment has also been marked by a selective emphasis, the trend towards conducting program trials of more accessible universal-selective home visitation may be related to the policy stance that several European governments have taken on prevention and intervention in the early stages of life. In some countries, early family interventions are backed by policies that support families through monetary supplements, paid and job-protected leaves from work for parents, as well as accessible health and child care (Kamerman, 2000). European health and social welfare services also provide a strong pre-existing framework to reach large numbers of service professionals and parents (Puura, et al., 2002). Specially designed post-secondary education for professional home visitors in European countries like the United Kingdom provide further support for bringing visitation efforts into the mainstream experience of all first time parents.

Kamerman (2000) offered a thought-provoking explanation for the apparent differences between the American and European experience in early family intervention and it is as follows:

> Clearly, a wide range of programs in Europe directly target very young children and their families or provide a strong foundation of support for families generally. Without the label, they include all that we in the United States would consider "early intervention" programs and more......other countries have established such policies and programs based on far less research than exists in the United States as the result of political will, not necessarily rigorous research. Building on commonly held values about children and their families, these countries have invested in these policies and programs on the assumption that children are important, that they must be well cared for, that the society has a large stake in the future of its children, and that over time there will be lessons from the program experiences that will lead to improvements......In the end, it is simply a matter of priorities and values. (p. 626)

While there still seems to be a gulf, it can be argued that the direction of American and European early intervention efforts are moving towards one another, with European early intervention researchers delving deeper into systematic program evaluation and American scientists working harder in the areas of social policy and program dissemination. A close marriage between innovation, evaluation, policy, and dissemination promises to benefit families on both sides of the Atlantic.

Future Directions

The family can play an integral role in the promotion of positive development of the individual. The following is a summary of ideas that may assist in the design, implementation and evaluation of future early family interventions.

- Among family interventions implemented in the zero- to five-year age range, few programs have exhibited as many positive outcomes as that of model home visitation and early educational enrichment initiatives.

- What is it specifically that makes model early family interventions useful? At this point it is safer to say that we know that various combinations of intervention components work well. Unpacking studies do exist, but there is clearly a need for more efforts along these lines.

- Exemplary visitation and enrichment programs should be further examined to better understand which approaches are most useful for which families.

- Answering the "what works" question is only the first step. Interventionists must strive for quality implementation. Program developers and other interested parties must address the challenge of making well-implemented, evidence-based programs available to families who can benefit from such initiatives.

Chapter Endnotes

[1]Illustrative theories are described throughout this book. It is beyond the scope of this review to go deeply into the many promising theories that have salience to the prevention and youth development field. While supported in the research literature, the reader should be aware that the theories described are not meant to provide the definitive last word in any given area. These theories have potential value in that they offer an explanatory framework for understanding why particular interventions maybe thought to work.

[2]The Nurse-Family Partnership was first tested with a research design that would allow the program designers to determine how much of the program was *enough* to generate a lasting effect. In this efficacy trial, mothers were matched and randomized into four groups. All participants were provided infant medical screening and referral services. This was the only intervention planned for the Prenatal Minimal Intervention Group One. The Prenatal Minimal Intervention Group Two was provided with free transportation to their child's prenatal and well-baby doctor visits. Prenatal Complete Intervention Group was provided all of the aforementioned services and was also visited by a nurse approximately nine times during the course of their pregnancies. The Pre/Postnatal Complete Intervention Group received all services and received visits from a nurse up to the age of two.

[3]In the Memphis trial, all participants were provided free transportation to their child's prenatal/well-baby doctor visits. This was the only intervention planned for the Prenatal Minimal Intervention Group 1. The Prenatal Minimal Intervention Group 2 was provided with free transportation plus infant medical screening/referral services. Prenatal Complete Intervention Group was provided all of the aforementioned services and was visited by a nurse during the course of their pregnancy and two times after the birth of their child. The Pre/Postnatal Complete Intervention Group received all of the aforementioned services and was also frequently visited by a nurse up to the age of two.

[4]At the age of three, IHDP intervention children had significantly higher IQ scores and fewer behavior problems in relative to a matched control condition. The intervention gains were most pronounced for the heavy LBW group in terms of IQ. Intervention effects for mothers included more months employed and a higher return rate to work relative to a control group. However, intervention mothers reported more brief illnesses/conditions in comparison to the control condition. Researchers suggested that this maybe due to the intervention mothers' increased knowledge about child health/development. At the age of five (two years post intervention), the heavy LBW intervention group had significantly higher scores on indices of cognitive development (e.g., IQ, vocabulary) than the heavy LBW control group. No other significant differences were found on behavioral competence or physical health outcome measures at the age of five.

[5]See the Blueprints web site at: www.colorado.edu/cspv/blueprints/Default.htm

[6]The Child Development Program's initial efficacy trial was conducted between 1980-1983 and drew program participants from six health authorities. Professional health visitors in each authority were matched and randomly assigned to either an intervention or traditional service control group. Intervention and control children were randomly selected from the visitors caseloads. Participants in the intervention group showed gains (from Year 1 to Year 3) in terms of improved home environment, immunization and hospitalization rates relative to the control group. Intervention children were less frequently registered on child abuse records and had fewer reported physical injuries relative to the control group. Intervention gains in educational and health home environment, mother's personality, child's personality, socialization and global development were also evidenced in the majority of the test regions. In the two regions where detailed dietary assessments were completed, there were intervention gains in the recommended daily allowance intake of nutrients for intervention versus control group (Barker & Anderson, 1988).

Chapter 3
Later Family Intervention

Introduction

Coercion theory (Patterson, 1982) offers an illustrative theoretical framework that connects important aspects of the family risk and protective factor research literature to a range of later family-related intervention efforts. This theory links the quality of parent-youth interaction in childhood and adolescence and a young person's adjustment across settings and developmental periods. In this perspective, the development of child and adolescent problem behaviors is largely framed in terms of the quality of family interactions.

A coercive cycle of interaction can take root in the challenging behavior of the child and poor parental readiness or practices. A definition of coercion is control through force or intimidation, which can be initiated by parents and/or children. An example of a coercive exchange begun by the child might be when the child begins to whine, cry or generally misbehave when wanting a toy in a store and the parent says no. When the parent gives the child the toy in order to stop the child's unpleasant outburst, this may positively reinforce the child's coercive behavior. The child will be more likely to try this tactic again because of the positive final outcome–a new toy. The next time, however, possibly the parent participates in their own kind of strategic behavior, beginning a cycle of coercive interchanges. Parents who are caught up in such a cycle are less likely to follow through with mild discipline for minor problem behaviors but tend to react inconsistently, sometimes retreating when conflict is at its height and at other times countering immediately with explosive, illogical, or harsh punishment (Biglan, et al, 1997; Scott, in press).

To decrease the chances of such a pattern of interaction beginning in childhood, Patterson and Narrett (1990) suggested that parents respond by ignoring whining or tantrums, thus removing the opportunity for the reinforcement of coercive behavior. Further, they asserted that consistent, mild, and non-physical punishment for misbehavior has been equated with lower levels of aggression in children. The interpretation of what constitutes mild punishment or an appropriate behavioral consequence varies within and across nations. The term *time-out*, for instance, has a variety of connotations. How a parent in a particular country or region administers a time-out may differ, with a child in one society spending a few minutes alone in his or her room or another parent in another country making use of some other method or socially appropriate place for the child and parent to calm down. Despite variation in practice, it can be argued that the core principle at the heart of time out is preserved as long as the child who is acting disobediently is not the recipient of a great deal of interest (Webster-Stratton, personal communication, 2002). This inattention will likely result in a decline in misbehavior.

Early coercive exchanges between children and parents may lay the groundwork for the persistent incompatibility of childhood to flourish in adolescence. Coercive interaction in the parent-child relationship is thought to teach the young person a number of expedient yet aversive behaviors (Coie, 1996). Coercion and aggression can yield many immediate benefits with peers in early childhood such as being first in line or getting a highly coveted toy. However, as the meaning of friendship grows to include an emphasis on material and emotional reciprocity, the profit margin associated with coercion begins to shrink (Hawley, 1999). Rejection by prosocial peers, the risk of enduring affiliation and identification with antisocial peers, and the escalation of problem behaviors may follow if children continue this style of interaction into late childhood and adolescence (Patterson, 1982). While these events transpire at school and in peer groups, a cycle of coercive parent-youth interaction also may endure in the family in the form of consistently poor communication, inadequate supervision, and inconsistent limit setting (French, Conrad, & Turner, 1995; Patterson, Reid, & Dishion, 1992; Stattin & Kerr, 2000). Taking deliberate steps to stop the cycle of coercive parent-child/adolescent interaction is considered to be a way to create a protective family context that becomes a resource the young person can draw on throughout her or his development (Dishion, Patterson, Stoolmiller, & Skinner, 1991; Patterson, 1992).

Chapter Organization

This chapter focuses on family interventions for school aged youth and their families. The first subsection offers a description of exemplar later family intervention elements and program illustrations. A best evidence synthesis of the later family intervention literature as it relates to the prevention of youth problem behaviors and the promotion of youth development then follows. This chapter concludes with a *Questions* and then a *Future Directions* subsection.

Exemplary Program Examples

In this subsection, exemplary family prevention programs conducted in the childhood to adolescent range have been organized around two categories: **family training and therapy**. This categorization was drawn, with some modifications, from an American expert group's classification of successful family interventions (Kumpfer & Alvarado, 1998, November)[1]. In the present review, the term family training is used to describe those prevention programs that have demonstrated utility with parents or families of children and teens who experience risk in the universal to selective range (*i.e., universal, universal-selective, selective – See Figure 1*). The generic content of family training regularly includes the provision of information and instruction in a number of skills. Training often involves both parents and young people.

Family therapy encompasses those later family programs that have successfully intervened with children, teens, and/or parents whose risk level falls in the selective prevention to treatment range (*i.e., selective-indicated, indicated, indicated-treatment – See Figure 1*). Family therapy has some of the same content features as family training, like focusing on skills development and improving the quality of family interactions. However, family therapy differs in that additional intervention components and more tailored strategies maybe used to address the needs of higher-risk youth and families. Intervention activities associated with family therapy may also be raised to a higher intensity level relative to family training   (c.f., *Program Examples* – Catalano, Gainey, Fleming, Haggerty, & Johnson, 1999; Park, et al., 2000).

Figure 1. Family Training-Therapy and Risk

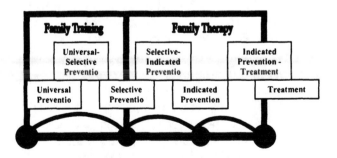

Model interventions, especially those that have a substantial history, are sometimes tested with samples that experience variable amounts of risk.

When initiatives show program-related effects with different samples, this makes for a more complex categorization of programs but also offers more precision in terms of understanding and documenting the limits of an intervention's generalizability. As Kumpfer and colleagues (1998) stated, "Thus while dichotomizing discussions, funding initiatives, intervention programs, and relevant literatures into categories of prevention and treatment can be useful, it can also be misleading if they are seen not as a continuum but as dichotomous alternatives" (p. 83). In the following subsection, an arguably less clean but hopefully accurate representation of the range of exemplary later family intervention work is presented.

Another organizational point that should be noted is that the risk and protective factors targeted for change in many later family interventions are empirically linked to a wide spectrum of youth problem behaviors (Kumpfer & Alvarado, 1998, November; Lochman & van den Steenhoven, 2002; Webster-Stratton, 2001). Yet, the prevention research literature on the topic has tended to be problem specific in focus (Kumpfer, Alexander, McDonald, & Olds, 1998; Tolan, Quintana, & Gorman-Smith, 1998). Because many family interventions for children and adolescents have been designed with a particular type of problem behavior in mind, the next two subsections describe promising, and well established, later family interventions relevant to the reduction of youth antisocial behavior, youth substance use, and risk due to parental addiction. Where appropriate, interventions that have demonstrated a spreading effect across problem domains will be noted and integrated into these subsections[2].

Family Training-Therapy: Preventing Youth Antisocial Behavior

Family Training. Examples of promising American and European family training programs with relevance to the reduction of antisocial precursors include DARE to be you (DTBY; Fritz, Heyl-Miller, Kreutzer, & MacPhee, 1995; Heyl-Miller, MacPhee, & Fritz, 1998) and Parent-Link (Davis & Hester, 1996). DTBY, for instance, works at the selective prevention level with at-risk families who have two- to five-year-old children. This intervention makes use of a family-focused intervention format in which parents take part in workshops and support groups to improve child rearing practices and corresponding skills like problem solving, communication, and child management techniques. Children also develop relevant skills by participating in games and activities that have parallel intervention content.

DTBY's efficacy trial took place over a two-year period in the American state of Colorado. The primary intervention was conducted over an eight- to 12-week period in the first intervention year, with regular **booster sessions** spread out over the second year of program activities. Relative to a control group, DTBY parents reported improved parenting practices, greater confidence in their care giving abilities, and viewed their child's behavior as less troublesome after one year of program activities. After the second year in the program, DTBY parents maintained earlier gains. As apart of its program development, school and community intervention components have been added to DTBY (Schinke, et al., 2002). See narrative reviews by Kumpfer and Alvarado (1998), Lochman and van den Steenhoven (2002), Scott (in press), and Sherman and colleagues (1997) for other successful program examples of this type.

Family Therapy. Well-established family therapies exist for higher risk children. Evidence now indicates that if high-risk children receive appropriate intervention early on, before antisocial behaviors become entrenched, the prospects for positive development can be greatly improved (Webster-Stratton, 2001). The Incredible Years Series offers an illustration of a well-established intervention that works toward the amelioration of child behavior problems. The Incredible Years represents a collection of interconnected programs that can be implemented with parents, children in the 3- to 10-year age range, child-care workers, home visitors, and teachers. Programs in the Series include: BASIC, ADVANCE, Dinosaur School, SCHOOL/Supporting Your Child's Education, and TEACHER. BASIC, the first intervention to be developed, is the best tested and most commonly used of all of the interventions in the Series. BASIC was first used in a university-based mental health setting in the United States. This intervention was originally a treatment designed to teach positive parenting practices to parents whose children have been diagnosed with clinically significant aggressive and/or oppositional behaviors.

Specifically, BASIC consists of a series of therapist- or interventionist-led parent workshop sessions. A well-elaborated, collaborative intervention model guides the use of a number of intervention strategies (Webster-Stratton, 1998c). A valuable technique is the use of videotapes that show everyday parent-child interactions with models of useful as well as counter-productive parenting practices. Videos provide opportunities for observational learning and group role-playing. Another strategy involves encouraging parents to practice learned skills in real-life situations via performance-based homework assignments. Other methods used to promote change include providing information through a parenting guide, establishing a parent Buddy network to give support and reinforcement, and involving parents in cognitive exercises like problem solving and cognitive reframing.

Published evaluations of BASIC, while numerous, have for the most part been small- to medium-sized in scale. Efficacy and effectiveness trials of BASIC, however, have consistently demonstrated significant, program-related benefits like improved parenting practices, parent-child interaction, and child behavior (Scott, Spender, Doolan, Jacobs, & Aspland, 2001; Taylor, Schmidt, Pepler, & Hodgins, 1998; Webster-Stratton, 1981; 1982; 1984; 1990a; 1990b;

1992). Programs in the Incredible Years Series are best known for intervention-associated declines in disruptive- and acting-out behavior in children, but programs in the Series have also demonstrated program-related decreases in child abuse rates and improvements in academic performance (Webster-Stratton, 1998a).

Among programs in the Series, BASIC currently has the most evidence in favor of its long-term utility. For BASIC, maintenance of pre- to post-test benefits have been shown up to three years post intervention (Webster-Stratton, Hollinsworth, & Kolpacoff, 1989; Webster-Stratton, Kolpacoff, & Hollinsworth, 1988; Webster-Stratton, 1990a). While one-year follow up benefits have been demonstrated relative to a traditional form of family therapy (Webster-Stratton, 1984) and Head Start services (Webster-Stratton, 1998b), the longer-term maintenance of intervention gains has not been evidenced relative to a control or alternative intervention group. In the majority of the BASIC evaluations, the wait-list control groups are regularly offered BASIC or some variation of BASIC while the original intervention groups undergo follow-up testing.

There are limits as to what we can say about the long-term utility of BASIC in particular and the Incredible Years Series in general. Yet, BASIC is one of the few interventions that have successfully undergone rigorous testing outside of its home country. BASIC has been implemented and evaluated in the United States, Canada, and the United Kingdom (Patterson, et al., 2002; Scott, et al., 2001; Taylor, et al., Webster-Stratton, 1998a), with an ongoing trial taking place in Norway (Mørch, et al., 2001; Mørch, 2003), as well as training activities in Sweden (K. Hansson, personal communication, 2003). At the time this review was written, three BASIC trials were completed: one in Canada and two in the United Kingdom. A particular strength of these trials is that three independent research teams carried out the evaluations in non-university affiliated mental health clinics (Scott, et al., 2001; Taylor, et al., 1998) and a community-based setting (Patterson, et al., 2002). The longest follow up conducted was six months. The overall pattern of results across these evaluations, in most instances, was generally comparable to intervention gains found in American program trials.

One can take the BASIC program evaluation conducted in South London-West Sussex as a case in point (Scott, et al., 2001). This study was implemented with one hundred and ten parents of children who showed elevated levels of conduct problems. BASIC was offered to parents through trained mental health therapists. A pre-/post-test design with block random assignment of parents to BASIC or a wait-list control was utilized. As in the American and Canadian program tests, British children whose parents underwent BASIC training in this study showed significant reductions in antisocial and problem behavior on multiple indices. These youngsters were also less likely to be diagnosed with oppositional defiant disorder. All program- related reductions were made relative to children in the control group. Relative to control parents, BASIC parents also showed significant improvements in parental practices.

In the final analysis, BASIC is arguably one of the most robust and well investigated later family interventions available today. Program evaluations of BASIC have used some of the most rigorous evaluation designs and methods available, such as random assignment to condition, the use of standardized, blind observational techniques, and multiple informants to assess behavioral change. BASIC has also undergone systematic testing in order to determine the most powerful and cost efficient combinations of intervention modalities and formats. BASIC outcome evaluations have indicated the program's reduced cost and relative utility compared to traditional therapeutic approaches. Finally, variations of BASIC and other interventions within the Series have also been successfully tested as prevention programs in non-clinical community settings such as Head Start centers, daycare centers, and schools (e.g., Spaccarelli, Cotler, & Penman, 1992; Webster-Stratton, 1998a; Webster-Stratton & Hammond, 1997; Webster-Stratton, Reid, & Hammond, 2001). Illustrations of other salient U.S. family therapies include Parent Management Training (Forgatch & Martinez, 1999; Patterson & Forgatch, 1987) and Family Effectiveness Training (Szapocznik & Williams, 2000). Reviews by Kumpfer and Alvarado (1998), Lochman and van den Steenhoven (2002), Scott (in press), and Sherman and colleagues (1997) offer examples of other successful family therapies for children.

A collection of well-established interventions for families with high-risk adolescents should also be mentioned at this point. Functional Family Therapy (FFT) offers an example of a family therapy of U.S. derivation tailored for use with troubled teens. FFT works with teens whose risk spans from a selected, at-risk status for delinquency, to juvenile offenders with or without a clinical diagnosis of conduct disorder. Individual families are usually referred to FFT through the social or justice systems as an alternative to incarceration or as an after incarceration transition program. The total number of intervention hours can range from eight to 30 hours across a three-month period. FFT's primary intervention principles are: 1) engagement/ motivation, 2) behavior change, and 3) generalization. The engagement/motivation period focuses on breaking down a family's negative expectations, affect, and thinking, as well as building of a respectful and positive relationship between the interventionist and the family. The behavioral change phase is guided by an assessment of the family strengths and weaknesses. The interventionist then designs a plan of action that is grounded in a range of evidence-based intervention strategies and used in accordance with the particular context of the individual family. The diversity of available intervention activities here can include, but are not limited to, training in social-, communication-, problem solving-, and conflict resolution skills for all family members as well as parent training. Intervention activities can also explicitly be aimed at siblings. Finally, the generalization stage is designed to promote the maintenance of long-term change by helping families deal with setbacks and linking them to existing resources in the community.

As of 1998, FFT was tested a total of thirteen times with experimental (e.g., Alexander & Parsons, 1973; Hansson, Cederblad, Höök, 2000; Klein, Alexander, & Parsons, 1977) and quasi-experimental designs (e.g., Barton et al., 1985; Gordon, et al., 1988; Gordon, Graves, & Arbuthnot, 1995). Published FFT trials have been empirically rigorous yet often small- to medium-sized in scale. Researchers have noted that across FFT's multiple trials, this program is 25-60% more successful than conventional approaches or no intervention at reducing reoffending and other institutional placements (Alexander, et al., 1998). Positive intervention- related results have been demonstrated in follow up studies that have spanned up to six years (e.g. Gordon, Graves, & Arbuthnot, 1995). Positive results have also been noted for siblings up to three years after intervention (e.g., Alexander & Parsons, 1973; Parsons & Alexander, 1973). Process-outcome analyses have linked FFT's intervention success to changes in family relations and communication styles, as well as the interventionists' pedagogical and relational skills (Alexander, et al., 1998).

A program evaluation conducted in the American state of Utah, offers an illustration of published FFT trials (Alexander & Parsons, 1973; Parsons & Alexander, 1973). In this case, participating teens and their families were referred by the juvenile justice system, predominately for first-time offenses. Seventy-five families were randomly assigned to FFT, an emotion-centered family therapy (Emotion), or a control group. A post-hoc, insight-oriented counseling condition with eleven families was also added when the follow up registry data was collected (Insight). In this study, FFT families evidenced improved family interactions relative to families in the emotion-centered family therapy and the control condition. Follow up data, at six- and 18-months post intervention, indicated that FFT youth had a significantly lower rate of reoffending (26%) relative to youth in both alternative intervention groups (Emotion=47%; Insight=73%), the control condition (50%), and county-wide rates of juvenile reoffending (51%). At a later follow up, two and a half to three and a half years later, recorded offenses for referred youths' brothers and sisters also showed a significantly lower rate of offending (20%) relative to siblings in the alternative intervention groups (Emotion=59%; Insight=63%) and the control condition (40%).

FFT is a well-established intervention that has undergone development and testing in the United States for over 30 years. FFT has been selected as a Blue Prints model intervention and is presently being implemented in up to 80 sites across the United States. Work on utilizing FFT with Swedish families began in the early 1980s, with the first randomized, controlled trial occurring between 1993-1995. To date, two trials have been conducted, one in Lund (Hansson, Cederblad, & Höök, 2000) and the other in Växjö (Johansson, Drott-Englén, Hansson, & Benderix, 2002). As in America, participating adolescents primarily came in contact with FFT via the justice or social welfare system. In the Lund trial, eighty-nine referred families were randomly assigned to either an intervention (I) or a control (C) condition. An examination of registry data at post-testing and after one-year post intervention showed that FFT youth had a lower rate of reoffending relative to control youngsters (Post test: I=33% versus C=65%; Follow up: I=41% versus C=82%). Within FFT families, intervention teens and their mothers reported pre- to follow-up improvements on indices of mental health. Complete youth- and mother-reported data was not available for the control families. The quasi-experimental trial conducted in Växjö showed similar pattern of results but with a smaller number of families. Relative to a matched sample of comparison youth (n=17) referred for an alternative treatment, FFT youth (n=45) evidenced a lower rate of reoffending at the 18-month, follow up assessment (I=35% versus C=65%).

Multisystemic Therapy (MST) offers an example of another well-established family therapy appropriate for use with high-risk pre-teens and teens (Borduin, 1999; Henggeler, et al., 1996). Interventionists and families work together to develop and tailor services based on the family's identified strengths and risks. Based on the family's needs and context, interventionists provide mental health services like addiction and marriage counseling, individualized therapy, strategic-, structural-, behavioral-, and cognitive-behavioral family therapies, as well as advocacy for social- and medical-services. Parents are often trained in positive parenting practices based on communication, problem solving, and conflict resolution skills as well as non-coercive behavioral management, monitoring of the young person's peer associations, and encouragement of youth academic and vocational efforts. Young people are also able to receive direct services from the interventionist such as social- and thinking-skills training and anger management. Other core features of MST focus on monitoring the process of the intervention on a regular basis, ensuring that intervention actions are not only contextually but also developmentally appropriate, promoting family empowerment, and working to transfer positive, intervention-related changes across contexts. Process-outcome analyses have associated MST's program success to interventionists' ability to maintain treatment fidelity, which, in turn, is linked to improvements in family interactions and reductions in deviant peer associations (Huey, Henggeler, Brondino, & Pickrel, 2000).

The MST approach was developed in the 1970's and has undergone comprehensive evaluations on multiple occasions in the United States (e.g., Borduin, Mann, Cone, Henggeler, & et al., 1995; Brunk, Henggeler, &

Whelan, 1987; Henggeler, Melton, & Smith, 1992; Henggeler, Melton, Smith, Schoenwald, & Hanley, 1993) with a recently completed trial in Canada (e.g., Leschied & Cunningham, 1998; 1999; in press). U.S. evaluations, while sometimes small- to medium-sized in scale, have yielded impressive results. For instance, an evaluation conducted in Missouri showed positive program effects up to four years post- intervention in terms of increased cohesion in family interactions, improved parent mental health, lower reoffending rates, and lower violent- and drug-related crimes. These gains were made relative to a group of young offenders who completed services as usual (individual therapy), a group who dropped out of usual services, a group of MST dropouts, and a group who refused participation in any program (Borduin, Mann, Cone, Henggeler, & et al., 1995). MST is one of the model Blue Print programs, is currently undergoing additional effectiveness trials in the United States, and is being tested in Norway (Ogden, 2001). Other examples of American family therapies that have a positive track record with this population of troubled adolescents include Brief Strategic Family Therapy (Szapocznik & Williams, 2000). Outcome evaluations of interventions conducted by Bank, Marlowe, Reid, Patterson, and Weinrott (1990) and Emshoff (1983) describe additional promising American program examples. Multidimensional Treatment Foster Care has also had considerable success in the United States (Chamberlain & Reid, 1998), with an ongoing trial taking place in Sweden (K. Hansson, personal communication, 2003).

Family Training-Therapy: Preventing Youth Substance Use and Risk Due to Parental Addiction

Family Training. Preparing for the Drug Free Years, now renamed Guiding Good Choices, is an example of a well established family training program (GGC; Hawkins & Catalano, 2003; O'Donnell, Hawkins, Catalano, Abbott, & Day, 1995; Park, et al., 2000). GGC is appropriate for use with the families of older children and early adolescents who experience low- to moderate-levels of risk. In GGC, parents take part as a group in five, two-hour training sessions. These workshops focus on parent training in youth management techniques and emotional regulation. This is facilitated by providing general information on youth development and drug education, helping parents to clarify their views on youth substance use, and encouraging the creation of a family alcohol and drug policy. In the majority of sessions, an emphasis is placed on activities that increase a young person's investment in the family. Youth join their parents in one training session that deals with the promotion of **social resistance skills** and also participate in parent-child homework. In a universal trial conducted in a rural part of the United States, GGC youth evidenced significantly lower alcohol initiation- and use-rates relative to control youth up to three and a half years after intervention activities ended. At this time point, GGC parents also still retained stronger views against adolescent substance use (Park, et al., 2000).

The Strengthening Families Program[3] (SFP; Kumpfer, Molgaard, & Spoth, 1996) offers a unique example of a later family intervention that has demonstrated its utility across the prevention to treatment spectrum. SFP is American in origin. It has been culturally adapted and implemented in English, French, and Spanish in various sites in the United States. International program trials have also taken place, or are ongoing. The SFP's core intervention components focus on increasing social bonds within the family and promoting connections to the community in an effort to delay youth drug debuts and curb existing use. Along with training in positive, non-punitive parenting practices, emotional regulation, communication, and conflict management, SFP parents are provided information on child development and health. Children receive similar training as a group and also join parents for some training sessions.

SFP was originally developed in the mid-1980s as a treatment for families who experienced high-risk due to parental drug addiction. This variation of SFP showed promise with this population of high-risk families (Kumpfer & DeMarsh, 1985). Further work was done to adapt the SFP for use as a prevention program for non-substance addicted parents who have school-age children and pre-adolescents (Kumpfer et al., 1996). The SFP has also had success as a prevention intervention. For example, a program evaluation in Iowa at the universal level showed lower alcohol initiation and use relative to the matched comparison group at post-testing and at one- and two-year follow-up assessments with a strengthening of intervention benefits at the two-year follow-up (Spoth, Redmond, & Lepper, 1999). Two other trials have tested the relative utility of GGC and SFP (Redmond, Spoth, Shin & Lepper, 1999; Spoth, Lopez, Ryes, Redmond, & Shin, 1999; Spoth, Redmond, & Shin, 1998). In these studies, both interventions showed enduring program benefits found in previous intervention trials, such as lower drug initiation rates and positive changes in targeted family constructs. For illustrations of additional promising U.S. drug prevention, family training programs see the Child and Parent Relations Project (Loveland-Cherry, Ross, & Kaufman, 1999) and the review conducted by Schinke and colleagues (2002).

Family Therapy. Focus on Families (FoF) offers an illustration of a promising U.S. family therapy designed to address parents' substance addiction problems and strengthen parents' skills as a way to promote the well being of their children (Catalano, et al., 1999). This program involves intensive parent training, a short family retreat, and a home visitation service. Parent training focuses on instruction in relapse prevention strategies, youth management techniques, emotional regulation, problem solving, social resistance, and communication skills. The home visitation service provides an opportunity to reinforce the training sessions and to provide individualized social and medical service advocacy. Intervention activities take place over one year. A FoF outcome evaluation indicated significant positive changes among intervention parents in terms of problem solving, rule setting in the home, domestic strife and drug use at a twelve-month follow- up assessment. All changes were found relative to a control group. A particular strength of this trial was that parents' reports of drug use were corroborated by random drug tests. Despite this program's utility with parents, children did not evidence a great deal of change (Catalano, et al., 1999). Other American interventions that have demonstrated utility with families who experience risk due to parental addiction include the Michigan State University Multiple Risk Child Outreach Program (Nye, Zucker, & Fitzgerald, 1995) and the Strengthening Families Program (Kumpfer & DeMarsh, 1985).

In a search of the European literature, a relevant descriptive example from Spain was located. ALFIL (Gual, & Diaz, 1999) is aimed at children of alcoholics, aged 12-16 years, and their parents seeking help for alcohol addiction. Parents undergo addiction treatment and attend two ALFIL sessions as a group to work on improving their parenting practices, communication and social skills with the aim of communicating an effective drug prevention message to their children. The youth-focused component brings adolescent children of alcoholics together in small groups for nine sessions to provide accurate alcohol- and drug-education including the clarification of risks associated with being a child of an alcoholic, and the process of addiction. The program also seeks to provide social support and reinforcement for drug-free attitudes and activities, as well as promote the development of decision-making, social skills and positive coping for risky situations.

In ALFIL's pilot test, intervention adolescents showed pre- to post-test gains in knowledge regarding addiction and problems associated with drug use. Intervention parents reported pre- to post-test improvements in family environment and dynamics such as communication and conflict resolution. This program evaluation is, however, limited in that there was no comparison group available for youth or parents. With the above noted exceptions, few later family interventions appropriate for use with substance addicted parents have undergone rigorous controlled evaluation and shown utility under such conditions (Dusenbury, 2000).

Synthesis

Core Later Family Intervention Components

While tailored to deal with specific problems and populations, exemplary later family interventions often share certain content features that incorporate a consideration of the risk and protective factor research literature as it relates to families and developmental transitions of childhood and adolescence (c.f. *Relevant Narrative Reviews* – Dusenbury, 2000; Kumpfer, Alexander, McDonald, & Olds, 1998; Kumpfer & Alvarado, 1998, November; Lochman & van den Steenhoven, 2002 – *Relevant Meta-Analysis* – Woolfenden, Williams, & Peat, 2003). On the topic of family risk and protective factors, the following questions are critical: How do family members really get along with each other? Are parents managing the behavior of their children in ways that promote the child's development, reduces the young person's exposure to harm, and strengthens family ties? Intervention components commonly found in successful later family interventions address these issues by: engaging families in activities designed to foster positive forms of family cohesion and involvement; offering parents' instruction in the use of developmentally appropriate and non-coercive youth management techniques; and providing families training in communication, problem solving, conflict resolution, and emotional regulation.

Developmental transitions addressed in the content of successful later family interventions recognize that young people will increasingly have: greater autonomy, more elaborate competencies, greater openness to peer socialization, and will be more likely to experiment or increase their involvement in problem behaviors. Intervention content that works in concert with such developmental changes include: Giving parents accurate information about the normative changes of childhood and adolescence and the creation of intervention programming that is directed at both parents and youth, with particular care taken to avoid activities that bring high-risk pre-adolescents and adolescents together. While further research into the subject is needed, current evidence suggests that concerns about grouping at-risk children are not warranted (See the *Questions* subsection for an analysis of the peer aggregation question). The content features described in this and the preceding paragraph can be called *core later family intervention components*, and have salience to much of the model prevention work being conducted with families who have children and teens (c.f. *Relevant Narrative Reviews* – Ashery, Robertson, & Kumpfer, 1998; Biglan, et. al, 1997; Dusenbury, 2000; Kumpfer & Alvarado, 1998, November; Lochman & van den Steenhoven, 2002; Scott, in press; Sherman, et al., 1997).

Connecting to Families

It should be noted that not all family interventions that offer parents instruction or tips on childrearing yield the same results. In a quantitative review of controlled prevention programs designed to improve the social and behavioral prospects of young people, Durlak and Wells (1997) found that parenting interventions alone did not yield significant benefits. The parent programs included in this meta-analysis were time-limited, worked strictly with parents in a group format, and were derived from an assortment of psychological traditions including the behavioral, humanistic, and psychoanalytic. Besides having sound programmatic content, successful later family interventions also,

> ...concentrate on skill development rather than on simply educating parents about appropriate parenting practices. Effective programs use interactive teaching strategies to present skills to parents and their children, allow for practices and feedback, assign homework, and then help family members refine skills that work and modify those that do not. (Etz, Robertson, & Ashery, 1998, p. 2)

So, it is the combination of *core later family intervention components* combined with *sound pedagogical strategies* that seems to yield results (Dusenbury, 2000; Kumpfer & Alvarado, 1998, November; Lochman & van den Steenhoven, 2002).

Beyond programming and pedagogy, successful family interventions also generally make use of strategies that promote family engagement, cooperation and investment. Methods thought to encourage greater family retention and involvement include: outreach activities; promoting interventionist–family interactions that are consistent and respectful; and minimizing practical barriers that block program access like scheduling, transportation, and child care. With more difficult to reach families, additional engagement strategies might involve: periodic home visits to promote mutual understanding; moving from a top–down training model to a family empowerment approach; and gaining the support of key family stakeholders, even if they are not direct intervention participants (Bailey, 2001; Celano & Kaslow, 2000; Cunningham & Henggeler, 1999; Dusenbury, 2000; Gerris, Van As, Wels, & Janssens, 1998; Kumpfer & Alvarado, 1998, November; Perrino, Coatsworth, Briones, Pantin, & Szapocznik, 2001; Prinz, et al., 2001; Scott, in press; Szapocznik & Kurtines, 1989). Such family engagement strategies represent hard won knowledge that comes from working directly with families. Yet, much of what we know about these techniques is based on examining exemplary multi-component family interventions and not through explicit studies designed to test the relative utility of different strategies with participants who experience differential amounts of risk. Developing and systematically testing engagement strategies like those just listed above, may go a long way in helping interventionists learn how to maximize family retention and engagement, as well as intervention benefits (Dusenbury, 2000).

Specific vs. Spreading Effects by Risk

Due to the problem specific organization of later family intervention literature, summative comments will be made on the state of these programs as they relate to the prevention of select youth problem behaviors and risk associated with parental dysfunction. As in the description of model later family programs, spreading program effects and a consideration of program utility by risk level will be noted where relevant.

Preventing Youth Antisocial Behavior. Within the later family intervention literature, there exist some controlled evaluations of universal-selective family training programs with particular relevance to the reduction of antisocial behavior or violent precursors. Those initiatives that have shown promise under adequate testing conditions span the childhood and adolescent periods, utilize core later family intervention components, and demonstrate immediate improvements in parenting practices, parents' well being, the quality of family interactions and in some cases behavior problems (c.f. *Program Examples* – Davis & Hester, 1996; Heyl-Miller, et al., 1998; Knapp & Deluty, 1989 – *Relevant Narrative Reviews* – Kumpfer & Alvarado, 1998, November; Lochman & van den Steenhoven, 2002; Sherman, et al., 1997). There is still much to learn, however, about the utility of such interventions in terms of producing enduring changes in parenting, family functioning, and youth antisocial behavior.

In contrast, the research literature on family therapies to reduce and prevent child behavior problems is extensive. Exemplar family therapies in this area make use of core later family intervention components and place particular emphasis on intensive parent instruction and practice in non-coercive child management techniques. Model therapies consistently show significant program-related reductions in acting-out behaviors among children through the pre-adolescent years. The extent of change in child behavior related to this particular type of intervention across meta-analyses tends to fall in the medium to large (ES=.50 to .67) effect size range (Scott, in press). Other benefits associated with participation in such programs include improvements in the quality of parent-child interactions and parents' well being (*Relevant Narrative Reviews* – Kazdin, 1998; Kumpfer & Alvarado, 1998, November; Patterson, Dishion, & Chamberlain, 1993; Scott, in press; Taylor & Biglan, 1998 – *Relevant Meta-analysis* – Serkitch & Dumas, 1996; Weisz, Weiss, Han, Granger, & Morton, 1995). In those instances where a follow up was conducted, intervention-associated benefits have been maintained for up to three years (Scott, in press). But as Webster-Stratton (2001) stated, "...we need studies to establish the link between reducing targeted family and child risk factors early in life and a decrease in later violence, crime, and drug misuse" (p. 7). Additional long-term evidence to support of the utility of these interventions is needed.

An important qualification to the findings just described is that the majority of outcome evaluation studies for this type of intervention were conducted in cases where an early onset of serious behavior problems was probable (c.f. *Relevant Narrative Reviews* – Greenberg, et al., 2001; Kazdin, 1998; Scott, in press). In other words, many of the best interventions in this area were developed as treatments for families with children who have clinically significant externalizing behavior problems. Some of these treatments have made their way into the prevention research literature as *selective-indicated* interventions or as elements of cross-context prevention programs. For instance, BASIC has undergone evaluation with both clinic- and community-derived samples (c.f., *Program Examples* –Patterson, et al., 2002; Webster-Stratton, 1981; 1982; 1998). Parent Management Training is a core part of the parent component in the Michigan State University Multiple Risk Child Outreach Program (Nye, Zucker, & Fitzgerald, 1995; 1999) and the Montreal Prevention Experiment (Tremblay, et al., 1992). Such prevention trials, while offering only preliminary evidence, do show a pattern of change in parenting, family relations-interactions, and child behavior that is consistent with the large number of positive trials of similar programs conducted with clinic referred samples. Additional *prevention trials* with at-risk samples and unpacking studies that partial out the unique contribution of the family intervention components in complex, multi-component, cross-context interventions would advance prevention programming in this area.

Another research area that is of current interest is family therapies for adolescents who are at risk for recurrent and serious involvement in the adult justice system. While appreciating a family's goals and values is a general feature of interventions that produce positive change (Berlin, et al., 1998), model family therapies for delinquent adolescents go to great lengths to: understand an individual family's basic structure and context; establish mutual respect between the interventionist and family; and form an accurate assessment or understanding of a family's strengthens and potentials, as well as experience of risk. Other features of exemplar family therapies in this area involve: 1) working on a family by family basis, thereby avoiding potential problems associated with bringing at-risk teens together for intervention activities, 2) using skilled, well trained and supervised interventionists, 3) tailoring the amount of program exposure to fit the progress of individuals families, with usually at least three- to four-months of active intervention, and 4) applying a range of evidence-based programming, including core later family intervention components, on a family's identified and malleable risk and protective factors. The targeting of risk and protective factors happens not only at the individual or family level but also across contexts. The contextual approach taken in many model interventions is drawn from social ecology theory (c.f. *Program Examples* – Alexander, et al., 1998; Henggeler, et al., 1996; Szapocznik & Williams, 2000 – *Relevant Narrative Reviews* –

Alexander, Sexton, & Robbins, 2000; Borduin, Heiblum, Jones, & Grabe, 2000; Brosnan & Carr, 2000; Greenwood, 1996; Henggeler, 1999; Huey & Henggeler, 2001; Kazdin, 1998; Kumpfer & Alvarado, 1998, November; Sherman, et al., 1998 – *Relevant Meta-analyses* – Gordon, Arbuthnot, Gustafson, & McGreen, 1988; Woolfenden, et al., 2003).

Successful family therapies in this area challenge the notion that little can be done to improve the life prospects of teenagers taking part in delinquent behavior. Exemplar programs have shown intervention-associated reductions in overall reoffending rates, violence-drug related crimes, and other institutional assignments. For interventions like Functional Family Therapy (FFT) and Multisystemic Therapy (MST), the scale of declines in reoffending in controlled outcome evaluations fall in the 25-70% range. To put these results in context, it is instructive to look at meta-analyses that have examined the utility of the diversity of programming directed at young offenders (c.f. *Relevant Meta-analyses* – Lipsey, 1992; 1995; 1998; Wilson & Lipsey, 2000b; Redondo, et al., 1999). Interventions included in such meta-analyses typically: have undergone controlled evaluation; represent diverse theoretical traditions; and differ in terms of content and change producing strategies, sometimes including family interventions in the meta-analysis and other times not. Across these quantitative reviews, intervention related reductions in reoffending rates fall in the 10-12% range. Furthermore, Woolfenden and colleagues (2003) in a meta-analysis of particularly rigorous program evaluation studies found that model family therapies, this included exemplar interventions like MST and Multi-dimensional Treatment Foster Care, evidenced a significant reduction on reoffending rates relative to comparison youth in the medium effect size range (ES = .565). This decline was over a one to three year follow up period. Significant differences in favor of the family therapies were also found for self reported delinquency and the number of days spent in institutional settings. Other, pertinent meta-analyses that included family therapies found that non-institutional family-focused interventions were among the most successful program types for working with young offenders and other high-risk youth (Hazelrigg, Cooper, & Borduin, 1987; Lipsey, 1992).

Follow-up in individual outcome evaluation studies also indicate that model family therapies in this area yield significant reductions in reoffending rates up to four- and six-years post intervention. Spreading program effects have also been recorded in domains such as teen-parent mental health, school attendance, running away and family-peer relations (c.f. *Program Examples* – Alexander & Parsons, 1973; Borduin, et al., 1995; Brown, Henggeler, Schoenwald, Brondino,& Pickrel, 1999; Chamberlain & Reid, 1998; Emshoff, 1983; Henggeler, Melton, & Smith, 1992; Henggeler, Melton, Smith, Schoenwald, & Hanley, 1993; Parsons & Alexander, 1973; Pickrel & Henggeler, 1996; Szapocznik & Williams, 2000). It should be noted that there may still be important differences between model family therapies (Woolfenden, et al., 2003). Therefore, systematic intervention comparison studies and unpacking studies will be critical for future advances within this field.

Samples in the relevant program evaluations in this area have primarily been adolescent, sometimes with and without a clinical diagnosis of conduct disorder, and usually with some type of contact with the child welfare or juvenile justice systems. Model family therapies in some instances have shown promise from the *selective prevention to treatment levels* (Kumpfer, Alexander, McDonald, & Olds, 1998). Brief Strategic Family Therapy (BSFT) and Functional Family Therapy (FFT) offer cases in point. BSFT and derivative programs have demonstrated utility with youth referred by school staff for suspected drug use to teens with a clinical diagnosis of conduct disorder or substance addiction (c.f. *Program Examples* – Szapocznik & Williams, 2000). FFT has been associated with significant reductions in offending and reoffending rates for youth referred to child welfare services, first-time teenage offenders, repeat juvenile offenders, and the siblings of young offenders (c.f. *Program Examples* –Alexander & Parsons, 1973; Alexander, Pugh, Parsons, & Sexton, 2000; Hansson, et al., 2000; Parsons & Alexander, 1973). As in the child behavior-problem literature, additional *prevention trials* with at-risk samples that follow participants into adulthood would greatly enhance intervention work in this area. Additional research on the dissemination of model family therapies with children and teens in Europe also promise to add to what is known about the generalization of intervention benefits cross-nationally and the knowledge base on family processes fundamental to positive youth development.

Preventing Youth Substance Use and Risk Due to Parental Addiction. Family-related drug prevention efforts have shown considerable progress over recent years (c.f. *Relevant Narrative Reviews* – Ashery, Robertson, & Kumpfer, 1998; Dusenbury, 2000; Kumpfer & Alvarado, 1998, November). While several of the newest interventions use a triage or multiple-gating approach and add cross-context elements to family-focused intervention activities (c.f., *Program Examples* – Dishion & Kavanagh, 2000; Sanders, 2000), promising drug prevention family training programs can be found in the research literature (c.f. *Relevant Narrative Reviews* – Kumpfer & Alvarado, 1998, November; Lochman & van den Steenhoven, 2002; Schinke, et al., 2002). Exemplar interventions of this type regularly include *core later family intervention components*, as well as *problem specific programming* such as: 1) giving parents accurate information about alcohol and drugs, 2) encouraging parents to clarify their own views about youth substance use, 3) efforts to define and enforce a family policy on youth substance use, and 4) involving young people and parents in social resistance training (c.f. *Program Examples* – Kumpfer, et al., 1996; Park, et al., 2000 – *Relevant Narrative*

Reviews – Bry, Catalano, Kumpfer, Lochman, & Szapocznik, 1998; Dusenbury, 2000; Kumpfer & Alvarado, 1998, November; Lochman & van den Steenhoven, 2002; Schinke, et al., 2002). Little is known about the relative utility of individual intervention actions, making component analysis studies important to ensuring future advances in the field (Dusenbury, 2000; Etz, Robertson, & Ashery, 1998; Lochman & van den Steenhoven, 2002).

Under what circumstances have these interventions been successful? To date, evaluations of promising family training programs that work to prevent youth drug use have primarily been family-focused with intervention activities offered to both parents and youth. The duration of successful interventions have ranged from five weeks up to one year of active intervention (c.f. *Program Examples* – Loveland-Cherry, et al., 1999; Park, et al., 2000). As a group, such programs have demonstrated utility at the universal to selective prevention levels, with older American children and early adolescents. Intervention during the transition from childhood to adolescence maybe particularly timely given that opportunities for drug experimentation become increasingly commonplace and patterns of substance use are likely to be forming during this transition period (Lochman & van den Steenhoven, 2002; Rhodes, et al., 1997). Family training at this time may be particularly important for parents, because such initiatives prepare parents for the changes their child will experience and offers parents tools that can help them to steer their children away from early- and heightened drug involvement (Bry, et al., 1998; Kumpfer & Alvarado, 1998, November).

In terms of spreading and specific effects, these model programs have shown both short- and longer-term promise especially in terms of lowering alcohol initiation- and use-rates, as well as improvements in parent-youth relations and interactions, family communication, and parental norms about youth substance use. Changes in alcohol and family variables have been found to persist between two- to three-and-half years post intervention (c.f. *Program Examples* – Loveland-Cherry, et al., 1999; Park, et al., 2000; Spoth, Redmond, & Lepper, 1999). Such program associated changes in youth alcohol use and the quality of family life provides corroborating evidence to support what is known from the risk and protective factors research literature about family functioning, parental drug norms, and youth substance use. Additional epidemiological and intervention process-outcome analysis studies promise to yield an even more precise understanding of the potential relationships between the family and youth substance use. Intervention work in Australia (Sanders, 2000) and an ongoing cross-boarder trial of SFP in Canada and America (Kumpfer, Molgaard, & Spoth, 1996) also offer to provide new information about the generalization of the benefits associated with model, family, drug prevention programs outside of the United States.

One may ask the question of, why do we not have equally strong group interventions for higher-risk youth and their families? Teens with more serious substance use difficulties, as in the case of higher risk youth with behavioral problems, may particularly benefit from family therapies that work with single families on a one-to-one basis (c.f. *Program Examples* – Szapocznik & Williams, 2000 – *Relevant Narrative Review* –Kumpfer, Alexander, McDonald, & Olds, 1998). A prevailing view in the family intervention field is that a family-by-family approach with high risk youth maybe the most desirable choice (Etz, Robertson, & Ashery, 1998; Kumpfer & Alvarado, 1998, November). Intervening with one family at a time protects the youngster from harmful peer aggregation effects and gives family members the opportunity to try out and practice new ways of interacting directly with one another. Group intervention formats for parents of higher risk teens may also be a viable alternative, when circumstances preclude a young person's participation or instances where a family-by-family approach is not feasible (c.f. *Program Examples* – Dishion, Andrews, Kavanagh, & Soberman, 1996; Irvine, Biglan, Smolkowski, Metzler, & Ary, 1999).

Turning to family therapies that aim to prevent problem behaviors in youth whose experience of risk is largely associated with their parents' drug abuse, it is evident that interventions in this area seem to be most successful when *explicit drug treatment for parents* is combined with *core later family intervention components*. Such interventions are family-focused and expressly treat parental addiction and relapse, codependence issues, as well as youth knowledge, attitudes, and expectations regarding alcohol and other drugs. As parental addiction issues are addressed, successful programs go a step further and instruct parents and youth in the important skills that characterize other exemplary later family interventions. Promising interventions in this area have been intensive, spreading program activities across one year of active intervention (c.f. *Program Examples* – Catalano, et al., 1999; Kumpfer et al., 1996 – *Relevant Narrative Reviews* – Dusenbury, 2000; Kumpfer, Alexander, McDonald, & Olds, 1998). It should be noted that few rigorously tested therapies for substance-addicted parents exist (Bry, et al., 1998). As in the home visitation field, substantial work with substance-addicted parents and their families is needed.

Tentatively, it can be said that the few model therapies in this area, however, do demonstrate that it is possible to bolster the quality of family life in high-risk families. Positive intervention-related changes parental drug-taking behavior and child problem behavior are also within reach (c.f. *Program Examples* – Catalano, et al., 1999; Kumpfer et al., 1996). In the Focus on Families efficacy trial, for example, declines in parental drug use and improvements in related family variables were found to endure up to one year after intervention activities ceased. However, the same level of success in reducing youth substance use has been more difficult to achieve. There is evidence that points to a possible trickle down intervention effect for children whose parents have successfully undergone addiction treatment (O' Farrell &

Feehan, 1999), and longer-term follow up of participating children would offer a more precise test of the potential benefits of such families therapies (Bry, et al., 1998; Dusenbury, 2000). Future work may also profit from a greater incorporation of youth-focused components that are tailored to the social and developmental changes taking place in childhood and adolescence. Consideration of the peer aggregation issue for adolescent programming would also be warranted here.

Questions

Particular issues become salient when working with families who have children and teens. An emergent issue addressed in the following subsection has to do with a consideration of the consequences of bringing high-risk children and adolescents together as part of an intervention. A question that cuts across the family intervention field is also revisited: Can evidence-based family interventions promote the success of families on a large scale?

Peer Aggregation Question

Peers have important functions to play in the lives of young people (Bukowski & Hoza, 1989; Coleman & Hendry, 1999; Piaget, 1932/1965; Youniss, 1994). It is clear that the type of peers that one associates with is important (Hartup, 1996). It has widely been demonstrated that deviant and non-deviant peers tend to congregate together and affiliation with deviant peers is a strong predictor of adolescent problem behaviors (Farrington, 1990; Lipsey & Derzon, 1998; Marcus, 1996).

Empirical studies consistently demonstrate that youth tend to choose friends who are like themselves in terms of demographics, attitudes, and behaviors (Dishion, Patterson, & Griesler, 1994; Kandel, 1978; 1985). As youngsters progress in their friendships, the socialization process is thought to continue to promote an increased level of similarity between friends (Cohen, 1977; Kandel, 1973; 1978; Mounts & Steinberg, 1995). Similarity and socialization processes have important implications for peer group formation and may, in the future, determine how interventions are designed.

Family interventions for older children and adolescents are often family-focused and include parallel program components. Parent components usually involve bringing a number of parents together into small- or medium-sized groups. Youth components either gather several young people together into groups for training and/or involve them in parent sessions. In the Strengthening Families Program (Kumpfer, Molgaard, & Spoth, 1996), for example, families attend workshops together and then break into child- and parent-only groups. They later come back together for family interaction sessions.

The utility of grouping older children and teens together as part of a family-focused intervention was examined in the Adolescent Transitions Program (ATP). This intervention was initially tested with a sample of families with young people (11-14 year olds) who experienced an elevated level of risk (Dishion & Andrews, 1995; Dishion, et al., 1996; Dishion & Kavanagh, 2000; Poulin, Dishion, & Burraston, in press). ATP featured four different formats: a parent-focused, a teen-focused, a combined parent- and teen-focused, and a self-directed program variation. In the parent format, a curriculum was designed to instruct parents in positive childrearing practices such as effective reinforcement, rule setting and enforcement, monitoring, problem-solving and communication skills in parent-adolescent interactions. Intervention strategies included discussions and structured activities. In the teen format, the curriculum focused on self-reinforced goal setting and attainment; encouraging pro-social peer affiliations; and teaching social resistance, problem solving, and communication skills. Intervention strategies were similar to the parent format. In the self-directed format, which has served as a type of control group, families were given the intervention's instructional materials, with no other support or interaction. A quasi-experimental comparison condition was also formed.

At post-test, all of the intervention conditions evidenced immediate reductions in the levels of negative family interactions and conflict, relative to the comparison group. Additionally, at this point, the parent format demonstrated a marginally significant pre- to post-test reduction in teacher-rated problem behaviors. However, at the one-year follow up, the teen-focused format showed a negative intervention associated effect. These participants in the teen format had more self-reported tobacco use and more teacher-reported problem behaviors. Further, the combined parent + teen format did not yield enduring decreases in youth problem behaviors. At one-year follow up, the parent only format showed a significant reduction in youth substance use. A three-year follow up study showed harmful effects in terms of increases in self-reported tobacco use and teacher-reported acting out behavior for the ATP teen and parent + teen formats relative to a comparison group that combined the self-directed format with the quasi-experimental comparison group. Subgroup analysis further showed that teens in the peer-oriented formats who had lower risk at program entry particularly suffered from their program exposure (Poulin, et al., in press). ATP program variations that brought at-risk youth together for intervention activities, teen and parent + teen formats, clearly showed enduring program related negative effects. It is important to note, however, that ATP's parent-only format did demonstrate utility in its initial program evaluation (Dishion, et al., 1996) and in a subsequent effectiveness trial (Irvine, et al., 1999), particularly in terms of improving parent-teen interactions, and reducing youth substance use and problem behaviors (Dishion & Kavanagh, 2000).

Dishion, McCord, and Poulin (1999), in a discussion of deviancy training and the peer aggregation problem, highlighted the negative effects found in the Cambridge-Somerville Youth Study (McCord, 1978). Intervention activities in this study were conducted with a sample of at-risk males aged 10.5- to 16-years old. Those youth that attended intervention-related summer camp experiences were especially likely to experience adjustment problems up to thirty years later. See Poulin et al. (in press) for other supportive and divergent program examples related to the peer aggregation debate.

It should be said that this aggregation phenomenon with teenagers might not occur in interventions with children. Several of the family interventions described thus far bring at-risk children together for intervention activities and yield positive results. Webster-Stratton's child-focused intervention, Dinosaur School, brings groups of children together to attend a series of workshop sessions (Webster-Stratton & Hammond, 1997). The foci for intervention change include the child's problem solving, communication, and conflict resolution skills. Dinosaur School uses intervention strategies employed in the other programs in the Incredible Years Series like the modeling of positive behaviors. Techniques unique to the program include the use of imaginary play, games, and full-size puppets. Children that attend Dinosaur School can range in age from 3- to 10-years old and are often considered at-risk or diagnosed with clinically significant levels of conduct problems. Program evaluations thus far have not shown harmful effects. On the contrary, Dinosaur School on its own or combined with parent and/or teacher training represents a promising mixture of intervention techniques that yields significant benefits (Webster-Stratton, 1998a; Webster-Stratton & Hammond, 1997).

Why might it be dangerous to bring at-risk teens together and not at-risk children together? By looking back at the research literature on peer relations one sees that as children move into adolescence, they spend an increasing amount of time with peers. Further, middle adolescence is the developmental period when peer influence has been thought to be at its greatest (Berndt, 1982; Fuligni & Eccles, 1993). When high-risk teens are brought together for intervention activities, we may unintentionally capitalize on socialization processes that Kandel (1973; 1978) and others have observed in naturally occurring friendships and peer groups. Peer relations become increasingly salient in adolescence and this may be one of the possible keys to the question of why aggregation may matter for teens but not for children.

Dissemination Research

How can successful programs, with a considerable evidence base, be brought to the families who need and want them? Domitrovich and Greenberg (2000) suggested that the coming test for the prevention field, "...is to help the consumers put 'proven programs' into place effectively, so that they reproduce effective outcomes shown when they were first developed and evaluated" (p. 194). In practice, an empirically validated intervention is a necessary but not sufficient condition for intervention success. Studies of the specific details of how successful programs work and how programs fair once they are disseminated are therefore critical to the development of a scientific-knowledge base on strategies to help people on the front lines of promotion and prevention work to conduct evidence-based programs. Efforts along these lines are becoming increasingly possible as government entities require the use of interventions with a sound scientific basis (Domitrovich & Greenberg, 2000). An initiative launched in Norway in the area of family intervention offers an illustration of just such an opportunity.

In response to a public debate on crime and dissatisfaction with strategies for intervening with antisocial youth, the Norwegian government launched an initiative to develop and institute a national strategy to help families with children and teens at risk for antisocial behavior problems (Mørch, et al., 2001; Mørch, 2003; Ogden, 2001). After a consideration of the scientific research literature, three, well established, American, family interventions were selected to make up the backbone of the government's strategy: The Incredible Years Series (Webster-Stratton, 1998a), Parent Management Training (Patterson & Forgatch, 1987), and Multisystemic Therapy (Henggeler, et al., 1996). The approach in each case has been to make minimal program modifications, seek training and supervision from program developers, integrate interventions into mainstream services, and to test for intervention effectiveness with scientifically strong evaluation designs. The programs do, however, vary in terms of models of dissemination and specific outcome evaluation strategies.

For example in this initiative, programs within the Incredible Years Series, BASIC and Dinosaur School, are offered to Norwegian families who have children, aged four- to eight-years old, with clinically significant symptoms of conduct and/or oppositional defiant disorder. These programs are first being integrated into the child-family mental health care systems in Trondheim and Tromsø before being disseminated nationwide. Within these cities, eligible families are referred for treatment at outpatient mental health clinics. An estimated 252 families will take part in a clinical trial over a two-year period, with random assignment to a wait-list control, BASIC, or combined BASIC plus Dinosaur School condition (Mørch, et al., 2001; Mørch, 2003).

The dissemination of Parent Management Training (PMT) in Norway differs from the aforementioned Incredible Years trial in that, from the outset, it is aimed at immediate national dissemination. While the type and severity of problems targeted for change have parallels to the Incredible Years, PMT is offered to Norwegian families with older children, in the six- to 12- year old range. In America, PMT has been developed and tested over the three decades. In this time, PMT has demonstrated utility in controlled efficacy and effectiveness trials (Forgatch & Martinez, 1999) and has influenced a number of successful interventions such as the Montreal Prevention Experiment (Tremblay, et al., 1992). PMT is based on a social interaction learning model and coercion theory (Patterson, 1982). Programmatic features of the intervention center on fostering improved parental monitoring, positive child management, skills development, family problem solving and positive involvement (Forgatch, personal communication, 2002).

PMT's dissemination in Norway is unique in that three successively larger cohorts of youth mental health therapists will be trained in PMT. These therapists are the regular service providers to youth who are at-risk for behavior problems and work out of mental health clinics nationwide. The first generation of 30 clinicians, who underwent an intensive three year training and supervision, are charged with the task of training two future cohorts of therapists. An intervention trial is embedded in PMT's dissemination. An estimated 100 families will participate in an outcome evaluation study, with random assignment to PMT or services as usual. Study participants will be drawn from the caseloads of first generation therapists. A dissemination study is also planned in which the training of therapist cohorts will be examined in terms of how program fidelity is maintained or loosened over the course of the intervention's national dissemination (Forgatch, personal communication, 2002; Ogden, 2000).

Multisystemic Therapy is also slated for immediate national dissemination. Unlike the Incredible Years and PMT, MST will be administered primarily through the child welfare system at the county level to 12- to 17-year olds referred for delinquent behavior. While training and supervision is being carried out in 17 out of the 19 Norwegian counties, the main program evaluation centers on how MST is implemented in five geographic regions (Akershus, Oslo, Rogaland, Telemark, and Vest-Agder). An estimated 100 families will participate in an outcome evaluation study, with random assignment to MST or services as usual. Training and supervision of MST therapists and supervisors in Norway differs from the multi-generation model used to disseminate PMT, in that MST teams in Norway were 'new hires' employed only to work with MST. MST also has a relatively quick yet concentrated training with an emphasis placed on close, ongoing supervision, and booster training (Ogden, 2001).

Results from the Norwegian government's effort to incorporate evidence-based family interventions into the regular services provided to families with children and teens at risk for antisocial behavior problems, as well as those youth with diagnosable behavior problems are yet to be published. Forthcoming dissemination and outcome evaluation studies, however, do have the potential to greatly add to what is known about large-scale dissemination and the effectiveness of these model family interventions outside of the United States.

Initiatives like the one just described help to ensure that the families that manifest high levels of risk or reach out for help get assistance. Yet, the widespread promotion of successful families remains as a lingering challenge. Taylor and Biglan (1998) suggested that we will not reap the full benefits of evidence-based prevention programming until we move from a clinical perspective to a public health perspective. These authors offered that non-clinical channels such as physical health care providers, schools, the media, and religious organizations can be used to more broadly disseminate science-based knowledge about successful family practices.

Helping broad cross-sections of parents to interact in an effective and promotive way with their youngsters is of considerable importance. Working preventatively with the general population of parents, however, is not without its own challenges. For example, parents who do not perceive their youngster to be at risk maybe difficult to engage in intervention efforts (Roker & Coleman, 1998). Dusenbury (2000) in a review of drug prevention programs, noted low rates of parental involvement even in successful, universal, cross-context interventions like the Midwestern Prevention Project (Chou, et al., 1998; Johnson, et al., 1990) and Project Northland (Perry, et al., 1996).

Despite upfront costs and practical challenges, there is a growing call for policy makers and practitioners to use the knowledge that is available to translate scientific intervention trials into successful services that are able to affect meaningful change in large segments of the general society (e.g., Domitrovich & Greenberg, 2000; Melton, 1997). Today, most countries consider a high quality, free education to be included in the basic rights of a child (United Nations, 1948). We may be at a point in the history of prevention and promotion work that can be likened to the time period when the benefits of free, high quality formal education first became accepted in wide sectors of the community. As the technology and knowledge surrounding intervention develops there may also come a time when effective evidence-based services for families becomes included in the fundamental rights of children.

Future Directions

Successful later family interventions confirm the importance of families in the development and amelioration of youth problem behaviors. What follows is a series of comments that may prove useful in future family-related prevention and youth development initiatives.

- Interventions should work in concert with the changing characteristics of families.
- The quality of family interactions is an important target for intervention across development.
- While exemplary early family interventions are unarguably important, later family initiatives also have a role to play in promotion of healthy child and adolescent development.
- As in the early family intervention literature, collaborative interventions strategies appear to hold promise. The utility of such approaches should be systematically tested.
- The effort put into evaluation should equal the energies spent on program development and implementation. In a time of greater accountability, and with the knowledge that interventions can cause harm, carefully designed evaluations that use multiple measures and informants, adequate samples, and long-term follow up are a must.
- As in the early family intervention literature careful unpacking studies are needed to identify what specifically makes model later family interventions successful.
- When working with adolescents who have moderately elevated or high-risk levels it may be better to intervene with parents, utilize intervention approaches that have been shown to be particularly useful with higher-risk teens, and avoid grouping these young people together.
- Although exemplary family training and therapies do exist, there is a need to further develop broadband initiatives that move beyond single problems and populations.

Chapter Endnotes

This expert group was charged with the task of identifying successful family interventions as apart of the J.S. Center for Substance Abuse Prevention's Prevention Enhancement Protocol System (Kumpfer & Alvarado, 1998, November). The group's first identified program type was behavioral parent training which consisted of interventions designed to help parents learn how to decrease coercive interactions. Another strong program variation was family skills training. In this type of intervention, parents of at risk children received behavioral parent training, children were exposed to their own training, and behavioral family therapy was available. Further, family skills training stressed intervention activities to improve family bonding. In the present review, behavioral parent and family skills training were collapsed into one category called family training and expanded to include low to moderate risk teenagers (e.g., universal, universal-selective, selective). The same expert group also identified a class of intervention aimed at bolstering family communication, dynamics, and relations in families with high risk adolesc In this subsection, the group's use of the term family therapy is expanded to include higher risk famil where the family's heightened risk can be attributed to the young person's and/or parents' adjustment difficulties. Further, in this review, family therapy is extended to include children who experience ris the selective prevention to treatment range (e.g., selective-indicated, indicated, indicated-treatment). Since this expert group's work, other family-related literature reviews have used program categorizat similar to the ones used in this review (e.g., Lochman & van den Steenhoven, 2002; Woolfenden, et a 2003).

[2]Educational enrichment activities with families of school aged children and teens are not described f the reason that this type of intervention when directed at older youth takes up a relatively small part o the overall family intervention literature. Although there is a scarcity of strong programs examples, parent involvement is common in successful cross context interventions that have produced academic school-related benefits for school age children (e.g., *Basic + SCHOOL: Supporting Your Child's Education* – Webster-Stratton, 1998; *Success for All* – Slavin & Madden, 2001) and pre-teens (*e.g., Valued Youth Partnership* – Cardenas, Montecel, Supik, & Harris, 1992). Cross context family plus school interventions are discussed in the *School* section.

[3]The Strengthening Families Program has elements of both family training and therapy.

Section 2
The School Context

During the early 1900s, improved access to education changed the lives of many children and adolescents (Tanner, 1972)[1]. Formal mandatory education helped to address the growing needs of increasingly industrial and technology-driven societies for well-educated workers. Yet, this key social transition also structured the lives of many youngsters more than ever before (Church, 1976). Furthermore, the day-to-day socialization or teaching of most children began to expand beyond parents to include formal educational institutions (Bronfenbrenner, 1979). Before mass public education, older family members and neighbors took primary responsibility for socializing young people. While the family and community remain key settings for teaching knowledge and standards for behavior, schools have gradually assumed more responsibility for not only instructing students in particular subject areas but also in helping young people develop an array of assets like: competence, autonomy, and social bonds (Lewis, Battistich, & Schaps, 1990). Therefore, the rise of mass public education provided broader and more uniform life experiences for many young people. It also has made it easier to apply new knowledge about prevention and youth development on a large-scale basis.

Chapter 4
Individual Focused School Intervention

Introduction

When one examines what is taking place within the school in terms of prevention programming, it becomes clear that intervention efforts within this setting are anything but simple, even in programs focusing primarily on individual-level change. School-based programs commonly include individual-level targets for change such as knowledge, skills, competencies, and behaviors (Greenberg, Domitrovich, & Bumbarger, 2001; SAMHSA, 1999; Weissberg & Greenberg, 1998). School-based initiatives are often designed to produce change at the individual level or, alternatively, in conjunction with efforts to change broader aspects of the school environment. Further, the type of intervention action taken, as well as the developmental level of program participants and the levels of risk they experience each introduce an additional layer of complexity.

Individual-level prevention programs, for example, are designed to yield direct changes in risk-protective factors such as the student's: academic skills, school investment, generic life competencies, as well as reductions in current problem behaviors. Possible methods for producing change at the individual level could include: academic tutoring or education-skills promotion in the service of a prevention- or promotion-related goal. Intervention actions taken at the individual level vary widely and depending on their developmental appropriateness, can be applied to children in primary school and/or adolescents in secondary school[2]. Many problem behaviors are targeted in school based initiatives including those specific to the school environment, as well as issues that transcend the boundaries of the school. Thus, the full range of youth problem behaviors is included as credible objectives or targets for school based prevention efforts (Black, Tobler, & Sciacca, 1998; Greenberg, et al., 2001; Hansen, 1992; Reppucci, Woolard, & Fried, 1999). Later in this chapter, examples will be presented of prominent theory and research that link individual and school-related risk-protective factors to given problem behaviors. In addition, this chapter will outline the select rationales guiding different forms of school related intervention.

Chapter Organization

This chapter first gives examples of specific school-based interventions that are known to be effective for producing change in individual-level aspects of students such as social competencies, academic abilities or problem behaviors. These interventions are organized by the domains of individual-level phenomena that are targeted for change. Programs described range from those directed at enriching children's general academic achievement to those initiatives aimed at reducing adolescents' risk for substance use, delinquency and sexual risk behaviors. This chapter reviews primarily successful school interventions with a single-level approach to intervening with at-risk youth. Next, a best evidence synthesis is presented for research literature regarding individual-focused intervention programs. Finally, several key questions regarding school interventions are addressed and future directions are offered.

Exemplary Program Examples

Academic Tutoring

There are a number of school-based interventions designed to promote academic competence in children and teens[3] (McLaughlin, & Vacha, 1992; Wood & O'Malley, 1996). School failure undermines optimal youth development through a diversity of paths (Slavin, Karweit, & Wasik, 1994). A consideration of the complex relations between academic skills development and **attributional biases** offers one avenue for better understanding the impact of school failure. As children transition into the formal school setting, they are routinely presented with academic tasks they must complete. Under normal circumstances, children experience both success and failure in the classroom. Based on these encounters, youth are thought to craft for themselves strategies for coping with achievement settings and the perceived expectations of others such as parents and teachers. Students who show steady competence in school are thought to apply appropriate skills to the task at hand, blame failure on transient factors outside themselves, and take personal credit for their success (Nurmi, Salmela-Aro, & Haavisto, 1995).

In contrast, less competent students' experiences with success and failure are related to the development of radically different ways of thinking about causes of events in school settings. Self-defeating attributional biases (e.g., negative, self-blaming thoughts about poor performance) that are based on a history of failure and skill deficits can influence students to behave in ways that reinforce these negative thoughts and increase their chances of actual failure (Nurmi, 1993a). For example, the development and strengthening of learned helplessness, involves escalating patterns of behaviors such as passivity, a lack of goal-oriented behavior, and the absence of a positive attributional bias that often buffers or shields children from the harmful effects of negative feedback. Self-handicapping, operates via a different path and is characterized by persons who are so busy trying to explain away their failures that they are not able to take proactive steps towards accomplishing a goal (Nurmi, Salmela-Aro, & Ruotsalainen, 1994). In the failure-trap scenario, the individual does not believe in her or his ability to achieve a given task, expects failure, and takes part in task-irrelevant behavior, not out of a desire to build an excuse as in self-handicapping but out of genuine interest in the off-task activity or as a means to blunt the stress associated with an achievement expectation (Nurmi, 1993b). In this case, failure in academic tasks strengthens the young person's sense of incompetence, negative expectations, engagement in task-irrelevant behaviors, and the internalization of self-defeating attributions (Nurmi, et al., 1994). Cross-sectional and longitudinal research provides support for connections between these negative achievement strategies, a range of youth problem behaviors, and adult adjustment difficulties, suggesting the importance of promoting early academic success and engagement among at-risk children (Au & Watkins, 1997; Calabrese & Adams, 1990; Costa, Jessor, & Turbin, 1999; Eronen & Nurmi, 1999; Nurmi, Berzonsky, Tammi, & Kinney, 1997; Nurmi, et al., 1994; Schulenberg, Wadsworth, O'Malley, Bachman, & Johnston, 1996).

Academic enrichment initiatives in the primary and secondary school years can take a number of forms. Yet, a common goal of these interventions is to bypass and disrupt negative developmental processes, such as the development of negative attributional styles, that increase risk for academic task failure, course failure, poor school bonding, and school drop out (Collins et al., 1995; Dryfoos, 1994; 1995). Common academic enrichment strategies consist of giving the young person frequent opportunities to build a sense of competence in achievement settings by strengthening the youth's basic academic skills. Strategies such as tutoring are often used to promote positive behavioral change in many academic enrichment programs (Cohen, Kulik, & Kulik, 1982; Greenwood, Carta, & Hall, 1988). This is a largely individual-level approach that pairs a tutor and student together in order to promote the child's development and retention of academic skills, pro-school attitudes, and other skills conducive to school engagement and success. Many types of people can conduct successfully one-on-one student instruction in school settings including: teachers, para-professionals, adult volunteers, or older and same age classmates. Tutoring can also take place inside or outside of the classroom and serve a wide range of children experiencing different types of adversities.

Adult Tutoring. An illustration of a tutoring intervention that has been shown to be effective among children with early literacy problems is Reading Recovery. This selective intervention was developed and first tested in New Zealand (Center, Wheldall, Freeman, Outhred & McNaught, 1995; Clay, 1979/1985; Glynn, Crooks, Bethune, Ballard, & Smith, 1989) with later evaluations taking place in Australia (Rowe, 1989; Moore & Wade, 1998), America (Shanahan & Barr, 1995), and England (Sylva & Hurry, 1995). When evaluated in different countries, Reading Recovery has undergone some changes to fit better with how schools are organized and how prepared children are at school entry. However, the core program focus on improving literacy through the individualized tutoring of children by a trained teacher has remained constant across evaluations. Reading Recovery activities usually take place for 30 minutes each day. The intervention may include between 30 and 60 lessons, which are spread across one or more school terms. Pupils finish the program when their tutors judge them to be functioning at an age-appropriate reading level. In the program's language, the student is 'discontinued' at this point (Shanahan & Barr, 1995).

A key criticism of Reading Recovery is that the discontinuation system may positively bias attempts to evaluate the program. Youth who are discontinued are successful program completers. Children who drop out of the program or who do not respond significantly to the intervention after 60 lessons are not always included in Reading Recovery outcome evaluations (Shanahan & Barr, 1995). Yet, in statistical analyses designed to control for this potential bias, youth who take part in Reading Recovery still demonstrate significant positive changes on measures of reading proficiency across the intervention period, compared to students who are not at risk, as well as pupils that are at risk for reading difficulties. Reading Recovery has had less success, however, showing that program gains in reading persist over time (Shanahan & Barr, 1995; Sylva & Hurry, 1995). Taken all together, the majority of well-designed Reading Recovery program trials show immediate positive gains in terms of improved literacy and have partial support for sustained program benefits (e.g., Rowe, 1989; Moore & Wade, 1998).

Peer Tutoring. Peer tutoring provides another potentially useful way to provide individually-based academic enrichment experiences to at-risk children. When conducted with entire classrooms, this type of intervention works across the levels of the school environment (individual-classroom) by providing students one-on-one instruction and making changes to the classroom reward structure. Classwide Peer Tutoring (CWPT) is a promising universal-selective illustration of this approach (Greenwood, Delquadri, & Hall, 1989; Greenwood, Terry, Arreaga-Mayer, & Finney, 1992). CWPT is American in origination. The structure of the intervention involves the random matching of students into pairs on a weekly basis. Student pairs are then assigned to one of two class teams and provided with lessons to review and teach to each other during the week. Tasks assigned can involve reading or math. The desirable level of student participation in CWPT activities is 90 minutes daily. Core CWPT program elements include: lesson plans and strategies for completing assignments that are constructed by teachers, new student pairings each week, and rewards contingent upon the performance of the tutoring pair and the entire team.

Several positive evaluations of CWPT exist demonstrating its effectiveness (Arreaga-Mayer, Terry, & Greenwood, 1998). One long-term program evaluation involved an experimental study conducted with at-risk 6 ½- to 7-year-olds starting in the beginning of the first grade and continuing with CWPT program activities into the fourth grade (Greenwood et al., 1989). One low socioeconomic status (SES) intervention group received weekly CWPT program activities for four years, while a low SES control and a high SES comparison group had instruction as usual. When followed up four years after the end of the study, the low SES CWPT group outperformed the low SES control group on several measures of academic achievement. At the 4-year post-intervention follow up, no statistically significant differences were found between the CWPT students and the high SES comparison pupils. This result can be interpreted as positive support for this program in that the low SES recipients of CWPT began to approach or exceed national age norms for reading, language, and mathematics skills and started to perform at a level comparable to their more advantaged peers.

Promising examples of academic tutoring by adults exist for individual-level (e.g., Reading Recovery – Clay, 1979/1985) and cross context *family-school* interventions (e.g., *Fast Track* – Bierman, Greenberg, & the Conduct Problems Prevention Research Group, 1996; *Success for All* – Slavin, Karweit, Wasik, Madden, & Dolan, 1994). CWPT represents only a sample of the peer tutoring initiatives that have been shown to be effective (Cohen, et al., 1982; Fantuzzo, King, & Heller, 1992; Greenwood, et al., 1988; Wood & O'Malley, 1996; Heller & Fantuzzo, 1993). Other successful American peer tutoring interventions include Classwide Peer-Assisted Learning Strategies (Fuchs, Fuchs, Phillips, & Hamlett, & Karns, 1995), Classwide Student Tutoring Teams (Maheady, Sacca, & Harper, 1987) and Reciprocal Peer Tutoring (Fantuzzo, et al., 1992). Tutoring is no doubt a well-used strategy in many European school systems (e.g., Schmidt & Moust, 2000; Sylva & Hurry, 1995). Yet, beyond those already programs mentioned, additional controlled interventions trials of European tutoring programs were by in large not found.

Education and Skills Promotion

One fundamental assumption behind the use of education to prevent unwanted developmental outcomes is that people need accurate information about certain behaviors and lifestyle choices in order to make informed and rational choices about them. For example, the Theory of Reasoned Action (Ajzen & Fishbein, 1980) attempts to explain how knowledge can provide a catalyst for behavior change. In this widely cited model, the chain of events leading to a specific behavior begins with the behavioral and normative beliefs that a person holds. Behavioral beliefs are an individual's evaluation of what is likely to happen if she engages in a given behavior. For example, what are the likely risks and rewards of smoking marijuana after school with friends? Normative beliefs involve an individual's evaluation of what significant others might think about her engagement in a given behavior. The person in question may believe that her parents will certainly object to smoking with friends, but the individual's perception of the peers' opinions may vary markedly across different peer networks. Behavioral and normative beliefs are several competing influences that result in variation across persons and settings in health-related attitudes, intentions, and behaviors. Thus, if a student were to believe that little good could come from smoking marijuana and/or there was sufficient social pressure from significant others to avoid the behavior, then the student would be less likely to choose to smoke. For several decades, this model of health behavior and behavior change has served as a strong conceptual core for a significant proportion of the early **health education** and drug prevention efforts conducted in both school and community settings (Evans, 1998).

Although knowledge-based education remains a mainstay of a great deal of universal prevention programs (Gullotta, 1994), contemporary education for prevention purposes is often supplemented with other program components based on other strategies to promote behavior change (e.g., Chou, et al., 1998; Botvin, et al., 2000; Flynn, et al., 1997; Kelder, Perry, & Klepp, 1993; Puska & Uutela, 2001; Zabin, et al., 1988). In recent years, multiple component intervention packages in school and community settings regularly pair knowledge-based education with **life competence promotion** strategies (e.g., Botvin, et al., 2000; LoSciuto, Rajala, Townsend, & Taylor, 1996; Perry, et al., 2000). Life competence enhancement occupies a central role in a wide range of school-based youth interventions due to its prominence in many theoretical models of the onset and maintenance of specific problem behaviors, as well as through its association with indicators of general adjustment (Davis, 1999; Elliott & Gresham, 1993).

But what is life competence? The basic elements of competence in life are, in part, made up of a broad set of skills that promote positive adaptation to expectable life challenges (Catalano et al., 1999; Ferrer-Wreder, Montgomery, & Lorente, in press; Luthar, 1993; Masten & Coatsworth, 1998). Key examples of abilities that enhance competence include cognitive problem solving and social-emotional skills. Both are instrumental for constructive interaction with others and they provide a foundation for youth to become socially adept and skilled at making decisions. The study of the development of competence has several conceptual models and empirical strategies including: social skill approaches for enhancing behavioral skills; social problem-solving to promote the development of cognitive abilities essential for sound decision-making; social perspective-taking to better understand others' motives in social interactions; and self-control training to evaluate one's own behavioral options prior to acting (Beelmann, Pfingsten, & Lösel, 1994). Each of these traditions in the study of competence and its enhancement contribute to improving a youth's ability to make flexible and intentional responses to the demands of social settings or to take advantage of opportunities offered in the environment (Waters & Sroufe, 1983; Weissberg, Caplan, & Harwood, 1991). These are skills needed to overcome expectable psychosocial challenges as children and adolescents encounter key development transitions. If these skills are not socialized in the course of early interactions within the family or later in early peer group or school settings, youngsters will be increasingly limited in their ability to form close lasting relationships, to recruit and maintain social support, and to make informed and adaptive decisions about their behavior and responses to the behavior of others (Cowen, 1994).

Education-skills initiatives conducted in school settings have historically been designed to address a particular category of youth problem behavior like drug use, violence, teenage pregnancy prevention or they have fallen under the rubric of health education. Because of this categorical emphasis, the next three subsections are organized by discrete problem behaviors commonly targeted for change in individual-level, school-based education-skills interventions. Salient multi-level and cross context program examples, as well as relevant initiatives that have demonstrated spreading effects will also be integrated into these subsections.

Education-Skills: Preventing Youth Antisocial Behavior. Elements of life competence promotion have long been used to plan and implement prevention programs to reduce youth aggression (e.g., Oden & Asher, 1977). Aggressive responses to unclear social interactions may stem from youths' biased beliefs and competence deficits including: pro-violence views and beliefs that violence is a normal and acceptable way to solve problems; the inability to generate prosocial alternatives to interpersonal coercion; the tendency to attribute hostile intent to others in ambiguous social situations; and, inadequate coping skills and decision making processes (Lahey, Waldman, & McBurnett, 1999; Pettit, 1997). Many of these biased attitudes and skill deficits are modeled and practiced in early home environments and further reinforced in primary school settings. When children enter primary school with inadequate levels of basic social competencies and little effort is expended to compensate for these deficiencies, they are left vulnerable to a host of adverse outcomes, for instance, through a process of increasing rejection by, and isolation from, prosocial peers (Reid & Eddy, 1997). Core goals of competence enhancement programs are: the promotion of cognitive, social, and emotional competence; reduction of coercive interactions; minimizing rejection by prosocial peers and enhancing acceptance by deviant peers; and, preventing the onset of conduct problems, juvenile delinquency, and adult criminality. This type of work is not limited to school settings but schools remain a key location for universal and selected prevention efforts (Taylor, Eddy, & Biglan, 1999).

The Second Step Curriculum (SSC) offers a useful illustration of this general approach (Grossman, et al., 1997). SSC has undergone testing with a universal sample of primary school students in the American State of Washington. In this evaluation, students were given a series of lessons designed to promote qualities such as empathy, emotional insight, and impulse/anger control through the use of exercises to improve perspective taking, problem-solving and emotional regulation. A key strategy used in this study to increase desirable behaviors was the discussion and role-playing of hypothetical social scenarios. Through exercises using these vignettes, skills were modeled by the teacher and practiced by students. An SSC program evaluation tested the intervention's impact after 17 months of weekly 30-minute training sessions. Twelve primary schools participated in this efficacy trial, in which students were assigned randomly to two conditions: the intervention or programming as usual. Few statistically significant results were found for parent or teacher ratings of children's behavior. Still, random observations of a subset of students in the intervention and control conditions (12 students from each classroom, n=588) showed that children who received the intervention showed significantly less physically aggressive behavior in the classroom, playground, and cafeteria. In addition, students who received SSC showed significant increases in neutral/prosocial behavior in the playground and cafeteria. These increases in desirable behaviors persisted at a six-month post intervention follow up.

The search for comparable European school based education-skills interventions did not yield many matches. One cross context example from Sweden, however, may be relevant. Social Emotional Training (SET) is presently undergoing testing in primary and lower secondary schools located on the outskirts of Stockholm, Sweden (Kimber & Sandell, 2001). Many of the youth attending these schools belong to ethnic minority groups that experience socio-economic disadvantage. Thus, SET is a selective intervention that has as its core, an individual level school based social-emotional competence promotion curriculum. Because SET was in the process of being tested at the time that this review was written, no conclusions about the usefulness of the program can be made. This intervention is described here because its evaluation design should yield an empirically sound efficacy trial and it provides an example of such an initiative designed for a European school setting.

The SET program draws its theoretical basis from the field of emotional intelligence (e.g., Gardner, Kornhaber, & Wake, 1996; Goleman, 1997; LeDoux 1998; Salovey & Mayer, 1990; Salovey & Sluyter, 1997; Sternberg, 1997). Program activities involve a series of developmentally-tailored exercises (i.e., increasing in complexity and duration for each grade) that teachers implement with their students during class periods. At the primary school level, 6- to 13-years-olds participate in 20-minute lessons twice a week. At the lower secondary school level, 14- to 16-years-olds participate in 45 to 60 minute sessions on a weekly basis. Each program activity deals with a specific aspect of social or emotional competence. Homework activities to be completed with the students' parents add a cross context element to the intervention. Two intervention and two matched comparison schools are currently participating in SET's efficacy trial. The evaluation design calls for pre- and multiple post-test assessments through the three years of intervention. Multiple informants and sources of data are integrated into the research design. Outcome evaluation results are expected in 2004.

Promoting Alternative Thinking Strategies (<u>PATHS</u>) is worth discussing at this point (Greenberg, et al., 2001). PATHS can be distinguished from many school-based interventions by its degree of development, i.e., a 15-year history, enhancement of multiple elements of social-emotional competence, and an explicit focus on the whole school environment that infuses PATHS into the everyday commerce of the school. With the implementation of PATHS as a part of Fast Track (Conduct Problems Prevention Research Group, 1999b), this well-established intervention has undergone controlled evaluation several times in America. The PATHS program has also been evaluated in the United Kingdom and the Netherlands.

Similar to the Second Step Curriculum and Social Emotional Training, PATHS uses a teacher-implemented curriculum that focuses on the promotion of social and emotional competence among primary school students. In PATHS lessons, a number of interactive techniques designed to promote key skills are presented to children. Enhancement of these skills is seen as an essential precursor of emotional adeptness and the ability to relate to others. The PATHS curriculum is comprehensive, involves up to 131 lessons, and it may be used over the entire span of primary school. Evaluations of PATHS typically are conducted after at least one year of exposure to program materials. Recently, PATHS materials have adapted to be developmentally appropriate for use with children in kindergarten.

In a randomized controlled trial using a non-clinical sample of children, PATHS was found to produce desired gains with regard to social-emotional competence, student reports of behavioral difficulties, and teacher reports of student adjustment, for a period of up to two years following program involvement. Notably, a strengthening of program effects was also found at the two year follow up (Greenberg & Kusché, 1998; Greenberg, Kusché, Cook, & Quamma, 1995). Comparable benefits from the PATHS intervention have been found when it has been used as a universal prevention program or applied to specific at-risk groups of children. In addition, there is growing evidence that the impact of PATHS spreads to children's internalizing symptoms (Conduct Problems Prevention Research Group, 1999b; Greenberg & Kusché, 1998; Greenberg, et al., 1995). Studies linking intervention processes to specific outcomes suggest that the effectiveness of PATHS is determined in large part to teachers' ability to maintain intervention fidelity, that is, to implement the program fully and consistently (Conduct Problems Prevention Research Group, 1996b; Greenberg, et al., 2001).

To date, European PATHS trials have been quasi-experimental, i.e., without the key features and controls of true experiments. As in some of the American program evaluations of PATHS, children participating in the European trials were hearing-impaired. Specifically, four schools for hearing impaired children and two hearing impaired units took part in the United Kingdom evaluation (Hindley & Reed, 1999). Children receiving the intervention (n=24) were pre-tested once and tested at 9 and 12 months after the initial assessment. Intervention activities took place over one year, with a follow up assessment nine months after PATHS activities ended. The wait-list control group (n=31) followed the same sequence of assessments, but they did not receive PATHS until program activities were finished in the intervention school. The wait-list group was evaluated after taking part in PATHS lessons for nine months.

The intervention group showed significant improvements on measures of emotional competence and adjustment soon after receiving PATHS compared to the wait-list group. At follow up, these gains were maintained for the intervention group for a measure of emotional competence, but not on measures of adjustment. It should be noted that no reference group was available for the follow up due to the wait-list design. After receiving PATHS, the wait-list comparison group showed similar intervention benefits for indices of emotional competence. These findings suggest that PATHS has demonstrated significant efficacy in enhancing key precursors of competence in both American and European samples of children.

Since 1989, PATHS has been integrated into the curriculum of some Dutch and Belgian schools for hearing-impaired children. A pilot test of PATHS, without a reference group, demonstrated significant treatment gains among children who received the intervention (N=33), for parent- and teacher-rated behavior, as well as social-emotional competence and problem solving (Joha, Luit, & Vermeer, 1999). While both included small samples, the United Kingdom and Dutch program evaluations offer preliminary evidence to support the generalizability of PATHS to European special education settings. Larger scale controlled trials are necessary to confirm these results and will result in additional insights into PATHS' cross national applicability and utility.

Many skills-competence promotion initiatives take place in schools, since the traditional educational mission of schools corresponds to the general notion of competence building among youth. A subset of these programs have demonstrated utility, particularly in terms of reducing youthful antisocial behavior and risk factors for adolescent problem behaviors. Successful universal and selective interventions from United States predominate this research literature, with programming available for primary school pupils (e.g., *Cognitive-behavioral intervention with aggressive boys* – Lochman, 1992; *Interpersonal Cognitive Problem Solving* – Shure, 1997; Spivack, Platt, & Shure, 1976; Spivack & Shure, 1982; *Interventions on the prevention of social exclusion* – Coie and Krehbiel, 1984; Oden & Asher, 1977; and others Hudley & Graham, 1993; Prinz, Blechman, & Dumas, 1994). Comparable programs are available for secondary school students (e.g., *Responding in Peaceful and Positive Ways* – Meyer, Farrell, Northup, Kung, & Plybon, 2000; *SMART Talk* – Bosworth, Espelage, & DuBay, 1998; Bosworth, Espelage, DuBay, Daytner, & Karageorge, 2000; *The Improving Social Awareness* – *Social Problem Solving Project* – Elias, et al., 1986; 1991; *Yale-New Haven Middle School Social Problem-Solving Program* – Caplan, et al., 1992). Interventions that add family components to school based education-skills curricula have also shown promising results (e.g., *Fast Track* – Conduct Problems Prevention Research Group, 1999a; 1999b; *Montreal Prevention Experiment* – Tremblay, Pagnai-Kurtz, Masse, Vitaro, & Pihl, 1995). We will return to these cross context interventions later in the next chapter.

Education-Skills: Preventing Youth Substance Use. The research literature on school based drug prevention is large and has a substantial history (Evans, 1998). In this subsection, emphasis is placed on the part of this literature that involves school-based education-skills interventions aimed at drug use prevention. These prevention programs exist for both primary and secondary school students, with a growing number of interventions specifically designed for children and early adolescents. These school based alcohol, tobacco, and other drug (ATOD) interventions often have a universal rather than selected focus, and they are delivered to all students attending a particular school. A key assumption of such programs is that later onset and lower levels of use for a range of licit and illicit substances leads to better short- and long-term outcomes (Allensworth, 1993; Collins et al., 1995; White & Pitts, 1998).

Class 2000[4] represents a promising European example of this type of skills-oriented prevention program at the primary school level (Bölcskei, Hörmann, Hollederer, Jordan, & Fenzel, 1997; European Commission, 2000; Hollederer & Bölcskei, 1999; 2000). This intervention, established in 1991, has been widely implemented throughout Germany with more than 130,000 children participating between 2002 and 2003. The program is typically implemented over a four-year period, from grades 1 to 4, among children from six to ten years old. Intervention goals include strengthening children's self-concepts, and bolstering their application of critical life skills, such as social resistance skills, to overcome everyday challenges to use drugs. Classroom based lessons are supplemented with up to three sessions presented by trained health workers. It is recommended that program activities be coordinated with parent involvement and changes to the school environment to provide further support for program goals. In a large quasi-experimental program trial (N=3,489) that measured behavior changes from the first to the fourth grades, this program was shown to produce significant reductions in cigarette smoking. At the end of the fourth grade, youngsters in the comparison group reported significantly more experience with smoking (t_1=10.6% to t_2=32%) relative to youth in the intervention condition (t_1=10.3% to t_2=25.2%). Also, significantly fewer Class 2000 students were regular smokers relative to pupils in the comparison group.

While American universal drug prevention programs for children under the age of ten have not shown a great deal of utility (Hall & Zigler, 1997), interventions for older children and adolescents have shown greater promise. Life Skills Training (LST), for instance, is a well established multiple level (individual, peer) program example commonly used with early adolescents. LST was developed in America and it is a domain-specific application of generic and social resistance skills training with coordinated lessons to delay the onset of, or reduce current levels of substance use (Botvin, Baker, Dusenbury, Botvin, & Diaz, 1995; Botvin, et al., 2000). This program can be implemented as either a universal or a selective intervention. Program content is based on cognitive-behavioral principles and key behavior change techniques include teacher and student facilitated role-playing, modeling, feedback, reinforcement, and practice via homework assignments to enhance skills to resist social influences to engage in substance use. LST combines social resistance skills with a broader approach to enhancing social competence, in a long-term, classroom based format implemented during the transition to secondary school (i.e., during the American 7th, 8th, and 9th grades).

Large-scale, long-term outcome evaluations of LST are promising and document significant reductions in mean levels of tobacco, alcohol, and marijuana use, especially among students who received 60% or more of the 30 lessons over the three year span. These gains were maintained in some evaluation samples for over three years following the conclusion of LST programming. In addition, the significant effects of the intervention were found to generalize to American teens who are ethnic minorities from disadvantaged backgrounds (Botvin, Schinke, Epstein, Diaz, Botvin, 1995; Botvin, Dusenbury, Baker, James-Ortiz, & Kerner, 1989).

The Oslo Youth Study[5] (OYS) is an example of a relevant multiple level (individual, peer) program from Europe (Tell, Klepp, Vellar, & McAlister, 1984). Unlike LST, however, the OYS was a school-based intervention with a brief format, approximately ten lessons over a 15-month period. Program components emphasized teacher and student led educational activities, resistance skills training, and a public commitment by youth to abstain from smoking. A significant strength of the OYS was the long term follow up of program participants, that resulted in little attrition of participants over time. Youth in the intervention and comparison groups were on average 13 years old when pre-tested at program initiation, and they had an immediate post-test, and a ten year follow up assessment (at an average age of 23). An evaluation at the end of the OYS documented significantly lower smoking onset rates for students receiving the intervention (16.5%) compared to those in the comparison condition (26.9%). Intervention youth also reported significantly more knowledge regarding the effects of smoking relative to youngsters in the comparison condition. Significant long-term benefits of the intervention were found only for males. Intervention males were significantly more likely to have never smoked (58% compared to 44%). Among smokers, intervention males also reported 15% less frequent weekly smoking relative to comparison group males (Klepp, Tell, & Vellar, 1993; Tell, et al., 1984).

Other methodologically sophisticated and rigorously implemented education-skills intervention programs have demonstrated that it is possible to make at least immediate and in a few instances longer lasting changes in substance use by older children and adolescents through school based intervention (*Alcohol Misuse Prevention Study* – Dielman, Shope, Leech, & Butchart, 1989; *Growing Healthy* – Connell & Turner, 1985; Smith, Redican, & Olson, 1992; *The Improving Social Awareness – Social Problem Solving Project* – Elias, et al., 1986; 1991). Schools also remain a principle setting for education-skills activities in successful cross context antidrug initiatives like the Midwestern Prevention Project (Pentz et al., 1989), Project Northland (Perry, et al., 1993; 2000), and the University of Vermont Study (Flynn, et al., 1997; Worden, Flynn, Solomon, & Secker-Walker, 1996).

Education-Skills: Preventing High Risk Sexual Behavior and Teen Pregnancy. In recent decades, systematic efforts have been made to describe and explain adolescent sexual behavior, with the ultimate aim of reducing the individual and social costs of preventable risky sexual behaviors or adolescent pregnancy (e.g. Cates & Berman, 1999; Jemmott & Jemmott, 2000; Paikoff, McCormick, & Sagrestano, 2000; Seidman & Reider, 1994). While sexual expression among adolescents is normative and potentially self-enhancing, it is also associated with a range of problematic health outcomes, and concurrent problem behaviors (Leigh, 1999; Tubman, Windle, & Windle, 1996).

Prevention programs focusing on adolescent sexual behavior have shown efficacy in reducing a range of behaviors that include unprotected intercourse, sexually transmitted diseases (STDs), and unintended pregnancy. A number of promising school based, education and skill development-oriented prevention programs significantly reduce harm related to adolescent sexual behavior, either via impacts on risky sexual behavior such as multiple partners and unprotected intercourse, or by improving contraceptive use. Important examples of promising interventions in the United States include those designed as universal programs (e.g., *Get Real about AIDS* – Main et al., 1994; *Reducing the Risk Program* – Kirby, Barth, Leland & Fetro, 1991), as well as those developed for at-risk adolescents (e.g., *Be Proud! Be Responsible!* – Jemmott, Jemmott, & Fong, 1992). These programs are designed to address the needs of adolescents who are either currently sexually active or at increasing risk for the initiation of sexual activity.

Program trials of two of the aforementioned universal school based programs provide a case in point. Reducing the Risk and Get Real about AIDS each were: tested with samples of predominately European American teens who had an average age of 15, supported by a strong theoretical basis, taught by teachers, integrated into comprehensive 15 session health education curriculum, interactive in nature, and oriented toward the modeling, rehearsal, practice, and discussion of key skills and social competencies. In addition, contraceptive use was integrated into the curricula. Evaluation of the Reducing the Risk program indicated that, in contrast to students in the comparison condition, who received sex education as usual, pupils in the intervention condition were significantly less likely to initiate intercourse, or if currently sexually active, were less likely to engage in unprotected intercourse (Kirby, et al., 1991). Positive behavior changes following intervention were also found in a quasi-experimental evaluation of Get Real about AIDS. In this study, students receiving the intervention were more likely to use condoms and to reduce their number of sex partners (Main et al., 1994).

Some pregnancy prevention programs have shown significant efficacy for selected targeted behaviors, using a range of conceptual approaches and strategies to implement change. Yet, most intervention programs promote the development of specific or generic skills designed to change knowledge and attitudes, sexual behavior or to enhance contractive use including: general sexuality education (e.g., *Education Now and Babies Later* – Kirby, Korpi, Barth, & Cagampang, 1995), selected examples of abstinence-oriented programs (e.g., *Postponing Sexual Involvement* – Howard & McCabe, 1992), and school based clinics that include counseling and skill development as part of contraceptive planning[6] (e.g., *Center for Population Options Study* – Kirby & Waszak, 1992).

Synthesis

The scope and heterogeneity of school based interventions has resulted in burgeoning research and practice oriented literatures that are often difficult to compare and to integrate due to differences in the goals, design, or implementation of specific programs. There is a significant need to define key themes in these literatures, not only to bring order to a rapidly growing research area, but also to provide recommendations to both researchers and practitioners regarding the utility of available prevention approaches. Specifically, it is essential to identify useful programs and best practices for altering risk-protective factors that have particular relevance to school performance, as well as those that have salience for a variety of problem behaviors. In addition, it is important to provide guidelines regarding the conditions that modify the success of intervention actions, to inform professionals planning programs of individual level amenability to prevention variables and barriers to program implementation. A best evidence synthesis of these emergent issues from the broad literature on school based prevention programs is outlined below.

Academic Tutoring

Tutoring appears to be particularly appropriate for promoting academic competence in children otherwise vulnerable to school failure. The majority of well tested and successful interventions in this area are directed at primary school children who have academic difficulties (c.f. *Program Example* – Shanahan & Barr, 1995 – *Relevant Narrative Reviews* – Durlak, 1997; Greenwood, et al., 1988; McLaughlin & Vacha, 1992; Slavin, et al., 1994 – *Relevant Meta-Analyses* – Cohen, et al., 1982). The promotion of numeracy and literacy skills seem to be, on the whole, equally responsive to this approach. The available evidence also suggests that not only are tutor-student relationships a useful method for improving functioning related to academic outcomes, but that better academic functioning and classroom behavior may promote improved social relations with peers (c.f. *Program Example* – Fantuzzo, et al., 1992). Therefore, selective tutoring interventions within schools may initiate processes that decrease the likelihood of school failure among specific subgroups of students, while simultaneously promoting resilient trajectories in other domains.

Promising tutoring programs appear to share several characteristics. First, successful tutoring engages a young person in learning tasks by making them more enjoyable, providing support for such activities, affirming the importance of academic endeavors, and building students' confidence that they can learn (Ellis et al., 1998; Terry, 1999). Second, tutoring programs demonstrate that adults and classmates care about the tutees and feel personally invested in them, potentially counteracting students' sense of alienation. Third, skills and competencies modeled in the tutoring experience reinforce prosocial skills related to success in school and other social settings, including: cooperation, teamwork, and on-task behavior (Muscott & O'Brien, 1999). Fourth, shared time within tutor-student relationships provides opportunities to model and practice skills more generally predictive of resilience, such as planning and goal setting, self-monitoring, and problem-solving (Blum & Jones, 1993).

School based tutoring interventions regularly show immediate program benefits in enhancing academic skills for children. Yet, a principal shortcoming in the tutoring literature is the general lack of evidence for program durability. Tutoring as a stand alone intervention is seldom assessed for enduring effects. Despite this limitation, the potential value of tutoring should not be dismissed casually. Tutoring initiatives with their focus on academic enrichment offer a high degree of overlap with the traditional educational mission of schools. Consequently, school stakeholders are likely to provide considerable support to tutoring programs. Tutoring is also a key component of comprehensive cross context interventions designed to improve at risk children's academic skills, positive school adjustment, social competence and interpersonal relations (c.f. *Program Examples* – Conduct Problems Prevention Research Group, 1999a; Dumas, Prinz, et al., 1999).

Adult vs. Peer Tutoring. Tutoring by adults is often directed at primary school children who experience risk for school failure and/or behavior problems in the classroom. The peer tutoring literature tends to target a broader universal-selective population of primary school students. Tutoring has been implemented successfully in school settings by a number of types of persons, with the more prevalent form of intervention being peer tutoring, due to its less intensive service delivery demands on school personnel.

Prevention programs have been designed that explicitly engage peers in the process of implementing program materials and procedures by including peers as tutors, sometimes in addition to their roles as recipients of program services. In their roles as tutors, students have opportunities to engage in forms of learning that diverge from a traditional classwide didactic format, thereby providing more intensive exposure to lesson materials (Greenwood, et al., 1988). In addition, students are challenged to master the material to the extent that they are comfortable presenting concepts to classmates. Reviews of the peer tutoring literature demonstrate that academic and attitudinal benefits accumulate for those who receive school based peer tutoring, as well as for those pupils who act as tutors (c.f. *Relevant Narrative Reviews* – Greenwood, et al., 1988; McLaughlin & Vacha, 1992 – *Relevant Meta-Analyses* – Cohen, et al., 1982).

It can be argued that tutoring delivered by teachers and other adult paraprofessionals takes the 'teaching advantage' away from youth and presents considerable practical complications or a significant drain on limited resources (Durlak, 1997). This intensive form of intervention, in contrast to didactic classroom instruction, requires significantly greater expenditure of resources, not the least of which is the instructional time required and the intensity of instructional effort. Furthermore, tutoring might be uncomfortable for some teachers who may be less at ease with more intense personal instructional relationships with their students. Teachers, even those who endorse the value of tutoring to promote adaptive academic outcomes, may also balk at additional responsibilities to their already overburdened schedules, even if their involvement is limited to the supervision of other adults providing classroom tutoring to students. Yet, if teachers are not involved in decisions about the tutoring their students receive, they may feel as if their role as professionals has been devalued.

Peer tutoring becomes increasingly attractive as a program alternative when the supervisory function of teachers is esteemed and making the most of limited resources is a high priority. It should be noted, however, that peer tutoring is not without its own limitations. Peer tutoring with a solid structure of activities for tutors and tutees has been associated with more pronounced program benefits (Cohen, et al., 1982). Consequently, a significant proportion of teachers' efforts must still be devoted to creating program materials and guiding peer tutoring sessions (e.g., Greenwood, et al., 1989). Furthermore, studies have shown that instruction of complex skills is more problematic in the peer format for tutoring (Cohen, et al., 1982; Greenwood, et al., 1989). When complex materials are taught, teachers must invest more time "up front" training peer tutors or organizing materials into manageable units for each tutoring session. Peer tutoring has been linked to significant improvements in students' knowledge, attitudes, and performance in specific academic subjects. Yet, peer tutoring programs tend to be less successful when tutors and tutees are the same age, and in particular when their grade level is third grade or lower (Cohen, et al., 1982). This finding and the results from similar evaluations of peer tutoring suggest the importance of program structure, proper preparation of lesson materials, and adequate supervision of participating students.

Education and Skills Promotion

Education. Universal and selective school interventions often have as an initial goal to raise students' basic level of knowledge regarding risk behaviors (Centers for Disease Control and Prevention, 1994; 1999, November). Lack of knowledge and comprehension of relations between risk behaviors and adverse outcomes is assumed to be a significant barrier to the reduction of youth problem behaviors (Dusenbury & Falco, 1995). For example, a traditional rational approach to fostering behavior change assumed that if young people were supplied with accurate information regarding the benefits and consequences of their behavior, they would make logical changes in their behavior (Ambtman, Madak, Koss, & Strople, 1990). The assumption that enhancing knowledge about a specific narrowly defined problem behavior like tobacco use will result in significant changes in attitudes, behavioral intentions or outcomes is dubious in absence of its integration into a theory based, comprehensive intervention that is fully integrated into the school curriculum (Flay, 2000; Lewis, et al., 1990). While a sufficient knowledge base is a useful foundation upon which to build specific behavioral skills and interpersonal competencies, information-only prevention approaches are generally seen as being less than developmentally optimal and less efficacious than comprehensive and interactive skills based approaches (Bruvold, 1993; Hansen, 1992). Thus an information only approach appears to be a valuable one if the specific targeted outcome for enhancement is also educational in nature. However, this approach appears to produce less positive results as a stand-alone program to reduce problem behaviors in schools or to transfer intervention gains to settings outside schools.

Many prevention oriented educators, practitioners, and researchers have recognized the limitations of curriculum based, education only approaches that seek to produce health behavior change. In contrast to a more traditional health instruction model, Allensworth (1993) suggested that interventions are more likely to be successful if they employ a more all-encompassing health promotion model. The health promotion model improves upon standard health instruction because didactic methods are only one of many ways to educate young people about promotive behaviors. Additional methods might include policy change and modifications to the school environment, media presentations, direct interventions, or modeling and role-playing. This integrative approach emphasizes activities and participatory learning that encourage the practice of key skills to increase the likelihood of positive behavioral change. Interventions influenced by a health promotion paradigm attempt to infuse health education into the broader academic curriculum, thereby providing consistent prevention messages from multiple sources and multiple opportunities to engage in health promoting activities.

Skills Promotion. Programs to enhance general social competencies or behavioral skills viewed as protective factors for specific maladaptive outcomes like drug use, teen pregnancy, risky sexual behavior are routinely included as components of school based universal and selective prevention efforts (Durlak & Wells, 1997; 1998). Attempts to enhance relevant skills (e.g., refusal skills, decision-making skills, or communication ability), as well as more general competencies (e.g., awareness of feelings, building options for coping, recognition of risk situations) are fundamental to health promotion efforts for a wide range of risk behaviors (Collins et al., 1995). Yet, preventionists designing programs must select some balance between enhancing generic individual and interpersonal competencies (e.g., decision-making, communication skills, negotiation and refusal skills, self-esteem and self-efficacy) or focused applications of these competencies (e.g., condom self-efficacy; drug refusal skill; sexual communication skills). Weissberg and Greenberg (1998) suggested that interventions that emphasize the transmission of a combination of generic and targeted skills are more likely to produce meaningful and sustainable behavioral change than are purely educational approaches to behavior change, or efforts that rely solely on the development of targeted skills. Similarly, a focus on generic skills at the expense of developing problem specific skills may result in the enhancement of competence in general without achieving the desired behavior change. Programs like Life Skills Training (Botvin, Baker, Dusenbury, Botvin, & Diaz, 1995; Botvin, et al., 2000) incorporate intervention actions to build generic and targeted skills, thereby providing a way to bridge the gap between general social competence and changes in specific problem behaviors. In general, such an intervention approach is not unique to anti-drug education-skills initiatives and may be applied to a broad range of problem behaviors.

Putting it All Together: Education and Skills Promotion. Education-skills initiatives that have demonstrated success in reducing a range of risk behaviors share several features (Weissberg & Greenberg, 1998). First, they are clearly supported by a coherent theoretical framework and an extensive base of empirical research. Second, they provide interactive learning opportunities through which they transmit both specific and general skills hypothesized to provide protection against one or more risk behaviors, in addition to problem-related knowledge. Clearly, peers as participants and as co-facilitators play significant roles in the process of implementing universal and selective prevention programs incorporating skills-training components. Peers' participation in dynamic prevention programs with interactive activities is one feature that makes these programs clearly superior to traditional, didactic, information based prevention models across a range of problem behaviors and health-related outcomes (c.f. *Relevant Narrative Review* – Dusenbury & Falco, 1995 – *Relevant Meta-Analysis* – Black et al., 1998). Third, problem-related information is presented in a manner that is developmentally and culturally appropriate, factually accurate, and contrasted with existing social norms and beliefs within the school and peer networks. Fourth, long-term, multi-year programs that start before the onset of a problem behavior are generally viewed as more desirable prevention strategies than programs that propose to reduce levels of ongoing risk behaviors (Lewis et al., 1990).

Specific vs. Spreading Effects by Risk. While there are programmatic and methodological similarities across education-skills interventions in schools, the literature on this topic is largely organized in a problem specific fashion. The following subsections summarize the school based education-skills intervention literature as it corresponds to the amelioration of specific youth problem behaviors. As in the description of exemplar school based education-skills initiatives, spreading program effects and a consideration of program utility by risk level will be noted where relevant.

Education-Skills: Preventing Youth Antisocial Behavior. Several comprehensive reviews of social skills and competence initiatives, as well as school based violence and crime prevention exist in the research literature (c.f. *Relevant Narrative Reviews* – Gottfredson, 1997; Taylor, et al., 1999 – *Relevant Meta-Analyses* – Beelmann, et al., 1994; Quinn, Kavale, Mathur, Rutherford, & Forness, 1999; Schneider, 1992; Wilson & Lipsey, 2000a). Many of these reviews, however, are not designed to answer the specific question of 'do school based education-skills promotion programs reduce antisocial behavior in youth?' While schools remain key staging grounds, education-skills initiatives may be implemented in community or home settings (c.f. *Relevant Narrative Review* – Taylor, et al., 1999). School and non-school based education-skills promotion initiatives are therefore occasionally mixed in meta-analytic analyses. Because these programs were not coded separately, it is becomes difficult to parcel out results in terms of relevant school based programs alone (e.g., Quinn, et al., 1999). Despite these challenges, interventions included in a good number of the above mentioned reviews met the program review criteria laid out in *Overview Chapter*, were school based, and had education-skill promotion as a main program element (c.f. *Relevant Narrative Reviews* – Taylor, et al., 1999 – *Relevant Meta-Analysis* – Beelmann, et al., 1994; Wilson & Lipsey, 2000a).

What conclusions can be taken away from this research literature? Salient school based programs exist for universal and selective student populations. Successful interventions in this domain often take an interactive and participatory learning approach that is paired with programmatic content that combines: 1) relevant knowledge such as information that challenges pro-violence beliefs and attitudes, 2) the promotion of generic life competencies such as coping and decision making skills, and, 3) problem specific skills training in areas like emotional regulation and the generation of prosocial alternatives to interpersonal conflict. School based education-skills initiatives relevant to the prevention of antisocial behavior have documented short-term behavioral improvements in child (c.f. *Program Examples* – Grossman, et al., 1997; Lochman, et al., 1984) and early to middle adolescent samples (c.f. *Program Examples* – Hudley & Graham, 1993; Farrell, Meyer, & White,

2001; Feindler, Marriott, & Iwata, 1984; Prinz, et al., 1994). A meta-analysis conducted by Wilson and Lipsey (2000a) puts the relative extent of such changes into perspective, while it offers clues as to which program components maybe more or less useful for producing these behavioral changes. This meta-analysis was particularly noteworthy in that the school based programs reviewed (N=201) were coded by their intervention content, thereby making it possible to compare education-skills promotion initiatives that emphasized emotional regulation (n=37) to programs focusing on social skills development (n=71). Programs emphasizing emotional regulation showed a uniform and significant, or in meta-analysis language a homogenous, ability to positively affect change on measures of aggressive and disruptive behavior in youth (ES=.43). As a group, the social skills interventions were found to yield a significant immediate impact on indices of aggressive and disruptive behavior (ES=.32), but analyses also indicated that these interventions showed different levels of effectiveness, in that not all programs yielded comparable positive results[7].

What is the reason for this diversity in program outcomes? One potential explanation is that the word 'social skill intervention' encompasses a diversity of programs, employing many different strategies to produce behavior change. Salient meta-analyses have also shown that some social skills programs may yield gains in specific indicators of social competence like problem-solving and social-cognitive skills, but these gains do not always translate into to behavioral change (c.f. *Relevant Meta-Analyses* – Beelmann et al., 1994; Quinn, et al., 1999). In addition, it should be said that social skills interventions are not always designed to work with children exhibiting behavioral problems. An objective of an intervention program targeting this at risk population may be to reduce social marginalization rather than overt aggression.

Relevant illustrations of this point may be found among those school based interventions designed to address social exclusion. In contrast to prevention programs aimed at reducing social skill deficits associated with aggressive or antisocial behavior, social exclusion-oriented interventions in general do not demonstrate reductions in violent behavior. This may be due in part to the type of samples involved in these interventions. Such initiatives often recruit diverse samples of children with a wide range of socio-metric characteristics. The available research literature suggests that the adjustment trajectories for popular, unpopular, neglected, controversial, and rejected children can be quite diverse depending on the outcome in question. Aggression, however, is not always synonymous with social marginalization, given that even popular children engage in some physical and relational bullying (Crick, 1997; Crick & Grotpeter, 1996). Different types of intervention strategies may be more or less appropriate for children in different socio-metric categories, as distinctly different developmental processes may be related to the onset or maintenance of social exclusion in different groups of children. Thus, social exclusion-oriented initiatives may not have program goals that necessarily fall squarely in the realm of violence prevention.

Returning back to the general results of the aforementioned meta-analysis (Wilson & Lipsey, 2000a), it can be argued that the findings of this investigation of the research literature indicate that school based education-skills initiatives have shown promise in terms of yielding immediate positive behavioral change. Short-term positive changes in cognitive-social-emotional competencies, peer acceptance, and cognitions-beliefs that are negatively related to antisocial behavior have also been demonstrated for child (c.f. *Relevant Program Examples* – Shure & Spivack, 1988) and early to middle adolescent samples (c.f. *Relevant Program Examples* – Bosworth et al., 2000; Caplan, et al., 1992). Yet, there is a need for greater specification of the content boundaries and objectives of particular types of education-skills initiatives, through fine grained component analysis of successful programs that have impacted youthful antisocial behavior and related risk-protective factors.

How durable are program benefits? In a recent review of randomized well-controlled evaluation trials of social skills programs to reduce aggressive and delinquent behavior, Taylor, Eddy, and Biglan (1999) for example, found little empirical support for the utility of these programs as free standing interventions, as they largely resulted in moderate and often short term reductions in conduct problems in selected domains. With regard to this issue, Weissberg and Greenberg (1998) distinguished between person-centered competence enhancement programs (e.g., skills training models) and ecologically based competence enhancement programs, emphasizing that more ecological approaches to the enhancement of social competence attempt to modify children's environments to facilitate the practice and reinforcement of newly learned skills. These authors suggested that it may be unrealistic to expect anything other than short-term retention of intervention gains if environmental supports do not exist to promote the use and subsequent generalization of new skills and competencies. Changes in environmental settings and the removal of barriers to skill generalization may be facilitated by training teachers and classmates, or alternatively parents, to use the same skills (e.g., decision-making, conflict resolution skills) thereby providing modeling, feedback, reinforcement, and opportunities for practice. In addition, broader changes in classroom and family settings, in relationships between people or the allocation of resources may serve to alleviate broader social influences that promote the continued expression of antisocial behavior (Reid & Eddy, 1997; Weissberg & Greenberg, 1998).

Another explanation for the lack of long-term program effects may be due in part to a general lack of effort to follow up program participants after intervention. For the few interventions in this area that have undergone long-term follow up, interesting results have sometimes been found. For example, an intervention for primary school pupils (c.f. *Program Example* – Lochman, 1992) and an initiative for middle school students (c.f. *Program Example* – Elias, et al., 1991) each showed long-term program benefits, but in the former case improvements at a three year follow up assessment were found for substance use and not for aggressive behavior. In the adolescent program, intervention gains were shown on measures of both substance use and aggressive antisocial behaviors at a six year follow up assessment. Although the ability of school based education-skills initiatives to make enduring changes in antisocial behavior, misconduct, and criminality on the whole has yet to be firmly established, such programming may have the potential to extend positive effects beyond antisocial behavior alone. At this time, there is significant need for additional rigorous and long-term evaluations of school based, skills oriented prevention programs designed to lower rates of antisocial behavior (Loeber & Farrington, 1998b).

Are these interventions equally useful across childhood and adolescence? Although successful program examples for adolescents can be identified, there is evidence to suggest boundaries for the timing and developmental appropriateness of this type of prevention effort. In a meta-analysis by Durlak and Wells (1997), for instance, interpersonal problem solving interventions produced significantly larger intervention gains for children aged seven to 11 than for children over age 11. To date, violence prevention curricula for older adolescents, as a group, have not yielded impressive behavioral results (Coben, Weiss, Mulvey, & Dearwater, 1994). The expression of antisocial behavior in adolescence varies by developmental factors such as the timing of onset, and different processes and mechanisms may underlie the antisocial behaviors of separate homogenous subgroups of adolescents (Loeber & Stouthamer-Loeber, 1998). Failure to account for the multiple pathways leading to problem behaviors may mean that certain adolescents within the general population of students may not have gotten an adequate amount of intervention at the right time and/or the type of programming did not fit a particular subgroup's risk-protective factor configuration. Taylor, Eddy, and Biglan (1999) argued for school based education-skills initiatives that are incorporated into a comprehensive prevention strategy for interrupting broader developmental processes maintaining antisocial behavior. In such a tailored and developmentally-graded approach, at risk primary school children could receive education-skills training linked to parent training and classroom management initiatives for teachers. In contrast, the needs of high risk adolescents maybe more appropriately addressed via intensive multi-modal approaches like Multisystemic Therapy (Henggeler et al., 1998).

Education-Skills: Preventing Youth Substance Use. To date, successful school based anti-drug education-skills initiatives primarily exist for older children and early to middle adolescents at the universal and selective prevention levels (c.f. *Relevant Narrative Reviews* – Botvin, et al., 1998; Evans, 1998; Hall & Zigler, 1997; Hansen, 1992 – *Relevant Meta-Analyses* – Bangert-Drowns, 1988; Tobler, 1992; Tobler, Lessard, Marshall, Ochshorn, & Roona, 1999; Tobler & Stratton, 1997). With the noted European exception of Class 2000, school based education-skills interventions for young school children typically show limited effectiveness. Drug Abuse Resistance Education (DARE), for example, is a universal prevention program targeting substance use in school children. A nationally recognized program, DARE is the most widely implemented program of its kind in American schools, reaching millions of children each year (Harmon, 1993). A meta-analysis of outcomes from evaluations of DARE suggested that program participation was more likely to impact attitudes about substance use rather than levels of actual use (Ennett, Tobler, Ringwalt, & Flewelling, 1994). Other substance use prevention programs targeting primary school children like the BABES Program (Abbey, Oliansky, Stilianos, Hohlstein, & Kaczynski, 1990) have reported similarly mixed findings (Hall & Zigler, 1997). It can be argued that the state of the science regarding what is now known about, "what works in the drug prevention" has not yet been extended downwards into the early school years. Future efforts along these lines would benefit from updated and systematic program development with young school children coupled with long-term program evaluation.

In terms of school based education-skills programs for older children and teens, successful interventions of this type are consistent with a health promotion perspective, backed by a strong conceptual and evaluation framework, in an intensive implementation format that often includes booster sessions (c.f. *Program Example* – Botvin, et al., 1995). Successful European program examples in this area, while varying in length and intensity, contain many of the same features that have been determined to be useful in comparable programs in the United States (c.f. *Program Example* – Klepp, et al., 1993). Specifically, prototype school based education-skills initiatives regularly have *more than one* of the following elements: 1) information about drug use and its consequences, 2) education regarding social norms for substance use, 3) social resistance skills training, and 4) generalized life competence promotion (Botvin, et al., 1998).

The first component, information, addresses the need for youth to have accurate knowledge when it comes to alcohol, tobacco, and other drugs (ATOD). As mentioned previously, one should be careful with information based intervention strategies. For instance, Ross, Saavedra, Shur, Winters, and Felner (1992) suggested that increased knowledge regarding substance use often has little impact on actual drug use or intentions to use because enhanced knowledge does not necessary translate into alterations in behavioral choices. Similarly, Bruvold (1993) found that smoking prevention programs based solely on knowledge enhancement produced far smaller intervention gains than programs using methods guided by social reinforcement, social norms, or developmental models. Others have contended that educational efforts to reduce substance use or other health risk behaviors isolated from efforts to enhance more basic skills or more comprehensive community based prevention efforts, are unlikely to overcome pervasive social influences such as the mass media, family or neighborhood norms or modeling, or an individual's learning history (Ambtman, Madak, Koss, & Strople, 1990; Pentz, et al., 1989).

The second component listed, norm education, touches on the need to provide young people with correct information about the prevalence of drug use among peers. Dusenbury and Falco (1995), for instance, summarized key components of successful drug prevention curricula and concluded that drug education is more effective if it is research based, theory driven and presents developmentally appropriate information including normative data regarding drug use. Studies have indicated that young people often assume that peers' ATOD use is more frequent and of greater magnitude than it really is. Therefore, youngsters may be overly enthusiastic to use ATOD in order to avoid being different from classmates (Botvin, Baker, Dusenbury, Botvin, & Diaz, 1995; Kandel, 1985).

The third and forth components deal with non-specific and problem behavior specific skills promotion. A considerable degree of consensus exists among experts in the domain of school based substance use prevention that generic and problem specific competencies, such as resistance skills are essential protective factors for the reduction of substance use in adolescence (e.g., Dusenbury & Falco, 1995). Social resistance training is in part based on the premise that drug use begins and escalates in social (e.g., peer) contexts. This type of training is aimed at helping youth identify social persuasion techniques and to respond more effectively to social influences to use alcohol or other drugs. Specifically, youngsters learn and get practice in how to turn persuasion tactics around for prosocial aims. Interactive group based exercises that allow the modeling and rehearsal of appropriate refusal skills, as well as better recognition of messages and settings promoting the use of substances are key features of empirically supported approaches to substance use prevention (e.g., Botvin, et al., 1998). Furthermore, nonspecific indicators of life competence such as problem solving or communication skills are often added to school based drug prevention programs. These multi-purpose skills are generally viewed as useful to youth in the wide range of life situations they encounter, including occasions when they will have to make decisions about whether or not to use drugs.

As in education-skills initiatives in other settings, model school based substance use interventions are interactive and often provide learning opportunities in the context of classroom and small group exercises to build social competence, and relevant skills to reduce the likelihood of the onset or maintenance of substance use (Black et al., 1998). Interactive and participatory teaching methods are regularly used to promote the acquisition and practice of important skills (e.g., refusal skills, decision-making skills) that are ideally integrated into a comprehensive health promotion strategy. Furthermore, it has been recommended that school based educational-skills efforts be culturally sensitive and include sufficient teacher and/or student training and support, as well as adequate coverage of concepts to ensure mastery.

Promising school based education-skills initiatives with salience to drug prevention commonly show short-term improvements on indices of ATOD use, as well as desired changes in related risk-protective factors. As in the previous subsection, enduring behavioral change is the exception rather than the norm. The overall lack of evidence for program durability could be due to the limited number of interventions that are evaluated for extended periods under adequate testing conditions. Among the few interventions of this type that have yielded long-term reductions, positive change has been noted on indices of ATOD use for up to three, six, and ten years post intervention (c.f. *Program Examples* – Botvin, et al., 1995; Elias, et al., 1991; Klepp, et al., 1993). While such long-term program benefits are not without qualification (e.g., in the Botvin, et al., 1995 greater program fidelity was linked to significantly improved outcomes, and in Klepp, et al., 1993, enduring improvements were found only for male program participants), such prototype programs demonstrate what can be achieved through the application of well implemented and evidence based school interventions. An examination of the broader literature on school based education-skills programs, however, indicates that not all interventions of this type meet with similar levels of success. Most drug prevention programs conducted in schools do not produce significant, immediate or longer lasting change in the drug use of students. The often transient and smaller than expected effect sizes obtained in many substance use prevention programs can be linked to wide range of factors including: narrow or information-only program focus, lack of intensiveness or follow up booster sessions, poor conceptualization, or inadequate evaluation (Hall & Zigler, 1997; White & Pitts, 1998).

Education-Skills: Preventing High Risk Sexual Behavior and Teen Pregnancy. In this intervention area, a range of viable strategies for risk reduction among adolescent samples exist (c.f. *Relevant Narrative Reviews* – Centers for Disease Control and Prevention, 1999, November; Kirby, 2000; Kim, Stanton, Li, Dickersin, & Galbraith, 1997; Ostrow & Kalichman, 2000 – *Relevant Meta-Analyses* – Kok, van den Borne, & Mullen, 1997). Efforts to decrease sexually transmitted disease (STD) exposure or adolescent pregnancy often focuses on limiting both sexual activity (e.g., delaying its onset, promoting abstinence, or reducing numbers of partners) or limiting risky sexual behavior (e.g., unprotected intercourse) (Gillmore et al., 1997; Kirby, et al., 1997). In addition, although sometimes controversial in certain communities, prevention efforts also do focus on the promotion of contraceptive use and related skills, attitudes and intentions among youth (Alstead et al., 1999). Successful school based education-skills initiatives that address adolescent sexual behavior, like other promising education-skills interventions make use of a combination of program elements that in this case include: 1) accurate information about sex, 2) sex specific norm education, and 3) social competence enhancement via the promotion of communicative competence, self-efficacy, self-esteem, and/or refusal-negotiation skills.

In terms of program utility, there is evidence to support the conclusion that school based education-skills programs can have a positive impact on the health behavior of young people. Kok and colleagues (1997) reviewed 14 meta-analyses of health education and promotion programs, which included school based education-skills programming. Within the meta-analyses, both youth and adult prevention programs for a wide range of substantive health behavior domains were represented. Regarding the extent of change found across such intervention efforts, the authors reported effect sizes of 0.55 for primary prevention education programs ($\underline{n}$ = 41) and an overall effect size of .46 across all other programs. Yet, Kok and colleagues' enthusiasm was tempered as they noted that most evaluation studies reported short-term rather than long-term outcomes. Similarly, outcomes in evaluations were often measured as attitudes, beliefs and intentions, rather than as actual reductions in specific behavioral targets such as risky sexual behavior or increases in other health-enhancing behaviors. While this and others recent reviews suggest that evidence exists to support the utility of school based, health related prevention programs, considerable gaps exist in the current knowledge base. This is especially the case with regard to school based prevention programs targeting adolescent sexual behavior. Research on adolescent sexual behavior has a number of methodological difficulties, sometimes lacks methodological rigor, and is subject to heated debates over appropriate intervention tactics (e.g., abstinence vs. harm reduction).

Given the current limitations of the literature, it can be said that certain features of health promotion programs seem to improve program utility. Kok and colleagues (1997) review of salient meta-analyses also offers some guidance on this point. These authors concluded that a key determinant of the success of the intervention approaches studied was the degree to which they fully implemented principles from social learning theory to transmit program objectives to students via the use of feedback, reinforcement, and facilitation. Another point for consideration was the timing of intervention efforts, and the types of risk-protective factors targeted for change. For example, one issue revolved around the question of whether it is more useful to attempt to prevent teen pregnancy or STD transmission by focusing on the immediate, specific causes of those maladaptive outcomes (i.e., unprotected intercourse) (Nitz, 1999) or to implement intervention actions earlier in relevant developmental processes, thereby attempting to promote general competencies predictive of a wide range of adaptive outcomes (Davis, 1999; Weissberg & Greenberg, 1998).

The implementation of early, comprehensive, cross cutting interventions, and in particular with at risk youth, may provide opportunities to enhance both general competencies and specific skills, thereby improving the likelihood of significant intervention gains. In addition, the implementation of such programming may be a more efficient use of limited prevention resources because this strategy may decrease the need for multiple, parallel selective interventions at a later date (e.g., for sexual behavior, substance use, proper nutrition, and exercise). It should be noted, however, that little is known about appropriate school based programming for young children as it relates to sexual behavior. Health promotion programs for primary school children do not typically address in depth aspects of sexuality education, due to the perceived lack of developmental appropriateness of this subject matter (c.f. *Program Examples* – Connell, Turner, & Mason, 1985; Resnicow et al., 1992). Since defining behavioral success in such early interventions requires long-term outcome studies, future work with in this area would benefit from more rigorous long-term evaluation studies of both child and adolescent samples, as well as additional program development for young students.

Questions

A number of key issues are embedded in the preceding description of exemplary school intervention programs. Some of these questions have been alluded to, and are revisited here in greater detail. First, what are the advantages and challenges of implementing prevention programs in schools? Second, who should be responsible for prevention programming that takes place within a school? Third, what is the optimal role of teachers in this process? These questions are addressed in turn.

School Based Prevention: Do the Benefits Outweigh the Challenges?

Schools have increasingly become important contexts for the design, implementation and evaluation of prevention initiatives (Dryfoos, 1995; Durlak, 1997). The basic structure of, and activities that take place within, schools helped to enhance this institution's emerging role as a laboratory for the implementation of prevention programs. The bureaucratic structure of schools makes possible the efficient sampling, scheduling, tracking and retention of participants. Program delivery in schools provides convenient access to large, representative[8] samples of children and adolescents (Romualdi & Sandoval, 1995). The relevance of school environments to key developmental processes in the young person's life, also suggests that not only are schools key settings for the expression of problem behaviors, but that by extension, they are fitting sites in which to try to interrupt processes that maintain problem behaviors.

An additional rationale for implementing prevention programs in school settings is that improvements in student behaviors influence how well schools are able to fulfill their established role as centers of learning. There are, therefore, pragmatic reasons for schools to support prevention programs since the intended outcomes of such initiatives may help to improve student functioning, both academic and social, during program participation and thereafter (Weissberg & Greenberg, 1998). At a more values oriented level, schools that endorse a traditional mission of providing education to, and improving the lives of young people, and in particular, those youth at risk for school failure and other adverse outcomes, are hard pressed to reject the aims of many universal and selected interventions (Cowen & Durlak, 2000).

Clearly, schools are well-situated settings in which universal, selected, or even indicated interventions may be conveniently implemented. Yet, there are several contentious issues that can create a tension between the traditional mission of the school and the increasing need to develop school based interventions to improve the life chances of young people. Ideas about how to negotiate between conflicts regarding the moral and social development of the young person and the dissemination of subject knowledge have long been central themes of discourse in the field of education (Dewey, 1916/1966). It may be difficult to strike the right balance between school time expended on purely academic pursuits and time spent participating in prevention programming that may or may not have an immediate academic payoff. School administrators and teachers, while endorsing the goal of a particular initiative, may consider a participatory role to be outside their more clearly defined educational duties (Gensheimer, Ayers, & Roosa, 1993).

Parents and social organizations might also vehemently object to prevention programs that are thought to usurp parental authority to socialize youth or are perceived to be in conflict with a specific group's moral teachings. Often, differences in the goals of an intervention and the values of stakeholders in the school system are not readily apparent until the specific content of the proposed intervention is revealed to all participants in the implementation process (Gensheimer et al., 1993; Perhats, Oh, Levy, Flay, et al., 1996). While involved parties may agree on the most general assumptions of a prevention initiative, they may disagree on the means to accomplish related goals or to whom program related principles apply.

For example, school based universal prevention programs have for a decade or more focused on reducing intolerance to diversity among students and other school staff (Carter & Vuong, 1997). While most educators may agree with the importance of the goals of programs that promote respect of others as a reflection of their personal values, or as an core element of citizenship, they may wish to restrict the promotion of tolerance to specific groups on the basis of ethnicity, sexual orientation, religious affiliation, or gender (e.g., Nichols, 1999). Similarly, the means to accomplish intervention goals may be hotly debated between program staff and school staff, or within school staff itself.

The viability of a given intervention is shaped in part by the degree to which a number of influences, including the prevailing values of the school, the broader community, and the prevention program are congruent, can be articulated, and may be operationalized into change producing procedures that can be realistically implemented (Danish, 1996). For example, the goals of many school-based initiatives focus on enhancing capacities among students that are thought to positively alter relations between early adversity and later educational, social, physical or mental health outcomes. These programs focus on changing intra-individual qualities like cognitions, emotional regulation, social competencies, and behavioral reactivity (Cummings, Davies, & Campbell, 2000). Yet, what are thought to be key aspects of children's functioning that are appropriate for intervention may vary depending on the informant (e.g., parents, children, teachers, or intervention "experts") and the perceived relevance of the proposed initiative to the lives of program participants (Dumas, Rollock, Prinz, Hops, & Blechman, 1999; Resnicow, Soler, Braithwaite, Ahluwalia, & Butler, 2000). That is, what may be considered important for optimum youth development may vary depending on culture, class, or other demographic factors. For example, regarding choice of targets for intervention, indicators of youth functioning and adjustment broadly defined as popularity or social status, or autonomy may be differentially valued in different groups of people and invested with markedly different meanings.

Similarly, what constitutes a risk or protective factor for undesirable or desirable outcome is determined, in large part, by the context in which that variable is expressed (Cicchetti & Aber, 1998). That is to say that "risk" or "protection" stem less from specific levels of variables in isolation, and more from developmental processes set into motion by changes in the levels key variables or their interaction with broader sets of factors found within the family and other social contexts. Standardized, school based prevention programs may not be sufficiently context-sensitive to ensure their success across a broad range of school settings, that serve diverse groups of students, who experience widely disparate families and communities (e.g., Aber et al., 1998; Dielman, 1994).

While school based interventions may be an efficient means for delivering services to either general or selected samples of children, substantial challenges obviously still exist (Wagner, Swenson, & Henggeler, 2000). Yet, Catalano and colleagues (1999) in their review of the youth development program literature, for instance, found that schools provided a main staging ground for intervention activities in 88% of the programs identified as well evaluated and successful. This was especially the case among promising and well-established cross context interventions. The centrality of the school in cross context intervention programming is also reflected in the wider prevention intervention literature with school related actions being routinely implemented along with parallel efforts within the home or community (e.g., Catalano, et al., 1998; Taylor, Eddy, & Biglan, 1999; Ward, 1998). This suggests that despite many ongoing challenges, school based prevention becomes increasingly more viable and even valued when a genuine consensus among key program stakeholders is reached regarding the seriousness of a social problem, priorities for desired outcomes, and acceptable pathways to obtaining those outcomes. However, even under the best of conditions, tensions can surface at any point in the intervention cycle regarding not only the foci and content of specific school based prevention efforts, but also the means used to promote positive change and where authority rests to make such decisions.

Top Down – Bottom Up Issues

A key question in the implementation of school based prevention programs is who assumes leadership for an intervention effort (Furlong, Morrison, & Pavelski, 2000). As in other prevention programs implemented in established agencies or settings, there may be a dynamic tension between program stakeholders over decision making authority related to the development of the program, specification of goals and means to achieve them, and to whom the program will be applied (e.g., Archie-Booker, Cervero, & Langone, 1999). A fundamental determinant of the direction and content of an intervention is the decision to implement a program that has been developed by prevention specialists from outside the school setting, in contrast to the development of a program within a particular school to address the needs of children within that setting (Meyer, Miller, & Herman, 1993; Thayer, 1996). While there are intermediate positions, such as employing outside consultants to develop a program specific to a particular school, programs will vary systematically by the degree to which the development and implementation of the new program is directed by stakeholders inside or outside the school, or by consultation between them (Everhart & Wandersman, 2000).

Experts, teachers, administrators, parents, and children may have different perspectives and levels of knowledge when developing and implementing a prevention program. Their perspectives depend, in large part, upon the values of the different parties and the degree to which adequate understanding exists of the developmental pathways to the outcomes targeted for change. For some child or adolescent outcomes, a large body of theory, research and practice exists, documenting well-validated sequences of person-environment transactions between risk-protective factors increasing the likelihood of adverse outcomes (Loeber & Farrington, 1998a). For example, in the area of conduct problems, a wide range of applied developmental studies and prevention demonstration projects have been conducted, documenting robust and generalizable developmental pathways across populations varying by ethnicity, social class, gender, and culture. Therefore, interventions addressing conduct problems in schools may benefit from expert leaders who can draw on current scientific knowledge from this area. In the face of a large body of validated research and practice, however, tension between intervention integrity and tailoring the program to the needs of the school can still be a significant roadblock to ensuring the effectiveness and generalizability of an intervention (Dumas, Rollock, et al., 1999; Forgey, Schinke, & Cole, 1997).

Even greater sharing of leadership roles may be warranted in the development of prevention programs intended to address maladaptive patterns of behavior for which a smaller body of knowledge exists regarding possible developmental pathways, e.g., for internalizing problems, substance abuse, or suicidal behaviors (Bartell, 1995; Nelson, Amio, Prilleltensky, & Nickels, 2000). Similarly, if little is known about the differential utility of a prevention program across heterogeneous groups of children and adolescents, then working partnerships between diverse stakeholders in the school are essential to enhance knowledge needed to tailor or customize the intervention. Critical information, provided in part by stakeholders within and outside the school, is key to enhancing knowledge of how target behaviors are maintained by different developmental processes for different groups of children, and the appropriate strategies for attaining program goals. Future development of culturally sensitive programs for children and adolescents highlights the need for partnerships between prevention specialists, school personnel, and children and their parents to ensure greater likelihood of program success for understudied problems in underserved populations (e.g., Jemmott, 1996).

Teachers and Program Utility

In school based-prevention programs, teachers will inevitably play important roles in program development and implementation (e.g., Conduct Problems Prevention Research Group, 1999a; 1999b). These roles may range from lower levels of involvement to full involvement. In particular, during program implementation, teachers will have some degree of involvement due simply to their position as key stakeholders in services delivered within school settings (Beland, 1996). Whether teachers function as front line staff in program delivery or assume lesser involvement in the process of implementation, their roles in the educational mission of their school are likely to be influenced by either the delivery of prevention services in their school or potential short- and long-term improvements in the functioning of their students. Therefore, the roles of teachers in the program implementation process and barriers to their full participation deserve further consideration (Everhart & Wandersman, 2000; Genaux, Morgan, & Friedman, 1995).

Teachers have been trained traditionally to function as educators, that is to facilitate students' acquisition of knowledge and their development of related skills. In contrast, most teachers have not been trained in the delivery of human services or as prevention specialists. Therefore, the more that the goals and objectives of a prevention program depart from the traditional educational mission of teachers, the more essential comprehensive training experiences will be to supplement teachers' knowledge and skills to insure proper implementation of intervention activities (Heller, Fredrick, Best, Dykes, & Cohen, 2000; Kronick, 2000). Appropriate training will provide sufficient in-service time to conduct a full review of program materials, as well as opportunities to ask questions and participate in demonstrations of interactive program activities. Studies of teachers' implementation of prevention programs describe positive relations between level of training received and teachers' perceptions of program effectiveness and their satisfaction with program implementation (Tubman, Vento-Soza, Barr & Langer, 2002). Therefore, adequate training opportunities are likely to improve program implementation via increases in both (a) teachers' motivation and confidence to deliver program materials and activities, and (b) increases in actual skill levels. Lack of such comprehensive training opportunities may diminish the success of school-based interventions.

While sufficient training helps to remove some of the barriers to teachers' successful delivery of prevention programs, other obstacles must be surmounted in order to empower teachers to deliver program elements (File & Kontos, 1992; Rohrbach, D'Onofrio, Backer, & Montgomery, 1996). For example, teachers will require adequate release time in order to reduce conflict between program delivery roles and other competing roles such as that of educator. In addition, teacher motivation to deliver programs will be enhanced by perceptions of support from administrators, parents, students, and the broader community (Keller & Tapasak, 1997). Administrative support can be demonstrated via policies that reinforce goals inherent in ongoing prevention programs, as well as by statements regarding the importance of teachers' efforts to the overall mission of the school. Recruitment of parents for their participation in prevention efforts also provides teachers with additional sources of support for their efforts (Evans, Okifuji, & Thomas, 1995). Finally, support for prevention programs and their full implementation is depends on sufficient financial and material support. As will be discussed in the *Synthesis* subsection of the next chapter, the provision of adequate training and support is also critical for intervention integrity in peer-led prevention programs (Black et al., 1998; Walker & Avis, 1999).

Future Directions

The design and implementation of successful individual-level school interventions is dependent upon a number of factors for which there exists significant collective wisdom and experience, as well as the results of many years of quantitative outcome evaluation studies. A number of recommendations can be distilled from accumulated knowledge and practice to suggest guidelines for future intervention efforts. These conclusions can be made regarding model individual level school interventions:

- Successful interventions have a strong conceptual foundation and are theory-driven. There are clear rationales for the questions that have been selected to test, the outcomes of interest, and the measures used to assess and evaluate them. In addition, there is a body of empirical evidence to support the efficacy of the key change-producing procedures selected to change target behaviors. These choices are linked to a developmental theory that explains why a specific problem behavior develops and how specific developmental processes can be interrupted.
- The success of an intervention depends on the fidelity of the implementation of program components. Standardization of delivery techniques and the monitoring of interventionists implementing program components across heterogeneous settings are essential to conducting a rigorous evaluation.

Conclusions with relevance to particular program variations include the following:

- Exemplar school based education-skills initiatives combine the provision of accurate knowledge regarding the development, maintenance, and consequences of problem behavior with the development of skills and competencies to replace targeted behaviors or to protect students from their onset. Skills and other competencies are best introduced, practiced and reinforced in the context of dynamic, interactive group exercises rather than in didactic, education-based formats.

- Program materials should be designed to engage the children and adolescents who are anticipated to be the key consumers and program stakeholders. Care must be taken to include program consumers in the process of designing or customizing program materials, e.g., through feedback obtained in focus groups or by directly soliciting input in the design phase. Similarly, care must be taken to ensure that program materials are developmentally appropriate and culturally sensitive.

- Interventionists (e.g., teachers) charged with implementing program materials are sensitive to negative feedback or lack of interest from other program stakeholders. Therefore, it is important that efforts be made to maximize "buy-in" from other stakeholders in the organization (from students, administrators, and other staff) by creating organization-wide recognition of the impact of the problem behavior and the potential benefits of the prevention program. Similarly, support from outside the school, such as that from parents, businesses, and community organizations may be essential to the implementation and the maintenance of the program and should be pursued via vigorous outreach efforts.

- It is essential that teachers, professional staff, or students implementing program components be adequately training, monitored, and supervised. In school settings, given inherent conflicts between the traditional educational and socialization missions of schools and the requirements of the prevention program, extra vigilance is warranted to maintain program integrity. In addition, care must be taken to minimize role conflicts and role overload for school staff as they assist in the implementation of program components.

Chapter Endnotes

[1] It is recognized that despite the advances that have been made, access to universal education is by no means uniform for all young people.

[2] The precise timing of school entry and completion differs within and across nations. In the United States, for example, some state governments or local school boards mandate that five year olds attend kindergarten. In other instances, kindergarten is not mandatory and only six year olds are required to attend first grade. The duration of lower and upper secondary school (i.e., junior and senior high) can differ but American teens usually complete secondary school (i.e., the 12th grade) at the age of 17 or 18. European nations also vary in terms of the time spent in primary and secondary school. In Sweden, parents have the option of placing their child in

primary school at the age of either six or seven, with typical entry at the age of six. Swedish teens finish mandatory lower secondary school approximately at the age of 15 and typically opt to attend upper secondary school for another three years, with the average completion age being 18 years old. Germany has a similar system, but children begin primary school between the ages of 5 and 6 years old. In outcome evaluations, grade levels and not ages are often used to describe young people taking part in a study. In the present review, a youngster's age will be used in sample descriptions, if it has been reported.

[3]Changes in teaching practices, small group instruction, and other alterations of the classroom are also important ways to achieve the same academic enrichment goals. These more structural approaches will be taken up in the next chapter.

[4]Due to language limitations, primary sources were not used here. Class 2000 program developers provided an English language summary of this program and its trial. The present description of Class 2000 is based on that summary.

[5]LST and OYS have elements of both individual and/or peer related intervention.

[6]School based and school linked clinics are addressed in greater detail in the *Community Chapter*.

[7]The effect sizes reported in Wilson and Lipsey's (2000a) meta-analysis were adjusted so that these statistics were recorded after taking the following factors into account: subject attrition, subject characteristics such as age and risk status, program duration, implementation quality, or who delivered the program.

[8]Youth who are excluded from school due to misconduct have been identified as a group in need of attention and services. School based interventions typically miss these youngsters. Alternative schools are one response to the problem of locating and aiding youth who might otherwise be excluded from school. This topic will be addressed in the *Synthesis Subsection*.

Chapter 5
Environment Focused School Intervention and Cross Context Family School Partnerships

Introduction

During the latter half of the 20th century, in both America and the nations of Europe, broad-based social changes have fundamentally altered the experience of childhood and adolescence (e.g., Mortimer & Larson, 2002; Shanahan, Mortimer & Krueger, 2002). Some of the most significant changes result in part from population-level demographic shifts in family composition (i.e., trends in rates of marriage, divorce and childbearing), or work force participation (e.g., maternal employment, the structuring of work and the emergence of the service sector). Other significant society-wide influences upon the experience of childhood or adolescence involve secular trends in crime, health care and technology (e.g., rapid changes in telecommunications and information exchange). In addition, cohort changes over the past several decades in norms for, and attitudes about personal behavior (e.g., substance use, sexual behavior, interpersonal violence) has resulted in growing scrutiny of the developmental processes most commonly resulting in maladaptive outcomes for youth (e.g., Jessor, 1998; Kandel, 2002; Schulenberg, Maggs, & Hurrelmann, 1997). In turn, improved understanding of the antecedents and developmental trajectories of problem behavior in childhood and adolescence has led to growing calls for early, comprehensive and sustained efforts to prevent the onset and acceleration of child and adolescent problem behavior (e.g., Ammerman & Hersen, 1997; Durlak, 1997; Dryfoos, 1994).

To growing numbers of researchers and practitioners, schools have been seen as playing a major role in not only the universal or selective prevention of maladaptive outcomes, but also in the promotion or positive development of adaptive outcomes (e.g., social competence, ethical values and behavior, social and civic engagement, among others). While the twin goals of prevention and positive development may still be seen by some as falling outside the traditional educational mission of primary and secondary schools, the significance of mandatory universal education as (a) a socializing agent and (b) a salient developmental context is undeniable. Neglecting schools as potential staging areas for effective prevention programs may mean that a large proportion of children and adolescents will not receive specific services necessary to (a) avoid developing maladaptive patterns of behavior or

(b) reach their full potential (Dryfoos, 1994). In contrast, inundating schools with well-intentioned but piecemeal programs designed to address multiple problems or to promote positive outcomes without a thorough understanding of the traditional mission and priorities of schools is likely to be less than optimally successful (e.g., Sarason, 1996). Instead, some experts in prevention science have argued that the mission of schools themselves, not only what they do, but how they do it, should be the focus of change efforts (Eccles & Appleton, 2002; Perry, 1999; Weissberg & Greenberg, 1998).

In this spirit, school based interventions can be implemented at many levels in addition to the traditional focus on individual level change efforts targeting students. Increasing emphasis on intervention efforts at broader ecological-contextual levels to influence the social and learning environments of schools (e.g., Bronfenbrenner, 1979) has meant that school based prevention programs are likely to become increasing complex and challenging to implement and evaluate. For example, a single program might involve implementing procedures to produce change in one or more of the following: individual students, peer groups, classroom interactions, or overall aspects of the entire school (Gottfredson, 1997; Weissberg & Greenberg, 1998). The content of a specific intervention and the diversity of the students, families and communities who are stakeholders in the participating school district may contribute significantly to the complexity of implementation efforts and ultimately, to likelihood of program success.

Similar to individual-level prevention programs, different environment-oriented school interventions have different goals. In general, environment-oriented interventions that take place in schools are based on the idea that a young person's life chances can be improved significantly by modifying the structure and functions of the school. While such interventions target the school environment itself for modification, these change efforts may be implemented in a variety of ways. Key risk-protective factors that may be targeted for change might include: prosocial peer rejection and associations with deviant peer groups, access to drugs and firearms, the school's standards related to academic achievement and social conduct, as well as social support to at-risk students and the consistent enforcement of rules by faculty, staff, and administrators (Gottfredson, 1997). Potential interventions in this case could include, in peer group directed interventions, efforts to establish prosocial norms in peer groups within schools; and in classrooms, the development of alternative techniques for classroom instruction and management. Whole school interventions are often aimed at changing a school's social climate by improving school buildings, setting new norms or rules, innovative scheduling and grouping of students in "schools within schools" or other alternative school organizations. In this chapter, examples will be presented of prominent theory and research that link school-related risk-protective factors to specific problem behaviors. In addition, this chapter will outline the select rationales guiding different forms of school related intervention.

Chapter Organization

This chapter first gives examples of specific school-based interventions that are known to be effective. These interventions are organized by the level of school environment that is targeted for change, specifically levels other than those focused on intra-individual change. Programs described in this chapter range from those directed at changing behavior in the context of existing peer networks to those initiatives aimed at the structure and organization of the school environment itself. Successful school interventions with a single or **multi-level approach** and cross context interventions that work with both families at home and school settings are integrated into the overview of programs presented in this chapter. Next, a best evidence synthesis of the research literature is presented. Finally, questions regarding school interventions are addressed, and future directions are offered.

Exemplary Program Examples

Peer Related Intervention

Peers have the ability to be agents of positive behavioral change and reduction of risk behavior throughout the life span (Berndt, 1982; Bukowski & Hoza, 1989; Hartup, 1996; Youniss, 1994). The peer context is not tied to a specific geographical location but exists in multiple settings. Yet, school presents youngsters with abundant opportunities for daily interaction with peers (Adler & Adler, 1998; George & Hartmann, 1996). Youth tend to choose or select friends who are like themselves in terms of demographics, attitudes, and behaviors. In turn, as friendships among young people develop, socialization processes are thought to promote increased similarity among peers (Cohen, 1977; Kandel, 1973; 1978; Mounts & Steinberg, 1995). The similarity/socialization phenomenon that operates and influences the development of peer networks has implications for the development of youth problem behaviors. The research literature clearly shows that the type of peers one associates with is important to the development of both adaptive and maladaptive behaviors (Hartup, 1996). Affiliation with deviant peers during adolescence is a robust predictor of juvenile delinquency, substance use, risky sexual behavior, and school failure (Hawkins, Herrenkohl, et al., 1998; Farrington, 1990). From the preventionist's viewpoint, a significant challenge lies in harnessing the similarity, socialization, and other processes related to peer association for prevention and enhancement goals. As stated in the *Overview Chapter*, the function of prevention is to not only to help people but it is also to generate new knowledge and to test theory. In the study of peer relations, where much still remains to be understood regarding processes of peer influence, peer related interventions are likely to provide significant new knowledge that will contribute to our understanding of how peers can facilitate the development of adaptive behavior patterns in adolescence.

How have peers been integrated into school based prevention programs? One strategy has been to have youth assume informal facilitative roles in intervention activities as models of prosocial behavior or other skills targeted in the prevention program. The inclusion of peers in interactive exercises that demonstrate, model, and practice skills engages students by having them communicate about course materials, participate interactively in group activities, receive feedback from classmates, and obtain realistic learning experiences. The small-group peer participation approach may be more highly valued by students that a purely teacher-delivered program format because they feel that their peers listen to and understand them, take their opinions seriously, and they are often more comfortable talking to peers than adults (Black et al., 1998). This intervention strategy relies on different facets of group process to provide opportunities for students to receive both multiple exposures to core skills and reinforcement for satisfactory participation. This strategy is made explicit and intensified when a young person undergoes formal training to become a program facilitator or co-facilitator.

Social resistance training (SRT) offers an example of how peers with prescribed and clearly defined roles can be included in a school-based intervention. Peer leaders and educators both have been used to implement resistance skills training exercises as prevention strategies to reduce youth substance use or risky sexual behavior. Promising American program examples include the Longitudinal Adolescent Alcohol Prevention Trial (Hansen, Graham, Wolkenstein, & Rohrbach, 1991) and Project SNAPP (Kirby, Korpi, Adivi, & Weissman, 1997). In each prevention program, resistance skills training focused on the use of trained peers to role-play key skills, lead games and group activities, as well as to facilitate discussions. Students were taught to recognize risky situations and barriers to the refusal of risk behaviors, as well as appropriate skills to overcome social pressure to engage in risky behaviors. Outcome evaluations at the conclusion of each program suggested that these interventions produced significant changes in adolescents' attitudes and intentions regarding target behaviors (e.g., alcohol use, plans to have intercourse or to use condoms), as well as knowledge about how to resist risk behavior and related skills. However, the programs did not produce changes in students' perceptions of peers' risk behaviors. While Project SNAPP did not produce significant changes in adolescents' risky sexual behavior, behavioral intentions rather than alcohol use behaviors were assessed for AAPT due to the young age of program participants.

The World Health Organization (WHO) Collaborative Study on Alcohol Education and Young People offers a promising cross-national illustration of the general strategy of integrating peers into the delivery of intervention programs (Perry, et al., 1989; Perry & Grant, 1991). The WHO study was conducted in schools at sites in Norway, Australia, Chile, and Swaziland. The intervention consisted of a five-lesson, school based alcohol prevention curriculum administered by students or teachers. Intervention components centered on general drug education, normative education, resistance skills training, and an invitation to make a public commitment to abstain from alcohol use until an older age. The specific strategies used to promote change included: games, modeling, reinforcement, and lessons (i.e., a peer-led, small group condition and a teacher-led, classroom based condition). The intervention was relatively brief and took place over the course of two months in 1987.

Participating schools were randomly assigned to one of two intervention conditions: peer-led (n=10), Teacher-led (n=9), or a control (n=6) condition. Participating students' alcohol use was assessed before and after the intervention and at a six-month follow-up. The results supported the effectiveness of the intervention for those who reported being drinkers and non-drinkers at the baseline measurement. In addition, the peer-administered condition resulted in greater reductions in risk behavior than did the teacher-led format for the majority of assessed measures. Results were similar regardless across the countries that participated in the program evaluation. Positive changes in alcohol-related knowledge and attitudes, and views of friends' alcohol use were related to subsequent reductions in alcohol use. Some results varied by gender, however, positive results were found for both males and females.

While the evidence to support the utility of peer involved and peer led prevention programs is at the present time mixed, it can be argued that peers are natural adjuncts in school-based education-skills training programs for youth. In the wider prevention research literature, program examples of successful interventions that have integrated peers into program activities do exist. Several of these universal and selective interventions are cross context multi-component initiatives that have yielded positive outcomes across a range of risk behaviors among children (e.g., *EARLY ALLIANCE Project* – Dumas, Prinz, Smith, & Laughlin, 1999; *Fast Track* – Conduct Problems Prevention Research Group, 1999a; 1999b; *Interventions on the prevention of social exclusion* – Coie & Krehbiel, 1984; Oden & Asher, 1977; *Montreal Prevention Experiment* – Tremblay, et al., 1995; *Seattle Social Development Project* – Hawkins, Catalano, Morrison, et al., 1992). In addition, several of the programs that integrate peers have evaluations that support their effectiveness for reduction of risk behavior among adolescents (e.g., *Life Skills Training* – Botvin, et al., 1995; *Midwestern Prevention Project* – Pentz, et al., 1990; *Minnesota Heart Health Program* – Perry, Kelder, Murray, & Klepp, 1992; *North Karelia Project* – Vartiainen, Paavola, McAlister, & Puska, 1998; *Oslo Youth Study* – Klepp, et al., 1993; *Project Northland* – Perry, et al., 2000).

Classroom Intervention

        Classroom interventions are designed to improve the instructional environment in schools. Students' classroom behavior often serves as the primary target for a specific intervention program. Coercion Theory (Patterson, 1982) as it was described in the *Later Family Intervention Chapter,* is a precursor of, and generalizable to, later relationships between at-risk children and their peers, as well as those between students and teachers. The socialization of oppositional or defiant behavior in early childhood through coercive exchanges with parents and siblings increases the likelihood that children will resort to aggressive behaviors in interactions with peers upon entry into primary school (Pettit, 1997). Therefore, school entry is a critical time for intervention because this transition to a new environment offers either opportunities for both the generalization and stabilization of social skill deficits, distorted attributes and cognitions about self and others or opportunities for positive change. Specifically, schools provide new social contexts for the generalization and stabilization of aggressive, undercontrolled behaviors in new relationships or, alternatively, the learning and practice of more adaptive and prosocial forms of interaction with new peers (Fergusson & Lynskey, 1998; Tremblay, Masse, Perron, & LeBlanc, 1992).
        Peers and teachers quickly label children who have problems with interpersonal relationships and who are disruptive in class as "troublemakers" or "problems." Rejection by peers and labeling by teachers as being difficult put children at greater risk for segregation into deviant peer groups. These forms of exclusion from networks of non-deviant peers greatly raise the likelihood that children will develop multiple problem behaviors (Dishion, Capaldi, Spracklen, & Li, 1995). Well-planned interventions to reduce children's off-task and/or aggressive classroom behavior and to increase their basic academic skills and socially competent behaviors predict both their better short- and long-term outcomes in multiple domains of functioning, and improvements in their classmates' ability to learn (Finn, Pannozzo, & Voelkl, 1995). If teachers devote smaller proportions of their time to correcting behavioral problems in the classroom, they have more time to devote to their traditional mission of promoting academic achievement. Therefore, prevention-oriented initiatives designed to reduce children's disruptive or off-

task classroom behavior have multiple benefits that generalize to the entire learning environment (Nelson, 1996).

As in the family, the setting and enforcement of rules in the classroom should follow a rational, proportionate and consistent approach. In this regard, it is the teacher who is ultimately responsible for managing students' inappropriate or disruptive behavior in the classroom, while still promoting a supportive environment where learning can coincide with investment and personal growth (Gettinger, 1988). Beyond managing the behavior of children in classrooms, teachers can act as role models to their students. For youngsters who experience considerable adversity in their daily lives, school may be the safest and most supportive place they encounter during the day. In addition, teachers often may be significant adult figures who can provide positive experiences that redirect a young person's life onto a path toward resilience (Kendall-Tackett, & Eckenroade, 1996; Rutter, 1989; Westerman & La Luz, 1995). A sound student-teacher relationship or learning partnership is linked to increases in academic skills, achievement motivation, and school bonding which in turn predicts academic engagement and the reduction of risk factors for academic failure, including marginalization, labeling, and tracking. Interventions that enhance interactions between students and teachers are key strategies for both increasing the quality of schooling experiences and the likelihood of multiple positive outcomes (Davis, 1999; Nelson, 1996).

Behavioral techniques have a long history of use in classroom settings to reduce the frequency of misbehavior or to improve the overall learning environment (Catalano, Arthur, Hawkins, Berglund, & Olson, 1998; McCain & Kelley, 1994; Skinner & Smith, 1992). For example, the Good Behavior Game (GBG) and Mastery Learning were tested over a six-year period in Baltimore, Maryland (Kellam et al., 1991; Kellam, Rebok, Ialongo, & Mayer, 1994). GBG is designed for primary school children and uses behavioral principles such as a token economy to reward and reinforce appropriate classroom behavior. Teams are formed within a classroom to strengthen appropriate behavior. During GBG sessions, that are gradually lengthened from ten minutes to three hours, teams are given points if the members displayed disruptive or off-task behaviors. Behaviors for which points are assigned are clearly specified to the students before the game begins. If a team accumulates more than four points during game periods, it can not win, although it is possible for all teams to win. In forming teams, disruptive students are randomly assigned to teams to make the game fair and to provide all at-risk children with access to prosocial peers who can model desired behaviors. Mastery Learning (ML) is a variation of the GBG that focuses on learning academic subjects. In this version, the team based behavioral approach used in the GBG is used in the context of learning literacy skills. In ML, the pairing of academic skills enhancement with systematic changes in the classroom reward structure is similar to the approach taken in some interventions emphasizing peer tutoring (e.g., *Classwide Peer Tutoring* – Greenwood, et al., 1992; *Reciprocal Peer Tutoring* – Fantuzzo, et al., 1992).

The GBG and ML have been rigorously evaluated using by matching participating schools and randomly assigned them to one of three conditions: 1) GBG, 2) ML, and 3) a control condition. After one year of program activities, immediate gains were shown for improved classroom behavior for the GBG condition and increased literacy skills for the ML condition compared to the control groups. After five years, however, there were no significant overall differences among the groups that would support the greater effectiveness of GBG over ML or the control conditions. Comparisons of subgroups of the more aggressive children in the sample suggested that the effectiveness of the GBG program was related to program participants' levels of aggressiveness at the start of the program. Specifically, GBG did not appear to protect children who were not aggressive at the onset of the program from developing aggressive behaviors, but males who were aggressive at first assessment showed significant reductions in aggressive behaviors compared to GBG males in the control condition. Therefore, the impact of GBG appeared to be modified by participants' levels of initial aggressive behavior. The effects of GBG appear to spread for boys with regard to lower rates of the initiation of cigarette smoking, relative to boys in the control condition. A similar program related benefit was documented for a subset of the ML pupils (Kellam et al., 1991; 1994).

The Smoke Free Class Competition (SF-CC) is a promising example of a European classroom based initiative that uses behavioral strategies to further a prevention aim (Vartiainen, Saukko, Paavola, & Vertio, 1996; Wiborg & Hanewinkel, 2002). In this case, however, the specific behavior targeted for change is tobacco use among early to middle adolescent students. The competition works like this: 1) at least 90% of the pupils in a class must decide if they want to take part in the competition, 2) if an agreement is reached, students sign a behavioral contract to abstain from smoking for a period of six months, 3) students' weekly smoking behavior is recorded through anonymous self reports, and 4) the class wins a prize (e.g., a trip) if no more than 10% of the students report smoking over the test period. While Smoke Free Class Competitions have been conducted in up to 15 European countries, rigorous evaluations have been conducted in only two nations: Finland and Germany.

During the test period in the Finnish trial, classes who participated successfully had significantly lower smoking initiation rates (2.3%) than classes that did not participate (5.1%), or the classes that dropped out of the competition (3.9%) (Vartiainen, et al., 1996). In the German trial, comparisons of the participating and non-participating classrooms found that intervention classes reported significantly less smoking (7.8%, a decline of 0.2%) than comparison classes (13.9%, an increase of 7.5%) (Wiborg &

Hanewinkel, 2002). While smoking rates for both groups increased at a five month follow up assessment, the increase in the comparison classes was significantly greater than that in the intervention classes. Although the German trial was large-scale, (Pre-test N=4,372), there was substantial program attrition of students (Pre-Post-Follow up N=2,142). Despite this and a few other limitations[1], the two positive evaluations of the Smoke Free Class Competition conducted by independent research groups does lend support for this intervention's utility for delaying the onset of teenage smoking.

A relevant multiple level (individual, classroom) intervention entitled Komet is currently undergoing evaluation in Sweden. Although outcome evaluation data for Komet was not available at the time this review was written, it is described here because the evaluation design should yield a rigorous evaluation of the program. Furthermore, some of Komet's intervention components have been evaluated successfully in the United States (Bierman, Miller, & Stabb, 1987; Greenwood, 1991; Lochman & Lenhart, 1993). An early variant of Komet called 'How Teachers Can Help Disruptive and Rejected Children' was pilot-tested in Sweden (Forster & Tegenmark, 1998). While this pilot test produced positive outcomes, it involved a small sample and its results should be interpreted cautiously.

Komet is implemented in the context of whole classrooms with program efforts focused on one high-risk child in each class who receives specialized intervention activities. Komet's behavior management component is directed primarily towards the content of the teacher's interaction with the identified high-risk child. Individually tailored behavior management programs are designed for each participating child. Teachers are also trained to use behavioral management principles as a means of working effectively with the entire class. Komet's social skills training component is designed to improve the conflict resolution skills of the identified high-risk child as well as the entire class. The peer-tutoring component of Komet is similar to the Class Wide Peer Tutoring model (Greenwood, et al., 1989; 1992).

Komet's utility is being evaluated in comparison to an alternative form of intervention and a wait-list control condition. The alternative intervention condition is Project Charlie [Chemical Abuse Resolution Lies in Education]. Project Charlie was originally developed in the 1970's as a drug prevention program in the United States (Storefront/Youth Action, 1987). Intervention materials have been modified and updated since initial program development in the form of a life-skills training curriculum with foci related to social competence building, drug education, and self-esteem enhancement. Project Charlie is used in schools across Sweden. At present, no controlled outcome evaluations of either Komet or Project Charlie have been completed in Sweden or the United States (Ahlgren & Merrick, 1984; Lepinski, 1984; Sharma & Griffin, 1999). A controlled study of Project Charlie, however, has been conducted in England. In this evaluation, immediate intervention related benefits were found for decision-making and drug knowledge, and a subsequent follow-up documented positive behavioral gains (Hurry, Lloyd, & McGurk, 2000; Hurry & McGurk, 1997). However, substantial attrition of participants occurred at follow up.

In an ongoing program evaluation, teachers of children aged 7 to 8 years in the City of Stockholm who are willing to participate will be randomly assigned to a Komet, Charlie, or waitlist control condition. To date, 50 teachers and approximately 1,000 students are currently participating in the study. It is anticipated that approximately 200 teachers and 4,000 children will eventually participate by the end of the year 2002. The evaluation design calls for pre- and post-test evaluations encompassing at least one year of intervention.

With the exception of Komet and the Smoke-Free Class Competition, the European research literature on classroom level interventions offers little in terms of controlled outcome evaluations. Initiatives designed to change elements of the classroom environment like child behavior, student-teacher interaction quality, the learning climate have shown utility in other American program trials, particularly as a strategy for yielding positive behavioral outcomes (e.g., Evertson, 1985; Evertson, Emmer, Sanford, & Clements, 1983). Some promising cross context interventions of American origin have also successfully integrated classroom behavior management with parallel program components that emphasize parenting skills (e.g., *EARLY ALLIANCE Program* – Dumas, Prinz, et al., 1999; *Seattle Social Development Project* – Hawkins, Catalano, Morrison, et al., 1992).

Whole School Change

The whole school approach is designed to engage all primary stakeholders in the school including students, parents, teachers, and administrators and to involve them in prevention efforts. Whole school change can also center on making improvements to the environmental features of schools and initiating prevention-oriented school policies. By making direct modifications to schools' learning or social environments that function as key contexts for youth development, it is thought that we can influence students' exposure to risk and protective factors. As a category of intervention programs, whole school programs take their inspiration from a number of sources and therefore can take on a variety of forms. This subsection will focus on one type of whole school intervention programs with demonstrated utility, namely anti-bullying initiatives.

Anti-Bullying Interventions. There is a long-standing international effort to better understand and prevent bullying in primary and secondary schools. This is one of the few prevention-related research literatures that is not dominated by American studies and prevention programming (e.g., Smith, et al., 1999). From reviews of this literature, we know that the traditional definition of bullying has equated bullying with overt or physical aggression and other forms of coercive behavior. In contrast, more recent definitions of bullying have incorporated increasingly gender-sensitive conceptualizations of bullying that include more covert or relational forms of interpersonal aggression such as social exclusion, relationship manipulation, and gossiping or rumor spreading (Crick, 1997; Crick & Grotpeter, 1996). Regardless of the particular forms of interpersonal aggression studied, several commonalities are apparent. Specifically, bullying behavior is systematic, in contrast to random acts of interpersonal violence, and bullying occurs in the context of peer relations and broader social networks in schools and other community settings. The particular forms that bullying takes and the context in which it develops and is expressed highlight the importance of a whole school approach to the prevention of bullying behavior among children and adolescents.

One of the first rigorously evaluated intervention programs to address bullying took place in Bergen, Norway. The Olweus Bullying Prevention Program (OBPP) aims to foster a safer school environment through a restructuring of schools in ways that discourage bullying (Olweus, 1993; Olweus, Limber, & Mihalic, 1999). At the school-wide and classroom levels, the intervention involves awareness raising activities, as well as the formulation and implementation of anti-bullying policies. When actual bullying takes place, victims receive social support and students involved in bullying are exposed to non-punitive consequences and receive clarification on the school's expectations for students' behavior toward each other. Parents are involved in this process and informed about incidents of bullying. During the time that the OBPP is ongoing, consistent and non-punitive consequences for bullying and reinforcement for prosocial behaviors are delivered systematically to students.

An evaluation of the O-BPP was conducted in the early 1980s, over a two and a half year period (Olweus, 1994). School children aged 11 to 14 years in 42 schools took part in the efficacy trial. The outcome evaluation was designed as a quasi-experimental **age cohort design**. In such a design, groups of pupils in the same grade level at different points in time (i.e., cohorts) are compared to identify group differences in outcomes. The timing of student assessments depends on whether or not pupils have been exposed to the intervention[2]. Comparisons of levels of target behaviors at follow up indicated that the bullying and victimization levels were significantly lower after 8 and 20 months of program exposure. The extent of these declines ranged from 50-70%, depending on the cohort group analyzed and indices of bullying or victimization measured. Significant reductions in the number of new cases of bullying were found in this evaluation. Students in intervention schools reported greater affinity towards school and improved class environment.

Finally, those classes with higher intervention fidelity demonstrated greater program benefits.

Since its efficacy trial, O-BPP has undergone additional testing in the United States and Norway. In an American program evaluation (Melton, et al., 1998; Olweus, et al., 1999), slight modifications to the O-BPP were made including: community promotional activities, school-wide anti-bullying rules, and the integration and extension of programming to church related activities. African-American youth living in a rural part of the United States participated in this study. The outcome evaluation was quasi-experimental with 11 intervention schools matched to 28 wait-listed comparison schools. Students in intervention schools reported approximately 25% less bullying after seven months of program activities compared to an increase in comparison schools. Intervention school students also did not escalate their involvement in several antisocial behaviors that increased among students in the comparison schools. O-BPP is one of the eight model Blue Print programs that are currently undergoing additional effectiveness evaluations in the United States.

A recent evaluation of O-BPP in Norway, entitled the New Bergen Project against Bullying, has extended the original intervention to include a series of meetings between teachers, program staff and the school psychologist, with the aim of strengthening intervention fidelity, or the quality of program implementation. In this multi-year quasi-experimental evaluation, school children (11 to 13 years old) in 14 intervention and 16 comparison schools are participating in the study. Age-cohort and longitudinal outcome analyses for the first intervention year show significant declines in the bullying and victimization levels following students' exposure to program activities. The Norwegian government has plans to disseminate O-BPP first to 200-250 Norwegian schools and then to all schools in Norway (Olweus, personal communication, March 7, 2002).

The Flemish Anti-Bullying Intervention (FA-BI) provides a promising example of an alternative approach to the problem of bullying (Stevens, de-Bourdeaudhuij, & Van-Oost, 2000; Stevens, Van-Oost, de-Bourdeaudhuij, 2000). As in the O-BPP, school wide efforts in the FA-BI focus on the formulation of an anti-bullying policy at the school and classroom levels and on raising student and staff awareness about bullying. FA-BI, departs from the O-BPP, however, due to its greater emphasis on combating bystanders' passive or active acceptance of bullying. Through a teacher-implemented classroom curriculum, students work to develop their own personal competence to successfully intervene and stop bullying when it occurs. As in the O-BPP, one-on-one intervention activities with identified bullies and victims consist of teachers working with bullies to increase their empathy towards victims, feelings of responsibility, making amends for the damage done, and their willingness to agree to behave in a more prosocial manner.

Work with victims emphasizes providing emotional support and social skills enhancement.

The FA-BI was tested over the course of 20 months (1995-1997) with students aged 10 to 16 years old. Participating schools were randomly assigned to either one of two intervention conditions: intervention with researcher support, intervention without researcher support or a control condition. The group of schools that received the 'Intervention with Researcher Support Condition' was provided with explicit teacher training and assistance from program designers throughout the implementation period. Schools receiving 'Intervention without Researcher Support' received a video and implementation manual, but no additional support. Primary school youngsters in both intervention conditions maintained the same or a slightly reduced level of bullying behavior compared to an increase in bullying in the control condition. There were no significant differences between intervention and control youngsters at the secondary school level. Additional analyses were conducted on those youth who were not regular bullies or victims. The subgroup analysis of "bystander students" indicated that among secondary school students, the intervention students' views on bullies and victims, their perception of their ability to successfully intervene in a bullying episode, and self-reports of intervention attempts all showed significant improvement across the intervention period. However, these indicators of program impact largely faded by the time of the follow up evaluation.

Evaluations of anti-bullying initiatives have been conducted in Belgium (Stevens, de-Bourdeaudhuij, & Van-Oost, 2000; Stevens, Van-Oost, de-Bourdeaudhuij, 2000), England (Eslea & Smith, 1998; Smith & Sharp, 1994), Germany (Hanewinkel & Knaack, 1997a; 1997b; Lösel & Bliesener, 1999), Norway (Roland, 2000), and Spain (Ortega & Lera, 2000). These program evaluations differ with regard to how the evaluations were designed and the content of the programs, with some interventions incorporating program elements found in the O-BPP and others testing strategies aimed at other aspects of bullying or the more general phenomenon of school violence. During the past several years, there has been growing interest in the design and implementation of prevention programs that reduce children's experiences of interpersonal conflict and violence in schools (Beauboeuf, 1995; Centers for Disease Control and Prevention, 1998). While bullying prevention programs are becoming more firmly established in the United States, Americans are more frequently looking to the international research literature on bullying prevention.

Cross Context Family School Partnerships

Cross context interventions work in more than just one environment. A number of rigorously evaluated cross context programs provide excellent examples of how theory-driven, coordinated programs with parallel components implemented in school and home settings can fundamentally alter a young person's experience of adversity and access to social resources. Well-established programs in this area include long-term follow up of participants, thereby documenting the degree to which program benefits persist over time. While the interventions described here may be organized on several dimensions, contrasts in this subsection will be made to highlight how specific implementation strategies used in selected prevention programs enhance their ability to produce sustainable change in targeted outcomes among samples of at risk youth.

The coordinated application of social learning and coercion theories, as well as a range of behavioral techniques in the classroom and at home form the core of the Montreal Prevention Experiment (MPE; Tremblay et al., 1992). MPE was a *selected* intervention designed to reduce disruptive behavior among primary school boys. The school component focused on promoting social competence and emotional regulation by stressing problem-solving skills, life skills, conflict resolution, and self-control. To complement school based components, a parent-training module fostered parenting skills that promote children's competence including: the management of family crises, behavioral monitoring, positive reinforcement for pro-social behavior, and effective behavior management without abusiveness. This component was modeled on the Parent Management Training program (Forgatch & Martinez, 1999). Interactive learning was a key intervention strategy for implementing these modules. Participants were boys (N=250) who were identified in kindergarten as disruptive, and subsequently scored above the 70th percentile on a standardized measure of behavioral disruptiveness in elementary school. Boys and their families received the intervention for two years, from 7 to 9 years of age. Program links between school and home were fostered through home visits by caseworkers that helped parents generalize desirable parenting skills, as well as in-school consultations between teachers and program staff.

The outcome evaluation of the MPE supported the long-term efficacy of this cross context intervention for reducing risk for continuation and escalation of children's antisocial behavior. Follow up comparisons were made among boys, ages 10 to 15 years, randomly assigned to one of three conditions (Intervention; n=43, Placebo control; n=82, and No attention control; n=41) on measures of school placement, juvenile court records, teacher-rated classroom behavior, and self-reported delinquency, substance use, perceptions of parent-child relations, as well as peer ratings of the target child. In early adolescence, boys who received the intervention were significantly more likely than the control group to: stay in age-appropriate classrooms, have fewer troublesome friends, have lower disruptiveness ratings by peers, and report less delinquency. By middle adolescence the positive outcomes continued among boys who received the intervention as they reported significantly less gang involvement, substance use, delinquency, and fewer troublesome friends compared to boys in the control condition. No long-term differences were noted in academic outcomes or registry offenses in middle adolescence.

Fast Track (FT) is a contemporary program similar to the MPE and provides another illustration of a cross context program linking school and home based prevention modules for children at risk for chronic antisocial behavior (Conduct Problems Prevention Research Group, 1999a; 1999b). In terms of differences, FT in contrast to the MPE has a universal component, began working with youth at an earlier point, targets a higher risk sample (top 10% versus MPE's top 30%), and has a greater diversity of program activities that extend over a longer period time. Yet, there are also notable parallels in the structure of the two interventions. As in the MPE, at risk children in FT also took part in regular supervised play with socially adept classmates at school and supplemental tutoring.

In addition, FT is a multi-component program that emphasizes the enhancement of individual skills and competencies while simultaneously modifying family- and school-level risk and protective factors for serious conduct problems. Coordinated program modules implemented in FT can be applied in either a universal or an indicated manner. FT was evaluated as a universal intervention, by randomly assigning matched pairs of primary schools (N=54) to either an intervention or a control condition. Universal activities administered to all children in intervention schools are exemplified by the teacher-delivered PATHS curriculum, which included an average of 48 PATHS sessions focusing on the promotion of emotional-social competence and prosocial behavior. In addition to PATHS, teachers were trained to use behavior based classroom and child management techniques. Therefore, as a universal prevention program, FT is comprehensive in its scope and cross context in its implementation.

Kindergarten students deemed to be at risk for later antisocial behavior were tracked towards FT's indicated intervention activities (e.g., after-school enrichment sessions). Children identified by parents and teachers as at risk for later antisocial behavior were recruited into the study and followed annually, in three successive cohorts. As in the MPE, coordinated modules were delivered to the identified child's parents. Representative parent activities included: training and rehearsal of noncoercive parenting practices, effective communication, and parent support of the child's academic engagement (Forehand & McMahon, 1981; Hawkins, Doueck, & Lishner, 1988; Webster-Stratton, et al., 1989). Children received skills training to promote social-emotional competence and individual tutoring to strengthen literacy skills. Parents and children participated in staff-facilitated group discussions to observe and practice together and solidify the skills-knowledge program content covered in both the parent and child training sessions. The content of these sessions was further reinforced by home visits and phone calls, as well as via individualized training in parenting and coping skills (Wasik, Bryant, & Lyons, 1990). During FT's original 10-year intervention span, specific program components were cumulative, varied in intensity, but were designed to be most intensive just prior to and during major life transitions, such as school entry, to facilitate successful mastery of these key developmental challenges.

The first outcome evaluation of FT as an indicated program with a sample of at risk, kindergarten students (N=891) their parents, and teachers documented significant immediate changes in multiple measures of child social competence, parenting behavior, parent-child interaction and academic performance. For parents receiving the intervention, significant positive changes were found for responses to hypothetical childrearing situations and level of involvement in their child's academic life. In addition, significant cross sectional differences at the end of first grade revealed that the children receiving the intervention had: better grades in language arts, more prosocial peer interactions, greater peer-rated prosocial behavior and popularity, as well as less special education instruction for boys as compared to children in the control condition. In addition, when FT was used as a universal intervention, significant positive changes from pretest to post-test were found for children in the intervention condition on indices of emotional competence, social problem solving, and responses to dilemmas in interpersonal vignettes (Conduct Problems Prevention Research Group, 1999a; 1999b).

A second outcome evaluation of FT's impact on at risk pupils at the end of the third grade (Conduct Problems Prevention Research Group, in press), demonstrated the maintenance of Year One program benefits on the following indices: improved child social competence, parenting behaviors, parents' endorsement of promotive childrearing techniques, as well as reduced use of special education services. Additional Year Three improvements included significantly higher levels of the following variables among children receiving the intervention: teacher and parent ratings of child behavior, classification as having severe behavior problems and classification as being free of serious behavior problems. Finally, the Year 1 intervention gains were shown to fade for peer-rated sociometric status and behavior, child academic performance, and parent involvement in school. The leveling off of these gains may have been related to changes in the content of intervention programming over time. Additional reports on FT's long- term effectiveness are expected as the universal and at risk samples are followed into young adulthood.

The Seattle Social Development Project (SSDP) offers another important program illustration (O'Donnell, et al., 1995)[3]. This intervention was designed to prevent school failure, drug use and delinquency among children living in high crime communities. Major elements of this universal initiative are applications of social learning theory, the social development model, and related behavioral principles to classroom and home settings. For example, the teacher intervention consisted of training teachers in the use of proactive classroom management, interactive teaching, and cooperative learning strategies. Key elements of the parent intervention included: instruction in child behavior management and social resistance skills related to child drug use as well as academic support (Hawkins, Lishner, Jenson, & Catalano, 1987; Hawkins, et al., 1988). The student intervention included developmentally appropriate social and emotional skills training in the first grade (*Interpersonal Cognitive Problem Solving*; Shure & Spivack, 1988). This program component focused on implementing skills training to improve competence in communication, decision-making, negotiation, and conflict resolution. In the sixth grade, skills training focused on improving refusal skills including: recognition and the legal naming of problematic situations, as well as the generation of potential consequences and positive alternatives to interpersonal and legal trouble.

The SSDP began in 1981 and involved students in eight primary schools for a six year period, beginning when students were in the first grade. When these students started the fifth grade, the study was expanded to include fifth grade students in ten other primary schools. Over the course of the study, there was random and non-random assignment to one of four conditions, full intervention (exposure to programming from the first to sixth grade), late intervention (programming in the fifth and six grades), parent-training only group (Preparing for the Drug Free Years, in the fifth and six grades only), or a no-intervention comparison group. Students have been evaluated on several occasions up to the age of 24.

While a number of short term program related results have been documented, long term program benefits have predominately been shown for students who received the full intervention. Evaluations in adolescence, for example, indicated that relative to comparison students, full intervention SSDP youth had better school bonding and achievement, less antisocial behavior, less lifetime sexual activity, and less heavy alcohol use (e.g., Hawkins, Catalano, Kosterman, Abbott, & Hill, 1999). At the age of 21, intervention benefits were once again recorded for the full intervention group, who reported safer sexual practices and behaviors, as well as fewer female pregnancies. These results were found relative to the comparison group (e.g., Lonczak, Abbott, Hawkins, Kosterman, & Catalano, 2002).

The Dorset School Intervention Programme (DSIP) provides a prominent example of a European cross context program (Bagley & Pritchard, 1998; Pritchard, 1998; 2001). DSIP was a selective intervention that employed multi-disciplinary teams of social workers and teachers in the United Kingdom to forge stronger linkages between schools and families. Targets for change included child and adolescent problem behaviors and a range of measures of school engagement. Project teams conducted a series of activities to promote opportunities for positive school-family interaction and positive behavioral change in children. Key activities included: several different individual-level change producing procedures (e.g., secondary school transition counseling, health-sex education, extensive follow up on absent students), direct education-skills training in group settings, as well as whole school programming (e.g., anti-bullying initiatives, after school activities). Teams also provided classroom crisis management of disruptive children and provided specialized services to these children and their families (e.g., improved links between school and family, family counseling and training, behavioral training of children, advocacy through interagency collaboration, and better parental educational expectations for their youngsters). This intervention approach was designed to both resolve immediate crises in school and to provide supportive services to families, explicitly integrating school based programs with external services to benefit vulnerable children and adolescents.

The DSIP continued for a period of three years with an initial sample of 1,300 at risk primary and secondary school students, aged 9 to 16 years. Children and adolescents enrolled in the program were recruited from local communities significantly above national and regional standards for measures of adult crime, unemployment, non-nuclear families, and use of free school lunches. In an evaluation of the DSIP program, individual records were not linked, i.e., data were collected from different sets of primary and secondary school children (attending the same schools) at the beginning and conclusion of the study. At time of testing, two intervention schools and two control schools were compared on mean levels of registry information related to educational (exclusions due to behavior problems, standardized test achievement, GCSE), criminal justice, and social welfare outcomes (child protection referrals). In addition, self-report data were collected from children regarding delinquent and substance use behaviors, as well as school and social attachment.

At the beginning of the study, primary school children in the intervention were significantly worse off than children in the comparison condition on measures of problem behavior and school attachment. In contrast, at the end of the program, children in the intervention schools had comparable rates of bullying and theft, comparable or higher levels of school attachment, a significantly lower rate of referrals to child protection agencies (a decrease of 76%) relative to countywide levels (an increase of 33%), and no school exclusions relative to the comparison schools' ten exclusions. These positive intervention results were found despite the fact that the intervention school had more potentially troublesome transfer students accepted for enrollment (n=28) relative to the comparison school (n=3). A two-year follow up of 48 of the primary school intervention children, at ages 14 to 16 years, compared them with a new comparison sample of 180 adolescents living in a similarly disadvantaged community and documented lower levels of behavior problems, delinquency, and substance use among children who received the intervention, as well as greater attachment to school and society in general.

Similar to younger program participants, secondary students attending intervention schools at program end showed less truancy, fighting, and substance use relative to students in comparison schools. Adolescents at the intervention school also demonstrated increased school attachment and more optimism regarding the future. The intervention and comparison schools had comparable numbers of school exclusions (9 vs. 8) even though the intervention school accepted a greater number of number of transfer students (37 vs. 14). Although this study had design flaws (i.e., non-equivalent schools), the short- and long-term aggregate gains made by students in the intervention schools suggests the potential value of building links between schools and families, and in particular with regard to the interdisciplinary team delivery of supportive services to children and families in crisis.

The preceding program examples provide evidence that a number of well-established American and European comprehensive cross context selected prevention programs exist and have generally been evaluated in a rigorous manner that documents their broad based efficacy. These comprehensive, multi-component longitudinal prevention programs for at risk children and others (e.g., *EARLY ALLIANCE Program* – Dumas, Prinz, et al., 1999; *First Steps Program* – Walker, Stiller, Severson, Feil, & Golly, 1998), have had significant immediate and long-term impact on relations with parents, teachers, and peers, and improved the quality of school experiences. Long term follow up evaluations of programs like MPE and the SSDP suggest that they promote delays in the onset of early adolescent problem behaviors (c.f. O'Donnell et al., 1995; Tremblay et al., 1992). Therefore, interventions to improve the overall learning environment and quality of family life appear to result in enhanced social relationships and social competence. These are program gains that serve a protective function for vulnerable children that deters the onset of adolescent problem behaviors, thereby increasing the life chances of program participants. The documentation of these effects, both short- and long-term, is essential and will aid in identifying critical points at which developmental systems that promote and maintain maladaptive patterns of behavior are open to modification.

Synthesis

Similar to individual-level, school based interventions, interventions focused on promoting changes at broader social levels in schools are heterogeneous, varying widely in goals, design, or implementation of specific programs. This diversity in conceptual underpinnings, content, and outcomes has resulted in outcome studies that are often difficult to compare and to integrate. The identification of key themes in these literatures is essential to enhance the comparability of existing studies and to suggest fruitful avenues for the improved evaluation and enhancement of current prevention approaches. In this chapter, efforts are made to identify useful programs and best practices for altering elements of broader social structures within schools to improve learning environments, as well as students' interpersonal behavior within school settings. Once again, we provide guidelines regarding the conditions that modify the success of intervention actions, to inform professionals planning programs of factors that can facilitate or act as barriers to program implementation. A best evidence synthesis of these emergent issues from the broad literature on school based prevention programs is outlined below.

Peer Related Intervention

The success of peer related interventions have been subject to some debate (Milburn, 1995; Walker & Avis, 1999). At present, evidence for the utility of school based peer interventions is mixed. For example, results of a recent meta-analysis of anti-tobacco and sexual health prevention programs suggested that *peer led* interventions in these areas are no more useful than alternative interventions implemented among comparison participants (c.f. *Relevant Meta-Analysis* – Posavac, Kattapong & Dew, 1999) which contradicts earlier meta-analyses (c.f. *Relevant Meta-Analyses* – Bruvold, 1993; Kok et al., 1997). Youth prevention programs conducted in a variety of settings yield examples of peer related interventions that support the potential usefulness of the informal participation of peers in the modeling, practice, and generalization of key skills, i.e., through associations with short and longer term improvements of problem behaviors (c.f. *Program Examples* – Bierman, et al., 1996; Botvin, et al., 2000; Coie & Krehbiel, 1984; Hawkins, Catalano, Morrison, et al., 1992; Klepp, et al., 1993; Oden & Asher, 1977; Pentz, et al., 1990; Perry, et al., 1992; 2000; Tremblay, et al., 1995; Vartiainen, et al., 1998). Yet, it is important to note that in many of these interventions peers are not the sole interventionists and participants are exposed to other evidence based strategies designed to complement peer administered activities.

One can take the research literature on school based peer led and peer involved violence prevention as an illustration of the challenges involved in charging young people with the task of being the principal agents of change in a school based intervention. Peer mediation is an example of a peer led intervention in which student arbitrators are trained to use specialized skills and to provide an interpersonal context that facilitates the negotiation of a solution to a conflict that is acceptable to involved students (Hawkins,

Farrington, & Catalano, 1998). Specifically, peer mediators, when requested to do so by students involved in a dispute, attempt to promote perspective taking by the involved parties and to suggest possible compromise positions. This process emphasizes listening and communication skills, leadership and problem solving ability, as well as the ability to suspend judgment and maintain confidentiality.

There is mixed support for the utility of peer led mediation programs. Evidence does exist in support of the utility of small-scale peer mediation projects, but these results have not generally been replicated on a larger scale (Bell, Coleman, Anderson, Whelan, & Wilder, 2000; Gentry & Benenson, 1993). Large, rigorously evaluated, peer led mediation programs have produced less than convincing evidence of program utility (c.f. *Program Example* – Orpinus et al., 2000 – *Relevant Narrative Reviews* – Hawkins, Farrington, & Catalano, 1998; Johnson & Johnson, 1996). An explanation for these mixed findings is that peer mediation programs do not appear to transfer key conflict resolution skills to students involved in a conflict. It is also unclear, the degree to which the use of mediation skills by peer arbitrators translates into changes in norms for the school or student behavior, e.g., lower incidence of fighting, disciplinary problems, and suspensions (Hawkins, Farrington, & Catalano, 1998; Johnson & Johnson, 1996). Curricular approaches to social competence and skill enhancement, on the other hand informally involve students in skills training activities and such programming has demonstrated utility in the reduction of antisocial behavior (c.f. *Program Example* – Farrell & Meyer, 1997). Beyond violence prevention, selected school based interventions where peers served as mentors to ameliorate problems other than interpersonal conflict have shown significant utility for child (c.f. *Program Example* – Dennison, 2000) and adolescent samples (c.f. *Program Example* – Eggert, Thompson, Herting, & Nicholas, 1994). Therefore, under specific well-controlled conditions, peer led interventions maybe useful for addressing some but not all problem behaviors.

As in the family intervention literature, interventionists who utilize peer facilitators and/or aim to promote a prosocial peer culture are coming to grips with the possible implications of mixing students with varying risk levels together for program activities. As a recent review has indicated, peer group change strategies my have unintended and harmful consequences. That is, deviant peers may socialize antisocial behaviors among more prosocial peers, rather than the reverse (Dishion, et al., 1999). This consideration maybe especially pressing for programming that relies heavily on peer modeling with adolescent participants.

While intervention efforts that informally involve peers are seen as potentially useful with regard to resistance skills training or other participatory educational modalities including social competence enhancement, recent reviews of *peer-led* interventions indicate that, in some instances, such programming may represent a threat to program fidelity if adequate peer training, monitoring and supervision are not ensured. Commonly cited problems with peer led intervention include: 1) a lack of clear program aims and objectives, 2) poor fit between project design and implementation environment, 3) lack of planning for, or management of peer intervention efforts, 4) inadequate training of peer leaders, 5) and poorly specified interpersonal boundaries. These objections to the use of peers in schools as the principal interventionists do not necessarily minimize the potential utility of well implemented programs, but they do emphasize the critical role of training and supervision (c.f. *Relevant Meta-Analysis* – Black et al., 1998). In sum, certain factors appear to modify the utility of peer involved prevention activities, these include but are not limited to the aforementioned issues surrounding program fidelity, training, and supervision, as well as the type of problem behavior targeted for change, the amount of exposure to other evidence-based intervention components, and the degree to which program elements are implemented in settings outside the school (e.g., family, community) (Samples & Aber, 1998).

Classroom Intervention

Successful classroom management programs often work with primary school and lower secondary students at the universal to selective prevention levels. Exemplar initiatives offer evidence to support the utility of classroom directed behavioral interventions, particularly if the goal is to produce immediate reductions in student misbehavior, as well as improvements in academic skills and performance (c.f., *Relevant Narrative Reviews* – Gottfredson, 1987; Durlak, 1997; Weissberg & Greenberg, 1998 – *Program Examples* – Evertson, 1985; Fantuzzo, et al., 1992; Greenwood, et al., 1992; Kellam, et al., 1994). Classroom interventions as stand alone modules do not typically show long-term program benefits (See Kellam et al., 1994 for a notable exception). However, the outcome evaluation literature in this area does show indications that such interventions may show promise as school based anti-tobacco initiatives (c.f., *Program Examples* – Kellam, et al., 1991; 1994; Vartiainen, et al., 1996; Wiborg & Hanewinkel, 2002).

What are the programmatic features and implementation strategies common to classroom level interventions that yield positive outcomes with regard to either pupils' academic performance or school behavior? Promotive classrooms are thought to be based on: robust teaching methods, teachers' use of clear rules for behavior and their consistent enforcement, positive reinforcement strategies in place of punishment, the close monitoring of the quality of both coursework and homework, and an emphasis on consistent attendance and academic performance (Gottfredson 1987; Loeber & Farrington, 1998b). These practices improve classroom organization and effectiveness because they clearly articulate norms and expectations for behavior (e.g., setting and enforcing rules) and they standardize effective educational practices (e.g., via consistent use of validated behavior management techniques). Durlak (1997) also characterized the promotive classroom environment as a social context in which there exists: 1) supportive interpersonal or teacher-student relationships; (2) commitment to achieving clearly specified goals; and, (3) structure and organization. Proposals for revamping classrooms, curricula, or schools themselves often emphasize these key elements (e.g., Cooper 1993; Nelson, 1996).

It is important to note that promising classroom-level initiatives are often grounded in behavioral theories, including social learning theory, and may incorporate elements of ecological theory (Catalano, et al., 1998). A firm basis in a theoretical framework provides a foundation for specifying more precise relationships between child or teacher behavior and other elements of classroom settings (e.g., norms and rules, rewards and consequences). Furthermore, a strong conceptual foundation aids in prediction by specifying what should happen under certain conditions, and aids in the interpretation of the results of programs after evaluation data are collected. Successful classroom based interventions are also informed about, and responsive to, the significance of timing. For example, some selective initiatives like the Good Behavior Game are specifically designed to address key organizational transitions like that of at risk children entering into the more structured learning environment of primary school (Kellam et al., 1994). Many prevention programs designed to promote school bonding, basic academic skills, and prosocial skills are characterized by their early timing which is geared to minimize the likelihood that children will fail to progress in their initial years of schooling (Greenwood et al., 1992; Grossman et al., 1997; Meyer, 1984). Other classroom interventions have addressed normative developmental transitions such as participation in exploratory risk taking or antisocial behaviors (Mayer et al., 1983).

Teachers undoubtedly play key roles in the development, implementation, and maintenance of promotive classrooms. Ward (1998) listed and elaborated a series of proactive, practice oriented procedures that teachers can implement in their classrooms to increase structure in learning situations and to assist students in building their own capacity for self discipline. Specific recommendations to enhance discipline included: holding high expectations for all students, coaching students to develop self-discipline, modeling appropriate behavior, providing instruction on conflict-resolution skills, and encouraging greater involvement in classroom activities by parents and community members. Promotive classrooms require considerable investment in both staff development and ongoing teacher training. For example, training, familiarity, and experience are essential to the development of respectful and culturally competent attitudes and interaction styles that are basic elements of supportive interpersonal relationships (i.e., learning partnerships) between teachers and students. While training is essential to assist teachers to address inappropriate and potentially dangerous situations (e.g., techniques for intervening in physical fights, skills for deescalating confrontations), training is also warranted to develop skills that teachers may use to facilitate a positive classroom environment to promote resilient outcomes such as appropriate communication styles or clear goal setting (Alexander & Curtis, 1995). Similarly, as classroom based prevention programs are implemented, and in particular, as program activities increasingly depart from traditional teaching methods, training is critical to insure the fidelity of the interventions administered (Dusenbury, et al., 1997). Therefore, both ongoing educational processes and prevention programs designed to modify them depend heavily on teachers' levels of training and preparedness to maximize the likelihood of successful outcomes.

The "ingredients that work" in classroom settings to promote competence among children who experience adversity have been summarized by several educational writers in order to distill the core elements of promotive teacher-student interactions (e.g., Benard, 1997; Florida State Department of Education, 1997; Wang, Haertel, & Walberg, 1997). The resulting documents are available and accessible to parents, teachers, administrators, and other child development specialists and provide concrete suggestions for changing the content and delivery of educational materials to enhance the likelihood of positive educational and behavioral outcomes among at risk children. Many of these recommendations regarding optimal classroom environments are consistent with summaries provided in meta-analyses of outcome evaluation studies aimed at reducing problem behaviors in the classroom. For example, reviews of school based programs to prevent or remediate aggressive or delinquent behaviors among elementary and junior high school students identify behaviorally based selective prevention efforts as being the most useful for changing a range of student behaviors in the classroom (e.g., Catalano, et al., 1998). More importantly, however, both popular treatments of best practices for classroom management and more scientifically driven evaluations of behaviorally based classroom level interventions converge to suggest that while results of such interventions are meaningful and encouraging, there is evidence that behavioral changes do not necessarily transfer from the classroom to other environments.

To enhance program utility and student retention, programs often forge links with families, attempting to increase parent involvement in school activities and support for program goals (e.g., Gottfredson et al., 1993). Outreach efforts by schools or school based prevention programs is essential to increase the engagement of parents in their children's educational experiences (via tutoring, monitoring attendance and homework, participation in school activities and decision-making, etc.) beyond the most motivated of parents (Durlak, 1997). Children whose parents are engaged in their schooling are more likely themselves to be engaged academically and their positive school experiences are related to positive educational outcomes or greater amenability to ongoing prevention programs (Garmezy, 1991). Therefore, an important plus of classroom based interventions is that they are often compatible with other programs operating in contexts outside the school (e.g., community and family settings) and can be linked with them if efforts are made to move beyond a stand-alone program within the school to co-ordinate the implementation of program elements across contexts (Dumas, Prinz, et al., 1999; Henggeler et al., 1998; Weissberg & Greenberg, 1998). Classroom based behavior management programs can be enhanced by coupling them with family training and individual level social competence training. This extends behavioral management and skills development across settings so that behavioral changes are generalized rather than remaining confided to a specific setting (O'Donnell, et al., 1995).

Whole School Change

A growing number of prevention programs, and in particular those that are school based and emphasize education-skills development, are person centered rather than ecologically oriented. In other words, young people are trained to use new skills without corresponding modifications to key social environments that would allow the practice and generalization of newly acquired social competencies (Weissberg & Greenberg, 1998). Whole school interventions are diverse, but a commonality among such initiatives is the emphasis on promoting not only individual level but also environmental change. The anti-bullying interventions previously highlighted in this chapter are not the only whole school interventions with demonstrated utility (c.f. *Program Examples* – Felner, et al., 1993; Felner, Ginter, & Primavera, 1982; Greenberg, et al., 2001). Yet, program examples in this area are notable in that they provide a model of a type of whole school intervention that has met with considerable, but not unqualified, success.

Anti-Bullying Initiatives. Whole school prevention programs for bullying have been conducted in the United States, as well as other countries such as Belgium, Canada, Italy, Norway, Spain, and the United Kingdom (c.f., *Relevant Narrative Review* – Smith, et al., 1999 – *Program Examples* – Arora, 1994; Okabayashi, 1996; Olweus, 1997; Pepler, Craig, Ziegler, & Charach, 1994; Ross, 1996; Sharp, 1996; Tattum, 1997). The success of such whole school programs across nations indicates the usefulness of continued investigation and evaluation of such programming. From this international research literature, well-controlled outcome evaluations generally support the utility of whole school bullying prevention programs. Exemplar interventions have demonstrated success particularly in terms of decreasing the incidence and prevalence of bullying-victimization, as well as improving in the learning and peer environments of primary and lower secondary schools. There is, however, evidence to suggest boundaries for the timing of anti-bullying initiatives, in that mixed program results appear to be more common among samples of middle to later adolescents (c.f. *Program Examples* – Hanewinkel & Knaack, 1997a; 1997b; Stevens, de-Bourdeaudhuij, & Van-Oost, 2000; Stevens, Van-Oost, de-Bourdeaudhuij, 2000). The reasons for this finding may lie in the organizational dynamics of primary and secondary schools or it could be related to developmental changes in the prevalence of physical and relational bullying.

How durable are intervention gains found in samples of children and early adolescents? While there is evidence within multiple year interventions that point to continued program benefits (c.f., *Program Example* – Olweus, 1997), there remains a substantial need to better document the post-intervention effects of whole school bullying initiatives. Future work also should be done to more precisely map out the boundaries of such interventions potential spreading effects into related problem behavior and mental health domains. Even within the area of bullying, future studies may expand the current focus on physical aggression to include both relational bullying and victimization. This would allow whole school programs to claim success in changing several different social processes that are all elements of the bully-victim syndrome. In addition, the unique role of families in the remediation of bully-victim problems requires further investigation.

What particular combinations of program components and strategies are commonly found across successful anti-bullying programs? School-wide changes promoted in the 'whole school' approach often involve clarifications in school rules and improved enforcement of anti-violence policies, increased awareness and ownership of rules across the entire population of the school, and active attempts to change norms regarding school violence (Gottfredson, 1997). Thus, a primary goal of the whole school approach in this case is to engage all primary stakeholders in the school including students, parents, teachers, and administrators and to involve them actively in efforts to reduce the incidence of bullying in school. While traditional programs often relied on a single teacher, counselor, or administrator to be in charge of the bullying problem for an entire school, programs with a whole school approach actively recruit support from across the entire school (Okabayashi, 1996; Olweus, 1993; Pepler, et al., 1994).

A key component of whole school bullying interventions has been awareness training for children and teachers, that is, to define a range of bullying behaviors for all participants in the school setting and to raise awareness of the impact of bullying on the victim. Awareness training for children has often been integrated into existing classroom curricula. This universal educational component is intended to create a more open forum for students to seek help. In turn, teacher and staff training is intended to develop improved detection and monitoring practices during break times, and strategies for offering less punitive responses to the victims of bullying, as well as clearer contingencies for students who bully their peers. Some multi-modal prevention programs attempt to develop linkages between key contexts for bullying by incorporating both school and home based training and outreach components in which parents of bullies are contacted and invited to talk with teachers to coordinate efforts between the school and home to interrupt bullying behavior (e.g., Ross, 1996; Sharp, 1996).

Anti-bullying initiatives are regularly implemented on a universal, whole school basis. Embedded within such interventions are selective, targeted program elements that are administered to identified bullies and victims. Programming in this instance often involves psychoeducational modules designed to enhance the social competence of bullies, typically by building social skills considered to be protective factors that buffer the expression of hostile exchanges in peer groups (Lochman, Lampron, Gemmer, & Harris, 1986; Yung & Hammond, 1998). In other cases, a prevention program may implement components designed to assist the victims of bullying. A study by Sharp (1996) examined the utility of victim-focused activities, using assertiveness training to enhance social skill deficits in children who were identified as the targets of bullying exchanges. The outcome of this study suggested that this prevention strategy resulted in at least short-term increases in the psychosocial adjustment of former victims. Although this prevention strategy appears to be promising, given the group processes involved in bullying, this prevention strategy may have unintended consequences if not implemented carefully as a component of a more comprehensive anti-bullying intervention that targets multiple factors maintaining these behavior patterns. For example, a stand-alone victimization reduction program may produce incidents where a victim's assertive interactions with a bully elicit further aggression rather than the desired nonaggressive response, thereby increasing the likelihood of increased social isolation for the victim.

Recent evaluations of bullying prevention programs, however, document that the whole school approach is not without variations in reported outcomes or efficacy in reducing targeted behaviors (Eslea & Smith, 1998; Young, 1998). For example, Young (1998) investigated the effects of peer conflict groups on ongoing rates of bullying behavior. The results of this particular study showed that although children reported lower levels of bullying and victimization, school personnel reported similar or increased rates of bullying. While this result highlights the importance of multiple sources and methodologies for the collection of outcome data, it also suggests that the impact of whole school prevention programs are by no means perceived uniformly by their participants. Similarly, Eslea and Smith (1998) demonstrated that the utility of whole school programs was determined in part by the degree to which program components were implemented in a systematic manner. Schools that deviated from a predetermined, standardized delivery format showed intervention gains of reduced magnitude, or in some cases, reported increases in the incidence of bullying. This evaluation finding is critical because it identifies a significant potential barrier to the effectiveness of whole school bullying prevention programs that are sensitive to both students' need for safety during educational activities and staff needs for anti-bullying programs that are convenient to implement.

Whole School Interventions with Mixed Evidence of Program Success. To date, whole school interventions such as alternative schools, school policy interventions, and school based situational prevention have met with mixed empirical results. Such interventions are frequently implemented without evaluation. The paucity of well-evaluated outcome and process studies may therefore contribute to the inconsistency of research findings. Because these forms of whole school intervention are increasingly implemented in schools, a brief commentary on these interventions is offered below.

Alternative Schools. In the United States, alternative schools are separate and distinct from traditional comprehensive public schools. There is substantial heterogeneity in the mission and content of alternative school programs, including last chance programs, remedial programs, and alternative learning environments (Raywid, 1994). While these settings can differ markedly, many alternative schools are intended to be contexts in which mainly secondary educational requirements are provided to adolescents who have difficulties adjusting to the demands of traditional school settings (Beauvais & Oetting, 1986). Poor fit between a young person's needs and the demand of traditional schools can also be complex, but in many cases it can be related to behavior problems, truancy or inadequate academic performance.

Although it can be argued that alternative schools are well positioned as selective and indicated prevention sites, evidence suggests that standard service delivery options at such schools (e.g., assessment and referral out for services, psychoeducational interventions) may not address key problem behaviors related to a pupil's alternative school placement. For example, alternative school students have been identified as a population at risk in adolescence for problematic patterns of substance use in comparison to traditional high school students, as well as violent and aggressive interpersonal behavior (e.g., Newcomb, Maddahian, Skager, & Bentler, 1987; Sussman, Dent, Simon, & Stacy, 1995; Sussman, Dent, & Galaif, 1997). In contrast to their disproportionately high levels of drug and alcohol use, the majority of alternative school students do not receive intensive substance abuse prevention programs (Sussman, et al., 1995). This is cause for concern given significant associations in this multi-problem population between interpersonal violence, other forms of juvenile offending, substance use, depression, and suicidality (Galaif, Chou, Sussman, & Dent, 1998).

If alternative schools are not staffed adequately or allocated sufficient funding to implement evidence based interventions, they may serve as structured learning environments that maintain or accelerate adolescent problem behaviors rather than providing services to remediate them. The notion that alternative schools may contribute to the perpetuation of the behavioral criteria that led to initial school placement is based in part on recent evaluations of school based substance abuse prevention programs. These data suggest that substance use-related features of the peer social environment (i.e., norms, role models, and opportunities) significantly predict recent alcohol use and problem use (e.g., Roski et al., 1997). The segregation of multi-problem youth into alternative schools may both exacerbate normative social pressures for conformity during adolescence and reduce access to the protective effects of non-deviant peers, thereby increasing risk for substance use problems among students in these schools (e.g., Allison et al., 1999). Furthermore, the findings of both developmental and prevention studies suggest that the segregation of adolescents into peer networks based on their levels of deviant behavior creates contexts where problem behaviors can escalate (Dishion, et al., 1999). This suggests that successful alternative school programs will need to counteract the segregating effects of alternative school placement by exposing students to comprehensive evidence based prevention programming, rather than simply segregating problem students from the general population.

School Policy Interventions. The formulation and articulation of policies for behavior within school settings is an essential component of a wide range of school-based interventions (Centers for Disease Control and Prevention, 1994; 1998). While formulation of school policies without active enforcement efforts or their integration into a broader intervention program is unlikely to produce meaningful short- or long-term changes in students' behavior, the role of policy in changing social norms in school settings and transmitting those social norms into broader community settings may be significant. Conversely, lack of clearly articulated and enforced anti-drug or anti-violence school policies may hamper the efforts of teachers and other school administrators to promote prevention programs due to increased conflict regarding program implementation and decreased consistency of the messages transmitted to students (Glynn, 1989; Rohrbach, D'Onofrio, Backer, & Montgomery, 1996). The salience of formal policy as a central program element that reinforces, guides, and supports health promotion efforts in schools is underscored by the initiatives of the United States' Centers for Disease Control and Prevention and other agencies. For example, these agencies have worked to develop and disseminate guidelines for the implementation of anti-tobacco programs, including specifying the core elements that should be covered in explicit policies (e.g. Centers for Disease Control and Prevention, 1994). The development of guidelines for school-based policies to create supportive organizational environments in which successful evidence based interventions can be implemented highlights and formalizes official commitment (e.g., by states and school districts) to program goals.

Yet, in the United States, official policy development does not necessarily ensure broad based adherence to policy goals at the state or school district level. Individual states do not necessarily provide clearly articulated statements, rules, or procedures describing policy violations and consequences, or how policy will be communicated or implemented, and state-level policies may differ from policies implemented at the school district level (Ross, et al., 1995; Tompkins, Dino, Zedosky, Harman, & Shaler, 1999). Therefore, the formulation and articulation of policies regarding school based interventions serve important purposes related to the adoption, implementation, and evaluation of new and continuing programs and provide the means for assessing the degree to which the priorities of state and federal agencies are realized. Yet, these efforts are only one element, but an essential one, of comprehensive, integrated prevention strategies for improving child and adolescent outcomes (c.f., *Relevant Narrative Review* – Flay, 2000 – *Program Example* – Gottfredson, 1997; Gottfredson, Gottfredson & Hybl, 1993).

Situational Prevention in Schools. Changes to environmental features of schools are sometimes attempted in order to affect positive change in students. By making direct modifications to the learning or social environments that constitute key contexts for child and adolescent development, it is thought that students' exposure to environmental risk-protective factors can be minimized. An example of the implementation of structural changes to school environments to reduce the levels or frequency of targeted undesirable behaviors involves the concept of situational prevention (Clarke, 1995). Situational prevention attempts to reduce undesirable behavior (e.g., interpersonal violence, property offenses, substance use) by a range of techniques that aim to either reduce opportunities to participate in the behavior, or increase the perceived difficulty or risk associated with the behavior. Examples of how situational prevention strategies are implemented in school settings include: improved monitoring via video surveillance, enforcement of policies regarding classroom attendance, use of interior and exterior common areas, restricted access to and exit from buildings, and searches of student property in lockers (Catalano et al., 1998). It is thought that such strategies provide visible guidance for appropriate behavior, as well as increase the perceived costs of engaging in misbehavior. Yet, such structural changes can also have the effect of raising important questions about individual freedoms within school environments.

To date, situational prevention has been employed more often in community settings to prevent street crime than in school settings to deter substance use or school violence. While there are some suggestions that situational prevention may have only small to modest effects for preventing crime as it is unlikely to have significant influence over individuals with either very high or very low levels of self-control (e.g., Wikstrom, 1995), this proposition remains to be tested in a rigorous school based evaluation. Therefore, forms of situational prevention remain organizational prevention strategies that await empirical support in a school context (c.f. *Program Example* – Astor, Meyer, & Behre, 1999). As in school policy interventions, such environmental approaches may result in a greater or lesser degree of success depending on the extent to which changes in school contexts are used to reinforce other evidence based interventions implemented in the same settings (Weissberg & Greenberg, 1998).

Cross Context Family School Partnerships

Successful and well-evaluated family plus school initiatives have primarily been multi-year programs that intervene with at risk samples during childhood (c.f. *Program Examples* – Conduct Problems Prevention Research Group, 1999a; 1999b; in press; Dumas, Prinz, et al., 1999; Tremblay et al., 1992). Exemplar interventions have demonstrated spreading program benefits that include short and long-term changes on indices of school achievement, antisocial behavior, substance use, and related risk-protective factors. These cross context intervention efforts may enhance the likelihood of producing significant behavioral change that is sustainable in long-term follow-ups because such strategies have the potential to alter the developmental systems that maintain conditions and processes linked to adaptive and maladaptive outcomes. These approaches acknowledge the importance of equifinality (Cicchetti & Rogosch, 1996) and the dynamic, multi-level person context systems that probabilistically increase the likelihood of the onset of maladaptive patterns of behavior. In addition, such comprehensive multi-level prevention programs incorporate the principle of multifinality by enhancing program utility via multiple points of entry into a targeted developmental system, to counteract ongoing processes that increase risk for maladaptive outcomes. Furthermore, likelihood of long-term program benefits may also be bolstered due to the intervention actions used in such efforts. Program components integrated into model family plus school interventions, in many cases have a positive evidence base as individual interventions (e.g., tutoring, classroom management, family training, etc.).

While there are many compelling reasons for integrating school based prevention programs with coordinated program components that are delivered to parents or in home settings, two of the most significant involve the concepts of adversity and social resources and their relation to adaptive or competent outcomes among children (Masten & Curtis, 2000; Masten et al., 1999). Specifically, the likelihood of competent outcomes among children is enhanced when the adversity experienced by children is reduced while access to social resources (e.g., warm, consistent parent-child relations) is increased. Conversely, risk for maladaptive patterns of adjustment increases significantly in developmental systems when severe, long-term and sustained adversity is present with little buffering by available social resources. Therefore, by providing parents and families with evidence based programs that are coordinated with intervention actions delivered at school, preventionists construct the conditions to: (a) reduce a young person's exposure to adversity within the home environment, and (b) increase the social resources available to the youngster. School-family linkages forged within a specific prevention program should provide greater consistency in the positive experiences of children across settings, and in particular with regard to their exposure to key change-producing procedures (e.g., reinforcement for desired behaviors, tutoring at home by parents, discussion of distorted cognitions). In addition, a cross context prevention effort is more likely to significantly impact multiple aspects of a developmental system that maintains maladaptive patterns of behavior (Cicchetti & Toth, 1998). Similarly, changes to the broader developmental system regulating individual behaviors, rather than simple change efforts aimed at individuals, puts in place conditions that provide opportunities for individuals to practice and consolidate behavioral gains made in the school setting, increasing the likelihood that these positive gains or new competencies will generalize to additional settings (Weissberg & Greenberg, 1998).

Questions

A number of issues are embedded in the preceding description of exemplary school intervention programs. Some of these questions have been alluded to, and are revisited here in greater detail. First, how do we accurately evaluate interventions that target systemic aspects of a school environment? Second, should indicated prevention initiatives have a place in schools? Third, why are integrated, comprehensive and sustained intervention efforts more likely to yield positive developmental outcomes among program participants?

Design and Evaluation Issues

The evaluation of school based prevention programs is based largely on the classic experimental design (Campbell & Cook, 1979; Lipsey & Cordray, 2000). In this design, individual participants are randomly assigned to either an intervention or a control group. In this case, the individual participant is the **unit of assignment**. Participants in an intervention group are exposed to some type of program activities or stimuli that is withheld from participants in the control group. Using a **cohort design**, responses are collected from participants in both the intervention and control groups before (pre-test) and after (post-test) the intervention group is exposed to the program activities. Participants' responses or data are then grouped together for members of each of the respective groups (intervention and control) and compared to each other to see what effect the prevention program may have had on those participants who experienced the intervention. In this situation, the **unit of analysis** is at the individual level. In environmental interventions, the unit of assignment or the 'participant' can be a context like a classroom, a school, a school district, or a community. When the unit of analysis is not at the individual level, evaluation data should be pooled by the particular environment targeted for intervention and not at the individual level.

There is a growing call for preventionists to match the unit of assignment with the unit of analysis in outcome evaluation studies (Biglan & Ary, 1985; Catalano, et al., 1999; Gottfredson, 1997; Hawkins, Farrington, & Catalano, 1998). It has been argued that a mismatch between the units of assignment and analysis yields a distorted picture of program utility (Biglan & Ary, 1985). In a recent comprehensive review of youth development programs, Catalano, et al. (1999) found that among 25 well-evaluated and successful interventions, a little less than half of these studies appropriately matched the unit of assignment with the unit of analysis. This finding suggests that current practice in the field of program evaluation may introduce bias into the outcome analyses of many studies.

Remedies to this methodological controversy have included the simple step of intervening with individuals and assigning them to intervention and control conditions, and analyzing the outcome data at the individual level. One problem with this approach is that not all prevention programs are implemented with the individual as the entity to which program materials are delivered. In many prevention programs, individual delivery of program materials is impractical or prohibitively expensive. Therefore, many interventions deliver program components to naturally occurring clusters of individuals, such as classrooms or other groups in after school or other community settings. For example, a common way to foster knowledge and skills development is to give an entire classroom a lesson on resistance skills and persuasion tactics (Botvin, Botvin & Ruchlin, 1998). This program delivery strategy has both practical (e.g., cost-effectiveness, convenience, efficiency) and theoretically compelling (e.g., fostering practice, modeling, or feedback) advantages.

Professionals planning the evaluation of prevention initiatives must also consider the integrity or equivalence of control or comparison groups (Gabriel, 2000). Implementation of programming for an entire school along with the measurement of target behaviors among non-treated students in a similar but geographically distinct control or comparison school represents a desirable situation (i.e., an adequate nonequivalent control group design). In this case, the preventionist does not to be as concerned about cross-contamination between the two groups. Yet, one can never really determine, with a high degree of certainty, the extent to which the intervention and control groups are equivalent without random assignment of participants to groups, given the possibility of unmeasured extraneous variables. In contrast, if control students are located in the same school as intervention students, protests over differential treatment, lack of access to valuable services, and unintentional exposure of control students to intervention activities can pose a serious but not insurmountable challenge to getting an accurate test of the intervention (Weiss, 1998). Therefore, the use of individuals as the unit of assignment and analysis remains a viable option in instances where this is possible and appropriate (e.g., teacher-administered tutoring programs).

Others have suggested matching the unit of assignment, if it is a school or community with the respective unit of analysis. In this case, the outcome evaluation data is pooled by the unit of assignment and then analyzed. One significant concern regarding this strategy is its tendency to reduce the statistical power available for analyses. In order for certain types of inferential statistics to function properly, a sufficient number of subjects must be included in the analysis (Kraemer & Thiemann, 1987). When the unit of assignment is matched with the unit of analysis, a study that might have had 2,000 students with pre- to post-test data and an adequate level of statistical power is transformed, with regard to comparison to, one intervention and one comparison school. The number of participants is reduced to an N of 2, and that in turn substantially reduces the level of statistical power. Preventionists have overcome this problem by assigning an adequate number of schools or communities to each condition (e.g., *Communities Mobilizing for Change on Alcohol* – Wagenaar, Murray, Gehan, et al., 2000) or by employing a multi-level data analytic strategy that allows one to avoid this problem (Catalano, et al., 1999). This discussion raises the following question: should we discount outcome evaluation studies that over the years have not matched the unit of assignment with the unit of analysis?

Contemporary reviews of the prevention literature seem to lean in a direction that views the mismatched study as still giving accurate information about the utility of a program but not at the same level of precision as properly matched evaluation studies. These reviews also stress that preventionists should be aware of this potential difficulty and that they should use available strategies to proactively address this issue in the design of future program evaluations (e.g., Catalano, et al., 1999; Gottfredson, 1997). In the present review, mismatches between the unit of assignment and analysis will be identified. As in other reviews of the prevention literature, information gained from a mismatched study will be considered valid but not as compelling as the correctly matched program evaluation.

Schools and Indicated Prevention

Indicated interventions in schools are far less common than universal and selected approaches. Provision of youth treatment services is more typically accomplished in hospitals or other clinical settings where internal validity may be high but external validity and the barriers to service provision may vary widely among settings (Kazdin, 1999; Wagner et al., 2000). However, with the growth curves for substance use and juvenile delinquency generally peaking in adolescence (e.g., Loeber & Farrington, 1998b) and with significant corresponding increases in human and social costs, it is important to intervene with troubled youth where we find them. High-risk youth have contact with, and in some cases, if even only conditionally, stay within school systems. Accepting that these youth are a valuable part of a school's student body supports the development of indicated prevention and treatment efforts in school settings.

There are examples of highly successful comprehensive indicated prevention-treatment programs with school-based components (e.g., *Multisystemic Therapy* – Henggeler, 1999). The practical utility and the ecological appropriateness of delivering indicated prevention and treatment level services in schools have long been recognized (e.g., Cowen & Lorion, 1976). Yet, provision of intervention services beyond assessment and referral to treatment outside the school, or relatively generic counseling strategies for youth manifesting problems and their families often exceed the boundaries of the intervention programs typically offered in schools. The current intervention research literature on school based indicated prevention programs, while faced with numerous methodological challenges, suggests the potential strengths of this approach.

For example, Student Assistance Programs (SAPs) are a common school based intervention for American teens with substance use and/or other behavioral problems. In general, SAPs have two main components: (1) the assessment of students for early identification of adolescent alcohol and/or other drug abuse or behavioral problems; and, (2) applications of selected and indicated prevention strategies for the reduction of adverse consequences associated with those problems. As such, SAPs differ fundamentally from universal prevention programs, which are directed at reducing the likelihood of substance use among the general population of students (Klitzner, Fisher, Stewart, & Gilbert, 1993).

To date, four evaluations of SAPs have been published (e.g., Carlson, 1993; Carlson, Hughes, & Deeback, 1996; Morehouse, 1984; Wagner, Dinklage, Cudworth, & Vyse, 1999), and none of these studies included a comparison group, engaged in systematic, repeated, follow up of students who took part in SAPs, or evaluated students on standardized alcohol and/or other drug use measures. Therefore, no truly systematic and rigorous evaluations of SAPs in the United States currently exist. Furthermore, none of these studies attempted to identify the active ingredients of their interventions or sought to ascertain why certain students responded to intervention while others did not. Given the importance of SAPs for preventing the escalation of adolescent substance abuse in schools, empirical tests of their utility are clearly needed.

The Teen Intervention Project (TIP; Wagner, Kortlander, & Leon Morris, 2001) is an intervention designed to address shortcomings in the present SAP literature. TIP tests the efficacy of a standardized SAP for adolescents who have alcohol and other drug (AOD) problems. TIP provides a school based, group-counseling (GC) program in which students receive 10 weekly sessions of in school, manual based intervention activities. This intervention is based broadly on the group counseling methods widely used in SAPs. Comparison groups receive assessment and referral (AR) to outside service providers, a standard practice with substance abusing students in the school system in which TIP is being implemented. Both groups are assessed at referral to the program, immediately after intervention (GC) or 12 weeks after referral (AR), and at 4, 7, and 12 months after referral. Assessment includes standardized measures of AOD use, as well as measures examining the mechanisms of change associated with the group counseling condition. In order to examine why some students respond to the program while others do not, the impact of several different amenability to intervention variables is assessed. Unfortunately, because TIP is in the middle of its outcome evaluation, no conclusions about the utility of this intervention can be made at this time.

While potentially useful and important, there are a number of barriers to the delivery of indicated programs in schools (Simeonsson & Simeonsson, 1999). One possible reason for the lack of indicated initiatives to address the needs of students with advanced drug use and antisocial behavior is that these youth may attend school sporadically. Indicated school intervention, however, takes on greater import as more and more troubled youth stay within or on the margins of school systems. Furthermore, Wagner et al. (2000) have suggested that long standing differences between school contexts and traditional intervention settings may complicate the provision of indicated prevention and treatment in schools. Specifically, the traditional clinical culture largely outside and independent of the bureaucracy of school districts and associated issues of oversight, autonomy, and accountability may impede the development of empirically based and rigorously evaluated indicated school based prevention programs. Yet, the delivery of indicated prevention services in school settings is both developmentally and ecologically appropriate. In addition, this mode of service delivery has significant implications for improving participant retention and access to diverse populations of at risk youth. The potential advantages of school based delivery of indicated prevention actions, in combination with calls for the implementation of comprehensive and multiple context prevention programming (e.g., Catalano, et al., 1998; Cowan & Durlak, 2000; Dumas, Prinz, et al., 1999) suggests that schools will play an increasing role in the delivery of indicated prevention services to young people (See Hibbs & Jensen, 1996 for other emerging program examples).

Comprehensive Integrated Interventions and Enhanced Program Efficacy

A significant criticism of current school based interventions is that they are often result in changes to students' behavior or in the broader social structures of the school environment that are difficult to sustain for more than a brief period of time. Part of this concern is that school based interventions are often implemented in a piecemeal manner, i.e., as single-focus programs to address a specific problem behavior such as substance abuse or school violence (Kolbe, Collins, & Cortese, 1997). In these efforts, risk and protective factors unique to the targeted problem behavior often become the focus of intervention efforts. Therefore, efforts to address a problem behavior proceed as if it is unrelated to other correlated problem behaviors, often without a great deal of attention to more distal, general risk and protective factors that may be antecedents for a wide range of problem behaviors. In addition, this fragmented approach to intervention, even when programs are based on a sound conceptual model, often means that intervention efforts are not part of an overarching conceptual framework that serves as the basis for academic instruction, the overall educational environment, and an intervention philosophy that spearheads both prevention of maladaptive behaviors and promotion of adaptive behaviors (Greenberg et al., i2003; Weissberg & Greenberg, 1998).

The significance of an overarching conceptual framework for efforts to implement school based intervention programs is far-reaching (Mrazek & Haggerty, 1994). First, the selection of a conceptual framework that clearly articulates an intervention philosophy improves the likelihood that linkages can be spelled out and coordinated among intervention goals and procedures, classroom instruction and student learning, the format and operation of classrooms and other social structure within schools, as well as facilitative experiences in family and community settings. Second, a broader conceptual framework buttressing intervention efforts would tend to highlight commonalities in the development and maintenance of correlated problem behaviors, emphasizing common rather than unique risk and protective factors and common pathways to maladaptive outcomes. Such an approach would provide a broad rationale for intervention, specification of targets and timetables for action, and emphasize early and sustained program implementation. Third, such an overarching conceptual framework can be integrated into the mission of a school district and used to shape policy regarding teacher training and supervision, accountability, evaluation, and ongoing program development. Finally, this comprehensive approach to intervention is likely to result in greater integration between efforts to prevent the onset or maintenance of problem behaviors (i.e., universal, selected prevention) and efforts to promote positive youth development (Weissberg & Greenberg, 1998).

An illustrative example of such a comprehensive, integrated approach to intervention is offered by the Collaborative for Academic, Social and Emotional Learning (CASEL). In their document, "Safe and Sound" (CASEL, 2003), this organization summarizes currently available social and emotional learning (SEL) programs that have been used and evaluated in school settings, evidence regarding their effectiveness, and identified best practices. The SEL approach is promoted in this document and others as one conceptual framework that has demonstrated significant effectiveness in school settings for coordinating goals for academic achievement, reduction of general risk factors for behavior problems, greater integration of goals among schools, families and communities, and the transformation of schools into supportive learning environments (Eccles & Appleton, 2002; Elias et al., 1997). Generally speaking, these goals are accomplished by approaching intervention efforts as comprehensive and integrated endeavors. Specifically, components of successful SEL programs include strategies to: (a) co-ordinate program planning across different school structures; (b) create supportive learning environments with a positive classroom climate; (c) increase teachers' use of effective instructional practices; (d) promote fuller participation in school activities by parents and their communities; and, (e) modify structures and co-ordinate among efforts units within schools to build support for program goals and activities. While SEL programs focus on a wide range a of issues (e.g., social competence, health, school violence) a common thread that runs through them is the focus on development of social and emotion skills as a precursor to adequate functioning in academic settings and the mastery of interpersonal challenges in childhood, adolescence and the transition to adulthood (Greenberg et al., 2003; Weissberg & Greenberg, 1998).

The continued development, implementation and evaluation of comprehensive, integrated intervention programs in school settings is one critical future direction for school based intervention to continue to develop a body of empirically-supported best practices. The lack of comprehensive integrated intervention programs for school settings, and in particular for adolescents, continues to be a significant gap in current intervention research and practice, although the growing support for the effectiveness of SEL-based programs provides a model for the development of other approaches to the integration of intervention efforts. While a number of universal and selective cross-context programs with significant empirical support involve school based components (e.g., *EARLY ALLIANCE Project* – Dumas, Prinz, Smith, & Laughlin, 1999; *Fast Track* – Conduct Problems Prevention Research Group, 1999a; 1999b; *Seattle Social Development Project* – Hawkins, Catalano, Morrison, et al., 1992), additional efforts are needed to shift current emphases from single focus, categorical interventions to integrative approaches in school settings.

Future Directions

As in the case of successful individual focused school interventions, a rapidly growing body of empirical evidence exists supporting the efficacy of school based interventions that seek to modify broader social structures within schools. The success of programs designed to change peer groups, classroom environments, school environments or linkages between schools and other social structures is determined by multiple factors that may differ widely across school settings. Yet, the results of multiple quantitative outcome evaluation studies, as well as the collective experiences of those who have conducted school based interventions suggest that certain commonalities can be identified across successful intervention programs. Several recommendations can be distilled from accumulated knowledge and practice to suggest guidelines for future intervention efforts. These general conclusions can be made regarding model school and family plus school interventions:

- Model interventions are rigorously evaluated using valid and reliable instruments, appropriate research designs, and adequate samples representative of a population of interest. Efforts are made to resolve potential confounds in the design and implementation phases of the program evaluation.
- A young person's exposure to prevention program components is critical. School and cross context interventions must be of sufficient duration and intensity to make programs meaningful to participating students and families. Given the competing demanding for both classroom and family time, this guideline is

often difficult to follow and requires careful balance among the goals and needs of different stakeholders.

Conclusions with relevance to particular program variations include the following:

- Prevention programs, and in particular those seeking to reduce harmful behavior (e.g., violence or substance use) may be more effective when backed by school-wide structures such as policies or other organizational or structural changes that are clearly articulated to all stakeholders and enforced at all levels of the school. Yet, it should be noted that policy change alone may not be enough to produce enduring behavior change.

- The success of traditional school based prevention programs may be enhanced by continued and expanded efforts to extend the targets of an intervention beyond discrete behaviors exhibited at the level of the individual. A growing body of innovative research and practice has attended to the influence of school context on the maintenance of problem behaviors among children and adolescents.

- The generalization and maintenance of newly created behavioral changes are enhanced when the contexts in which children are developing offer them opportunities to practice socially competent and appropriate behaviors. Therefore, consistent efforts should be made to forge links between school-based programs and other key domains in children's lives such as family, neighborhood, and peer networks. Such links may be constructed within a comprehensive, cross context program or by more informal coalitions.

Chapter Endnotes

---

[1] Individual students were used as the unit of analysis in the German Smoke Free Class Competition trial (Wiborg & Hanewinkel, 2003).

[2] See the *Questions* subsection for a more detailed discussion of the unit of assignment and analysis issue.

[3] In addition to the authors, David Hawkins and Rick Kosterman made significant contributions to this description of the Seattle Social Development Project.

Chapter 6
Community Intervention and Community Related Cross Context Interventions

Introduction

Humans have the capacity to adapt to changing environmental conditions. We personally experience and see this phenomenon unfold around us. Through communities and other forms of social organization, we are able to transform adaptive responses into customs or rules for living. These lessons of life help to shape the foundation of our shared social knowledge, which can come in a diversity of forms. The community, like the family and school, provides an important staging ground for the creation and transfer of social knowledge. The community, as a primary context for youth socialization, offers an opportune setting for reaching young people.

Reviews of the research literature provide further support for the importance of the community in the explanation of youth development and the formation of problem behaviors (e.g., Berlin, Brooks-Gunn, & Aber, 2001; Booth & Crouter, 2001; Derzon & Lipsey, 1999; Hawkins, Arthur, & Olson, 1997; Hawkins, et al., 1998; Leventhal & Brooks-Gunn, 2000; Lipsey & Derzon, 1998; McElhaney & Effley, 1999; Rhodes, et al., 1997; Sherman, et al., 1997; Spooner, 1999). Specific aspects of community life that have been found to regularly co-occur with youth problem behaviors include: Community disorganization and disengagement, access and permissive attitudes towards firearms, alcohol, and other drugs, local transience or resident turn over, repeated exposure to crime and violence, poverty, and a lack of community resources. These risk factors are linked to the development of aggressive behavior (e.g., Attar, Guerra, & Tolan, 1994; Gorman-Smith, Tolan, & Henry, 1999; Loeber, Farrington, Stouthamer-Loeber, & Van Kammen, 1998; Loeber & Wikström, 1993; Preski & Shelton, 2001) and have also been associated with youth drug use, school drop out, early childbearing, risky adolescent sexual behavior, and child maltreatment (e.g., Coulton, Korbin, Su, & Chow, 1995; Hardwick & Patychuk, 1999; Herrenkohl, et al., 2000; Lee & Goerge, 1999).

Increasingly, risks within the community are being fought through the blending of a diversity of intervention ingredients, which are intended to come together to yield a positive end effect (Weissberg & Greenberg, 1998). One can take the metaphor of cooking oil, flour, sugar, and salt as an example. Although each of these ingredients plays an essential role in many recipes, different combinations yield quite different results. Intervention ingredients commonly used in the community have involved:

- Bringing individuals within the community together to act in service of a prevention goal.
- Limiting youngsters' access to alcohol and tobacco.
- Helping youth to develop the knowledge and skills that will enable them to proactively participate in their own lives and the life of their communities.
- Providing opportunities for young people to make personally and socially meaningful connections to society.

Chapter Organization

This chapter begins with a description of basic *program elements*. These are the primary ingredients commonly used in community-related programs: Community Mobilization, Access Restriction, Education-skills, and Opportunity plus Education-skills. After briefly outlining the basic characteristics, *program examples* in early and later childhood and adolescence will be presented to give an illustrative theoretical and/or empirical rationale that supports the identified intervention content areas. A discussion will follow in the *Synthesis* subsection of the ways in which these approaches have been successfully combined within communities and across contexts. Following this, the *Questions* subsection will discuss issues relating to community and community related cross context interventions. This chapter ends with a list of *Future Directions* drawn from the chapter.

Program Elements

Community Mobilization: Bringing Individuals within the Community Together to Act in Service of a Promotion or Prevention Goal

Grass roots social action inspired by community mobilization is certainly not new (cf. Catalano et al., 1998; Davis & Lurigio, 1996). What is new is the emerging intervention literature concerned with the examination of practices that either facilitate or forestall community-based mobilization movements. In this literature, there are a number of collaborative intervention models and case studies of researcher—community run intervention initiatives (e.g., Alstead, et al., 1999; Baldwin, 1999; Bryant, Forthofer, Brown, Landis, & McDermot, 2000; Buysse, Wesley, & Skinner, 1999; Evans, et al., 2001; Maurana & Clark, 2000; McCormick, et al., 2000; Paine-Andrews, et al., 1996; Randall,

Swenson, & Henggler, 1999). Another area of the prevention mobilization literature is aimed at the development of methods for measuring community readiness, as well as community leader perceptions of youth problem behaviors and the need for subsequent intervention (Edwards, et al., 2000; Plested, et al., 1999; Sosale, et al., 1999).

In what ways have communities mobilized to prevent youth problem behaviors and promote positive development? The nature of mobilization efforts range from community meetings where residents are simply informed of the planned intervention activities and asked to support these actions *-a more top-down approach-* to those that invite diverse groups of individuals within the community to take part in program planning and implementation *-a hybrid tactic-* to those that spontaneously form among community residents with little outsider input *-more bottom-up methods-*. Mobilization efforts in the community can be facilitated by participant observations, pre-intervention surveys, risk assessments, attempts to integrate participants' culture into the intervention, and efforts to create lasting decision making and administrative bodies that will remain active in the intervention district after an official research project ends.

The underlying rationale behind mobilization goes past the risk-and-protective-factors model to encompass notions of basic democratic rights of expression, opportunity to participate in social decision making, and empowerment (Bloom, 1996; Weissberg & Greenberg, 1998). Empowerment theory, perhaps fittingly, cannot be easily credited to one particular person, school of thought, or discipline (Beeker, Guenther-Grey, & Raj, 1998). There are, however, a number of theories and traditions of intervention work that fit within an empowerment framework. One can take as a theoretical example, Paulo Freire's (1970/1983) ideas on transformative education and social action. The essence of this approach is to empower those who are marginalized by creating a forum where they can build a critical understanding about their exclusion from the mainstream. Once marginal groups in society begin to take steps to act on the basis of this understanding, the prospect of gaining more control over the environment and direction of their lives becomes an ever greater possibility. Freire's (1970/1983) view of transformative education and action is largely geared towards groups who lack social, political, and, economic influence. However, it can be said that, "...the expression of empowerment is like the expression of democracy in action" (Bloom, 1996, p. 213). Therefore, it could be argued that democratic social action is the inherent right of all citizens within a given community. Freire's transformative pedagogy implies several possible avenues for social change such as raising community residents' level of consciousness about a social problem or by making the marginalized status of a particular group's or one's own group evident. Each of these strategies can provide a basis for bringing people together in a common pursuit.

Collaborative Community Action Research, the Development-in-Context Evaluation Model, and Comprehensive Community Initiatives each offer an example of a line of scientific investigation consistent with the idea of empowerment. Collaborative Community Action Research, for instance, is based on a hybrid intervention approach that views the community—scientist relationship as a mutually rewarding partnership. Researchers working within this tradition are particularly mindful of the history and ecology of the local setting, take careful steps to work in a collaborative manner, and pay attention to the unique strengths of the participating community (Weissberg & Greenberg, 1998). In a similar spirit, the Development-in-Context Evaluation model advocates a collaborative community intervention approach with an emphasis on making explicit the meta-theoretical foundations of such efforts and supports the use of more inclusive methods for program improvement and evaluation (Lerner, Ostrom, & Freel, 1995; Ostrom, Lerner, & Freel, 1995; Peterson, 1995; Zeldin, 1995). Comprehensive Community Initiatives take an analogous approach with a stress on viewing the community holistically as well as making community residents active players at all levels of intervention action (Berlin, et al., 2001).

Communities that Care® (CTC; Hawkins, 1999; Hawkins, et al., 1992) is a mobilization strategy that illustrates of how communities can be active and retain control over intervention initiatives, while still making use of the best scientific knowledge available on successful interventions and services. CTC has been likened to a computer 'operating system' which provides users with an easy to use and understand framework or platform for launching different software programs. Based on individual needs, a person will have different types of programs on their computer like word processing, statistical and drawing or photo-related programs. However, there is a standard range of software that one can buy and which should meet certain consumer quality requirements (Hawkins, et al., 1992).

CTC functions in a similar way in that CTC staff provide communities with a series of organizational steps that provide a framework for community action: 1) build an alliance of all individuals who have a stake in the welfare of the community, public and service officials, 2) elect a representative management board that will function as a decision making body for the CTC program, 3) hire a program coordinator in charge of daily administration, networking, support, and fund raising, 4) evaluate state of risk and protection in the community through a youth self-report inventory and official registries, 5) evaluate strengths and weakness of existing programs and services within the community, and 6) management board selects risk/protective factors to target, redirection of existing services to that aim, and selection of new evidence based programs to address targeted risk-protective factors (Hawkins, et al., 1992).

As with the computer operating system metaphor, CTC does not tell communities which programs to use or which problems to fix. CTC does, however, provide a range of scientifically sound support services to communities like standard survey instruments-data gathering procedures, a menu of scientifically sound intervention programs in family, school, and community settings to select from, support for community decisions and actions, and help with process and outcome evaluation efforts (Hawkins, et al., 1992).

CTC program development began in United States in 1990 (Hawkins, et al., 1992). Over its history, CTC has been used by approximately 400 communities (Channing Bete Company, 2003, June 26). CTC is also being implemented and tested in the United Kingdom and the Netherlands (e.g., Ince, Beumer, Jonkman, & Pannebakker, 2001; Utting, 1999). For example, 23 communities in England, Scotland, and Wales have used CTC to begin organizing local intervention initiatives (France & Crow, 2003). At the time this review was written, process (e.g., Arthur, Ayers, Graham, & Hawkins, in press; France & Crow, 2003; Harachi, Ayers, Hawkins, Catalano, & Cushing, 1996) but not outcome evaluation reports were available for CTC test communities. A process and outcome evaluation for United Kingdom test sites is anticipated in the near future (France & Crow, 2003). Comprehensive evaluation of community mobilization efforts such as those highlighted in this subsection promise to contribute to what is known about community mobilization, as well as yield science based methods that help communities come together to take effective action.

Access Restriction: Limiting Youngsters' Access to Alcohol and Tobacco

The effort to systematically limit a young person's access to alcohol and tobacco has taken on renewed momentum (e.g., SOU 2000/01:20; Substance Abuse and Mental Health Services Administration, 1996; World Health Organization, 2000; 2001). Regrettably, it is not particularly difficult for American and European teens to get a hold of these substances. Consider these findings:

- In the vast majority of studies on the subject, most youth irregardless of any demographic characteristic or frequency of use report that their main source of alcohol, tobacco, and other drugs comes from a social connection like a friend, family member, or other adult acquaintance (e.g., Centers for Disease Control and Prevention, 2000; Forster, Wolfson, Murray, Wagenaar, & Claxton, 1997; Harrison, Fulkerson, & Park, 2000; Robinson, Klesges, & Zbikowski, 1998; Wagenaar et al., 1996).
- Above and beyond social sources, commercial outlets also represent a credible point of access for youth. Shopping trials, in which a young **confederate** enters a shop in an attempt to purchase alcohol-tobacco, show that youth usually have about a 50% or better chance of making an over the counter purchase (Arday, et al., 1997; Dalenius & Romelsjö, 2000; Forster, et al., 1997; Landrine, Klonoff, Campbell, & Reina-Patton, 2000; Mattsson & Romelsjö, 1999).

In the face of this and other evidence that identifies drug availability as a significant community level risk factor (e.g., Hawkins, et al., 1998; Sherman, et al., 1997); it seems unrealistic to believe that contextual factors like access do not facilitate substance use.

Policy can be a catalyst for change in the community (Cowen & Durlak, 2000; Holder & Reynolds, 1997). The term policy refers, "...collectively to any voting decisions, referenda, ordinances, written regulations, licensing requirements, funding agreements, or statements that represent public agreement about a course of action..." (Pentz, 2000, p. 258). The reliance on policy as an instrument for prevention is largely based on the premise that this approach has the potential to yield population level changes in youth problem behavior and adult conduct. Analyses of alcohol- and tobacco- related public policy offer evidence in favor of this position (e.g., Bruun, et al., 1975; Holder, et al., 1998; Holder & Wagenaar, 1994; Pekurinen & Valtonen, 1987; Sulkunen & Simpura, 1997). For example, Leifman (1995) in an examination of historical trends in alcohol consumption observed that a spike in aggregate consumption levels from 1965-1977 in Sweden co-occurred with the introduction of medium strength beer (3.6% alcohol content) in grocery and convenience stores. An overall decline in consumption later coincided with the removal of this item from store shelves in 1977 and the introduction of other alcohol restrictive policies enacted in the late 1970s to mid 1980s. As Sweden entered this drier period, both youth and adult consumption levels showed declines (e.g., Romelsjö, 1987), with decreases in youth alcohol use being attributed in part to the hardening of access to the drug of choice among teens at the time, i.e., medium strength beer (Leifman, 1995).

Analyses of access interventions provide useful techniques that help to take a more proactive control over alcohol and tobacco use. These analyses also help to inform the alcohol and tobacco policy-making and maintenance process (e.g., Biglan & Taylor, 2000; Reynolds, Holder, & Gruenewald, 1997; Wagenaar, et al., 2000).

Policy Making: Advocacy. Policy advocacy is a core component of many access interventions. As a part of this strategy, concerned individuals and groups take steps to enact policies that encourage a community environment less conducive to underage drinking and smoking. Examples of such policies would include restrictions on beer kegs and alcohol in public places and events, and increased legal sanctions and liability for adults that provide youngsters with alcohol and tobacco (Alcohol Epidemiology Program, 2001, October, 16; Harrison, et al., 2000). Increased taxes to drive up retail prices, planning and zoning, represent additional ways to address the problem of youth alcohol-tobacco consumption through policy (e.g., Manley, et al., 1997a; Reynolds, Holder, & Gruenewald, 1997).

Policy Maintenance: Shopping Trials. The utility of a policy is partly tied to its enforcement. Shopping trials play a supportive role in realizing a public stance on the unacceptability of youth drug use. A shopping trial is designed to check the alcohol-tobacco vendor's level of compliance with existing laws that prohibit the sale of these substances to youngsters. Shopping trials usually consist of an adolescent confederate entering a shop, restaurant, or bar in an attempt to purchase alcohol or tobacco. These pseudo-consumers are trained to follow a standard buying protocol. The teens that take part in the shopping trial could be over the legal purchasing age yet have been judged to look younger than they really are (e.g., Grube, 1997; Wagenaar, et al., 2000) or may actually be underage (e.g., Jason, Billow, Schnopp-Wyatt, & King, 1996; Preusser & Williams, 1992). The deception involved in a shopping trial is weighed against the need to get an accurate indication of how easy it is for a young person to purchase alcohol or tobacco and to enforce compliance with existing laws prohibiting such sales or service. Certain precautions are usually taken in order to protect the confederate from possible harm. These include training, unobtrusive observation by a second teen confederate or an adult human service or law enforcement professional during the shopping trial, surprise breath analyses as a check against confederate alcohol use, and putting purchased alcohol-tobacco beyond use. After the purchase attempt, the confederate completes a survey or interview that documents the details of the shopping episode.

Education-Skills: Helping Youth to Develop Knowledge and Skills

Education-skills promotion enters into community prevention in a number of ways. Parallels to similar efforts in the school and family contexts are many. Because theories that support the education and skills approach were described in the preceding chapters, primary emphasis is placed on describing the shape that these actions can take on in the community.

Small Groups. One strategy is to utilize locations within the community to reach and work with youngsters. Small group training figures as a prominent example. In this case, an education-skills curriculum is implemented, for instance, in a recreation center or community-based clinic (c.f. *Program Examples* – Stanton, et al., 1996; St. Lawrence, et al., 1995). While small group education-skills training is often directed towards youth in a community setting, the students who receive this type of program can vary from medical personnel to restaurant workers and shop owners. Responsible beverage service or sales training (RBS/S) offers a case in point. RBS/S exposes shop personnel, servers, managers, and owners to educational-skills promotion activities that are aimed at raising awareness of existing laws and obligations, practice in identification checking, sales refusal and negotiation skills, and the development of a written and manager supported alcohol-tobacco service/sales policy (Grube, 1997; Saltz & Stanghetta, 1997).

Large Groups. Large forums for the exchange of information and skills may include didactic presentations to local residents and decision makers or interactive town hall meetings. Other education-skills programming salient to large groups include the use of media to publicize a prevention message (c.f. *Program Example* – Flynn, et al., 1997). Campaigns can use a wide range of media to reach a target audience including commercials, promotional materials, and internet sites (Goldberg, Fishbein, et al., 1997; UNAIDS, 1998; Tammi & Peltoniemi, 1999). Increasingly, the media is being used to put promotion and prevention issues on the public agenda, increase public concern and support for intervention actions, and provide an impetus for public officials to act. In this strategy of **media advocacy**, individuals that have a stake in the success of a particular initiative are trained to attract and efficiently manage news media attention (Holder & Treno, 1997).

Opportunity plus Education-Skills: Providing Opportunities for Young People to Make Personally and Socially Meaningful Connections

In the community intervention literature, there is an assortment of programs that seek to maximize a young person's attachment to people and lifestyles that are collectively defined in a given culture as prosocial. The Social Development Model (SDM; Catalano & Hawkins, 1996) can be used as a framework to provide an explanation for why these types of interventions should work. The SDM combines what we know thus far from empirical studies of youth problem behaviors, with contemporary notions of lifespan development. In addition, this model draws concepts from psychology (e.g., *Social Learning Theory* – Bandura, 1977) and criminology (e.g., *Control Theory* – Hirschi, 1969; *Differential Association Theory* – Matza, 1969).

An overriding idea in the SDM is that the development of pro and antisocial behavior is significantly impacted by our social interactions. More specifically, children will form social bonds to significant others if the following conditions are met: The child must think that there is a viable chance for a social interaction to take place; the child has to actually engage in a social encounter; children and their partners must have adequate skills to successfully interact; and the child expects that the social exchange will be a rewarding experience. In any given interpersonal encounter the opportunity to participate, level of involvement, ability, and reinforcement coincide to give the youngster an indication of what to expect from future interactions. Through this additive and cyclical social learning process children are able to develop lasting attachments. Day to day social exchanges with an array of people, whose influence varies over the lifespan, further modifies the strength and normative quality of social attachments. Over the course of many interactions, a social bond takes on a life of its own and leads to the internalization or the buying into a set of beliefs and a corresponding lifestyle that significant others represent or actively promote. The internalized belief system stabilizes as children grow yet it continues to be moderately open to the reshaping of attachments and beliefs via the accumulation of daily social experience and major social transitions.

As in Control Theory (Hirschi, 1969), the SDM offers that the existence of social bonds is a potent deterrent against deviant behavior. Further, the absence of strong relationships makes the costs, or consequences, of antisocial behavior seem not so bad. The SDM, does however, differ from Control Theory by asserting that the existence of a social bond does not in all cases guarantee prosocial behavior. In Control Theory, delinquents are often characterized as experiencing a social deficit that inhibits their ability to make meaningful connections to others. As a consequence, youth with weak attachments would lose very little socially if they engaged in risky behaviors.

In the SDM, the moral compass of the person that the child becomes attached to is critical. If this person advocates or engages in outright antisocial behavior then this will facilitate the child's identification with an antisocial identity and lifestyle. If the person is on the whole a positive role model then the social bond will function as it is postulated in Control Theory. The chances of detection and possible reward also factor into the equation in the SDM. If there is a low probability of being caught and big payoff for deviant behavior, then antisocial behavior is possible even in the presence of a prosocial attachment.

Thus, the SDM offers a reinterpretation of Control Theory which includes the possibility of antisocial behavior as a function of a lack of social attachments or attachments to role models of dubious character. Further, among those with prosocial attachments, the possibility of engaging in antisocial behavior if conditions are favorable to being undetected. However, in the final analysis, the SDM postulates that, "The relative weight of prosocial and antisocial influences will determine whether children begin to use drugs and engage in delinquent behavior..." (Catalano & Hawkins, 1996, p. 174).

The SDM also has arguable relevance in discussions of other problem behaviors. In a review of pregnancy prevention programs, for example, a category of intervention was described that stressed the idea that youth can be steered away from restrictive life choices by offering them "...opportunities for involvement and service in the present, as well as a clearer sense of possibilities for the future. Life Options program models give teens 'other things to do'..." (Miller & Paikoff, 1992, p. 267).

Opportunity interventions seek to tip the balance in favor of prosocial attachments and lifestyles. Initiatives like community service, mentoring, and recreational activities each in their own way attempt to foster at least one of the constituent elements of a promotive social bond. These elements include: Reducing the concrete and psychosocial barriers that discourage youth from taking part in interactions with prosocial others; deepening the young person's level of involvement in prosocial interpersonal exchanges; strengthening relationship skills; and providing social recognition and reinforcement for successful participation.

Community Service. Young people conduct volunteer work as a part of their service learning experience (Muscott, 2000; Yates & Youniss, 1999). The nature of community service can vary markedly and may be self-selected or, as is the case with adjudicated youth, court-mandated. The placement and supervision of youngsters is usually overseen by an adult such as a teacher, school counselor, program staffer, or juvenile justice official. The specific mechanisms by which community service is thought to be beneficial are many. These include: encouraging ability, building promotive relationships with adults and other youth, increasing the young person's investment in mainstream social institutions and organizations, and creating a history of activism in the community that can serve as a basis for the development a civic identity and future participation in democratic decision making (Youniss, McLellan, Su, & Yates, 1999; Youniss & Yates, 1999; Zoerink, Magafas, & Pawelko, 1997).

Mentoring. Mentoring relationships can be broadly conceptualized as a relational context in which emotionally positive experiences and specific forms of social learning can take place (Tierney & Grossman, 2000). Relationships with highly functioning adults or more advanced peers have long been considered as a means by which youth may gain access to significant resources like: support, guidance, care and concern, and the chance to further develop a range of life skills (Masten et al., 1999). As a selected or tertiary prevention strategy, mentoring is thought to fill a gap in the lives of at-risk youth who have insufficient contact with prosocial role models. Mentoring in this case can be linked to the promotion of resilience (Davis, 1999; Roth, Brooks-Gunn, Murray, & Foster, 1998). This intervention strategy is congruent with a resilience framework because significant contact with a well-functioning, caring mentor may fundamentally alter the future relationships of the young person. One hope of mentoring programs is that the relationship created and the ensuing intensification of a promotive social bond will function as a positive turning point in the life of the young person (Rutter, 1989).

Recreational Activities. An emergent research literature provides evidence in support of the proposition that a young person's leisure activities are meaningfully connected to their involvement in problem behaviors (Csikszentmihalyi, Rathunde, Whalen, & Wong, 1993/1997; Dryfoos, 1999; Halpern, 1999; Jones & Offord, 1986; Mahoney & Stattin, 2000; Mahoney, Stattin & Magnusson, in press). The mechanisms by which certain, free-time activities appear to protect or put youth at-risk are more complicated than simply busying idle hands. Going back to research literature described in the *Family and School Sections*, we know that peer relations are important predictors of youth problem behaviors (Farrington, 1995; Herrenkohl, et al., 2000) and that deviance training can occur among at-risk adolescents (Dishion, McCord, & Poulin, 1999; Poulin,

Dishion, & Haas, 1999). Thus, successful community-related initiatives are alert to the possibility of antisocial peer influence and act accordingly. A potential reason for why participation in certain kinds of free time activities is either favorable or harmful maybe based on whether the activity provides links to either competent or antisocial adults and peers (Cziksentmyhali, et al., 1993; Fletcher, Elder, & Mekos, 1997; Mahoney & Magnusson, 1998; Sherman, et al., 1997). Other explanations have centered on the possible association between certain types activities and skills development (Bloom, 2000; Jones & Offord, 1986). Clearly more research is needed in this area.

In sum, the program elements discussed here are embedded in a strong theoretical and/or rational foundation. Efforts to mobilize communities to promote positive youth development highlight the importance of communities and scientists working in a collaborative manner. With regard to limiting a young person's access to alcohol and tobacco, it was noted that well thought out and maintained policy can be a powerful vehicle for change. Community-based education and skills efforts can range from teaching small groups of liquor store clerks to educating large groups of people using broad media forms. Finally, communities looking for positive change can turn to providing resident youth with opportunities for prosocial connections, either through positive relationships or from doing something for the community themselves. Programs that have used either one or a combination of these elements have shown positive outcomes and are highlighted in an upcoming subsection.

Exemplary Program Examples

Early Community Intervention

Early intervention programs such as home visitation and enrichment initiatives have historically focused on working directly with infants and young children or reaching them through caregivers (Karoly, et al., 1998). However, it stands to reason that the provision of services to families and the creation of child-parent welfare institutions in the absence of community-wide change is an uphill battle (e.g., Gorman-Smith, et al., 1999). Of late, the community mobilization strategy offered by the Comprehensive Community Initiative (CCI) approach has been reformulated as a framework for supporting community-wide efforts to promote early child development (Berlin, et al., 2001; Lambert & Black, 2001). CCI advocates argue that the influence of the community on development can be pervasive (Berlin, et al., 2001).

CCI offers a rationale and organizational mechanism for: encouraging families and community residents to become full partners in the process of early intervention; initiating public policy change supportive of sound early child development; and bolstering traditional early intervention efforts with prevention programming intended to address risk and protective factors in the local ecology. There are examples of CCI inspired early child development programs (e.g., Berlin, et al. 2001; Brown & Richman, 1997) however, evidence of the utility of such initiatives remains largely an empirical question that awaits comprehensive testing.

Exemplary Program Examples

Later Community Intervention

As mentioned earlier in this chapter, many youth-oriented community interventions utilize multiple program components and strategies that are pulled together to create an overall intervention package. With the aspiration of producing a synergistic effect, these packages frequently address as many relevant risk and protective factors as possible. Cross-context interventions extend on this theme by implementing a coordinated series of actions across socialization contexts. Interventions that work in the community and subsume one or more microsystems are considered to be salient and are therefore incorporated into the review of programs presented here[1]. Also in this chapter, illustrative examples of exemplary community and cross-context interventions for school age children and teens are organized into three domains based on the content of the intervention actions taken:

- Access Restriction
- Education-Skills
- Opportunity plus Education-Skills

Access Restriction initiatives are designed to reduce the supply of alcohol and tobacco to young people primarily through the initiation and enforcement of anti-drug policies, with education-skills components playing a supportive role. Education-Skills and Opportunity plus Education-Skills intervention packages combine education, skills, and/or opportunity as the main form of intervention action. The degree to which a given prevention program is designed to mobilize community residents to take part in the intervention process varies across the three approaches.

Access Restriction Initiatives. The universal alcohol prevention program entitled Communities Mobilizing for Change on Alcohol (CMCA; Wagenaar, et al., 2000) demonstrates the potential benefits of using a dual policy making and enforcement approach. CMCA's efficacy trial was conducted for two and half years in 15 Minnesota and Wisconsin communities with an average of 20,836 inhabitants per community (Wagenaar, Murray, Wolfson, Forster, & Finnegan, 1994; Wagenaar & Perry, 1994). The program trial utilized a randomized group design with **nested cohort-cross sectional sub designs** (Wagenaar, et al., 2000) and **time series analysis** of registry data (Wagenaar, Murray, & Toomey, 2000). Seven intervention and eight control communities were block randomized to condition. As a part of the nested sub designs, groups of persons and environments that should be impacted by the intervention (e.g., merchants, youth, alcohol outlets) were pre- and post-tested. Although the persons and settings surveyed at pre-testing are not necessarily the same individuals or environments involved in the post testing, the people and settings tested at pre- and post-testing are still associated with the affected group or environment (e.g., merchants, youth, alcohol outlets). Comparable groups and environments in the control communities (e.g., merchants, youth, alcohol outlets) were pre- and post-tested in a similar manner. The design used to evaluate CMCA is appropriate because the target for intervention and unit of assignment was the community[2].

CMCA's programmatic aims included the mobilization of community residents to start and maintain environmental change within the community. CMCA used different strategies to mobilize the community. These included: designated drinking areas at community events, increased attention to the enforcement of existing laws prohibiting underage alcohol sales through shopping trials, police compliance checks, and RBS/S (Wagenaar, et al., 1999).

CMCA's efficacy trial showed that the initiative had the most impact on older teens and young adults. Driving while under the influence (DUI) arrests for 18-20 year olds in the intervention communities showed a decline during the pre-intervention period from 1987-1992 as well as through the 1993-1995 intervention period (Wagenaar, Murray, & Toomey, 2000). Eighteen to twenty year olds in the control communities also evidenced a decline during the pre-intervention period with a significant increase in DUI arrests during the intervention period. Other important results, a significant 17% decline in providing alcohol to younger peers among 18-20 year olds residing in the intervention communities relative to the older adolescents in the control communities (Wagenaar, et al., 2000).

There are indications that CMCA may have had some influence on the service practices of restaurants, bars, and other **on premise** establishments. Supporting evidence comes from a series of marginally significant (p=.06 or .07) changes in favor of the intervention communities in terms of increased checking of identification and sales refusals for teen confederate purchase attempts at on premise sites. Marginally significant changes in favor of the intervention community were also found for self-reported alcohol use and purchase attempts among 18-20 year olds (Wagenaar, et al., 2000). CMCA's efficacy trial is particularly notable for its scale of implementation, the rigor of its randomized design, and its use of multiple measurement sources like shopping trials, registry data as well as self-reports from merchants, high school students, and older teens and young adults.

The Community Trials Intervention to Reduce High-Risk Drinking (CTI) offers another promising example of an access intervention (Grube, 1997; Holder & Reynolds, 1997; Holder, et al., 1997;

Holder, et al., 2000; Millar & Gruenewald, 1997; Reynolds, Holder, & Gruenewald, 1997; Saltz & Stanghetta, 1997). Like CMCA, the CTI was a multi-year (1991-1996) universal intervention. The CTI, unlike the CMCA, targeted both the older adult and the youth population and used a quasi-experimental design that matched three intervention and three comparison communities. This initiative took place in the American states of South Carolina and California.

The CTI's goal was to reduce alcohol-related harm at the community level by working to produce change in four overlapping intervention domains: drinking and driving behavior, beverage service-sales, youth alcohol access and use, and the geographical redistribution of alcohol outlets. Techniques aimed at changing driver behavior included the implementation of consistent and well-publicized driver sobriety checks, improved preparation for law enforcement officials, and the use of more precise alcohol detection equipment. RBS/S activities dealt with the prevention of adult drunkenness and drunk driving as well as underage alcohol sales.

The bulk of intervention actions directed towards adolescents focused on limiting access to alcohol from off premise commercial outlets. This was accomplished by creating or better enforcing laws that prohibited the sale of alcohol to minors, publicizing police and community members' efforts to increase shop owner/clerk compliance with the law, and RBS/S training for off premise shop merchants and employees. Efforts to redistribute the geographic distance between alcohol outlets were mainly focused on initiating changes in local policies regulating zoning and licensing of alcohol outlets.

The CTI's efficacy trial, like the CMCA, had nested sub-designs and included time series analysis of registry data. Random, cross-sectional surveys were conducted with managers and members of the general public in the intervention and comparison communities at time points before, during, and at the conclusion of intervention activities (e.g., 1993, 1995, 1996). Repeated, random, cross-sectional shopping trials of on- and off-premise establishments in the intervention and comparison communities also took place. Finally, public policy adoption and geographical analysis of the density of alcohol outlets and the spatial distribution of alcohol-related harm in the local community were measured.

Outcome analyses indicated an approximate 10% overall yearly reduction in alcohol-involved traffic accidents from 1993 to 1995. There was increased adoption of on-premise alcohol sales policies in the intervention versus comparison communities. Shopping trials also showed a significant overall reduction in sales to teenage confederates in the intervention versus comparison communities. No spatial changes in outlet distribution were reported.

In Europe, two Swedish access initiatives were identified. Stockholm Prevents Alcohol and Drug Problems (STAD) is a universal-selective intervention designed to work in three arenas: primary health care, beverage service-sales, and youth prevention programming (Andréasson, 2001; Andréasson, Lindewald, Rehnman, 2000). STAD's principle goal is to encourage the creation and better adherence to preventative policies across the targeted intervention domains. Intervention actions used to achieve this aim include community mobilization, policy and media advocacy, increased vendor compliance checks, licensing, and education-skills training. Because this initiative is still in the process of implementation (1995-2005), a comprehensive accounting of the intervention's impact is yet to be reported. STAD's 10 year (1995-2005) assessment period should, however, yield valuable insight into the potential of policy initiatives to ameliorate community level problems associated with substance use.

The second access intervention was entitled the Trångsund-Skogås Alcohol and Drug Prevention Program (Dalenius & Romelsjö, 2000; Mattsson & Romelsjö, 1999). This intervention offers a promising example of an access enforcement initiative. The program consisted of a series of shopping trials at off-premise commercial outlets (e.g., gas stations, grocery stores, and kiosks) paired with RBS/S training for shop merchants. The purchase attempts followed a standardized protocol in which younger-looking adolescents (the teens in fact met or were over the legal purchasing age) attempted to purchase alcohol and tobacco. After the first shopping trial, health researchers and local police went out into the community to meet with area merchants. Intervention representatives and shop owners discussed the goals of the Trångsund-Skogås program, the legal age limitations for purchasing alcohol-tobacco, and the results of the first shopping trial. Shop owners were informed of the possibility of future compliance checks. Training meetings for local merchants were also organized. The topics covered included the status of local teen drug use, the levels of commercial purchases from shopping trials, and what challenges counter personnel face in selling alcohol and tobacco. Local newspapers publicized intervention activities.

The intervention was evaluated with a quasi-experimental cohort design. Because there was only one intervention and one comparison community in the Trångsund-Skogås Program, the unit of assignment-analysis issue is not relevant here due to the nature of data. A series of shopping trials were conducted on a rolling basis over a two-year period (1998 to 2000). The Trångsund-Skogås core program components of merchant education and policy enforcement via shopping trials yielded promising results over the intervention period. The 25 shops in the intervention community evidenced significant pre (57%) to multiple post test reduction (38%, 14%, 47%, 0%, 5%) in the number of over the counter alcohol purchases made by teen confederates relative to the pre (48%) to post test changes (32%, 39%, 80%, 23%, 52%) shown in 39 comparison community shops. Tobacco sales evidenced a similar pattern of positive intervention associated change.

The CMCA, CTI, and Trångsund-Skogås Program provide a representation of access interventions that have a significant focus on programming for youth and can boast of their success under scientifically strong evaluation conditions. Other interventions that have shown promise with American youth include the Border Binge Drinking Reduction Program by Voas and colleagues (Schinke, et al., 2002) and several interventions that have dealt with commercial tobacco access (c.f., *Program Examples* – Altman, Rasenick-Douss, Foster, & Tye, 1991; Biglan, et al., 1996; Jason, Billows, Schnopp-Wyatt, & King, 1996; Jason, Ji, Anes, & Birkhead, 1991; Keay, Woodruff, Wildey, & Kenney, 1993).

Education and Skills – Recreation Centers. In neighborhoods across the world, the tradition of setting aside a building in the community where young people can come together and take part in shared activities is kept alive (c.f. Boys and Girls Clubs of America, 2000; Swedish National Board for Youth Affairs, 1997; Young Men's Christian Association, 2001). The promotion of youth development is central to the work of many time-honored facility or center-based service organizations like the Swedish Youth Clubs and Recreation Centers, European Confederation of Youth Club Organisations, Boys and Girls Clubs of America, Young Men's and Women's Christian Associations, and Girls Incorporated. Center-based programs operate from a relatively consistent location in the community, which is typically owned by the parent service organization or the local government. Relative to interventions that are not tied to an established location, like mentoring, community-based recreation centers are more likely to be staffed by paid adults rather than non-paid adult volunteers and offer more programming throughout the week (Quinn, 1999).

The extent to which center-based service organizations have subjected their youth programs to scientific scrutiny varies. An examination of the European research literature on community-based recreation centers offers very little in terms of controlled outcome evaluations. Program trials of promising American recreation center initiatives are also in short supply. Yet within the pool of available program examples, well-evaluated programs offered through recreation centers have tended to be curriculum-based, education-skills training initiatives (Quinn, 1999; Sherman, et al., 1997).

The Focus on Kids (FK; Galbraith, et al., 1996; Stanton, et al., 1996) efficacy trial demonstrates that it is possible to implement education-skills prevention programming in a community-based recreation center with some degree of success. Before FK was tested several steps were taken to place the intervention on a sound footing within the community. Meetings with local residents and participant observations helped to promote greater acceptance of FK's intervention goals. Other strategies used to make the intervention less intrusive and more user-friendly included collecting assessment data in easily accessible locations, integrating participants' culture into the program activities, and implementing intervention actions that had a chance of being carried on after the formal research project ended (Stanton, et al., 1995).

The preteens and teens who took part in FK were predominately at-risk African American youth. For the most part, program sessions took place in local recreation centers. FK is a selective intervention that has an eight-week education-skills development curriculum at its core. The content of the curriculum dealt with the promotion of social decision making skills in situations related to sexual behavior, relationships, school, theft, and drug trafficking. FK used a **snow ball technique** to recruit study participants. Youth who expressed an interest in the program were asked to invite three to ten same gender friends to also take part in FK. These friendship groups were then randomly assigned to either the intervention curriculum or a general health education course. Thus, the unit of assignment in the FK trial was the friendship groups. Youth in the control group were provided with correct health information and were then able to freely discuss these issues. Control youth did not have to attend the health education sessions with members of their friendship group.

Outcome analyses were reported with the individual as the unit of analysis. Six months after program activities ended, intervention youth who were sexually active reported improved condom use rates relative to their counterparts in the control group. The difference in favor of the intervention group was 24% (Stanton, et al., 1996). Positive outcomes were also recorded for increased intention to use condoms, favorable views on condom use, and an increased sense of personal risk for HIV infection. All intervention gains faded at the 12 month follow up assessment. Interestingly enough, youth in both conditions (i.e., FK and control) were given access to condoms during the intervention period. The curriculum therefore seemed to, at least in the short-term, help bridge the gap between having access to condoms and using them.

Other American, center-based service organizations with education-skills programs do exist. Well tested and promising program trials of such initiatives include Bicultural Competence Skills (Schinke, Botvin, Trimble, Orlandi, Gilchrist, & Locklear, 1988) and Boys and Girls Clubs of America's SMART Program Series (Schinke, Orlandi, & Cole, 1992; St. Pierre, Kaltreider, Mark, & Aikin, 1992; St. Pierre, Mark, Kaltreider, & Aikin, 1997; St. Pierre, Mark, Kaltreider, & Campbell, 2001).

Education and Skills – Clinics and Schools. Promising community-based clinic and school-linked clinic initiatives can be found in the American research literature (c.f. *Community Program Examples –* Metzler, Biglan, Noell, Ary, & Ochs, 2000; St. Lawrence, et al., 1995 – *School-Linked Program Examples –* Koo, et al., 1994; Zabin, 1992). The cross-context, school-linked approach (school + community clinic) has not been frequently tested but the trials that do exist demonstrate that it is possible to improve outreach and modify school- or community-wide outcome indicators. The Baltimore Pregnancy Prevention Program, also known as the Self Center, gives us a promising program illustration (Zabin, 1992; Zabin, et al., 1988). This selective intervention provided reproductive services, education, and counseling in secondary schools and a nearby clinic. Program participants were African American adolescents who experienced social and economic disadvantage. Students were given information about the intervention project and services offered at school and in the clinic. Interaction between program staff and teens was of a voluntary nature, with youth seeking out services and activities. Intervention actions taking place in the schools largely consisted of information- giving talks, small group discussions among students and intervention workers, the provision of counseling services, and the training of teen intervention workers.

The teen clinic provided activities during and after school. Clinic-based actions dealt with further reproductive education, counseling, referral services, and medical service provision related to reproductive health including the distribution of contraceptives. Strategies used to initiate information sharing and discussion included games, videos, and written materials. Targets for change were decision making and goal setting, personal responsibility, and the analysis and reconsideration of existing beliefs regarding relationships, emotions, substance use, school attitudes, teen parenting, and different aspects of reproductive health including sexual behavior and contraceptive use.

The intervention was tested with a quasi-experimental, cross sectional-cohort design. Anonymous cross sectional pre- and post-testing took place over a three-year intervention period. Students within two intervention and two comparison schools took part in the trial. Youth taking part in the pre- and post-testing did not have to necessarily make use of clinic services to be included in the outcome evaluation, therefore, the target of intervention and unit of assignment was the whole school. Results have been reported with the school and the years of program exposure and grade level as the units of analysis (Zabin, 1992). Among intervention and comparison schools, a 30% pre- to post-test decline in pregnancy rates was found for females attending the intervention schools relative to a 58% increase among female students in the comparison schools. Program associated benefits were also found for later median onset of first sexual intercourse and contraceptive use among females with two or more years of program exposure (Zabin, 1992).

Another promising intervention was the School-Community Program for Sexual Risk Reduction among Teens (S/CP; Koo, Dunteman, George, Green, & Vincent, 1994; Vincent, Clearie, & Schluchter, 1987). As in the Self Center initiative, young people taking part in the S/CP trial were predominately at-risk, African-American adolescents. In both of these multi-year, selective interventions, students were provided with comprehensive sex-contraceptive education and, at least in the initial years of the S/CP intervention, access to contraception in school and through a nearby community-based clinic. S/CP differed from the Self Center initiative in that it utilized media advocacy, offered graduate-level, sex education courses to teachers, and educational outreach to concerned adults in the community like decision makers, parents, and religious leaders. Another notable difference is that the Self Center was tested in an urban setting, while S/CP was conducted in a rural part of the United States.

The outcome study conducted by Koo, et al., (1994) provides the strongest evaluation of the intervention to date. In this quasi-experimental, outcome evaluation, the S/CP community was compared to three close by and three distant comparison communities. Time series analysis of community-wide pregnancy rates among 14-17 year olds during the pre-intervention (1981-1982) and initial intervention (1984-1986) period indicated a significant decline in annual teen pregnancy rates in the S/CP community (from 77 to 37 pregnancies per 1,000 women between the ages of 14-17) relative to one adjacent (from 84 to 82 per 1,000) and three distant comparison communities (from 74 to 75; 75 to 82; 79 to 72 per 1,000 respectively). During the later intervention period (1987-1988), the S/CP community's pregnancy rates came close to returning back to pre intervention levels (66 per 1,000). The increase in the pregnancy rate of the S/CP community in the later program period was attributed to political controversy and state legislation towards the end of the early program period that first required parental consent to receive contraceptives and then made it illegal for a school-linked clinic to provide youth with contraception. Other challenges encountered towards the end of the initial and through later intervention periods included program staff-teacher turnover and struggles to keep the multi-year intervention message novel.

Community-based and school-linked clinic efforts are readily found in several European countries. Yet, controlled evaluations of these types of initiatives are rare. The Swedish Youth Health Centers (SYHC) offers an illustration. The SYHC have an extensive track record of delivering education-skills components along with teen medical services in schools and through community-based health clinics. Unlike American program examples, the SYHC have relatively stable financial and political support that allows adolescents and young adults to reliably access services[3]. However, no center has yet undergone a controlled evaluation (Jarlbo, 1998:17; Socialstyrelsen, 1996: 7; Swedish Society for Youth Centers, 1994; 1997).

Education and Skills – Schools and Community Activities. Another important program variation consists of cross-context interventions that pair school-based knowledge and skills development with a variety of community wide intervention efforts. The Minnesota Heart Health Program (MHHP) provides an example of just such a promising initiative (Kelder, Perry, & Klepp, 1993; Kelder, Perry, Lytle, & Klepp, 1995; Luepker & Perry, 1991; Nothwehr, Lando, & Bobo, 1995; Perry, Kelder, Murray, & Klepp, 1992; Perry, Klepp, & Sillers, 1989; Prokhorov, Perry, Kelder, & Klepp, 1993). The MHHP was a universal prevention program conducted in North Dakota and Minnesota across a ten year period (1980-1990). Community-wide activities included the dissemination of educational messages through mass media techniques, promotion of nutritional food labeling, easier access to cardiovascular disease screening, and smoking cessation contests. Embedded within this larger effort was a youth specific component entitled the Class of 1989 Study. The youth component lasted for six years (1983-1989) and was intended to serve as a complement to the more adult oriented community activities. The core of the youth component was a teacher- and peer-led education and skills development program that took place within area schools. The Class of 1989 study was evaluated with a quasi-experimental, cohort design. The unit of assignment was the community. Outcome evaluations of the MHHP's youth component typically describe what happened in one intervention versus one comparison community. Thus, the unit of assignment-analysis issue is a mute point because of the characteristics of reported data.

The intervention condition in the Class of 1989 study consisted of a group of students living in the MHHP's intervention community who participated in the Class of 1989 program activities (i.e., the school-based curriculum). A group of students living in the MHHP's comparison community served as the reference condition. By the study's end, weekly smoking rates for youth in the intervention community were significantly lower than youngsters residing in the comparison community. There were positive results for a number of health behaviors, with reduced smoking being the principal enduring intervention associated improvement for youth problem behaviors[4].

A similar intervention to the MHHP was the Finnish North Karelia Project (NKP) (Puska & Uutela, 2001; Puska, Vartiainen, Pallonen, & et al., 1982; Vartiainen, Paavola, McAlister, & Puska, 1998; Vartiainen, Pallonen, McAlister, Koskela, & Puska, 1986; Vartiainen, Pallonen, McAlister, & Puska, 1990). Like the MHHP, NKP was a universal intervention aimed at preventing cardiovascular disease. NKP was conducted in eastern Finland for several years with youth activities taking place over a two year period (1978-1980). As in MHHP, NKP utilized media campaigns and cessation contests aimed at adults and tested the utility of a school-based education and skills curriculum. NKP's school curriculum placed a particular focus on tobacco prevention via social resistance skills training and education on the dangers of smoking. NKP departs from the Class of 1989 study in that NKP tested the utility of using health educators and peer leaders to administer the program contrasted against implementation by teachers.

In the NKP, communities and their respective schools elected to participate in the intervention (n=4) or serve as a comparison (n=2). Similar to the MHHP, NKP's main result for youth problem behaviors was a decrease in tobacco smoking. Unlike MHHP, NKP was able to follow up on 71% of the original sample of young study participants up to 13 years after youth program activities came to an end (up to the age of 27 to 30). Early findings showed short-term intervention related benefits for baseline tobacco users and non-users alike. More specifically, youth self-reports of tobacco smoking significantly declined in the intervention condition at post-testing and at the two-year, post-intervention follow-up. This decrease is relative to the self-reports of comparison youth. At later follow-ups, the outcome results differed depending on who administered the program (adult health educator + peer versus teacher implementation). At the six-year follow-up, for example, significant decreases in smoking were found only for the teacher-administered version of the intervention. At the 13-year follow-up,[5] NKP's overall pattern of findings showed enduring benefits on measures of tobacco smoking. NKP's long-term results are particularly notable given the only two years of youth program activities.

As in the MHHP and NKP, other promising American interventions have utilized a school-based, anti-drug, education-skills curriculum as well as a community intervention format (e. g., *Midwestern Prevention Project* [6] – Johnson, et al., 1990; Pentz, et al., 1989; 1990; *Project Northland* – Perry, et al., 1993; 2000; *University of Vermont Study* – Flynn, et al., 1997; Worden, Flynn, Solomon, & Secker-Walker, 1996). All of the aforementioned interventions do however differ in terms of what is done in the community and who is targeted, with the MHHP and NKP seeking to effect change in both adult and youth behavior and the University of Vermont Study, Midwestern Prevention Project, and Project Northland working primarily to alter youth behavior.

Community Service plus Education-Skills. The research literature on community service is largely derived from program trials conducted in the United States. The Teen Outreach Program (TOP) offers an illustration of a promising cross-context intervention that combines community service with a classroom-based curriculum that corresponds to the youngsters' service learning experience <u>and</u> has an emphasis on life competence promotion. TOP is a universal intervention that is usually implemented over the course of one school year. Adolescents take part in at least 20 hours per year of community work and participate in weekly, teacher-implemented classroom meetings. TOP's history dates back to its inception in 1978 and has been implemented in Canada with national dissemination taking place in the United States.

While TOP has undergone testing in the past (Allen, Kuperminc, Philliber, & Herre, 1994; Allen, Philliber, & Hoggson, 1990), the strongest program evaluation was conducted with a subsample of 695 teens who were randomly assigned to condition (Allen, Philliber, Herrling, & Kuperminc, 1997). These youngsters were predominately African-American females who had an average age of 16. After statistically controlling for extraneous factors, intervention youth evidenced pre- to post-test declines in self-reported course failure, misbehavior in school, and teenage pregnancy relative to the control group. Results from previous program evaluations (e.g., Allen, et al., 1990; 1994) lend support to the pattern of findings found in this more rigorous test of the intervention (Allen, et al., 1997).

Other promising American program examples with a community service plus education-skills emphasis include the Reach for Health Community Youth Service Program (O'Donnell, et al., 1999) and the Quantum Opportunities Program (Lattimore, Mihalic, Grotpeter, & Taggart, 1998). See Schinke and colleagues (2002) for additional relevant program examples.

Mentoring plus Education-Skills. The majority of well tested, community-based mentoring programs are also American in origination (Sherman, et al., 1997; Tierney & Grossman, 2000). Across Ages (AA; LoSciuto, et al., 1996; Taylor, et al., 1999) offers a particularly interesting program illustration because its efficacy trial tested the relative contribution of mentoring to a multi-component intervention package. AA was a selective, cross-context intervention that provided at-risk youth with adult mentors, opportunities to participate in community service that benefited older adults, and teacher-administered, life-skills training in the classroom. Adult mentors were unpaid volunteers over the age of 55 years old. Mentors went through a standardized selection, training, and supervision process. Mentors had contact with one to two youth on a weekly basis over the course of a year.

Mentor–teen activities included academic and school oriented tasks and events, time spent engaged in leisure activities and community work with elderly adults. Classroom, life- competence promotion activities allowed youth to discuss their impressions of their service experiences and to develop life skills in the following domains: Coping, self-confidence, problem solving and decision making, health and drug knowledge, and relationships. Decision making in situations where substance use is likely was emphasized. Parent training and the encouragement of greater parental involvement was promoted through weekend activities for teens, parents, and mentors.

AA program activities take place over the course of one year. AA was evaluated by collecting pre and post test data on successive cohorts of sixth graders. Over a five-year period (1991-1996), the sixth grade classrooms of three middle schools were randomly assigned to one of the three conditions: Full intervention, intervention without the mentoring component, or a control group. Relative to the control condition, youth who experienced the full intervention FI showed improvement in terms of their views of school, the future, adults, the elderly, and community service as well as their knowledge of adults and decision making in drug use situations. The intervention minus mentoring (I-M) condition also evidenced improved knowledge of older people relative to the control condition.

Analyses that tested the contribution of the mentoring component showed that adolescents in the FI evidenced improvement in terms of their views on adults, school and the future in comparison to youth that received the intervention but did not have a mentor (I-M). A marginally significant (p=.056) result was found in favor of the FI on the frequency of substance use relative to the I-M. Researchers noted the possibility of a floor effect for substance use among intervention and control youth, suggesting that there was little room for improvement on this index at post testing. Overall, teens who received the complete intervention including mentoring had better results than the other two groups (C and M-I). This effect was also shown for registry reports of school absences.

Other promising American multi-component intervention packages that combine mentoring, education-skills, community service, or recreational activities include CASASTART (Center for the Study and Prevention of Violence, 2000, June, 6) and the Woodrock Youth Development Project (LoSciuto, Freeman, Harrington, Altman, & Lanphear, 1997; LoSciuto, Hilbert, Fox, Porcellini, & Lanphear, 1999). A review of programs by Schinke and colleagues (2002) offers descriptions of additional successful program examples in this area.

Recreational Activities plus Education-Skills. Recreational activities are a largely taken for granted part of many youngsters' lives (Bloom, 2000). Despite its commonplace standing in many countries, controlled evaluations of the recreation oriented interventions have just begun to accumulate (e.g., Quinn, 1999; Wilson & Lipsey, 2000b). The Woodrock Youth Development Project (W-YDP), for example, was tested as a selective, cross-context intervention with at-risk, ethnic, minority children and adolescents. Project development began in 1991 with subsequent testing taking place in the American, east-coast city of Philadelphia. W-YDP utilized a weekly classroom-based knowledge and life-skills development course. Great attention was directed at correcting youngsters' misperceptions about the prevalence of youth substance use, encouraging ethnic identity exploration, and promoting a value on cultural understanding. Family-directed intervention actions consisted of monthly parent skills training and home visitation. School representatives and parents took part in some anti-drug mobilization efforts. W-YDP's opportunity intervention components consisted of academic tutoring and mentoring by peers, after school activity clubs, and weekend outdoor retreats (LoSciuto, et al., 1997).

The most comprehensive program evaluation of the W-YDP drew data from two randomly assigned cohorts of youth who participated in W-YDP during the 1995 and 1996 school years (LoSciuto, et al., 1999). Pre- to post-tests showed that those youth who took part in intervention activities evidenced lower, self-reported substance use relative to youth in control classrooms. Significant intervention related improvements were also found for cultural competence-tolerance and school attendance.

An efficacy trial from Poland offers a promising European illustration of a community-based, recreation-oriented intervention package (Moskalewicz, et al., 1999). The Prevention and Management of Drug Abuse in Poland initiative took a multiple-pronged approach with intervention activities aimed at the general population, high-risk adult groups, and youth. Initiative components consisted of a community-wide, anti-drug promotional campaign, efforts to improve access to parent training-counseling and adult drug treatment services as well as the education of teachers, journalists, community leaders, and teens in drug prevention and treatment strategies.

The main youth component of this intervention was entitled Odlot. Local youth took part in a competition to name the program. The title decided upon, Odlot translates into English as 'take off'. The use of this term represents a challenge to the idea that substance use was the best way to attain joy and lead a complete life. A central theme of Odlot was that a healthy lifestyle allows one to achieve these goals. Odlot's main action was to provide funds and organizational support to existing youth leisure associations. Associations that were defunct due to a lack of funds were reopened and new associations were created on the basis of local demands. Seventy part-time activity leaders were employed. Leaders were encouraged to redesign activities to accommodate a larger more diverse group of youth. Associations offered activities in schools and in the community for extended hours, over holidays, and were promoted through a series of events.

The evaluation of Odlot, examined the impact of the intervention on adolescents residing in two intervention and one comparison community over the course of a year. Odlot was tested with a quasi-experimental, cohort design. Evaluators reported the outcome results for each intervention community versus the comparison community. In this case the unit of assignment and analysis matched, but statistical tests on the relative comparability of the intervention and comparison communities were not reported in the English language description of Odlot's efficacy trial (Moskalewicz, et al., 1999).

In the community versus community analyses, youth living in the first intervention community reported a significant pre to post test increase in prosocial home activities (e.g., doing homework, helping parents) relative to a decrease in comparison youth. Intervention youth within this community also reported a significant increase in one-year abstinence from all drugs in comparison to a decrease in the number of teen abstainers living in the reference community. The only significant results in the second intervention community came in the form of registry data. Such information was not available in the first intervention community. At the height of Odlot's implementation, the number of juvenile crimes and the number of youngsters using **sobering up stations** in the comparison community was twice that of the intervention community. Sub-group analyses examining the impact of the intervention on two age groups (14-15 year olds; 17-18 year olds) indicated that both groups surveyed in the two intervention communities showed improvement in the quality of how they spent their free time at home and evidenced stability or a decline in alcohol or sedative use relative to increases among comparably aged youth living in the reference community (Moskalewicz, et al., 1999).

There are other controlled trials of European programs within this category of intervention. One intervention yielded mixed results (e.g., *Community-Based Addiction Prevention Project* – Centre de Prévention des Toxicomanies, 1999) and two other trials were in the process of being tested at the time this review was written *(*e.g., *Evaluation of Stockholm Alcohol Prevention Program* – Romelsjö, 1998; Romelsjö & Haeggman, 2000; *Örebro Prevention Project* – Koutakis, Ferrer-Wreder, & Stattin, 2001; Stattin, 2000). For other American program examples, Project Northland and Creating Lasting Connections Program are promising interventions with a substantial emphasis on education-skills promotion and recreation (Johnson, et al., 1996; Perry et al., 1993; 2000). We will come back to Project Northland in greater detail in the *Questions* subsection. Other salient examples with recreational and education-skills program elements can be found in Schinke and colleagues (2002).

Synthesis

Later Community Intervention

Later community interventions have shown varying levels of accomplishment in promoting youth development and preventing problem behaviors. Universal and selective intervention initiatives are most common in this literature. These programs span the child and adolescent periods. The existence of quality programs for older youth is encouraging, but makes stark the need to develop community interventions that have relevance to young children and infants (Berlin, et al., 2001). By examining later community and cross-context interventions, we can see that the most successful programs creatively bring together a diverse yet complementary set of intervention actions to bear on the problems of youngsters and the communities in which they live. Considering the wide range of potentially useful interventions, a best evidence synthesis of individual program variations are presented below.

Access Interventions. To date, the most successful policy initiatives and access interventions have worked at the universal level and initiated several of the following actions in the community: 1) increased taxation of alcohol and tobacco products, 2) enacting and enforcing laws that make government officials and community residents more accountable for underage drinking-smoking, 3) raising awareness and creating a public mandate to reduce youth alcohol-tobacco access, 4) licensing of alcohol-tobacco vendors, 5) strengthening policy adherence through RBS/S training and compliance checks that result in social and material reinforcements-penalties for alcohol-tobacco vendors, and 6) mobilizing community residents to create, take part, and support intervention activities (c.f., *Program Examples* – Altman, Rasenick-Douss, Forster, & Tye, 1991; Biglan, et al., 1996; Dalenius & Romelsjö, 2000; Holder, 2000; Jason, Billows, Schnopp-Wyatt, & King, 1996;

Mattsson & Romelsjö, 1999; Wagenaar, et al., 1999; 2000 – *Relevant Narrative Reviews* –Biglan & Taylor, 2000; Flay, 2000; Holder, 2001; Pentz, 2000; U.S. Department of Health and Human Services, 1992). With the general lack of component analysis studies, it seems premature to draw conclusions about the relative value of these individual intervention actions [See Holder and Treno (1997) and Grube (1997) for a notable exception to this statement].

Under what conditions have access intervention packages shown promise? As a group, these programs have been most successful with adolescents and adults. The lack of success with children may stem from these youngsters' greater reliance on social connections to gain access to alcohol-tobacco. Social relationships still are the primary channel through which drugs become accessible to children and adolescents. In order to be truly successful, future interventions must develop strategies that target both social and commercial access (Forster, et al., 1997; Wagenaar, et al., 1996).

The potential long-term promise of access initiatives is still in question. Even among the more successful and rigorously tested access interventions, there has been little systematic follow up of what happened in the intervention communities after post testing. The follow up evidence that does exist indicates that in the absence of regular enforcement, underage sales are likely to return to pre-intervention levels (e.g., Altman, et al., 1991). One program trial suggested that a compliance check once every two or at least four months provides the best insurance that declines in illegal sales will remain low (Jason, et al., 1996). The available evidence does support the idea that informed and enforced policy does yield immediate benefits, but at present there is little evidence to support the long-term utility of this approach.

It should also be noted that access interventions have as a group been most successful in reducing underage alcohol-tobacco sales. However, questions have been raised about the extent to which a reduction in overall sales equals changes in actual consumption. Access interventions evaluated with multiple measurements do find marginally significant or significant changes in underage sales as well as youth consumption rates or indices of harm (e.g., Wagenaar, et al., 2000; Wagenaar, Murray, & Toomey, 2000). To improve the effects and measurement of access interventions, target groups and environments should be more precisely specified, measurement should be wider, and statistical analyses should be employed that link intervention change to outcome change (i.e., mediation models).

On the question of spreading versus specific effects, access interventions have shown promise in addressing both the youth alcohol and tobacco problem as well as altering the service and sales practices of both on- and off-premise outlets. Because the commercial distribution systems of hard and soft drugs differ, it is an empirical question as to whether commercial access restriction techniques have any direct relevance in fight against the illicit drug trade. Better methods for dealing with social access may go a long way in informing future work in the drug prevention field.

In terms of violence prevention, extensions of access intervention principles in the form of gun, buy-back programs and firearm regulations have met with little empirical success in the United States (Hawkins, et al., 1997; Sherman, et al., 1997). Problems applying access strategies to the problem of community violence may originate from social controversies surrounding violence. Biglan and Taylor (2000) have presented a thought-provoking commentary that contrasts the success tobacco control against the sluggish progress made in the field of community violence prevention in America. According to these authors, tobacco control has been successful and violence prevention has not because there is: 1) agreement on the causes and consequences of tobacco use, 2) agreement about the useful policies and intervention strategies, and 3) support from powerful and stable social organizations that communicate a simple yet evidence-based account of the problem and the best course of action to the general public and policy makers. Biglan and Taylor (2000) went on to argue that the requisite scientific evidence on violence exists and it is up to preventionists to put a clear case together and start promoting this message widely. Policy is at the heart of access interventions. A public policy represents a community's stand on a particular issue and a group commitment to action (Holder, 2001; Pentz, 2000). Thus, it seems that access intervention strategies may have import to violence prevention but while social division is pervasive, it maybe difficult to apply interventions that are highly dependent on public consensus to the contentious problem of community violence.

Education and Skills – Recreation Centers. Community-based recreation centers are well positioned as a potential launching point for promotion and prevention efforts in the community (Quinn, 1999). Youth service organizations continue to show considerable staying power as valued community resources that have remarkable outreach. Consider these statistics:

- European Confederation Youth Clubs consist of approximately 18,000 centers serving 3.5 million youth throughout Europe (European Confederation of Youth Club Organisations, 2003, February, 7).

- Boys and Girls Clubs of America have 2,851 locations offering programs to 3.3 million boys and girls across the United States and its administrative regions (Boys and Girls Clubs of America, 2000).

Not all recreation centers are the same, with marked variation possible on factors like the: nature of activities provided, environmental characteristics present, quality of adult leadership, amount of community support, and risk experienced by participating youth. There is little scientific evidence about the constituent elements of a successful recreation center (Quinn, 1999). The extent to which these centers promote or endanger youth development remains a largely untested empirical question (Sherman, et al., 1997). [See a prospective longitudinal study in Mahoney and Stattin (2000) and Mahoney, Stattin, and Magnusson (in press) for notable exception to this statement].

A few empirically sound trials of recreation center-based, education-skills promotion programs exist (c.f., *Program Examples* – Nicholson & Postrado, 1992; Schinke et al., 1988; 1992; Stanton, et al., 1995; St. Pierre, Kaltreider, Mark, & Aikin, 1992; St. Pierre, Mark, Kaltreider, & Aikin, 1997; St. Pierre, Mark, Kaltreider, & Campbell, 2001 – *Relevant Narrative Reviews* – Quinn, 1999; Sherman, et al., 1997). On the whole, these initiatives have shown short-term benefits in terms of encouraging safer sexual practices, reducing substance use, and changing related variables for the better. These programs span the late childhood and adolescent periods and have been found to work with American youth that experience moderate risk. Based on this preliminary evidence, it can be argued that evidence-based, youth development and prevention programs may have a role to play in the everyday activities of community-based recreation centers and warrant further investigation.

Education and Skills – Clinics and Schools. In contrast to community-based recreation centers, there is a sizeable research literature on the utility of community-based clinic programs for youth. In the United States, these programs most often work with adolescents who experience moderate to elevated risk. Similar European initiatives concentrate on teens whose risk level falls in the universal prevention to treatment range (Swedish Society for Youth Centers, 1994; 1997). Community-based clinics are useful venues for education and skills training (Nitz, 1999; Seitz, 1996). A meta-analysis of 32 North American program evaluations (Corcoran, Miller, & Bultman, 1997), for example, showed that community-based clinics were significantly associated with increased adolescent contraceptive use (ES=.6062) and decreased adolescent pregnancy rates (ES=.2753). The provision of education about contraception and access to contraceptives also were significantly linked to sought-after changes in these areas. These impacts were of greater magnitude for community-based programs than for school-based programs, and larger for programs based in clinics rather than other settings. This advantage for community-based and/or clinic based programs maybe related to the greater likelihood that such sites would provide youth with access to contraception.

This meta-analysis by Corcoran and colleagues (1997) also concluded that the prevention programs examined had little overall impact on the amount of participants' sexual activity. That is, as narrative reviews in this field concur, accurate and explicit contraceptive- and sex-education is not linked to increases in sexual activity. Further, program success is thought to be associated with time-intensive programs that emphasize decision-making, problem solving, and resistance skills in general.

Further, in specific situations where sexual behavior is salient, the acknowledgement of the impact of social influences on adolescent sexual behavior is important. Finally, these successful programs are implemented by well-trained and committed health specialists (c.f. *Relevant Narrative Reviews* – Kirby, 1997; Miller & Paikoff, 1992).

A community-based clinic is one of the places where a young person is likely to gain access to high-quality, education-skills training and services, but getting youth to come in and utilize the clinic remains a challenge (Nitz, 1999). In an effort to improve outreach, clinics have been relocated into schools and comprehensive prevention programming has been extended back and forth between schools and community-based clinics (e.g., Fischer, 1997; Kirby & Waszak, 1992; Koo, et al., 1994; Zabin, 1992). Program trials of school-linked clinics are important to highlight because these multi-front interventions have demonstrated an ability to yield pre- to immediate post-test change on population level indices of adolescent sexual behavior and childbearing (c. f. *Program Examples* – Koo, et al., 1994; Vincent, et al., 1987; Zabin, 1992).

Yet, long-term promise of these interventions remains largely untested. As in the field of violence prevention, it can be argued that widespread public disagreement about adolescent sexual behavior complicates American intervention work in this area. European school-linked efforts like the Swedish Youth Health Centers are informative given that these centers have several decades of consistent program delivery and function in a climate where there is greater social unanimity on what constitutes appropriate teenage sexual behavior (Seitz, 1996). Moreover, Sweden ranks consistently low in comparisons of adolescent birth rates among industrialized countries (Nitz, 1999). Direct evaluations of the Swedish Youth Health Centers and other European initiatives could substantially further knowledge development in area of teenage pregnancy prevention and add to the social debate on adolescent sexual behavior.

Education and Skills – Schools and Community Activities Promising and well established, cross-context, education-skills intervention packages have combined several of program components. These include: 1) school-based drug prevention activities that emphasize accurate drug information and opportunities for life-resistance skills training; 2) campaigns with savvy packaging that are communicated through multiple media; 3) media messages that are targeted, create alternatives in the minds of the audience, and promote skills development; and 4) cardiovascular disease prevention activities in the community at large (c.f., *Program Examples* – Flynn, et al., 1997; Pentz, et al., 1989; 1990; Perry, et al., 1989; 1992; Puska, et al., 1982; Vartiainen, et al., 1990; 1998; Worden, et al., 1996 – *Relevant Narrative Reviews* – Durlak, 1997; Flay, 2000; Hawkins, et al., 1997; Weissberg & Greenberg, 1998; Worden, 1999).

As Flay (2000) stated, conclusions about the relative utility of individual actions with these program packages are not possible due to a lack of component analysis. From the available studies, we have strong reason to believe that a well formulated media component can substantially add to the overall utility of a school-based drug prevention curriculum (Hawkins, et al., 1997; Worden, 1999). Conversely, the combination of a non-program linked media campaign and mobilization activities is not as useful as a full intervention package with media, mobilization, and school- and home-based programming (e.g., Pentz, et al., 1989; 1990). Based on the model programs highlighted and other salient reviews of the literature, it can be concluded that a media campaign that does not link to other evidence-based intervention activities has little chance of producing meaningful change in drug taking behavior (Flay, 2000; Hawkins, et al., 1997; Worden, 1999). Likewise, community mobilization will yield few meaningful benefits if this action only serves as an occasion for public saber rattling and does not function as a platform for evidence-based intervention action (Hawkins, et al., 1997; Treno & Holder, 1997).

Cross-context, education-skills programs have demonstrated short- and long-term effects on indices of substance use among older children and teens, with two interventions showing enduring program related effects over time (*Program Examples* – Flynn, et al., 1997; Puska, et al., 1982; Vartiainen, et al., 1990; 1998; Worden, et al., 1996). In terms of spreading versus specific effects, these interventions have generally been most successful in reducing tobacco use with one program evidencing benefits for a wide range of drugs (*Program Example* – Pentz, et al., 1989; 1990). For the most part, these interventions have been multi-year universal initiatives in which whole communities or only young people in a given community are targeted for intervention. Contrary to the universal access interventions described earlier, the design of choice here has largely been a cohort design.

Community Service plus Education-Skills. From American, cross-sectional and longitudinal research on youth activism, we know that adolescents who get involved in community service differ from those that do not, in terms of their engagement in deviant behavior and later participation in voluntary social organizations (Youniss, et al., 1999; Youniss & Yates, 1999).Community service is an increasingly common experience for many American teens (Youniss & Yates, 1997). The extent to which this type of intervention would benefit youth outside of the United States remains to be seen. The few well tested, controlled trials of community service and school-based, education-skills training in America have been primarily tested as a universal or selective intervention for adolescents. As a group these interventions have yielded immediate and significant reductions in school misbehavior, violent and risky sexual behavior, and early childbearing as well as improvements in academic performance and educational attainment (c.f., *Program Examples* – Allen, Kuperminc, Philliber, & Herre, 1994; Allen, Philliber, & Hoggson, 1990; Allen, Philliber, Herrling, & Kuperminc, 1997; Lattimore, Mihalic, Grotpeter, & Taggart, 1998; O'Donnell, et al., 1999). The available studies also indicate that teens with a more intensive community service experience seem to reap greater benefits from program participation (e.g., Allen, Philliber, Herrling, & Kuperminc, 1997; O'Donnell, et al., 1999). While one program example has shown evidence of post-intervention benefits (*Program Example* – Lattimore, et al., 1998), the long-term effects of such interventions remains, for the most part, an empirical question. In the final analysis, community service plus education-skills is a small but arguably up-and-coming part of the evidence-based intervention literature that should be studied in greater detail.

Mentoring plus Education-Skills. Mentoring represents another up-and-coming program variation. While mentoring is a time honored tradition in many countries, empirically sound evaluation has not, until recently, played a substantial role in the development of mentoring programs. Program trials with a significant mentoring component have for the most part been tested as selective interventions for American children and adolescents (Tierney & Grossman, 2000; Sherman, et al., 1997). Mentoring has shown promise as a single program element (e.g., Tierney et al., 1995) and also when it is paired with academic enrichment activities (Tierney & Grossman, 2000). The Big Brothers and Big Sisters (BBBS) intervention trial in particular demonstrated that youth service organizations can validate their methods and gain substantial insight through rigorous program evaluation. In a randomized, wait-list control trial that lasted for an 18-month period, at-risk older children and early adolescents who took part in a mentoring relationship showed a greater delay in the onset of substance use, less truancy, and fewer reports of hitting others (Tierney, Grossman, & Resch, 1995).

Further, mentoring as one aspect of a multi-component and context intervention has also shown promise (c.f., *Program Examples* – LoSciuto, et al., 1996; Taylor, et al., 1999; Center for the Study and Prevention of Violence, 2000, June, 6; LoSciuto, et al., 1997; LoSciuto, et al., 1999 – *Relevant Narrative Review* – Catalano, et al., 1999). Only a handful of well evaluated studies exist, but they are noteworthy. These studies add to what is known about mentoring and indicate that mentoring benefits at-risk preteens and teens by yielding immediate reductions in substance use and delinquent behavior. The long-term effects of mentoring alone, and mentoring as it is found in a multi-component intervention package, remains largely untested in the contemporary research literature (Sherman, et al., 1997).

Based on the available research, can we glean a preliminary idea about what constitutes high quality mentoring? Interventions with a significant mentoring component have been evaluated. As a group, these interventions have not always shown the same level of promise as BBBS (Sherman, et al., 1997) or recent multi-component mentoring programs like the Across Ages. BBBS's program success has been attributed to the organization's decades of program delivery experience, the considerable amount of time mentors and youth spend together, and BBBS's comprehensive screening, training, and supervision process for mentors

(Sherman, et al., 1997; Tierney & Grossman, 2000). Like BBBS, programs like Across Ages puts considerable effort into the selection and supervision of mentors and allows sufficient time for youth and mentors to establish a meaningful relationship. While mentoring can not be billed as a panacea just yet, well formulated and supervised mentoring does seem to benefit youth, and even perhaps mentors, and certainly deserves greater investigation in the future as a single intervention strategy and as a part of multi-component program packages (Philip & Hendry, 2000; Sherman, et al., 1997; Tierney & Grossman, 2000).

Recreational Activities plus Education-Skills. Recreational settings can serve as a promising venue to launch an intervention initiative or recreation in and of itself may serve as a form of intervention (Gullotta & Plant, 2000; Petitpas & Champagne, 2000; Vries, 2001). Not all types of recreation are equal, with considerable variation possible in terms of the nature of the activity, level of adult guidance, and risk levels of participating youth. Recreation is often lacking in troubled communities and the opportunity to test one's limits in a prosocial non school activity may have particular salience for youth who do not have ready access to recreation due to economic disadvantage or social-political change (Fukuzawa, 2000; Moskalewicz, et al., 1999; Sherman, et al., 1997).

The promotion and prevention research literature as it relates to recreation is scattered, with a study here showing that recreation can work well as a single program element (e.g., Jones & Offord, 1989); a meta-analysis there indicating that intensive outdoor challenge programs help troubled youth stay out of custody (Wilson & Lipsey, 2000b); and yet still another set of intervention trials showing that recreation plays an unknown part in promising multi-component program packages (e.g., Johnson, et al., 1996; LoSciuto, et al., 1997; 1999; Perry et al., 1993; 2000). If one seeks to make a patchwork quilt out of these findings, a few plausible conclusions become evident. The promising interventions that have made use of recreation, as a group, tend to yield immediate benefits on indices of adolescent substance use and delinquency (c. f. *Program Examples* – LoSciuto, et al., 1999; Moskalewicz, et al., 1999; Perry et al., 2000 – *Relevant Meta-Analysis* – Wilson & Lipsey, 2000b). Long-term effects are yet to be established. Recreation oriented initiatives have been implemented as universal, selective, and indicated programs with preteens and teens. The available evidence also indicates that intensive recreational activities seem to yield greater benefits (Komro, et al., 1996; Wilson & Lipsey, 2000b).

The majority of a teen's waking life is occupied with leisure activities (Csikszentmihalyi, et al., 1993/1997). Young people can choose to spend this time in a number of ways. This time can give indications of the young person's personal interests, competencies, and affiliations with various types of peers and adults. This is a particularly important field of inquiry that certainly merits further study, especially in terms of its implications for youth development and prevention programs.

Questions

Coming to Terms with the Community

How is the word community used in the prevention and promotion literature? In practice, the term has many meanings (Allamani, 1997; Barry, 1994; Berlin, et al., 2001; Limber & Nation, 1998). Communities can be defined on the basis of sharing a particular objectively defined administrative region such as a city, a county, or voting district. Government demarcations are important because they reflect political or economic realities, but there is also our subjective experience of where we live to consider. As a result, researchers and government officials have been known to ask residents to define for themselves the boundaries of their own community or neighborhood (e.g., Nash & Bowen, 1999; Shumow, Vandell, & Posner, 1998).

Every ten years, for example, the U.S. Census Bureau is responsible for a demographic and economic survey of the United States. Since 1998, community resident boards have assisted in the drawing of census tracts through the U.S. Census Bureau's Participant Statistical Areas Program. In most areas, census tracts have a range of 1,500 to 8,000 inhabitants and are further delineated by existing official boundaries or physical landmarks like roads or electrical lines. Once defined, the census tracts are then surveyed and this forms of the basis of the national census (U.S. Census Bureau, 2001a). American researchers sometimes use census tracts to define neighborhoods because it signifies an approximation of local residents' subjective perception of where they live and also provides demographic and economic information about the people living within the tract. The census does not, however, use the term community as an official geographic entity. Larger geographic areas used in the census such as a city and its boroughs, a county, or a state are defined mainly through preexisting administrative borders (U.S. Census Bureau, 2001b).

Other criteria used to define communities or neighborhoods rest on notions of relative size or resident cohesion. Neighborhoods can be defined as a smaller and unique subsection of a larger community or as in the American literature, is specifically identified as a particular census tract. Neighborhoods tend to reflect a more circumscribed geographic space, with a tight knit sense of cohesion among neighbors. Garbarino, Kostelny, and Barry (1998) stated that the word neighborhood can be associated with "...interaction patterns, a common understanding of boundaries and identity, and a set of shared feelings of belonging" (p. 288). In contrast, the word community at times can imply a spatially larger area than a neighborhood with weaker social ties among residents (Nash & Bowen, 1999; Seidman et al., 1998).

The use of the term community is not always connected to a place. Community is sometimes used to describe a geographically, free-floating group of individuals. A collection of people may form on the basis of a shared interest, purpose, or experience. Unlike other definitions of the community which specify geographical boundaries, communities of like minded individuals do not necessarily have to be tied to a particular physical location.

Finally, technology may have implications for the use of the word community in the intervention literature. The Prevnet Euro Project (PnEP) offers an interesting illustration of this point (Tammi & Peltoniemi, 1999). The PnEP was a two year pilot intervention (1998-2000) aimed at developing and testing methods for using information technology and telecommunications (i.e., telematics) to prevent youth and community-wide substance abuse. Institutions experienced in drug prevention were commissioned to develop web sites and other telematic methods. Across five European countries, the types of activities most frequently carried out were: recording all national internet drug prevention web sites, creating adult and youth oriented web sites, offering phone-in services, and providing easier access to videoconferencing. The primary content on program web sites included: fact and shared databases, news and discussion areas, knowledge and self assessment tests, games, data gathering, post cards, individual counseling, public consultation, providing links to other sites and services. The majority of the web sites provided information in multiple languages. Server records allowed program evaluators to measure the level of web site activity, what pages are being seen by the viewer-user and for what duration, the user's country, and the search engines used to locate a web site. If a web site survey or self-test was completed, more details about site users and participation levels could be collected (Tammi & Peltoniemi, 1999). Internet-based interventions, like PnEP, present the program evaluator with the challenge of defining the appropriate target group or community. Although current indicators of use (i.e., 'hits') and the user's country provide needed information, the anonymous and global characteristics of the internet complicates attempts to precisely identify who might be benefiting from intervention activities.

Despite diversity in criteria and the potential wrinkles caused by new technology, it can be said that a common thread in most current usages of the term community involves one or more the following elements: people, organizations, and/or a physical space (Barry, 1994). Because the terms community and neighborhood mean different things to different people, interventionists should strive to be explicit about how they came to define their intervention communities and neighborhoods.

Individual vs. Environmental Change Models

In the absence of strong agreement on shared definitions for the community or neighborhood there is, oddly enough, an evolving consensus regarding broad conceptual outlines or models of community life. Systems metaphors (Bronfenbrenner, 1979; Sameroff & Fiese, 2000) are found at the center of this convergence of opinion, in part because they offer a means for capturing some of the complexity and fluidity of the community (c.f., Brooks-Gunn, 1995; Holder, 1998; Tolan & Guerra, 1994; Weissberg & Greenberg, 1998). A systems perspective helps us to recognize that within a given locality there is a diversity of individual children, teenagers, adults, families, organizations, and institutions. Each person, relationship, and social structure is in some way linked to the other thereby creating a patchwork of interaction that is itself embedded in a broader culture and history. Communities are multifaceted environments, and as such, provide opportunities to directly intervene on the risk and protective factors found within and between the individual, relationships, and the local ecology.

Community initiatives can vary in terms which risk or protective factors are targeted for intervention. Individual models seek to change risk or protective factors directly associated with a given program participant (e.g., a child's knowledge about the harmful effects of drugs or skills to resist offers). A discrete group of participants is exposed to a series of intervention actions which in turn yields a well-defined cohort whose progress can be followed over time. Environmental models, on the other hand, seek to make changes to systemic risk or protective factors connected to the community itself (e.g., policy controls on the legal and illicit drug distribution systems). People are thought to be changed when they come in contact with the altered environment. Interventionists that subscribe to an environmental approach have begun to develop design and measurement techniques aimed at capturing the extent of contextual change and its impact on affected individuals (Gruenewald, 1997; Holder, 1998; Murray, Clark, & Wagenaar, 2000). There is debate as to which model offers the greater utility and durability (Cummings, 1999; Holder, 1997). Some maintain that both types of models have value with each model fulfilling a needed function (Norström, 1995; Worden, 1999). Advocates of the Community Systems Perspective argue that if we are to make a meaningful dent in a given social problem that has at least a partly ecological cause, then we must not only seek to change individuals but the environment must also be altered (Holder, 1998). Furthermore, an intervention that assumes an individual change model is destined at some point to take on an environmental model if it is to have any staying power in the community (Holder, 2001). For example, it has been suggested that environmental techniques, like policy advocacy, are a good way to ensure the sustainability of a successful individual oriented prevention project (Pentz, 2000). Long-term programs in the community, even individual-oriented ones, can only be maintained by obtaining stable funding and creating or revamping administrative infrastructures.

While this still remains a point of debate, some community and cross-contexts interventions have experimented with an individual plus environmental model (c.f. *Program Examples* – Biglan, et al., 1996; Holmila, 1995; 1997; 1999; 2000; LoSciuto, et al., 1997; 1999; Manley, et al., 1997b; Pentz, Bonnie, & Shopland, 1996; Pentz, et al., 1990;

Romelsjö, Andren, & Borg, 1993, September; Wagenaar, et al., 2000). Yet, the available program trials are usually slanted towards one side of the individual–environmental continuum and make use of a similarly weighted evaluation strategy. Project Northland provides an illustration of this point and offers a glimpse of what future individual plus environmental intervention models may look like.

Project Northland (PN; Perry, et al., 1993; 2000) was an American multiple component and context intervention aimed at influencing early adolescent drug use. Individual oriented intervention actions included educational events, newsletters, and home- based activity booklets. These activities were largely aimed at the provision of accurate information about alcohol, tobacco, and other drugs (ATOD), as well as giving parents and teens a chance to talk about drugs. Other individual level program activities dealt with school- based curricular activities and leisure opportunities. Environment oriented components involved the formation of an adult community coalition that had a mandate to reduce teen access to alcohol. The targets for change in this case were the passage of more restrictive laws and ordinances in support of RBS/S training, as well as seeking material rewards from local businesses to reinforce youth who made a public commitment to abstain from ATOD.

When PN is described in the research literature the focus is typically on a large cohort of students that took part in intervention activities or served as a member of the control group over a three year period. For the program trial, twenty school-districts and respective communities were matched then randomly assigned to either an intervention or a control condition. Analyses that controlled for pre-test differences found that by the study's end intervention associated improvements, intervention versus control, accrued on multiple indices of alcohol consumption, beliefs regarding the utility of alcohol, and parent-teen communication. The outcome results were particularly favorable for those teens in the intervention condition that were not alcohol users at the start of the intervention, relative to nonusers in control school districts.

For the environment-oriented aspects of the intervention, it was reported that eight alcohol-restrictive policy changes were recorded in three out of the ten intervention communities over the course of the three year study period. A baseline survey of the intervention group's parents, local alcohol vendors, and community leaders was conducted. Pre-test shopping trials or purchase attempts also took place. According to a principal investigator associated with the study, post test results on purchase attempts showed significant reductions in intervention communities (Perry, personal communication, 2003). In the cohort sample, youth perception of alcohol access in the community did not show a significant difference between conditions, intervention versus control. Although PN met its main goal by influencing early drug-use patterns for the better, an opportunity to capture a more precise reflection of the intervention's impact on the community at large may have been missed by the focus on the study's cohort design. Studies that thoroughly test individual, environmental, and individual plus environmental change models within the same intervention trial could only help in determining the relative durability and utility of working directly with individuals and/or environments.

Future Directions

A number of future directions can be taken away from the model programs described in this chapter and available reviews of the community intervention literature (e.g., Hawkins, et al., 1997; Sherman, et al., 1997; Weissberg & Greenberg, 1998; Wilson & Lipsey, 2000b). Interventionists can view these recommendations as a good starting place, but as this review hopefully demonstrates, firm conclusions about the utility of individual intervention actions should only be reached after faithful implementation and careful local evaluation. Future intervention work in the community can be facilitated by taking the following practical steps:

- Reach a community-level consensus on the nature of youth development and local problem behaviors. Formulate community supported policies that specify a course of action.
- Target commercial alcohol-tobacco access with evidence-based restriction strategies. Develop and test new strategies for tackling social ATOD sources.
- Offer drug and sex education-skills training of known utility and contraceptive services at an easily accessible location within the community and school.
- Communicate well formulated and program-linked media messages.
- Provide abundant opportunities for young people to get involved in community service and mentoring programs. Select service sites and mentors with care. Monitor youngsters' progress while they are in the midst of their service learning or mentoring experience.
- Offer young people accessible and meaningful recreational opportunities that allow them to increase their level of exposure to prosocial peers and adults.
- Remain mindful of the possibility of antisocial peer group dynamics in community intervention settings, especially among adolescents. Examine the risk levels of youngsters participating in community-based intervention activities. Provide high risk youth with intensive individual or family program activities of known utility.

Chapter Endnotes

---

[1] Cross-context interventions covered in this chapter include: community + school; community + family; community + school + family. Note that family + school programs were addressed in the *School Chapter*.

[2] See the *School Chapter–Questions Subsection* for description of the unit of assignment versus analysis issue.

[3] The number of Swedish Youth Health Centers has steadily increased since their inception in the 1970's. Today, there are more than 200 centers in operation. Sweden has roughly 8.8 million inhabitants with about 11% of this population being categorized as children and adolescents (Swedish National Board for Youth Affairs, 1997).

[4] Significant intervention related improvements in alcohol consumption levels among intervention versus comparison condition youth were found in the Class of 1989 study, but the intensity of these benefits faded in later adolescence (10th-12th grades).

[5] The reporting of the NKP's 13-year, follow-up results provides an illustration of the unit of assignment versus unit of analysis issue. Results described up to the 13-year, follow-up are based on survey responses given by all participants and were pooled together across the four intervention and two comparison schools. In this case, the individual subjects in the intervention versus comparison condition were the unit of analysis. While employing this analytic strategy, a difference emerged between baseline smokers and non-smokers with only non-smokers still reporting significantly less smoking at the 13-year follow-up (relative to baseline non-smokers in the comparison group). In the NKP, the unit of assignment was the community. The alternative analytic strategy used in the 13-year follow-up matched the unit of assignment with the unit of analysis. In these outcome analyses, the baseline smoker/non smoker distinction did not hold for the 13-year follow-up. An intervention-related improvement in terms of reduced lifetime tobacco exposure (22% less) was found for youth who participated in school-based intervention activities in contrast to those youth in the comparison condition. This result was found irregardless of baseline smoking status. Thus, depending on the way the outcome analyses were conducted, one can draw a different conclusion about NKP's long-term success with baseline smokers. However, an examination of NKP's short- and long-term findings when the individual was the unit of analysis and the evaluations where the unit of analysis was the school-community both indicate a pattern of enduring intervention associated benefits for tobacco smoking.

[6] The Midwestern Prevention Project and Project Northland are more elaborate interventions with additional components that emphasize systemic change within the community and direct intervention with families to reduce drug taking behavior in youth. Project Northland also has a recreational component.

Chapter 7
Prevention and Promotion across Borders

Introduction

Long held notions about human development maybe set to change in the near future. "Culture and context are becoming increasingly significant constructs......The changes in conceptualization that are being demanded are not minor. They may well require a shaking of the foundations..." (Mistry & Saraswathi, 2003, p. 267). Authors such as Mistry and Saraswathi (2003) posited that this shift in thinking comes from within the sciences and in reaction to external influences.

In the field of psychological study, one can observe a change that signals the mainstreaming of culture and context into our fundamental ideas about development. Mistry and Saraswathi (2003) linked this movement in psychology to problems encountered in global prevention and promotion efforts. This sea change is also encouraged by a wider acceptance of approaches like human ecology, and the lifespan and developmental systems perspectives. The views of Bronfenbrenner (1999) and Super and Harkness (1999; 2002) are examples of approaches that attempt to explain how culture fits into the context of human development.

In Bronfenbrenner's (1999) ecological systems approach, culture is conceived as part of the macrosystem, a distal or somewhat removed layer of the nested systems that make up developmental contexts. The example of a macrosystem influence given in *Chapter 1 – Overview* described how a cultural belief, i.e., 'it is good to bring and keep infants physically nearby adults during their work', may translate into caregiving practices that afford children particular experiences and how that in turn may influence their understanding of the world. Some have argued that this way of thinking about culture may be too distant from the individual and that culture may really have a more direct impact on the developing person (Super & Harkness, 1999).

In contrast to distant macrosystem influences, the idea of a developmental niche brings culture more intimately into our lives (Mistry & Saraswathi, 2003). Specifically, Super and Harkness (1999) theorized that culture is deeply woven into all aspects of a developmental niche. A developmental niche is made up of three culturally linked components that directly relate to the developing person[1]. These components consist of "the physical and social settings, the historically constituted customs and practices of child care and child rearing, and the psychology of the caretakers, particularly parental ethnotheories which play a directive role and are, by definition, shared with the community" (Super & Harkness, 2002, p. 271).

Despite the different depiction of the processes by which culture relates to development, there are commonalities in Bronfenbrenner's (1999) and Super and Harkness's (1999; 2002) perspectives. Both theories view the individual as active and consider the interplay of culturally-linked and non-linked facets of the environment as dynamic and each potentially influential. Additionally, these theorists highlight the holistic and pervasive nature of culture and its impact on the context of human development. Whether culture is considered proximal or distal to development, there is a growing recognition that the ecology of human development is itself in a state of development, it is multidimensional in nature, and culture is inextricably linked to the environment and human development (D'Andrade, 1990; Friedman & Wachs, 1999; Stearns, 2003, May 2).

Mistry and Saraswathi (2003) also suggested that external influences outside of the sciences are pushing culture and context to the forefront. The introduction of new technologies and social historical changes are helping to make our social world smaller (Barber, 2001, September). The shrinking of the social globe may be facilitated by the more widespread use of computers and the Internet which gives immediate access to email, websites, and chat rooms, the expanded use of satellite television with the ability to receive social mores from distant lands, and the mobility of populations through tourism or migration. Arnett (2001) commented that, "It is ironic that this attention to culture comes at a time in world history when the boundaries that give cultures their distinctiveness are becoming steadily fainter" (p. 25). An integrated global culture may be particularly relevant for young people who, while they may live across the world from each other, may still listen to similar music, play some of the same video games, drink the same soft drinks and wear the same brands of blue jeans and athletic shoes (Arnett, 2001; Kaufman & Rizzini, 2002).

With culture, context, and a smaller social world at the forefront of our thinking, we come back to some fundamental questions. How can culture be understood, adequately measured, and influenced? Culture and context have vast theoretical and practical implications for intervention efforts (Mattis, 2002). Today, individuals interested in human development and intervention often focus on how cultural processes can be scientifically understood and then harnessed to help improve the lives of young people.

Chapter Organization

This chapter summarizes the findings of an interview study with people who have taken part in cross-national interventions trials. We interviewed individuals who developed the programs and those that implemented them in a second or third country (See Figure 2).

Figure 2. Cross-National Interview Study Participants

Family Interventions
Incredible Years Series

Carolyn Webster-Stratton	Program Developer	US
Moria Doolan & Ivana Klimes	Program Implementers	UK
Willy Tore-Mørch	Program Implementer	Norway

Functional Family Therapy (FFT)

James Alexander & Tom Sexton	Program Developers	US
Kjell Hansson	Program Implementer	Sweden

Multisystemic Therapy (MST)

Scott Henggler	Program Developer	US
Alan Leschied	Program Implementer	Canada
Terje Ogden & Bernadette Christensen	Program Implementers	Norway

Parent Management Training (PMT)

Marion Forgatch	Program Developer	US
Terje Ogden & Elisabeth Askeland	Program Implementers	Norway

School Interventions
Olweus Bullying Prevention Program

Dan Olweus	Program Developer	Norway
Susan Limber	Program Implementer	US

Bullying Intervention Variations

Peter Smith	Program Implementer	UK
Reiner Hanewinkel	Program Implementer	Germany

Promoting Alternative Thinking Strategies (PATHS)

Mark Greenberg	Program Developer	US
Kees van Overveld	Program Implementer	Holland

In all cases, these are well established programs, with a supportive evidence base, at the very least in their home countries. Additional controlled effectiveness trials were either completed or in the midst of completion in the United States or Europe. The programmatic content, efficacy and effectiveness trials associated with these exemplar interventions have been described elsewhere in the book[2].

This interview study was not designed to be comprehensive. Instead, it represents a select sample of those persons involved in cross-national intervention work. However, through these interviews, it was possible to get indications of what people on the front lines of this issue have experienced and what they advise in terms of implementing programs across countries. All respondents were asked a standard set of semi-structured questions. In light of their unique experiences with different facets of the intervention process, separate sets of questions were sometimes posed to the program developers and implementers. The interviews were tape recorded[3] and transcribed in order to conduct an ethnographic content analysis[4].

Cross-National Collaboration and Intervention Research

Several questions were posed to the entire panel on the general theme of cross-national collaborative intervention research. Salient questions dealt with the following points:

- What do you think can be gained by *cross-national collaboration* and testing of interventions outside of their home countries?
- In your opinion, what are the necessary elements of a successful and sustained *cross-national collaboration*?
- What do you see as the biggest barriers to making *cross-national collaboration* happen on a more regular basis?

On the Benefits of Cross-National Collaboration and Intervention Trials

An important consideration is whether it is worthwhile to do cross-national intervention work, in the first place. Stearns (2003, May 2) encouraged researchers to explore the impact of culture in order to expand what is known about the human condition. "In a global age, the impact of cultural variation has greater significance than ever before, and we need a new generation of comparative scholarship to explore what's involved" (Stearns, 2003, May 2, p. B11). From the field of health promotion, Oldenburg (2002) wrote that countries all over the world should adopt a more international view and that health strategies will have to take into account social, environmental, and economic determinants. Our panel also recognized the advantages of collaboration and research on an international scale.

Response From Program Developers: It Strengthens an Intervention. Overwhelmingly, the developers commented that they felt that anytime a program is put into a different context it provides an opportunity to strengthen it (e.g., Forgatch, personal communication, 2002; Henggler, personal communication, 2002; Olweus, personal communication, 2002). Further, a respectful and collaborative relationship between program developers and implementers allows for a dynamic give and take in which ideas and methods are constantly being improved upon (Sexton, personal communication, 2002).

> Every time I train anybody, I learn a ton......the idea of training people in different cultures......from a program development point of view, you begin to see what are the themes, trends in cultures, you begin to see the problematic areas....I think it helps you communicate better......collaboration is really very, it's pretty neat, I mean, for me to sort of see what does transcend across the ocean......where the stumbling blocks are, as feeding that back to me.......I just re-did the leader manuals, partly because of my experience in feedback...things I might not of thought to tell people about, and that'll get put in the manual, or ideas that get shared with me......it's like everybody's helping......they're helping me continually improve the program... (Webster-Stratton, personal communication, 2002)

Other program developers echoed a similar sentiment. Along these lines, James Alexander (personal communication, 2002) commented that, "The whole idea of having to articulate something......you have to pay more attention to what it really means, and I have found that to be a delightful process". According to program developers, cross-national trials can clearly strengthen even an already good intervention.

Response from Program Implementers: Starting from Scratch Is It Really Necessary? As this book hopefully highlights, there is a growing worldwide body of evidence about what works in terms of advancing positive development and preventing youth problem behaviors. In an address to the Society for Research on Child Development (1997, April), Hillary Clinton, then first lady of the United States and an advocate for children, implored the room of researchers, practitioners and students to make their research accessible to those who need it. Many of the well established interventions described in this book have decades of careful epidemiological and applied research studies as a foundation. If such a knowledge base has been built up and good intervention results have been consistently demonstrated, then its seems reasonable to put these carefully studied ideas into practice whenever possible.

For program implementers, a main idea within their comments was that the creation of interventions from the ground up was not always necessary. If good interventions already exist, then such programs have the potential to address pressing local and national problems. Susan Limber (personal communication, 2002) remarked the following regarding the Olweus Bullying Prevention Program's dissemination in the United States:

When we were looking at it originally, it was not very well known in this country. I think it's a great example of how we should be looking globally for models for violence prevention or prevention generally. Let's not reinvent the wheel. What's out there that makes good sense and is consistent with what we know and what would work. Clearly, you need to look for what would make sense for our culture. But I think the best programs that I know are built on a set of principles about what works in preventing violence. That is usually translatable to other cultures. You need to tinker probably in many cases with the day-to-day, how those principles are translated into practice. But I think that we have a lot to learn from experience with what works and what doesn't work in other cultures.

Other program implementers reiterated the idea, that when possible, we should avoid reinventing the wheel (e.g., Hansson, personal communication, 2002; Klimes, personal communication, 2002; van Overveld, personal communication, 2002). As Elisabeth Askeland stated (personal communication, 2002), "...we need better intervention methods. And if you don't have it, we have to look and search for them".

Yet, it was noted that there is sometimes a belief that homegrown solutions are the only valid solutions to a local problem (e.g., Leschied, personal communication, 2002). Referring back to our conversation with Susan Limber (personal communication, 2002) once again,

...from the standpoint of folks looking to adopt a program......I hear an awful lot 'well,   we're not Norway or we're not England. We've got very different issues from other   countries. Why should we look to them to solve the problems we've got in our own school?' So, I think from the consumer's standpoint, there may not be so much recognition of the commonality of problems that are faced.

Portions of the risk-protective factors research literature described in this book, like international research studies on the phenomenon of bullying, tell a different story. While it is clear that there are significant cultural differences within and between nations, our shared humanity may make us more similar than we initially think (Leschied, personal communication, 2002).

Response from the Entire Panel: Interventions Inform Theory. A key sentiment in the responses of the entire panel was that cross-national intervention trials inform how we think about the basic phenomena we seek to change as interventionists. This can result in both theoretical and practical advances. Interview respondents remarked that cross-national intervention research represents a unique opportunity to see how the mechanisms of development work in different settings (e.g., Ogden, personal communication,

2002). If more can be learned about the processes of change, then this may improve our ability to promote positive development and prevent problem behaviors in a variety of settings. For instance, it was noted that Multisystemic Therapy (MST) is based on some fundamental ideas about how families and child-parent relations work (Ogden, personal communication, 2002). The developer of the program, Scott Henggler (personal communication, 2002) added:

> I think this probably holds across cultures. Antisocial behavior really fits within a multi-determined framework, and whether you are in Germany, Norway, Japan, or somewhere else. Hanging out with other kids who are really into drugs and crime, is going to be conducive to your antisocial behavior. Parents who just let you do whatever you want, it's going to be conducive to your antisocial behavior…

Further, Carol Webster-Stratton (personal communication, 2002) commented that there should be at least some common goals that all parents can share, such as wanting their child to have friends, obey their parents, and be successful in school. Program trials in various settings help determine if these goals and phenomena are indeed shared or in some ways universal. If there are parallels across settings, then we can learn more about how such similarities are specifically expressed in different contexts.

Elements of a Successful and Sustained Cross-National Collaboration

> *Response from the Entire Panel: Funding and Relationships Are Key.*
The panel's responses in this case centered on the need to establish an adequate and stable funding source, as a key concern. Another important consideration was the nature of the relationship between program developers and implementers (e.g., Christensen, personal communication, 2002). The majority of the panel commented on the significance of good relationships at this level. As with any good relationship they highlighted the importance of mutual respect, trust, readiness to share knowledge, and above all, good communication. While the value of Internet and phone contact was acknowledged, personal contact and direct training from the developers was noted to be of particular value.

> …I think when you want to adopt such a program, you need to have a meeting with the persons who developed the program. You need some personal contact, you have to have training from those persons. When PATHS came to Holland, Mark Greenberg came also to Holland, and he had some workshops for the Dutch teachers, and I think that's a very good idea. You need to know why those

developers made these lessons like they made them. (van Overveld, personal communication, 2002)

Members of the panel also suggested that there needs to be plenty of time for listening and working together to understand one another (e.g., Henggler, personal communication, 2002). Mark Greenberg (personal communication, 2002) added that:

> A sufficient time to understand each other's goals at the beginning is important, so that the collaboration that develops is going to be mutually beneficial, and really uses the expertise on both sides. Regular travel, face to face, as well...as other kinds of communication are necessary to really develop the model over time.

Furthermore, it was thought that having developers personally promote an intervention helps, because they cannot only give the details of why particular components appear and work as they do, but also continually stress the need for a scientifically strong program evaluation (e.g., van Overveld, personal communication, 2002).

Cross-National Collaboration, Why Doesn't It Happen More Often?

Response From the Entire Panel: Time, Money, and Energy. There was substantial unanimity among panel members regarding the challenges related to cross-national collaboration. The main sentiment was that key barriers related to this kind of work were finding adequate time, financial support, and personal energy (e.g., Askeland, personal communication, 2002; Klimes, personal communication, 2002; Olweus, personal communication, 2002). Many of the respondents remarked upon the rarity of finding a funding source interested in explicitly supporting cross-national intervention research. "...there's not a lot of sponsoring agencies and organizations and governments who have the vision to know why it's important..." (Leschied, personal communication, 2002). Other respondents noted that within the academic world such time-intensive research and outreach is not always rewarded.

> ...you don't get a lot of credits in an academic environment. You get it from publishing, and all this sort of stuff takes you away from publishing......You know, I came to this realization after twenty years......If I was spending twenty years doing all these randomized controlled studies, and I had no intention of anyone else ever using it, why did I do it? Because the hope is that you'll find something that you can pass on to other people......and they can

take it the next step forward. (Webster-Stratton, personal communication, 2002)

Ivana Klimes (personal communication, 2002) touched on a related issue: "...so much good psychology research......it just stays where it was done, and doesn't come out of the setting in which it was done, which is a shame".

In terms of beginning to address these obstacles, it was suggested that some type of organizational structure, either national or international, was needed to help support cross-national collaborative intervention efforts on a more consistent and explicit basis (e.g., Leschied, personal communication, 2002; Ogden, personal communication, 2002). It may also be helpful to raise awareness about the unique scientific and social benefits associated with conducting cross national intervention research.

Tailoring Interventions to Culture and Context

Beyond finding good professional partners and establishing a supportive environment for interventions to take root in, there are a number of issues related to successfully launching and maintaining a prevention or youth development program. A great deal of decision making occurs across the different phases of an intervention trial. Frequently, there is a sense of tension in which on the one hand, there is a need to tailor the program to fit the setting and on the other hand a desire for fidelity to the original model. "Adaptation defines the degree to which a program undergoes change in its implementation to fit needs of a particular delivery situation" (Schinke, et al., 2002, p. 21). However, there is also the concern about not changing an intervention to the extent that you lose the qualities that made the program successful in the first place. "Fidelity defines the extent to which the delivery of a prevention program conforms to the curriculum, protocol, or guidelines for implementing that program. A program delivered exactly as intended by its originator has high fidelity" (Schinke et al., 2002, p. 21).

Fidelity and adaptation is a concern when an intervention is implemented in any new setting, but what happens when the program in question was developed in another country? What then goes into the decision making process? In what ways are the choices similar or different from the choices normally made when an intervention is introduced to a new community, school, or family? The following questions were asked to the entire panel in an effort to tease apart this multi-faceted issue:

- In your opinion, what are the critical factors that have to be considered when implementing interventions cross nationally?
- Replication is an important part of the scientific process. Do you think that cross national replications should be as true to the original

as possible? If it is not, can we really say that the intervention worked
or did not work in another cultural context? Is exact replication an
unreachable or undesirable goal? What are your thoughts on the need
and limitations that should be placed on reinvention?

This question was posed only to program developers:

- How is the idea of cultural appropriateness dealt with or built into the
  intervention?

These questions were asked only of program implementers:

- In the program trial that you are or were involved in, what challenges
  did you encounter? How were these barriers addressed?
- How did language figure into this process, was it a substantial or
  superficial barrier?

The Qualities of Interventions Likely to Succeed in Another Country

*Response from the Entire Panel: Interventions with an Evidence Base
Have Clear Advantages.* When deciding on what program to import, the panel
overwhelmingly stressed the need to look at interventions that have a sound
scientific evidence base (e.g., Klimes, personal communication, 2002; Ogden,
personal communication, 2002; van Overveld, personal communication,
2002). A rigorously tested intervention that has demonstrated positive
outcomes in its home country is a good place to start. When talking about
exporting Functional Family Therapy (FFT), James Alexander (personal
communication, 2002) said:

> It would be foolish to try to adopt a program that hasn't been
> demonstrated to be effective no matter what the culture. In other
> words, the first place you'd look is at effective programs. The idea
> is you start there then you say, 'now could it also be effective with
> us?' But to start with other programs that are popular but haven't
> been demonstrated to be effective, that takes a greater leap of faith.

Program implementers involved in the dissemination of programs in
their own countries, consistently mentioned that a strength of adopting an
evidence-based intervention was that it allowed them to talk about and
highlight an intervention's record of positive, program-related benefits (e.g.,
Leschied, personal communication, 2002). From funding agencies to
participants, when implementers were able to point to the evidence-base of an
intervention, there was a stronger perceived commitment to taking on the
intervention. With more business-savvy companies getting into the youth
promotion and problem prevention arenas, our developers and implementers
cautioned against programs that may present magazine-quality lessons,
accompanied by glossy pictures, but do not have a sound evidence base (e.g.,

Alexander, personal communication, 2002; van Overveld, personal communication, 2002).

Response from the Entire Panel: Does the Intervention Fit the Particular Setting and Culture? The panel talked in depth about the importance of pragmatic appeal or cultural fit of an intervention (e.g., Christensen, personal communication, 2002; Smith, personal communication, 2002). Terje Ogden (personal communication, 2002) said regarding interventions under consideration for adoption, "...when professionals look into them and also politicians hear about them, do they seem sensible......they shouldn't be too exotic or too far away from some kind of common sense ideas in the Norwegian public". In a similar vein, Willy Tore Mørch (personal communication, 2002) remarked, "...to be informed about how the culture is looking at the topics and problem you are dealing with in the program is very important". It was also noted that costs associated with adopting an intervention should be in line with cultural expectations (Hansson, personal communication, 2003).

North American panelists repeated some of these sentiments and gave examples from their own experiences introducing interventions in a diversity of settings in their home countries (e.g., Henggler, personal communication, 2002; Webster-Stratton, personal communication, 2002). "You just can't take a program and impose it, because there is so much variation in the context of program implementation" (Leschied, personal communication, 2002). Hybrid and other collaborative approaches that combine elements of top-down and bottom-up intervention models are often explicitly designed to foster high levels of community or stakeholder mobilization and program investment. Regarding the preparation that goes into a program implementation, Carol Webster-Stratton (personal communication, 2002) said:

> You can't just go into a community and just say, 'here I am. I want to deliver this program'. So it's kind of making communities do their need assessment, figuring out if this is what they want, how it might meet their needs and how they can be invested in it, how they can have ownership in it, how they can be part of that process.

Productive collaborative relationships between interventionists and communities or stakeholders do not form overnight. Scott Henggler (personal communication, 2002) suggested that there should be substantial time committed to site development. During this preparation time, the candidate intervention can be discussed with stakeholders and the program developer can get feedback from implementers in terms of "...how does this fit with your system, with your culture, what has to be changed? Every site has issues that come up, so it's not unique to a particular country" (Henggler, personal communication, 2002). Insight into a community and culture as well as readiness to embrace a new intervention strategy can significantly weigh into the intervention implementation process and thereby affect program outcomes. Such considerations are also important when thinking about ways to create contexts more likely to sustain interventions over time (Trickett, 2002).

Replication, Reinvention, and Culture

An idea behind replication is that this practice is related to the discovery of true constants (Rosenthal & Rosnow, 1991). But in the world of prevention and youth development, true constants may be out of the realm of possibility. Yet, replication is still done as a way to carefully examine intervention programming and processes thought to be essential for yielding positive change. Exact replication demands high fidelity to the original intervention model. Terms like culturally appropriate or culturally sensitive imply some amount of tailoring, adaptation, or reinvention. However, looser forms of replication may allow us to gain insight into how disseminated interventions can be adapted to new settings, while maintaining or even maximizing the impact of key mechanisms of change. In a cogent treatment of this issue, Schinke and colleagues (2002) concluded:

> Research in other fields suggests that adapting programs is acceptable up to a 'zone of drastic mutation,' after which modification will compromise the program integrity and effectiveness (Hall & Loucks, 1978, March). Clearly, the limits of this zone need to be known and shared with the field. In so doing, we can find and disseminate prevention programs that are flexible and effective. Programs need to anticipate and allow for modifications that can promote a sense of ownership. In turn, that sense may contribute to the success and durability of a prevention program. (p. 21)

The panel's responses to several of the interview questions helped to clarify where, in their own experience, the boundaries of this zone of drastic mutation lie.

Response from the Entire Panel: The Core Principles of an Intervention Should be Left Intact, Until There Is Compelling Scientific Evidence that Points to the Need for Change. In responding to the question on replication and reinvention, the majority of the panel emphasized the need for close replications in new program settings. "...it's really important for replication that the program have integrity and quality......and that the developers really...articulate what that is" (Webster-Stratton, personal communication, 2002). Mark Greenberg (personal communication, 2002) put it this way:

> One of the fundamental issues is for developers to have a good sense of what are the fundamental skills we want to teach children, and good ways to do it, but also that they can be adapted quite a bit, without...changing...the fundamental nature of the interaction. And that flexibility is very important working cross nationally. There has to be an agreement that there are some things that cannot be changed, and the developers make that clear, and its respected. At the same time, the developers need to really have flexibility to understand the context.

Program implementers, for the most part, were also adamant on the importance of close replications (e.g., Christensen, personal communication, 2002; Klimes, personal communication, 2002). Willy Tore Mørch (personal communication, 2002) remarked:

> I believe that the first time you're doing a replication it should be as true as possible. Sometimes it's necessary to do some smaller changes just to make the program fit into your culture, but it should be as true as possible. And then it could be necessary after you have done the first replication, to look at the necessity of doing changes......So, I think it is at least a two-step process.

Other members of the panel commented that different forms of replication yield different types of information, each with its own value. Peter Smith (personal communication, 2002) explained,

> ...literal replication, where you pretty much as exactly as possible, do what someone else did. Might even be the same investigator doing it [*the intervention*] again...in a new sample of schools. Then you've got a constructive replication, which is where you've read what...someone wrote in their publication. You try and do pretty much what they did, but of course really following the details that are in the publication.......Then there's what's called operational replication, which is where you just take a general idea...and then you do it the way you think best...they're all useful and depending on what you're trying to find out.

On the notion of reinventing a program from the start, Moria Doolan (personal communication, 2002) said:

> I can remember, for example, going in, talking about the Incredible Years...and asking...who was familiar with the program and so on.

> And quite a few said they were quite familiar and some were even
> using it...but then you hear... 'Well, I only used this bit or that
> bit'......Now, they're using it in ways that...may be very helpful to
> them and the parents that they're seeing, but they're not
> implementing the program. And I think it's that kind of clarity that
> is...necessary in terms of saying...is it *[the program]* useful in a
> different context.

Another strategy to negotiate the replication and reinvention issue, is
through intensive site development. During the ground work that happens
before an intervention is adopted, perceived mismatches can be aired and
addressed. A close and careful examination of the fit between an intervention
and cultural values of the host nation was thought to be a way to bypass
potential mismatches (e.g., Hansson, personal communication, 2002; van
Overveld, personal communication, 2002). "...when you start considering a
program, you have to go through it, someone has to do that......we first go
through the program and find it acceptable..." (Ogden, personal
communication, 2002). However, once the program is seen as a good fit Terje
Ogden (personal communication, 2002) suggested:

> ...when we import a program or method to our country, we
> should...do it on the basis of the research results, we should try to
> implement the program very much as it is. And then after we've
> tried it, unless it's totally unacceptable, after you try it, adjust it,
> after evaluation, and not change it before hand.

*Response from Program Developers: Attention to Culture and
Context Lies at the Heart of a Good Intervention.* Resnicow, Soler,
Braithwaite, Ahluwalia, and Butler (2000) proposed that one of the ways to
come to terms with the problem of making adaptations based on the need for
an improved cultural fit, was to consider the deep and surface structure of an
intervention. The deep structure refers to aspects of the intervention that
reflect or account for culture-related factors known to influence behavior.
Surface structure refers to messages and materials that correspond to the
behavioral and social characteristics of a community. While deep structure is
thought to directly relate to an intervention's ultimate success, surface
structure relates primarily to initial receptivity or getting in the front door with
a program participant (Resnicow, et al., 2000).

When thinking about the notion of a deep program structure, an
important question arises. Does the intervention in question allow for the
influence of culturally-related phenomena that might be linked to program
outcomes? Incorporating an understanding of how participants and
stakeholders within the community perceive the cause and appropriate course
of action for dealing with a given problem can be critical to achieving desired

intervention outcomes. Some individuals within Latino communities in the United States, for example, view the causes of mental illness as both physical and spiritual (Tazeau, 2003, June). Consequently, persons suffering from mental illnesses who have such belief systems may seek a cure from mainstream American psychiatric medicine, as well as from traditional indigenous healers, sometimes called *curanderos*. Instead of viewing a client's faith in traditional healing systems as an obstacle, these channels for healing can be used as vehicles for change. For clients whose healing beliefs systems have spiritual foundations, the inclusion of indigenous healers or other religious authorities on mental health consultant teams can help to create treatment plans that are coordinated, meaningful to clients, and still grounded in the science-based world of psychiatric medicine (Tazeau, 2003, June). Interventions that gloss over or completely ignore such considerations as culturally linked beliefs, may in fact lose program participants and valuable opportunities to generate positive change.

Despite the emphasis on close replication, there was a widespread recognition throughout different parts of the interviews that culture and context should not be disregarded or treated lightly (e.g., Christensen, personal communication, 2002; van Overveld, personal communication, 2002; Webster-Stratton, personal communication, 2002). This was particularly clear in the program developers' responses to the question of how cultural appropriateness was addressed within their interventions. Some developers came to a strong recognition of the importance of culture and context through practical challenges that emerged in the program development process. Mark Greenberg (personal communication, 2002), for example, commented:

> I think PATHS has been going on for 20 years, so there are a number of phases in our development that way. Because PATHS was originally developed and first formed for deaf children, we were more concerned about culture issues in relation to deafness, than ...for example ethnicity...or cross-cultural sort of things. And that was very important, because it meant that because we're working in sign language. Sign languages are different...from the beginning we had to consider culture very carefully.

Developer's responses' predominately indicated that attention to culture and context was so important that was embedded within the core principals of their interventions. That is, flexibility, openness, as well as attention to culture and context, in many cases, were central facets of the intervention themselves. Program developers stressed that the actual translation of core principles to specific intervention settings was where this flexibility can come into play. "We're not talking about a paint by the numbers integrity, we're talking about an integrity of the therapeutic process and the mechanism that fit to the contexts. That's important. It's more a fundamental, philosophical principle..." (Sexton, personal communication, 2002). Marion Forgatch (personal communication, 2002), recognizing that interventionists tend to be creative people, offered that programs should allow them to use a wide range of tools to facilitate change.

> ...in our approach you have to have these parenting skills that you're teaching. And you need to use every clinical skill you have in order to pull it off. So that makes it not rote, in fact, that puts it back in art, and therapists are artists that's why they're doing it, they want to help people, and they want to be creative.

Many of the program developers mentioned that a good intervention begins with an openness to listening and addressing each participant as an individual with their own needs and goals. "What it ends up kind of getting down to, is that what's regarded as cultural competence, in terms of clinical practice, from our perspective, it's just good clinical practice" (Henggler, personal communication, 2002). That is, it is not necessarily particular to cross-national intervention work, but in all settings interventionists should approach each participant, whether they come from rural America or Norway, with an open ear and mind.

> FFT asks that the interventionist, the prevention specialist, therapist, probation officer, whatever it is, immediately begin to understand the information as it comes in, in terms of how it's represented to the family and what it means to the family in the context in which they live....everything that follows needs to be designed in order to help them be adaptive in their own culture and given their value system, rather than forcing them to adapt to some other culture that is of the therapist or the law or whatever... (Alexander, personal communication, 2002)

Tom Sexton (personal communication, 2002), also of FFT, agreed that a good family intervention should begin with the family and not with a set of assumptions.

> It's a very much start with the family and move outward, rather than begin with an a-priori......we've tried really hard to separate out the content of the issues that the families struggle with, the values that they have, the ways that they live their lives, the things that are important to them, from the therapeutic process.

Regarding the process of change, however, it was noted that there is a set of principles that a program like FFT follows. "FFT is a way to think, FFT is a process that you follow, FFT is a set of principles" (Sexton, personal communication, 2002). Carol Webster-Stratton (personal communication, 2002) likened this need for balance in making culture and context specific adaptations to programs, to the use of a blue print to build a home:

> It's important to have a structure, core principles, like a plan for building a house that is based on certain building or engineering principles. Now how you decorate it can be up to the leaders within that country or that culture to try to make it meaningful, to use the language, to use the metaphors, to make it something that they can relate to that's relevant. If you've got good principles about building a foundation from an engineer......you're not going to violate those or the whole thing will fall down.

This does not mean that culture and context are trivial or secondary considerations, another statement by Carol Webster-Stratton (personal communication, 2002) made this point clear:

> It's not enough to just colorize your vignettes. It also has to be the whole way in which people are respected. The tie-in between the discussions about what their childhood was like. We wouldn't say, 'what was it like to be from a Korean family?' We might say, 'what was it like in your family?' and a Korean parent would describe her experience. We try not to assume things......there's a lot of generalization in the literature. So the process is one of trying to learn as much as we can about these families' experiences in their culture.

There have been cautions in the research literature against using 'culture as an address' (Lopez, Edwards, Ito, Pedrotti, & Rasmussen, 2002; Shweder & Jensen, 1997, April). That is, beware of making generalizations about individuals based on an ethnic or cultural title. Within the United States, "Broad labels such as 'Latino' and 'African American' obscure intracultural differences and lead researchers to assume homogeneity of culture where little homogeneity may exist" (Mattis, 2002, p. 4). In remarking on her experiences in the United Kingdom, Moria Dolan (personal communication, 2002) said:

> ...we've had a lot of different people from a lot of different kind of cultural and ethnic backgrounds in the program, and I think this is an incredible individual variation...it isn't just cultural...so within the same culture, you'll see a lot of difference, in terms of the way people respond. So, I don't think you could kind of pick out one thing and say...that doesn't fit culturally, but you know I think,

> different people according to their own view and such about their
> culture, would give a different kind of...description...

European countries such as Sweden, once thought to be largely homogenous, today in fact are not. "In Sweden as a whole, one in four people is foreign-born or of foreign parentage" (The Economist, 2003, June 14, p. S4). Inattention to diversity within ethnic, cultural, and national groups may make it more likely that an intervention is out of step with its participants and eventually results in poor program outcomes (Resnicow et al., 2000).

Culture can intersect with a number of factors in complex ways (Cardemil, 2002; Lopez et al., 2002). It is therefore, important to be open to the uniqueness of any intervention setting, while at the same time not losing what is fundamental to making an intervention successful. In many model interventions, program developers have anticipated these types of challenges and offer strategies that can help implementers achieve a balance between necessary adaptation and the level of program fidelity needed to produce positive change.

Response from the Entire Panel: The Challenge of Translating Principles into Practice. At many points during the interview, panel members suggested that sound, well-evaluated intervention principles were likely to be relevant across cultures. The day-to-day translation of these principles, however, would always need fine tuning to better fit any given intervention setting. For our panel, this fine tuning dealt primarily with surface structure changes in images, program exercises, and more generally with language. As mentioned earlier in this chapter, the surface structure refers to how intervention messages and materials link to the implementation setting or life experiences of program participants. Relevant surface structure is thought to increase the acceptance and comprehension of an intervention (Resnicow, et al., 2000)

Through our conversations with the panel, we were able to get a better understanding of the nature and extent of the adaptations that have been made in order to better translate core intervention principles to specific situations or contexts. Panel responses in this subsection were drawn primarily from answers to questions posed separately to program developers (*How is the idea of cultural appropriateness dealt with or built into the intervention?)* and implementers (*In the program trial that you are, or were, involved in, what challenges did you encounter? How were these barriers addressed? How did language figure into this process, was it a substantial or superficial barrier?).* How surface structure changes could be made, while retaining close replication of the model interventions was of concern to many. The panel's responses to these questions, also gives us another glimpse at where the lines were drawn around each of the respective interventions' zones of drastic mutation.

Programmatic Content and Activities. Firstly, are the intended messages being received and understood? Mattis (2002) warned that, "…it is not sufficient to be deliberate in how images and symbols are deployed, nor is it sufficient to focus on intended meanings……researchers must seek to understand how signs and images are received, interpreted, understood, and used" (p. 7). Regarding surface structure changes made to the PATHS program in Holland, Mark Greenberg (personal communication, 2002) shared: "One surface issue was changing the stories or the pictures so instead of a child running out of cereal in the morning, they run out of butter for their bread". Addressing the same program, a Dutch collaborator for PATHS, Kees van Overveld (personal communication, 2002) added, "the challenge encountered was to translate and adapt the program to the Dutch situation because a lot of text and illustrations were very American. For instance, there were a lot of pictures with boys with baseball caps. Well, in 1987 there were no Dutch boys with baseball caps".

Program exercises can also present challenges. Intervention activities that may be taken for granted as acceptable in one community, may not exactly translate in the same way for another community (Roosa, Dumka, Gonzalez, & Knight, 2002). For instance, one of the tenets of the PATHS program is that labeling and discussing feelings rather than immediately acting out on them leads to positive behavior change in young people. How does such an exercise work in a culture in which children are not encouraged to discuss their feelings? "Who you talk to about your feelings…is very different across cultures" (Greenberg, personal communication, 2002). Making a similar point, based on her experiences with the Incredible Years Series and the program activities it involves, Ivana Klimes said: "…apart from language issues, there are actually issues that have got to do with whether it fits the culture in general and what is acceptable within the culture".

When developing and testing ideas that form the basis of programmatic content and activities, it is critical to take cultural variations into account (Greenberg, personal communication, 2002; Smith, personal communication, 2002). Ivana Klimes (personal communication, 2002) commented that the idea of giving lots of praise to children, a key part of the BASIC parent program, was not initially accepted by some British participants. Parents, in some instances, thought that the use of a great deal of praise was 'over the top' or typically 'American'. This challenge was overcome by working with parents to find comfortable ways to translate the idea of supporting a child's positive behavior into their own familial language. By working in such creative ways interventionists are able to reshape the content of an intervention to better fit an implementation context, while still coming to the same endpoint or goal, which is to facilitate positive change.

Language. There are obvious advantages to having program materials appear in a participant's own language and at an appropriate reading level (Resnicow, et al., 2000). Language fit into the program implementers' experiences primarily as it related to the translation of program materials and communication during the supervision-training process. In some cases, only small modifications were made to videos or handouts to help make the materials better fit the implementation context (Klimes, personal communication, 2002). In other instances, program materials like videos were given voice-overs or re-shot for the new implementation context (e.g., Limber, personal communication, 2002). Even in the United Kingdom, some of the program materials in American English, such as the parent training videos for the BASIC parent program were given voice-overs.

> ...there were some people, not all, who found the American accent quite difficult......actually got all of them [*the videos*]......dubbed, for people with English accents. And you know, there's no question......there's quite a few people who prefer it. (Doolan, personal communication, 2002)

In other cases, trials of the imported interventions were originally conducted with program materials in American English and program materials were eventually translated (e.g., Hansson, personal communication, 2002; Mørch, personal communication, 2002; Ogden, personal communication, 2002).

In terms of getting a good or accurate translation of program materials, some respondents said that the best translations usually were produced by someone who understands the deeper meaning of the key concepts (e.g., Askeland, personal communication, 2002).

> We had also a proper translation office that engaged people to do it, but I also had a look on it. Because people not from the field maybe sometimes translate it in a very formal way which is not the thinking of the book. (Hanewinkel, personal communication, 2002)

Program developers' comments also touched on this issue of identifying the deeper meanings of words, so accurate translations can take place.

> An example would be the word upset. Upset is a very general word about negative uncomfortable emotions in English, but it's quite specific in Dutch. Another example of that is we have lessons that are about the differentiation of problems that children face in English language, so for example, the word guilty in English can be both a behavior and it can be a feeling. You can be guilty and not feel guilty. And you can feel guilty and not be guilty. It's very confusing for children. Another example of that is sorry. You can

feel sorry or your can act sorry, and often times when children act or they say they're sorry, they don't feel sorry at all. Now that one is one that we didn't need to have in Dutch, the Dutch just dropped that lesson. Because they have different words for feeling sorry and saying you're sorry. Another example is people in England who are mad are crazy. But we use angry and mad as synonyms in American parlance. (Greenberg, personal communication, 2002)

Language also came into the supervision-training process for program implementers. This primarily was the case for those interventions in which in depth training and supervision was necessary (e.g., Hansson, personal communication, 2002). In these situations, program implementers and developers or trainers had to communicate on a regular basis. Some respondents mentioned that in the supervision process there were occasional difficulties in getting nuanced or complex meaning across, even when both parties spoke English well (e.g., Askeland, personal communication, 2002; Ogden, personal communication, 2002).

Sometimes this communication gap was turned around to the advantage of both the program implementer and developer. For example, in the implementation of Parent Management Training (PMT) in Norway, Norwegian translators living as students in Oregon transcribed 800 intervention sessions into English. This was done so the trainers in Oregon could have the full understanding of what actually happened in sessions with Norwegian families (Askeland, personal communication, 2002). It was noted that this was an important process because through these transcriptions the full, deeper meaning of the interactions between the families and therapists was clearer. The transcriptions allowed for detailed feedback as to what was done well and what the interventionists could do differently (Forgatch, personal communication, 2002).

The overall sentiment among panel members was that language was a sometimes difficult but manageable challenge, if addressed in ways that ensured that the program implementer and/or intervention participant were able to be understood and understand what was taking place. As Susan Limber (personal communication, 2002) commented on the subject, "it's a continual process to make sure things are as consumable as possible".

Policy and Cross National Intervention

How society deals with the question of helping its young people, is in part, a reflection of that society's historical, social, and political values and mores (Kaufman & Rizzini, 2002; Shweder & Jensen, 1997, April). Our panel was asked about the policy context that they functioned in within their home countries. We wanted to know how policies in their home countries related to their own intervention efforts. Through a series of questions, we were also able to hear the panel's recommendations about future policy directions that might hold promise. Because any nation's youth and family policy is multi-faceted and wide ranging, our policy questions to the panel were narrowed to focus on a particular content area, namely antisocial behavior. The members of our panel were in each of their own ways concerned and knowledgeable about the developmental course of antisocial behavior, and in some cases were internationally recognized scientific experts in this area or a related field. Comments summarized in this subsection were drawn primarily from the panel's responses to these questions:

- On the whole, how do social institutions within your country approach the problem of youth aggression and/or delinquency? Is it a question of public health, a matter for the mental health or justice systems, or is the response split up in a number of different ways?
- More generally, what are your thoughts about the youth and family related social policy in your country? Do the current policies help or hurt, in terms of the promotion of youth development and preventing youth aggression and/or delinquency?

Whose Job Is It to Work with Troubled Youth in Your Country?

Response from the Entire Panel: Justice, Child Welfare, Mental Health, and Education. Is antisocial behavior a justice, mental health, child welfare, or educational concern? Whose domain should it fall under? Who is assigned to work with young people who show behavioral problems? The panel consisted of persons working in the intervention field in several European countries, the United States, and Canada. North American respondents commented that this job often falls under the purview of the juvenile justice system (e.g., Leschied, personal communication, 2002; Limber, personal communication, 2002). Some respondents also mentioned that the response can come from other systems depending on the circumstances of the young person (e.g., Greenberg, personal communication, 2002). For example, Tom Sexton (personal communication, 2002) remarked on the basis of his experiences in the United States:

> I think it's a bit of a fragmented response......I think there's
> actually a changing scene here......in the past, there have been
> large walls between different institutions or systems that deal with
> kids...there were kids with the very same pattern, clinical pattern,
> violence, delinquency. They could be a mental health kid because
> they were...in the mental health system. They could be in the child
> welfare system. They could be in the juvenile justice system. When

you look at the clinical profile, they look very much the same, but they sort of get...labeled because of the system they're in.

Respondents within European nations said that the general societal level response was that child welfare or mental health systems were charged with helping troubled children. The justice system would only come into the picture when the youngster was a mid-adolescent or young adult (e.g., Askeland, personal communication, 2002; Doolan, personal communication, 2002; Hanewinkel, personal communication, 2002). Referring to Norway's historical response to troubled youth, Willy Tore-Mørch (personal communication, 2002) said: "The younger children, the mental health system has taken care of them. And, the adolescents, it is child protection services...And adults, in the criminal system, that's a description of how they are moving from system to system".

Future Policy Directions

Response from the Entire Panel: Future Policy Directions Concerning Troubled Youth Should Be Coordinated and Evidence-Based. The panel emphasized the need for future policy to move in directions that would ensure that troubled young people receive a timely, coordinated response from all social institutions that have a stake in the welfare of young people. This sentiment was shared across panel respondents, regardless of their home country or whether the respondent was a program developer or implementer. In many cases, respondents noted that their respective countries were in fact moving towards multi-sectoral, coordinated responses. On this issue, Susan Limber (personal communication, 2002) said,

> I may be a little too optimistic, but I think that we're going in the right direction to broaden the view. It's not just an education issue, it can't just be a justice issue, if we're really going to stem it early and make a difference, we've really got to look at all the other avenues of prevention.

From across the Atlantic, in Norway, Willy Tore Mørch (personal communication, 2002) shared this hopeful outlook: "I think it's more interest...intervening in the kid's contextual relationships...I think that's a change I have seen. Ten years ago and before, I think we are looking at a delinquent boy of 10 years as a hopeless guy...but not so much these days". Also from Norway, Dan Olweus (personal communication, 2002) added, "...the government tried to coordinate society's resources...the department of justice, the department of education, the department of children and family affairs and there were some absolutely good effects...". Moria Doolan (personal communication, 2002) further remarked on the policy changes taking place in the United Kingdom, "...one of the terms that this government is using is 'joined up thinking', and not just in this area but across the board...trying to push...mental health, education, social services...to work together, to then try and create...more coordinated programs". Tom Sexton remarked on the current situation in America:

> ...it's clear that people are now talking about these issues, trying to overcome those   system service delivery barriers, and realizing that there's a common profile of kids, meaning that they cross over those. How's that practically occurring? There are some places in which it's starting to make a difference.

Other respondents' optimism was tempered by the reality of their own experiences championing and implementing interventions within a variety of settings in their home countries. A strong sentiment was that governments are starting to look at troubled youth in a broader, more comprehensive way. Further, macro-level policies were headed in promising directions, but that there is still a long way to go on the ground. Today, troubled young people are often on the receiving end of fragmented responses and services that limit large-scale progress (e.g., Christensen, personal communication, 2002). From Holland, Kees van Overveld (personal communication, 2002) made this point: "You can say the collaboration is inadequate... ...everyone has the intention to help, but I don't think they have much influence, because all those activities are cut up". Elizabeth Askeland (personal communication, 2002) added,

> ...I think in Norway, we have principles that all different social institutions should collaborate. So, I think as a principle and as a structure we have it......Nobody wants really to do this job, because it's so many persons who have to do this job. Both neighbors, and school persons, and all the people who are working and seeing this.

Carolyn Webster-Stratton (personal communication, 2002) talked about the current real life consequences of disjointed policies and thinking using her own experiences in American schools as an illustration. She remarked that in schools,

> ...a lot of times the training has been in academic competence, and they see social and emotional curriculums as kind of icing on the cake. It's not going to improve their scores, which is what they're tested on......If you, as a child feel good about yourself and have some friends in the class and aren't afraid of the bully...have an

environment where you're...feeling safe, you'll learn more...one
feeds the other.

The effects of narrow, uncoordinated policies are not only felt in schools. The
American justice system is also touched by similar problems. Scott Henggler
(personal communication, 2002) gave this example:

> ...I think at the federal level...whether it's...the National Institute
> of Drug Abuse or the National Institute of Health...or the Centers
> for Disease Control...I think there is an attempt to frame this as a
> public health issue...but the decisions about how states and counties
> deal with these problems are really local......if a state legislature
> says...we're going to have a 'one-strike' law...everybody's going
> to do time, if they commit the crime, and it doesn't do a lot of good.

An analogous type of disconnect between local and national policies was
noted in Norway, "...in a way the current policies help now...but...it is more
local political decisions that are making programs for kids" (Mørch, personal
communication, 2002). Thus, for promising future policy directions, members
of the panel emphasized the need for more 'joined up thinking' that would
result in a wider range of coordinated programming and services that benefit
young people. As Mark Greenberg (personal communication, 2002)
concluded:

> We think of them in a very fragmented way......we think of it less
> as a building resiliency or protective factors in children, as a general
> model that will protect children from a variety of these
> outcomes......almost every time it's a response to a problem, and of
> course that's a fragmented model......in spite of the fact that the
> best writing on prevention science is an integrated model.

Another focal point was that such policies should be informed or
evidence-based. "I mean, we've got thirty years of research on some of these
principles that we know work...it should be available for people" (Webster-
Stratton, personal communication, 2002). From his own area of the
intervention field, Scott Henggler (personal communication, 2002) offered a
comparable conclusion.

> There are several states that have made commitments to the use of
> evidence-based practices, and I think as that happens it is useful not
> just to our work but to other evidence-based practices and to getting
> better outcomes in the field...... that is a very important policy
> push. We have this treatment model, where if its used right we can
> get some reasonable outcomes, but its not worth a dime if you don't
> have policies and funding structures that support the application of

the model. It's all for naught unless the folks at the policy level are
pushing the right kinds of initiatives.

Like the efforts to mount coordinated or comprehensive policies, the emphasis
on data driven programming and services represents a policy area in which
some progress has been made, but substantial advances are still pending. As
Marion Forgatch (personal communication, 2002) noted, "...it's only recently
since we have accountability coming in, saying...we don't want to waste our
money on programs that don't have any evidence, that's very recent and even
still we don't evaluate very well, we spend very little money on evaluation of
programs".

In summary, it was the combination of coordinated, evidence-based
programming and services that was of general importance to the panel. It
should be noted that the overall sentiment of the panel was that good,
practical tools now exist in many intervention areas. "I believe pretty
strongly...that these kids can be turned around. If their families are offered
help, these kids can be turned around, tripped off that track" (Webster-
Stratton, personal communication, 2002). Translating what we know works
into policy, and having those policies reflected in the thinking of persons
charged with helping young people, was seen as the key next steps to
advancing the life prospects of young people in a variety of countries.

Conclusion

The topic of context, culture, human development, and intervention
can be approached in many ways. As individuals interested in cross-national
intervention work, we decided to take a practical tact. This interview study
represents one way of addressing the intersections between context, culture,
human development, and intervention. This is a profoundly important and
tremendously large topic. Each approach taken in an effort to understand
these phenomena often can only tell a small part of what is a great saga. Yet,
it was our hope to offer some potentially useful knowledge by integrating
elements of the scientific research literature on this topic with the real life
experiences of individuals directly involved in cross-national intervention
work. Here, we offered our part of the story.

Historically scientists have shared their findings across borders. In
our thinking about borders, we viewed the concept of a border not only in the
geographical sense, but also in light of the disciplinary and professional
borders encountered in the everyday settings in which intervention work takes
place, such as schools, daycare facilities, or in the home (Oldenburg, 2002).
This book was written, with the hope of passing on potentially useful
knowledge across those borders.

Chapter Endnotes

[1]Super and Harkness (1999; 2002) explain in some detail how culturally linked facets of a developmental niche relate to developmental outcomes. This account centers on processes such as contemporary redundancy, thematic elaboration, and chaining. Specifically, contemporary redundancy refers to the repetition of similar influences in different parts of a developmental niche or environment. This repetition reinforces or strengths development in a particular way. An illustration of this phenomenon is the ability of Moken children living on islands off the coast of Thailand to change the size of their pupils to improve their under water vision. The need to see underwater becomes apart of the everyday experience of these children. The ability to accommodate for distortions underwater represents a valued skill that develops over time. Thematic elaboration deals with patterns of communication through core symbols or systems of meaning that reinforce cultural rules of performance. A salient example here would be children's ability to regulate specific emotions and their expression in social situations in a way that is appropriate to the expectations of the culture, such as the socialization of dependence in traditional Japanese culture (Super & Harkness, 2002). Finally, a third way culture coordinates environmental influences is by chaining. Super and Harkness (2002) described this process as follows, "no single element of the environment is sufficient in kind to produce a particular outcome, but the linking of disparate elements creates a qualitatively new phenomenon" (p. 272). Chaining, for instance, can occur in situations where there is a spread of a physical disease. In this situation, the high rates of disease are clearly linked to known pathogens in the environment, like certain high risk sexual behaviors. Ethnotheories can play into difficulties understanding the causes of a particular disease and the failure to take steps to alleviate it. Culturally linked customs can compound the effects of ethnotheories and permit an even greater outbreak (Super & Harkness, 2002)

[2]For more on the interventions discussed in this chapter refer back to: Functional Family Therapy (p. 53); Incredible Years Series (p. 51); Parent Management Training (p. 71); Promoting Alternative Thinking Strategies (PATHS) (p. 85); Multisystemic Therapy (p. 55); Olweus Bullying Prevention Program (p. 123).

[3]Interviews with panelists were conducted over a three month period, from January to March, 2002. Some follow up correspondence occurred from June to August 2003.

[4]Constant comparative analysis was used to classify the interview content into categories (Strauss & Corbin, 1998). One coder conducted all analyses. Representative comments were grouped into descriptive categories. The general properties of a given category were articulated (e.g., These comments are all similar because they involve challenges related to the translation of program materials) and a final set of categories was then generated. There was no restriction on the number of descriptive categories the coder could generate; nor was there any restriction on the type of criteria the coder could use. The second step in this process consisted of determining how the categories generated in the first step relate to one another or form a pattern. This second step consisted of a comparative analysis that paralleled the coding procedure used in the first step. More specifically, the coder generated hypotheses regarding possible relationships between the categories and articulated the criteria used to formulate her hypotheses (e.g., Taking a collaborative individual oriented approach with intervention participants, in many cases, can help to bypass cultural and contextual barriers to successful program implementation). Then a final set of hypothesized patterns was generated. There was no restriction on the number of hypotheses the coder could generate; nor was there any restriction on the type of criteria the coder could use.

Part III
Resource Guide

Chapter 8
The Glossary[*]

Academic enrichment: actions taken to enhance a young person's intellectual development and school performance (e.g., tutoring in subject areas like math or languages).

Age cohort design: an assessment of students in the same grade and approximately the same age is made as a part of an outcome evaluation study. Student responses or behavior are sampled at different time points depending on whether or not pupils in that grade have been exposed to a given intervention. See Olweus and Alsaker (1994) for a more complete discussion of age cohort designs.

Attributional biases: an individual's typical way of thinking about, explaining, and/or predicting his or her own behavior (or performance) in a particular type of situation.

Best evidence syntheses: in this review, a synthesis of the research literature is offered in the cases where enough evidence has accumulated. The synthesis technique used here involved equating a qualitative analysis of the exemplary programs described in this review with relevant narrative reviews and meta-analyses that already exist in the research literature. This variation of a best evidence synthesis of the research literature (Slavin, 1995) is used to make summative statements about particular areas of prevention research.

Booster sessions: refer to additional intervention related activities that participants experience after a program is completed. These are usually less intensive activities or sessions that recap an intervention's key points. This is also sometimes called booster training or booster activities.

Bottom-up intervention model: here, program participants have input into the intervention process and in some instances have predominate or complete control over an intervention.

Cohort design: in discussions of intervention outcome evaluations, a cohort design can refer to a study in which individual participants are assigned to an

---

[*]This glossary is designed to explain how the authors thought about and utilized key terms in the present review.

intervention or control group. Responses are collected from the same participants in both groups at pre and post-testing.

Confederate: in experimental research designs, the word confederate has a particular meaning. This person, the confederate, is in league with the researcher and acts as though she or he is a naturally occurring part of the environment. For example, the confederate in a shopping trial pretends to be a real customer and does not inform the shop keeper in advance that the purchase about to be made is apart of a research study.

Control and comparison group(s): a key for adequate program evaluation has to do with the use of a control or comparison group. Members of control and comparison groups usually only have minimal contact with program staff during project recruitment and assessment (pre-post testing and follow ups). These groups do not take part in activities associated with the tested intervention program. Some authors use the terms control and comparison group interchangeably. In this review, a distinction was made in that a control group implies that random or block random assignment to condition was used. The term comparison group denotes non-random assignment to condition. This design can provide a satisfactory quasi-experimental test of a program's utility depending on how the comparison group was formed and which post-hoc statistical controls are used to ensure the comparability of groups (intervention versus comparison) before the intervention takes place (Campbell & Stanley, 1963). When in question, the baseline comparability between intervention and comparison groups is noted in the review.

Cross context interventions: these initiatives are designed to work with individuals and environment(s) or within two or more environments (e.g., family–school– community).

Cross-national (interventions): in this review, this term is often used in relation to interventions that have or are being conducted in both the United States and Europe.

Disaggregating: to take apart or dismantle. See the glossary entry for 'unpacking or component delivery studies'.

Early educational enrichment: exposes children and/or parents to intellectual and social developmental activities. The site for intervention is typically the child's early school or daycare environment. In some cases, the intervention activities are extended to the child's home.

Effect size(s): Lipsey and Wilson (2001) stated that an appropriate effect size statistic shows:

...both the *magnitude* and the *direction* of a relationship, not merely its statistical significance. In addition, they are defined so that there is relatively little confounding with other issues, such as sample size, which figures prominently in significance test results (p. 5).

The benefit of using an effect size statistic, beyond its descriptive advantages is that all results irregardless of how they were measured can be placed on a single measurement scale. Results across studies that use this common metric then become easily comparable thereby facilitating synthesis of the research literature (Lipsey & Wilson, 2001).

Equifinality: is a core concept from general systems theory and developmental psychopathology that states there are multiple influences on the development and expression of both adaptive and maladaptive patterns of behavior. Because these influences vary widely in their combination and strength across people, there are likely to be multiple processes and pathways that lead to development of patterns of adaptive and maladaptive behavior.

Family therapy: the term therapy, in many cases, implies the treatment of individuals who meet the diagnostic criteria for a mental disorder. While some family therapies described in the *Family Section* were developed as mental health oriented treatments, these interventions have also been tested and shown promise as prevention programs with relevance to amelioration of youth problem behaviors and associated risk-protective factors. In the present review, the term family therapy encompasses later family interventions implemented at the selective prevention to treatment levels [selective-indicated, indicated, indicated-treatment]. Intervention efforts can be focused at parents and/or youth.

Family training: is a broad term in the intervention research literature. In the present document, family training specifically refers to universal–selective prevention programs [universal, universal-selective, selective] for parents and/or youth. For further elaboration see Later Family Intervention Figure, the discussion of family training in the later family intervention chapter.

Follow up: involves measuring the phenomena that the intervention is trying to change after the intervention has ended and participants have been post-tested. Some authors use the words post-test and follow up interchangeably. In this document, however, the term follow up means that a measurement has occurred after post testing. Follow up testing allows a preventionist to make sound conclusions about the durability of an intervention-related effect.

Health education: in the prevention literature, the term health education can imply a multiplicity of intervention efforts aimed at a variety of outcomes. Desired program benefits in youth or student populations can range from reductions in smoking, alcohol, and other drug use to declines in violent injury to lessening the occurrence of high risk sexual practices to the promotion of better exercise, nutritional and dental habits. While exercise, nutrition, and dental health fall outside of the direct mandate of this review, health education initiatives that have demonstrated a positive program related impact on youth problem behaviors or corresponding risk and protective factors have been included in this document.

Home visitation: is usually provided to expectant and/or new parents. Visitors can be professional or non-professionals. Goals of visitation include preparing parents for their care giving roles and connecting them to essential resources (e.g., pre-natal care). Sherman and colleagues (1997) noted, "The common core of home visitation is a visitor who cares about child-raising sitting down in a home with a parent and a child" (p. 100).

Indicated (prevention): works with those persons individually identified as at risk for chronic-severe problem behavior, adult adjustment difficulties, and/or known diseases-disorders.

Intervention(s): some authors use the word intervention to refer to treatment. In this document, the terms intervention, initiative, and prevention program are used interchangeably and in all cases refer to forms of prevention. See *Classification Systems for Prevention, Promotion, and Treatment – Chapter 1* for a discussion on the distinction between prevention and treatment.

Intervention group: those individuals exposed to a given prevention program. This is also sometimes called the treatment or experimental group.

Life competence promotion: activities designed to foster skills that are useful in making the best of (or adapting to) a range of situations and/or challenges.

Media advocacy: concerned individuals can be trained to become more aware of communication and its effects. An important part of this training has to do with becoming more savvy or adept in the use of types of communication to deliver an intervention message (e.g., writing newspaper editorials, attracting television or radio attention, public announcements, and billboards).

Meta-analytic review(s) or meta-analyses: the research literature on a certain topic is gathered and categorized by the individual(s) conducting the meta-analysis. The results of the collected studies are then statistically combined. Conclusions about the research literature are made based on analyses conducted across studies. This is sometimes also called a quantitative review. It should be noted that quantitative reviews or meta-analyses still retain an element of human judgment in the coding program characteristics or in the interpretation of results, but rely primarily on the statistical combination of results across several studies to make an overall conclusion about the utility of particular types of intervention or ways of working.

Multifinality: is a core concept from general systems theory and developmental psychopathology that states there are wide differences in the likelihood that particular individuals will develop a specific adaptive (e.g., school graduation) or maladaptive (e.g., a psychiatric disorder) outcome. Many youth experience multiple risk factors for maladaptive outcomes but do not manifest them. The influence of a specific risk factor upon the likelihood of a specific outcome is dependent upon the totality of influences present in a relevant developmental system.

Multi-level approach: school programs can be designed to work in more than one facet of the school environment, (e.g., at the individual and classroom levels). In this document, these types of interventions are called multiple-level approaches or programs.

Narrative reviews: there is debate about the merits of qualitative and quantitative research synthesis (e.g., Corcoran, Miller, & Bultman, 1997; Durlak, 2000; Mullen, Muellerleile, & Bryant, 2001; Lipsey & Wilson, 2001). Qualitative or narrative reviews involve a human synthesis of the literature. More specifically, a narrative review is when an individual examines the research literature on a given topic and then makes conclusions based on this analysis. This is sometimes also called a qualitative or expert review.

Nested cohort-cross sectional sub-design(s) or designs: in terms of intervention outcome studies, a nested cross sectional design can be used when the unit of assignment is an environment such as a classroom, school, school district, or community. In this case, no individual person is selected for intervention. The environment itself is the target of intervention. People that have contact with this environment or a control/comparison environment provide responses at pre and post testing. In contrast to a cohort design, it is not necessary for the exact same people to provide data at both the pre and post testing. However, individuals giving responses at pre and post testing should have contact with the particular environment targeted for change or the control/comparison environment. When the target for intervention is an environment and not a particular individual, a cohort design where the same group of people is followed from pre to post testing is not necessarily the most precise reflection of the program's potential impact (Gruenewald, 1997; Murray, Clark, Wagenaar, 2000). The Community Trials Intervention to Reduce High-Risk Drinking (CTI; Holder, et al., 2000) as it is described in the *Community* chapter is a good example of this design. Notice that in the CTI, the design elements of pre to post testing and an intervention with control/comparison group are still retained. Who or what is thought to be the participant does however differ. When the nested cross sectional approach is just one element of a larger design, it can be referred to as a sub-design. If the nested cross sectional approach is the main focus of a study and the only design in use, then the it can be called a design.

On premise (versus off premise alcohol vendors): alcohol outlets are usually licensed by government entities to sell or serve alcohol for off and/or on premise use. Examples of off premise alcohol establishments are grocery and convenience stores, privately or state run liquor stores. On premise alcohol outlets include restaurants, cafes, bars, pubs, and discos. The on and off premise distinction is typically not made for tobacco retailers who may or may not be licensed to sell alcohol.

Opportunity interventions: offer young people the chance to develop promotive social bonds. Examples of such initiatives include community service, mentoring, and recreational activities.

Outcome evaluation(s): at present, there is still disagreement among preventionists regarding how outcome evaluation studies should be conducted or results expressed (Catalano, et al., 1999; McCall, Green, Strauss, & Groark, 1998). Outcome evaluation studies typically emphasize statistical analyses that answer the question of whether or not an intervention had a significant impact on those persons exposed to program activities versus those that did not take part in the planned intervention actions. This is also sometimes called a program evaluation, intervention trial, or outcome study.

Parent capacitation: actions that assist and/or bolster parents in their role as caregivers.

Pre-post test research design: an indication of adequate program evaluation is the existence of pre and post testing. A pre-post test research design means that testing occurs before the program starts (at the pre-test) and the same type of testing happens sometime after the program concludes (at the post-test). Testing that takes place during pre and post testing usually involve measuring the things that the intervention is trying to change, like a child's aggressive behavior at school or new parents' responsiveness to their infant. Sometimes the words pre-test and baseline are used interchangeably.

Problem behaviors: are defined as undesirable by the mainstream culture of a given society. Problem behaviors are therefore characterized by their socially determined meaning and consequences they can elicit. In regards to young people, problem behaviors are often grouped into the following categories: 1) violence and criminality, 2) substance use and abuse, 3) teen pregnancy and risky sexual behaviors, and 4) school failure. In this document, the terms problem behavior and youth problem behavior are used interchangeably and in all cases refer to four problem domains listed above. See Jessor (1998) for more on this topic.

Process evaluation(s): deal with the question of how an intervention was actually implemented and how changes associated with the intervention came about (i.e., the process of change, how did it happen?). This type of information is vital in terms of refining theory and in developing the next intervention.

Program attrition: in this document, refers to the number of program participants that drop out of a program evaluation study between data collection points (i.e., pre to post test or post test to follow up).

Promising: refer to interventions with statistically significant and predominately desirable results in at least one empirically sound outcome evaluation.

Protective factors: can be individual attributes or aspects of the environment that have been found in scientific studies to increase the likelihood that a person will not experience significant problem behaviors and/or adjustment difficulties. An illustration of a protective factor linked to positive youth development is a family's positive and promotive daily interactions (Kumpfer & Alvarado, 1998). Protective factors can interact with risk factors and problem behaviors in different ways. See these resources for more on this topic: Coie, et al. (1993), Luthar (1993), Luthar and Cicchetti, (2000), and Rutter (2000).

P-value(s): many test statistics yield p-values. The p-value approach is particularly vulnerable to problems related to sample size. For example, if the number of participants per condition is too few then there will be little statistical power to detect change. A sole reliance on p-values also makes studies with different sample sizes hard to compare. In this review, if no effect size was described in the original program evaluation, then reported p-values were used to determine the statistical significance of an intervention-related change (i.e., no effect size statistics were calculated by the authors).

Random and block random assignment versus non-random assignment: random assignment to condition is widely considered to be a strong experimental test of a program's utility because it reduces the chance of systematic bias. In random assignment, all participants have the opportunity to be in the intervention or control group before the program trial begins. What determines the participant's group membership is the outcome of a randomization procedure that the program evaluator should not influence, like the flipping of a coin, with all heads going to the control group and all tails being assigned to the intervention group. Other evaluators draw participants' names or subject numbers out of a hat, use a table of random computer generated numbers, or make use of other randomization procedures. A frequently used variation of the randomization procedure involves matching participants on important variables such as gender or ethnicity and then randomly assigning them to a condition. This is called block random assignment and is usually categorized as an experimental design. Random and block random assignment procedures should minimize average group differences on outcomes of interest prior to the implementation of an intervention, making the effect of the program more readily apparent. Illustrations of non-random assignment to condition are when participants volunteer to take part in the intervention or comparison group or are placed into a group for some reason. This is regularly called a quasi-experimental design. Pre-test differences between the intervention and comparison groups if significant can distort the results of a program evaluation. This difference can work in favor or against an intervention. For example, if an intervention is designed to reduce reoffending in juvenile delinquents and the intervention group is comprised mostly of hardened repeat offenders and the comparison group is made up of primarily first time offenders, then it maybe be more difficult for the intervention to demonstrate a positive result because the two groups are not similar at the outset. Examination of group comparability (intervention versus comparison) and post-hoc statistical controls can be used to address these problems, if they arise. See Campbell and Stanley (1963) for a discussion of this and other related topics.

Resilience: normal or optimal functioning in the presence of exposure to ongoing risk.

Risk factors: can be individual attributes or aspects of the environment that can endanger a person's development and/or adjustment. Examples of risk factors associated with youth problem behaviors include, family dysfunction, school and community disorganization, and exposure to violence and substance abuse (Hawkins, Herrenkohl, et al., 1998). The link between the risk factor and the outcome can be established through scientific studies (e.g., cross sectional/ longitudinal) that examine human development. As risk factors accumulate, the individual is placed in increased danger.

Science-based prevention: involves making decisions about intervention programming and implementation on the basis of evidence derived from commonly accepted scientific principles and methods.

Selective (prevention): in this document selective interventions are defined as those prevention programs that identify and intervene with subgroups in a given population based on a consideration of empirically known risk. The usage of this term is in line with the Institute of Medicine report (1994).

Snow ball technique: participants are recruited to be in an intervention or research student through word of mouth campaign (i.e., people already in the intervention or study ask friends and/or acquaintances if they would also be willing to take part).

Sobering up stations: designated locations within a community where an intoxicated youth can receive immediate medical and/or social services (i.e., emergency treatment of physical injuries, safe waiting area, or transportation home).

Social resistance skills: typically involves the use of interactive skills training to assist children or adolescents to recognize media appeals, to identify high-risk situations, as well as to model and practice assertive responses to subtle or overt pressures from peers to engage in substance use, risky sexual behavior, or other problem behaviors.

Spreading effects versus specific effects: in this document, a specific program effect refers to an instance where a prevention program has demonstrated an intervention-related benefit that has relevance to one problem behavior domain: 1) violence and criminality, 2) substance use and abuse, 3) teen pregnancy and risky sexual behavior, or 4) school failure. A spreading program effect refers to an intervention that has shown a range of benefits in at least two problem behavior domains.

Sub design(s): a design within a design

Time series analysis: any of a large body of univariate or multivariate statistical techniques developed to describe and model data collected in experimental or quasi-experimental longitudinal research designs. A key feature of time series analytical techniques is that they provide ways, when modeling or drawing inferences from time series data (i.e., multiple observation of, or reports from the same persons), to control for the dependence among the individual data points.

Top-down intervention models: in this case, non-program participants have primary control of the intervention process.

Treatment: the term treatment, in this text, is used in relation to socially defined youth problem behaviors and known mental health disorders. In the first case, a young person's entry and exposure to programming in an adult rehabilitative setting, like an adult prison, is considered an instance of treatment. Treatment also retains its traditional meaning in that individuals who meet the diagnostic criteria and receive services to address a mental disorder are viewed as the recipients of treatment. Interventions dealt with in this review were in some instances created as mental health treatments. To be included in this review, the treatment must have also demonstrated utility as prevention program with relevance to amelioration of youth problem behaviors and associated risk-protective factors.

Unit of analysis: information gathered from an intervention outcome evaluation study can be analyzed in different ways. An important consideration is whether or not the intervention attempted to change individuals and/or environments. If the intervention is aimed at individuals then participants' responses in the intervention group are pooled together. The responses of persons in the control condition are also grouped together. The responses of these two groups (intervention versus control) are compared against each other across the pre and post test assessments as a way to test the effects of a given prevention program. When an intervention is aimed at making environmental changes, then participants' responses are pooled according to condition (intervention versus control) and the environmental unit (e.g., classroom, school, school district, community). For example, if an intervention attempted to change the classroom structure, scheduling, and the content of classroom instruction in 15 schools, then student responses would be grouped at the level of the individual schools that make up the intervention group. The same would be done for control schools, and then a comparison would be made of these groups (intervention versus control) across time in order to test the effects of the prevention program.

Unit of assignment: in intervention outcome evaluations, people or environments can be assigned to an intervention or control group depending on whether the intervention is designed to make changes in an environment or individuals. If one is conducting an environmental intervention, then the unit of assignment should be the environment targeted for change (e.g., classroom, school, school district, community). For example, several communities can take part in intervention activities. Comparison/ control communities should also participate in the outcome evaluation as a reference group. In this case, communities and not people become the unit of assignment.

Universal (prevention): in this document, this term is defined as a prevention program that does not select program participants based on any consideration or assessment of risk. This usage of the term universal prevention is in line with Institute of Medicine report (1994). Youth development programs are also categorized as universal prevention programs. The placement of youth development programs into a universal prevention framework diverges from the Institute of Medicine (1994) classification system.

Unpacking or component delivery studies: these studies dismantle successful interventions by pitting various program components against each other and testing their relative utility. This allows the program designer to determine which intervention actions are essential for producing an effect.

Well established: in the present review, initiatives that have shown their utility under repeated and scientifically strong outcome evaluations and/or have demonstrated positive long-term program related effects in a single trial are called well established.

Young people: in the present review, the term young people is used in a generic sense and includes infants, children, and adolescents (i.e., 0-21 years of age). Also in this document, the words youth, youngsters, and young people are used as interchangeable terms.

Youth development program(s) (versus prevention): youth development programs often deal with the promotion of strengths, well being, health, and optimal functioning (Catalano, et al., 1999). In contrast, prevention is typically designed to reduce problems and foster positive development by reducing risk and increasing protective factors. In this review, youth development programs are classified as a type of universal prevention program. This is the only instance where there is a divergence from the Institute of Medicine (1994) classification system used throughout this document (i.e., for the terms universal, selected, and indicated prevention).

Chapter 9
Program Examples

Program Classification: American Home Visitation

Program Title: Nurse-Family Partnership

Developmental Period: Prenatal/Infancy/Early Childhood

Amount of Protection/Risk: Selective

Where was the Program Conducted? United States – Multiple sites: Semirural area in upstate New York; Memphis, Tennessee; Denver, Colorado

Stated Theoretical Basis: Human Ecology (Bronfenbrenner), Social Learning Theory (Bandura), Attachment Theory (Bowlby)

Who Implemented the Program? Nurses, trained non professional home visitors

Program Description (Elmira, New York): In the Elmira trial, the Nurse-Family Partnership was aimed at promoting the positive development of infants/children and their primary caregivers. All participants were provided infant medical screening and referral services. This was the only intervention planned for the Prenatal Minimal Intervention Group 1. The Prenatal Minimal Intervention Group 2 was provided with free transportation to their child's prenatal/well-baby doctor visits. Prenatal Complete Intervention Group was provided all of the aforementioned services and was also visited by a nurse approximately nine times during the course of their pregnancy. The Pre/Postnatal Complete Intervention Group received all of the aforementioned services and was also frequently visited by a nurse up to the age of two. For 6 weeks after delivery, the nurse made weekly home visits. From 6 weeks to 4 months, the nurse visited biweekly. From 4 to 14 months, the nurse visited every tri-weekly. From 14-20 months, the nurse visited every 4 weeks and from 20-24 months, the nurse visited every 6 weeks. Under crisis conditions, the nurse visited weekly. The nurse home visitation protocol consisted of social support, parent education on infant/child development, parent training in problem solving/goal setting and social skills as well as the mobilization of social support within the family and community (e.g., helping caregivers to help themselves in accessing basic services). **Program Duration:** The Elmira trial was conducted from 1977-1982. This was a prenatal to two years old program. **Program Language:** English. **Notes:** This program is listed as a model intervention on the Blue Prints Web site: www.colorado.edu/cspv/blueprints . Total cost of the complete Pre/Postnatal program per participant (infant/child-mother dyad) is estimated at approximately U.S. $8,000 (Note: This is estimated using 2002 U.S. dollar value). An economic analysis of the Elmira trial estimated a benefit-cost ratio of 4:1, with ratio only holding for unmarried mothers and families who experience socio-economic disadvantage (Karoly, et al., 1998).

Program Description (Memphis, Tennessee): The Nurse-Family Partnership was subsequently revised and tested with predominately ethnic minority families who lived in an urban setting. In the Memphis trial all participants were provided free transportation to their child's

231

prenatal/well-baby doctor visits. This was the only intervention planned for the Prenatal Minimal Intervention Group 1. The Prenatal Minimal Intervention Group 2 was provided with free transportation plus infant medical screening/referral services. Prenatal Complete Intervention Group was provided all of the aforementioned services and was visited by a nurse during the course of their pregnancy and two times after the birth of their child. The Pre/Postnatal Complete Intervention Group received all of the aforementioned services and was also frequently visited by a nurse up to the age of two. The Memphis visitation protocol was similar to the original Elmira trial with the addition of a stronger emphasis on parent capacitation (inclusion of additional mastery activities; Barnard's Keys to Caregiving program – NCAST feeding scale; Sparling's Partners Learning program) and greater articulation/action on the program's theoretical foundations. Home visitors also used a questionnaire to explore parents' health attitudes with this survey forming the basis of parent education. **Program Duration**: Prenatal to two years old program.

Outcome Evaluation (Elmira, New York): **Participants:** Predominately semi-rural European American first-time mothers and their infants (mothers were either adolescent, experienced socio-economic disadvantage and/or unmarried). **Design:** Participants were stratified by region and demographic characteristics and randomized into four intervention groups: Prenatal Minimal Intervention Group 1 (n=94), Prenatal Minimal Intervention Group 2 (n=90), Prenatal Complete Intervention Group (n=100), and Pre/Postnatal Complete Intervention Group (n=116). Final number of participants: Prenatal Minimal Intervention Group 1 plus Prenatal Minimal Intervention Group 2 (n=148), Prenatal Complete Intervention Group (n=79), and Pre/Postnatal Complete Intervention Group (n=97). **Measures:** Interviews with mothers (e.g., family characteristics, mothers' psychological and physical health/practices, social support) and medical/social services records were collected from the pregnancy up to the age of 15. **Results:** Outcome evaluation information presented here does not include 46 ethnic minority mothers. See Olds et al., 1983 for a complete report. Participants in the Pre/Postnatal Complete Intervention Group had the greatest and most enduring gains in terms of reduced health and social welfare problems for mothers and children (e.g., Birth outcomes: Better maternal prenatal health, knowledge/use of child development services, fewer low birth weight and pre-term births; Childhood outcomes: Fewer cases of child abuse, fewer child injuries, fewer emergency-room contacts and fewer child behavioral/coping problems; Adolescent outcomes: Fewer cases of child abuse, juvenile arrests/convictions, youth substance use and risky sexual behavior, greater rates of maternal entry into paid work; fewer maternal arrests and substance use related problems). This gain is in comparison to the other three intervention groups.

Outcome Evaluation (Memphis, Tennessee): **Participants:** Predominately urban African American first-time mothers and their infants (mothers were either unmarried and/or experienced socio-economic disadvantage). **Design:** Participants were randomized into four intervention groups: Prenatal Minimal Intervention Group 1 (n=166), Prenatal Minimal Intervention Group 2 (n=515), Prenatal Complete Intervention Group (n=230), and Pre/Postnatal Complete Intervention Group (n=228). Final number of participants: Prenatal Minimal Intervention Group 2 (n=443) and Pre/Postnatal Complete Intervention Group (n=203). **Measures:** Interviews with mothers and medical/social services records. **Results:** Participants in the Pre/Postnatal Complete Intervention Group evidenced pre to post test (at the child's age of two) program benefits on indices of child abuse (e.g., number and hospitalization for accidents). This benefit was found relative to the Prenatal Minimal Intervention Group 2. Five year post delivery benefits were also found for in the Pre/Postnatal Complete Intervention Group mothers (e.g., fewer later pregnancies, less utilization of social welfare programs) relative to mothers in Prenatal Minimal Intervention Group 2.

Further Reading/Materials:

Karoly, L. A., Greenwood, P. W., Everingham, S. S., Hoube, J., Kilburn, M. R., Rydell, C. P., Sanders, M., & Chiesa, J. (1998). *Investing in our children: What we know and don't know about the costs and benefits of early childhood interventions.* Santa Monica, CA: The RAND Corporation.

Olds, D. L. (1997). The prenatal/early infancy project: Fifteen years later. In G. W. Albee & T. P. Gullotta (Eds.), *Primary prevention works* (pp. 41-67). Thousand Oaks, CA: Sage.

Olds, D. L. (2002). Prenatal and infancy home visiting by nurses: From randomized trials to community replication. *Prevention Science, 3*(3), 153-172.

Olds, D. L., Henderson, C. R., Birmingham, M., et al., (1983). *Final report: Prenatal/Early Infancy Project. Final report to Maternal and Child Health and Crippled Children's Services Research Grants Program,* Bureau of Community Health Services, HSA, PHS, DHHS, Grant No. MCJ-36040307.

Olds, D. L., Henderson, C. R., Cole, R., Eckenrode, J., Kitzman, H., Luckey, D., Pettitt, L., Sidora, K., Morris, P., & Powers, J. (1998). Long-term effects of nurse home visitation on children's criminal and antisocial behavior: 15 year follow-up of a randomized control trial. *Journal of the American Medical Association, 280,* 1238-1244.

Olds, D., Robinson, J., Song, N., Little, C., & Hill, P. (1999). *Reducing risks for mental disorders during the first five years of life: A review of preventive interventions.* Washington, DC: Center for Mental Health Services.

Program Classification: European Home Visitation

Program Title: EU/WHO Multi-Center Psychosocial Promotion Project

Developmental Period: Prenatal/Infancy/Early Childhood

Amount of Protection/Risk: Universal

Where was the Program Conducted? Cyprus; Greece; Portugal; Federal Republic of Yugoslavia; Republic of Slovenia; Turkey

Who Implemented the Program? Primary health care workers (family doctors; pediatricians; professional and student health visitors); researchers

Program Description: This EU/WHO Multi-center Psychosocial Promotion Project is focused on supporting parents' sense of their own problem solving/coping capacity and it addresses the general population. This home visitation program conceptualizes visitor – parent interaction as an intimate, respectful, and collaborative relationship. Home visitors use a semi-structured interview to explore with parents a variety of topics related parenting and childrearing. This discussion forms the basis for exploration, problem solving and planning activities, parent capacitation, information giving, support for positive parenting practices, clarification of parenting and child development beliefs, and in cases of need parent – visitor advocacy for social/medical/psychiatric services. This EU/WHO Project is marked by its multi-national dissemination. **Program Duration:** The program is a three-year intervention that works with families/children from the pre-natal period until the beginning of the third year of life. **Program Languages:** Translation into the respective languages of the test site countries.

Outcome Evaluation: **Participants:** A Project Center was selected in each participating country (a primary health care center/institution). Primary health care workers (n=20) from each Center volunteered to participate in the program. **Design:** Workers were randomly assigned to condition (Intervention; Traditional health service visits). Target families (n=10) were randomly selected from each workers pre-natal visiting caseloads (families received the same condition assignment as their health care workers; N=200 mother – infant pairs; n=100 Intervention, n=100 Control per center). **Measures:** Outcome evaluation assessments are taken at six weeks, six months, 12 months, and 24 months. Mother report: Mother's adjustment/well being (Edinburgh Postnatal Depression Scale, EPDS, at six weeks, six, 12, and 24 months); mother's satisfaction as a parent (Daily Hassles Scale, DHS, at 12 and 24 months); mother's view of the infant/child (Bates Infant Characteristics Questionnaire, BICQ, at 24 months. Observational measures: Psychologist observations the quality of the caregiver – infant/child interaction, home environment (at six weeks, 6, 12, and 24 months), infant/child psychosocial development (Bayley Scale, BS, at 6 and 12 months), and language development (Bzoch-League Receptive Expressive Emergent Language Scale, REEL, at 24 months). **Results:** Intervention mothers evidenced a number of benefits relative to the comparison group (increased ease in care giving/the caregiver role, improved mother well being and positive parenting practices).

Further Reading/Materials:

Papadopoulou, K., Tsiantis, J., Dragonas, Th., & Cox, A. (2001). Maternal postnatal emotional well being and perceived parenting hassles: Does community intervention with normal population make a difference? *International Journal of Mental Health Promotion* 4(3): 13-24.

Tsiantis J., Dragonas Th., Cox A., & Papadopoulou K. (1997). Promotion of Children's Early Psychosocial Development In F. Anagnostopoulos, A. Kosmogianni, & V. Messini (Eds.), *Contemporary psychology in Greece. Research and application in the areas of health, education and clinical practice.* Athens, Greece: Ellinika Grammata Publications. [In Greek]

Tsiantis, J., Dragonas, Th., Cox, A., Smith, M., Ispanovic, V., & Sampaio-Faria, J. (1996). Promotion of children's early psychosocial development through primary health care services. *Paediatric and Perinatal Epidemiology, 10,* 339-354.

Tsiantis, J. & Papadopoulou, K. (in press). Primary prevention and promotion of children's early psychosocial development: The implementation of a programme through primary health care services in the general population. In *Promoting Positive Mental Health: A practical guide to planning, implementing and evaluating mental health promotion programmes.* WHO Collaborating Centre, Institute of Psychiatry.

Tsiantis J., Smith, M., Dragonas Th., & Cox A. (2000). Early mental health promotion in children through primary health care services: A multi-centre implementation. *International Journal of Mental Health Promotion, 2,* 5-17.

Program Classification: American Family Training-Therapy

Program Title: Strengthening Families Program (SFP)[1]

Developmental Period: Pre-school/Childhood/Adolescence

Amount of Protection/Risk: Universal/Selective/Indicated

Where was the Program Conducted? United States –almost all states, with research published on SFP versions for Alabama, Colorado, Hawaii, Utah, Michigan. SFP has also been implemented in Australia – Queensland; Canada – British Columbia, Montreal, Ontario; Costa Rica; Spain; and Sweden.

Stated Theoretical Basis: Resiliency Model; Social Ecology Model of Adolescent Substance Use

Who Implemented the Program? Trained program staff

Program Description: The Strengthening Families Program was originally developed as a 14-session, 2-hour program for high risk children of addicted parents in treatment by Dr. Karol Kumpfer at the University of Utah in the mid-1980s. It has subsequently been age- and culturally-adapted for the following populations – African American, Asian, Pacific Islanders, Spanish-speaking, and Indian/indigenous families (see Kumpfer et al., 1996; Kumpfer, Alvarado, Smith, & Bellamy, 2002). SFP combines three types of skill training, one for parents, one for children, and one for families. Meals, transportation, and child care are included to reduce barriers to attendance. About 8 families are an ideal size. Home practice assignments and behavioral change are stressed in all versions as well as family reunions at 6 and 12 months (Kumpfer, personal communication, 2003). SFP has been implemented/tested in locations as diverse as Iowa, Hawaii, Alaska, and British Columbia, Canada. In Iowa, the program was implemented as a universal intervention. The 7-session, Iowa Strengthening Families Program (ISFP), now called SFP 10-14, attempted to foster family-related protective factors/reduction of risk as a means for delaying the initiation of alcohol and drug use of children. Parents were provided development/health education, training in effective/positive parenting practices (rule setting and non-punitive enforcement/reinforcement), emotional regulation, communication, and conflict management. In Hawaii, the program was culturally adapted and implemented as a selective intervention with at risk Pacific Islander/Asian children (6-12 years old) and their families. Intervention parents were provided the aforementioned Strengthening Families training. Needs assessments and building links between family/community were especially stressed in this program. Intervention strategies were similar to the Iowa program. **Program Duration:** The pre-school and elementary school SFP version is 14-sessions long. The universal pre-teen and adolescent SFP version (e.g., ISFP) is 7-sessions long (Kumpfer, personal communication, 2003). **Program Languages:** English, French Canadian, Spanish. **Notes:** There is a cross-boarder comparison trial of SFP in (Buffalo, New York/Ontario, Canada) currently underway. Costs are US$250 for a CD with all program materials and limited site license to reproduce all trainer manuals, Implementation Manual, Evaluation instruments, and Parent and Children's Handbooks; approximately $ 2,500 (plus travel costs) for 2 day training (Kumpfer, personal communication, 2003).

[2]Outcome Evaluation (Utah) **Participants:** Families with children of addicted parents in treatment, methadone maintenance and outpatient mental health clinics. **Design:** Pre-post test, with families (N=90) randomly assigned to one of four groups: Wait-list control (WLC; n=30), parent training (PT; n=20), PT plus child training (PT/CT; n=20), PT plus CT plus a family relationship focused intervention (SFP; n=20). **Measures:** Parent/Child Report: Child Behavior Checklist, Moos Family Environment Scale, Cowan, and Olsen Family scales. **Results:** PT was associated with reduced negative behaviors among children and improved parenting skills. CT showed an intervention related improvement in child social skills. SFP was associated with improvements in a wide range of family related variables (e.g., family cohesion, organization, and communication) and reduced self reported substance use among SFP children (Kumpfer, personal communication, 2003; See Kumpfer & DeMarsh, 1985).

Outcome Evaluation (Utah) **Participants:** Children and families with children in primary school. **Design:** Pre-post test with random assignment of schools (N-12) to one of four conditions: I Can Problem Solve (ICPS; n=256 children); SFP plus ICPS (SFP+ICPS; n=56 families); SFP parent training only plus ICPS (SFP-PT+ICPS; n=21 families); Control group (CG; n=322 families). **Measures:** Parent/Child/Teacher Reports: child behavior and competencies; family characteristics (e.g., Moos Family Environment Scale). **Results:** Among the different study conditions, SFP+ICPS showed the strongest and broadest intervention benefits with positive changes evidenced on the child's school bonding and performance, as well as competence. Improvements were also found on family related variables (e.g., family relationships) and parenting skills. Declines in children's negative behaviors were also evident (Kumpfer, personal communication, 2003; See Kumpfer, Alvarado, Tait, & Turner, 2003).

Outcome Evaluation (ISFP- Iowa): **Participants:** Families with children/adolescents. **Design:** Pre-post test with one, 2 and 4-year follow up (n=374 pre-post test; n=317 at one year follow up; n=294 at two year follow up). Schools were matched on SES and size of the community's population, then randomly assigned to an intervention or control condition. **Measures:** Child's alcohol use (Alcohol Initiation Index). **Results:** The intervention group showed lower alcohol initiation/use relative to the control group at one and two year follow-up testing (a strengthening of the gain was reported at follow-up two).

Outcome Evaluation (Hawaii): **Participants:** Families with children/adolescents. **Design:** Pre-post test with an intervention and matched comparison group. **Measures:** Parent measures: Family relations (Family Environment Scale), parental attitudes and practices (Adult-Adolescent Parenting Inventory), parent psychological stress (Brief Symptom Inventory, Center for Epidemiological Studies Depression Scale), parent's substance use, parents' perception of child's use. Teacher ratings: Child problem behavior (Child Behavior Checklist). **Results:** Second cohort of families (Program year 2) showed significant reductions in family conflict relative to the comparison group.

Further Reading/Materials:

Aktan, G., Kumpfer, K. L., & Turner, C. (1996). The Safe Haven program: Effectiveness of a family skills training program for substance abuse prevention with inner city African American families. *International Journal of the Addictions, 31*, 158-175.

Coalition for a Drug Free Hawaii (2000). *Strengthening Hawaii Families – Program summary report*. Honolulu, HI: Coalition for a Drug Free Hawaii.

Harrison, S., Boyle, S. W., & Farley, O. W. (1999). Evaluating the outcomes of a family-based intervention for troubled children: A pretest-posttest study. *Research on Social Work Practice, 9* (6), 640-655.

Kumpfer, K. L., & DeMarsh, J. P. (1985). Prevention of chemical dependency in children of alcohol and drug abusers. *NIDA Notes, 5*, 2-3.

Kumpfer, K. L., Molgaard, V., & Spoth, R. (1996). The Strengthening Families Program for the prevention of delinquency and drug use. In R. D. Peters & R. J. McMahon (Eds.), *Preventing childhood disorders, substance abuse, and delinquency* (pp. 241-267). Thousand Oaks, CA: Sage.

Spoth, R., Redmond, C., & Lepper, H. (1999). Alcohol initiation outcomes of universal family-focused preventive interventions: One-and two-year follow-ups of a controlled study. *Journal of Studies on Alcohol, Suppl. 13*, 103-111.

<u>Program Classification</u>: Trans-Atlantic Family Therapy

<u>Program Title</u>: Functional Family Therapy (<u>FFT</u>)

<u>Developmental Period</u>: Late Childhood/Adolescence

<u>Amount of Protection/Risk</u>: Selective/Indicated/Treatment

<u>Where was the Program Conducted</u>? United States, Sweden

<u>Stated Theoretical Basis</u>: Theories on information processing, social cognition, and emotion; systems perspectives; behavioral and social learning theories

<u>Who Implemented the Program</u>? Clinicians, researchers, trained para-professionals (correctional, mental health, and social workers, college students)

<u>Program Description</u>: FFT is a comprehensive family focused intervention (complete in terms of its stated theory, mechanisms for insuring treatment fidelity, assessment, and dissemination). Individual families are usually referred through the social/justice system to FFT as an alternative to incarceration, post-incarceration transition program, or form of diversion or probation. This program is designed to work with youngsters who are at risk (delinquency, substance abuse) to those with clinically significant conduct/oppositional disorders. These are the primary steps of the intervention: 1) engagement/motivation, 2) behavior change, and 3) generalization. The engagement/motivation period focuses on building of a collaborative and positive relationship between the interventionist and family. Special attention is paid to setting optimistic (yet realistic) expectations for the intervention and the family as a whole. The behavioral change component is guided by an empirical and clinical assessment of the family strengths and weakness. Then the interventionist designs plan of action that is grounded in a range of evidence based intervention strategies (i.e., a menu) that are used in accordance with the particular intervention needs of an individual family. Activities here can include training in social, communicative, problem solving, and conflict resolution skills for all family members, parent training, the reconsideration of one's thoughts about the youngster's problem behaviors and the nature of family interactions (this is sometimes called cognitive reframing), gaining better insight into interpersonal needs and the developmental course of youth problem behaviors, specific treatment of parent psychopathology (if relevant). In recognition of the increased risk associated with having deviant family members, FFT behavior change strategies also explicitly direct activities to the sisters/brothers of young offenders. The generalization component is aimed at the maintenance of long term change by helping families to deal with setbacks or relapses and connecting them to existing resources in the community. Techniques used to promote change include modeling, reframing/reattribution, behavioral training, case management/advocacy. **Program Duration:** FFT has been developed and tested in the United States for over 30 years (1969 to the present). The total number of intervention hours (direct contact) can range from 8 to 30 hours spread over a three-month period. The Swedish trial of FFT was conducted between 1993-1995 (families had between 3 and 32 sessions, with an average of 10). **Program Languages:** English and Swedish. **Notes:** Special Features: The Functional Family Therapy—Clinical Services System is a computerized program, which helps the interventionist plan, implement, and assess the intervention. FFT is listed as a model intervention on the Blue Prints web site: http://www.colorado.edu/cspv/blueprints. Estimated costs from $US 1,350.00 to $US 3,750 per family (average of twelve home visits).

Outcome Evaluation (United States-Utah)[3]: **Participants:** Adolescents referred by juvenile justice system for mostly first time offenses (aged 13-16 at program start) and their families. **Design:** Random assignment to FFT (n=46 families) or an alternative intervention #1 (a family-interventionist discussions on emotional aspects of family life; n=19 families) or control group (received no special intervention actions; n=10 families). Pre to post testing. Follow up registry data was gathered at six to 18 months post intervention for the referred youth and 2.5 to 3.5 years after the intervention ended for siblings within treated families (not the originally referred youngster but their brothers or sisters). A post-hoc alternative intervention #2 (an insight oriented counseling program) was added when the follow up registry data was collected (n=11 families). **Measures:** Quality of family interactions, registry data on referred youth and their siblings reoffending. **Results:** FFT families showed improved family interactions relative to families in the alternative intervention #1 and the control condition. Follow up data (6-18 months) on recorded offenses for referred youth showed a significantly lower rate of reoffending for FFT youngsters (26%) relative to target youth in both alternative intervention groups (#1=47%; #2=73%), the control condition (50%), and county-wide rates of reoffending for juveniles (51%). At a later follow up (2.5-3.5 years) on recorded offenses for referred youth's brothers and sisters showed a significantly lower rate of reoffending for FFT siblings (20%) relative to target siblings in both alternative intervention groups (#1=59%; #2=63%), and the control condition (40%). See Alexander and Parsons (1973), Klein and Alexander (1977), Parsons and Alexander (1973).

Outcome Evaluation (United States-Ohio): **Participants:** Adolescents (age 15 at program start) referred by juvenile justice system for one or more minor to serious offense(s) and their families. **Design:** More serious offenders (with a mean of two offenses per youth) were referred to FFT plus standard probation (n=27 families) and a group of less serious offenders (with a mean of one offense per youngster) who were to receive standard probation services were randomly selected to serve as a comparison group (n=27 families). Follow up registry data was gathered at approximately two to three and five to six years (FFT n=23; Comparison n=22) after the initial referral. At the last follow up the target youth were young adults (age 21). **Measure:** Registry data on reoffending (non-traffic-related crime). **Results:** Follow up data (2-3 years) on recorded offenses showed a significantly lower rate of reoffending for FFT plus probation youngsters (11%) compared to the regular service condition (67%). At a later follow up (5-6 years), recorded offenses for FFT plus probation youth were significantly lower (8.7%) than youngsters provided with regular services (40.9%). **Notes:** Intervention youth had a significantly greater number of pre-test offenses relative to comparison teens. However, this difference should make it more difficult to demonstrate an intervention-related gain. This program was administered by trained and supervised graduate students. See Gordon, Graves, and Arbuthnot (1995), Gordon, Arbuthnot, Gustafson, and McGreen (1988).

Outcome Evaluation (Lund, Sweden): **Participants:** Adolescents under 18 years old who have had contact with the justice and social welfare systems from 1993-1995. **Design:** Pre-post testing with a one year follow up. Random assignment to an intervention (I, n=49) or control group (C, n=40). **Measures:** Registry Information: Reoffending. Mother report: Psychiatric symptoms (SCL-90), youth behavior (CBCL). Youth report: Internalizing/externalizing behavior, other psychiatric symptoms (SCL-90, CBCL), criminal behavior, sense of coherence (KASAM -- Antonovsky). **Results:** Intervention youth showed a lower rate of reoffending relative to the control youngsters at post testing and follow up (Post test: I=33% versus C=65%; Follow up: I=41% versus C=82%). **Notes:** 21 out of 40 control group families did not provide youth or mother reports for the post or follow up testing, however, registry information was gathered for all control families. Within the intervention group reductions in clinically significant symptoms were found for intervention youth (CBCL, SCL-90) and their mothers (SCL-90) from pre to follow up testing. See Hansson, Cederblad, and Höök (2000).

<u>Outcome Evaluation</u> (Växjö, Sweden): **Participants:** Adolescents under the age of 18 who had contact with the justice and social welfare systems. **Design:** Pre testing and a 18 months after first contact follow up assessment. Intervention youth were referred to FFT by a social worker. A comparison group was formed. After an initial meeting with a social worker, 17 of comparison youngsters were provided services as usual and 26 received no additional services. **Measures:** Registry Information: Reoffending [FFT youth (Pre-Follow up n=45) versus comparison youth (Pre-Follow up n=43)]; Youth Report [FFT youth only (Pre-Follow up n=36) – no comparison youth]: Family Climate, family relations, internalizing/ externalizing behavior (CBCL, YRS), sense of coherence (KASAM–Antonovsky), Ladder of Life (Wiklund, 1992). **Results:** Relative to those comparison youth (n=17) who were referred for additional services, FFT youth (n=45) evidenced a lower rate of reoffending at follow up (I=35% versus C=65%). **Notes:** Comparison youth (n=26) who were not referred for additional services fared better, i.e., had significantly lower reoffending rates (15%) than those youngsters who were referred to FFT (35%) or treatment as usual (65%). See Johansson, Drott-Englén, Hansson, and Benderix (2002).

Materials:
Alexander, J. F. & Parsons, B.V. (1982). *Functional Family Therapy*. Monterey, CA: Brooks/Cole.

Further Reading:
Alexander, J., Barton, C., Gordon, D., Grotpeter, J., Hansson, K., Harrison, R., Mears, S., Mihalic, S., Parsons, B., Pugh, C., Schulman, S., Waldron, H., & Sexton, T. (1998). *Blueprints for Violence Prevention, Book Three: Functional Family Therapy*. Boulder, CO: Center for the Study and Prevention of Violence.
Alexander, J. F. & Parsons, B.V. (1973). Short-term behavioral intervention with delinquent families: Impact on family process and recidivism. *Journal of Abnormal Psychology, 81*, 219-225.
Alexander, J., Waldon, H. B., Newberry, A. M., & Liddle, N. (1990). The functional family therapy model. In A. S. Friedman & S. Granick (Eds.), *Family therapy for adolescent drug abuse* (pp. 183-199). Lexington, MA: Lexington Books/D. C. Heath and Company.
Barton, C., Alexander, J. F., Waldron, H., Turner, C. W., & Warburton, J. (1985). Generalizing treatment effects of Functional Family Therapy: Three replications. *American Journal of Family Therapy, 13*, 16–26.
Gordon, D. A. Graves, K., & Arbuthnot, J. (1995). The effect of functional family therapy for delinquents on adult criminal behavior. *Criminal Justice & Behavior, 22*, 60-73.
Hansson, K., Cederblad, M., & Höök, B. (2000). Funktionell familjeterapi -- en behandlingsmetod vid ungdomskriminalitet. *Socialvetenskaplig Tidskrift, 3*, 231-242.
Johansson, P., Drott-Englén, G., Hansson, K., & Benderix, Y. (2002). *Funktionell familjeterapi i barnpsykiatrisk praxis: resultat av en samarbetsmodell vid behandling av ungdomskriminalitet utanför universitetsforskningen*. Manuscript submitted for publication.
Klein, N. C., Alexander, J. F., & Parsons, B. V. (1977). Impact of family systems intervention on recidivism and sibling delinquency: A model of primary prevention and program evaluation. *Journal of Consulting and Clinical Psychology, 45*, 469–474.
Parsons, B. V. & Alexander, J. F. (1973). Short-term family intervention: A therapy outcome study. *Journal of Consulting and Clinical Psychology, 41*, 195-201.

<u>Program Classification</u>: Trans-Atlantic Family Therapy

<u>Program Title</u>: Incredible Years: Parents, Teachers and Children Training Series

<u>Developmental Period</u>: Childhood

<u>Amount of Protection/Risk</u>: Universal/Selected/Indicated

<u>Where was the Program Conducted</u>? United States – Seattle, Washington, Canada – Thunder Bay, Ontario, England – London, Oxfordshire, Norway – Tromsø

<u>Stated Theoretical Basis</u>: Cognitive Social Learning Theory (Patterson's Social Learning Model; Bandura's Social Learning Theory)

<u>Who Implemented the Program</u>? Therapists/interventionists (of varied educational/training levels); researchers; parents; teachers

<u>Program Description</u>: The Incredible Years Series is a collection of interconnected programs that can be implemented with multiple (e.g., with parents, children, and teachers) or a single audience type (e.g., with children only). The Series has a history spanning over 20 years. BASIC, the first component to be developed, is the best tested and most widespread of the all of the programs in the Series. BASIC is designed to train parents in positive/effective parenting practices (limit setting/non coercive enforcement; problem solving skills). Attitudes and emotions clarification regarding parenting is also addressed. The standard BASIC training consists of a series of therapist/interventionist lead parent workshop sessions. Several parents attend these group sessions. Therapists/interventionists utilized a number of intervention strategies to promote change. A well-elaborated collaborative intervention model guides the use of these strategies. Strategies often include: The use of a series of video tapes that show everyday parent-child interactions with models of effective and counter productive/negative parenting practices (providing opportunities for observational learning and group role playing); practice of parenting skills in 'real life' situations via written/verbal and performance-based homework assignments (parents are provided individualized feedback on their homework using a portfolio method and through weekly telephone calls); parent education through informational materials (parenting book/guide); group and therapist/interventionist reinforcement (group members have a 'Buddy' network); cognitive exercises related to parenting issues (problem solving; cognitive reframing). A number of studies have been conducted to determine how to best provide the BASIC training program. These studies have systematically tested a variety of intervention modalities/formats (video tape only; video tape with brief consultation; group parent training with and without the use of the video tape series; group parent training versus one-family training). BASIC was first used in a mental health setting with families who have children diagnosed with clinically significant aggressive and/or oppositional behaviors. This program has also been tested in non clinical community settings in order to demonstrate its cross context transferability. BASIC has undergone revision and been expanded (e.g., ADVANCE; SCHOOL/Supporting Your Child's Education). For example, the ADVANCE program takes place after BASIC training is completed (an additional 14 weeks of sessions). ADVANCE makes use of intervention strategies employed in BASIC program (e.g., video modeling) but the content of the intervention targets the quality of family interactions on a broader level (beyond a specific focus on parenting practices). Targets for change include parent's emotional management/regulation, coping, problem solving, communication, and conflict resolution skills. The child-focused edition of BASIC is entitled, Dinosaur School (<u>DS</u>). Groups of children (5-6) attend a series of workshop sessions. The targets for intervention change include the child's problem solving (perspective taking; empathy training),

communication, and conflict resolution skills in the context of everyday relationship situations (home, school). DS uses intervention strategies employed in the other programs in the Incredible Years Series (e.g., video modeling, small group problem solving; self-talk). Special DS techniques include the use of 'pretend' play, games, creative program activities (drawing, story telling); informational materials (child homework, regular information to teachers and parents on child program activities), role playing/modeling of self-regulatory, attentive, and cooperative behaviors. The teacher focused edition of BASIC is entitled TEACHER program. Core components of this program include the quality of teacher-student-parent interactions (classroom control/learning; communication; involvement). Teachers are also provided training on how to incorporate socio-emotional competence building activities in the classroom. **Program Duration:** BASIC (12 weeks); BASIC + ADVANCE (22 weeks) SCHOOL (BASIC + academic enhancement program for use with children up to the age of 10 years old); Dinosaur School (22 weeks); TEACHER program. **Program Languages:** English (American and English Accents), Spanish, Norwegian, and segments in Vietnamese. **Notes:** Estimated costs **(United States)** Start up: Program materials (curriculum/videos) and initial training: U.S. $3,200-4,200 Maintenance: Therapist/interventionist salary: U.S. $1,800 per training series (12 weeks of sessions) – **(United Kingdom)**: Eligible families receive the program free of charge. Scott, Doolan, Jacobs, & Aspland (2001) estimated a cost of £571 per family through National Health Service Child and Adolescent Mental Health Centers – **(Norway)**: Eligible families receive the program as a part of national health/welfare service.

[4]Outcome Evaluation (BASIC vs. Family Therapy vs. Control Group): **Participants:** Clinic referred sample. Design: Pre-post test with one year follow up. This study is a comparison of the BASIC parent training (pre-post test n=13; follow up n=15) with traditional family (individual) therapy (pre-post test n= 11; follow up n=16) and a wait-list control group (n=11). **Measures:** Parent report: Child behavior (Child Behavior Checklist, CBCL; Eyberg Child Behavior Inventory, ECBI; Parent Daily Reports, PDR). Teacher report: Child behavior (Behar Preschool Behavior Questionnaire, PBQ). Observational measures: Observer-rated parent-child interactions at home. **Results:** On pre-post test indices both intervention groups showed improvements compared to controls (e.g., less non-compliance). Follow up results indicated maintenance of gains for the intervention groups relative to one another. This study highlights the reduced cost and relative utility of the BASIC program compared to traditional family therapy approaches for conduct problem children. See Webster-Stratton (1984).

Outcome Evaluation (BASIC vs. BASIC + ADVANCE): **Participants:** Clinic referred sample. **Design:** Pre-post test with one and two year follow up. Random assignment to condition (BASIC n=39 families; BASIC + ADVANCE n=38 families). **Measures:** Parent reported: Marital satisfaction (MAT) Brief Anger Aggression Questionnaire (BAAQ); depression (Beck Depression Inventory); stress in the parent-child relationship (Parenting Stress Index, PSI), child behavior problems (CBCL and ECBI). Observational measures: Parent-child interaction at home (DPICS); parent problem solving/ communication/emotional regulation strategies (PS-I CARE); child problem solving skills (SPST-R). **Results:** Both intervention groups reported significant pre-post-follow up improvements in child behaviors, parent-child interactions, and parent stress. Particular intervention gains associated with the ADVANCE program included improved parent problem solving/communication and child problem solving relative to the standard BASIC program. This outcome evaluation is one of two studies testing the ADVANCE program's utility. See Webster-Stratton (1994).

Outcome Evaluation (BASIC + Teacher Training + Head Start vs. Head Start Only): **Participants:** Non clinical (but at risk) community-based sample. **Design:** Pre-post test with one year follow up. Eight head start centers were randomly assigned to condition: BASIC +

Teacher Training + Head Start, B+TT+HS (pre-post test: n=264 families, follow up: n=189 families) or Head Start Only (pre-post test: n=130 families, follow up: 107 families). B+TT+HS parents had their children in a Head Start preschool and under went standard BASIC training (video tape combined within a series of interventionist lead parent training sessions). Teachers were informed of the content/strategies of the BASIC program and were encouraged to develop new ways to engage parents in school life. Head Start only parents engaged in Head Start related activities with their children enrolled in a Head Start preschool. **Measures:** Parent report: Parent's mental health (CES-D, Brief Anger-Aggression Questionnaire, BAAQ), parent's own childrearing history, parent's life events (Life Experience Survey), parenting practices (Daily Discipline Interview, DDI), parent-teacher involvement (INVOLVE), child behavior (Social Competence Scale, CBCL, ECBI). Teacher reports: Child behavior (Social Competence Scale, CBCL), parent-teacher involvement (INVOLVE). Observational Measures: Parent-child interactions (DPICS-R); parenting style (Coder Impression Inventory – Parenting Style). **Results:** Pre-post-follow up self-reports and home observations indicated that B+TT+HS parents evidenced significant improvement in parenting practices and the quality of parent-child interactions relative to the Head Start only parents. A similar pattern of intervention gains was found for child behavior at home. Teachers reported higher levels of parental involvement in the child's academic life for the B+TT+HS versus the Head Start only group. This outcome evaluation is one of two studies testing BASIC's utility as a community-based prevention program. See Webster-Stratton (1998).

<u>Outcome Evaluation</u> (Dinosaur School vs. BASIC + ADVANCE vs. Dinosaur School + BASIC + ADVANCE vs. Control Group): **Participants:** Clinic referred sample. **Design:** Pre-post test with one year follow up. Random assignment to condition: Dinosaur School (pre-post test: n=27 children, follow up: n=24 children) or BASIC + ADVANCE (pre test to follow up: n=26 mothers and 17 fathers) or Dinosaur School + BASIC + ADVANCE (pre test to follow up: n=22 children, 20 mothers and 16 fathers) or Wait-list Control (pre-post test: n=22 children, 22 mothers and 18 fathers). **Measures:** Parent reports: Child behavior (CBCL, ECBI, PSI, PDR). Teacher reports: Child behavior (PBQ) and preschool problem solving (Wally Child Social Problem-Solving Test, WALLY). Observational Measures: Parent-child interactions (DPICS-R); parent's problem solving and communication (PS-I CARE); child-peer interaction in a laboratory setting (PPS-I CARE). **Results:** The three intervention groups showed pre-post test improvement in child behavior relative to the control condition (parent reports, child-peer observation). Follow up assessments indicated that the intervention groups maintained the majority of their gains relative to one another. Among the intervention groups, the combined Dinosaur School + BASIC/ADVANCE program was the most successful relative to the other two intervention conditions at pre-post and follow up testing (in terms of parenting practices, child behavior and problem solving/conflict resolution skills). See Webster-Stratton and Hammond (1997).

<u>Outcome Evaluation</u> (Thunder Bay, Ontario, Canada – BASIC vs. Eclectic Family Therapy vs. Control Group): **Participants:** Clinic referred sample. **Design:** Pre-post test. This study was an effectiveness trial of BASIC parent training (n=46 families) with a non-manualized eclectic/ecological family (individual) therapy (n=46 families) and a wait-list control group (n=18 families). Families were triaged into a nonspecific intervention or wait-list comparison group. Intervention families were then randomly assigned to the BASIC or eclectic intervention conditions. **Measures:** Parent reports: Child behavior (CBCL, ECBI, PDR), parent's mental health (BDI, Brief Anger-Aggression Questionnaire, BAAQ), parent's perception of parent-child relationship (Dyadic Adjustment Scale), parents' perception of social support (Support Scale). Teacher reports: Child behavior (CBCL, Matson Evaluation of Social Skills with Youngsters, MESSY). **Results:** On pre-post test indices both intervention groups showed improvements compared to controls (e.g., fewer parent reported behavior problems with

children). BASIC program participants evidenced greater reductions in parent reported behavior problems in comparison to the eclectic intervention group. This study highlights the reduced cost and relative effectiveness of the BASIC program compared to traditional family therapy approaches for conduct problem children. It also demonstrates the cross context transferability of the BASIC program in a 'real life' clinic (non-university clinic) in another socio-cultural context (Canada). See Taylor, Schmidt, Pepler, and Hodgins (1998). This effectiveness trial is one of four that have been conducted in North America. These studies show the same general pattern of findings found in other tests of the BASIC program. However, these programs were conducted with community and daycare-based samples of parents (and teachers in one case).

Outcome Evaluation (South London/West Sussex, United Kingdom – BASIC vs. Wait-List Control Group): **Participants:** Clinic referred sample of children (3-8 years old) identified as showing elevated levels (above the 97th percentile) of conduct problems and their parents. **Design:** Pre-post testing using a permuted block design that consisted of an intervention (I; Pre-test = 90; Pre-post test = 73) and wait-list control (W-LC; Pre-test=51; Pre-post test=37) condition. **Measures:** Mother report: Child behavior and competence (Parent Account of Child Symptoms Interview, Strengths and Difficulties Questionnaire, Child Behavior Checklist, Parent Defined Problems Questionnaire, Parent Daily Report Questionnaire). Observation: Parent-child interaction (blind rater); Clinical diagnosis: ICD 10. **Results:** Children whose parents underwent BASIC training showed significant reductions in antisocial and problem behavior on multiple indices and relative to control group children. Intervention children were less likely to be diagnosed as having Oppositional Defiant Disorder relative to control children. Intervention parents were also found to interact in a more effective and non-harsh manner with their children on an observational task in comparison to control group parents. **Notes:** This study supports previous work indicating BASIC's utility in a non-university clinic settings and in another socio-cultural context. See Scott, Spender, Doolan, Jacobs, and Aspland (2001).

Outcome Evaluation (Oxfordshire, United Kingdom – BASIC vs. No-treatment control): **Participants:** Parents of children (2-8 year olds) who evidenced behavior problems in the top 50% (median split) of a general population sample on the Eyberg Child Behavior Inventory. **Design:** Block random assignment to BASIC or no treatment control group. Pre, post, and six month follow up (Pre N=116 parents; 56 control, 60 intervention; Post N=96 parents; 50 control, 46 intervention; Follow up N=92 parents; 46 control, 46 intervention). **Measures:** Parent reports: Child behavior (Eyberg Child Behavior Inventory – EBCI; Strengths and Difficulties Questionnaire – SDQ), parent adjustment/mental health (General Health Questionnaire – GHQ, Parenting Stress Index, Rosenberg Self-Esteem Scale). **Results:** Intervention and control parents both reported a decline in the intensity of child problem behaviors (EBCI – Intensity Score) at the six month follow up, with intervention parents reporting a significantly greater reduction. Intervention and control parents also reported a decline in child conduct problems (SDQ – Conduct Problem Score) at post assessment and six month follow up, with intervention parents reporting a significantly greater decline. Relative to control parents, parents who took part in BASIC training evidenced pre-post test reductions in parental social dysfunction (GHQ) at the immediate post test, with a fading of this effect at the six month follow up. **Notes:** The training of interventionists in this trial (i.e., health visitors and nursery nurses) was conducted by the Family Nurturing Network. This trial supports other studies that have indicated the potential of the BASIC program as a community-based intervention implemented by trained non-specialists. See Patterson, et al. (2002). A second randomized controlled trial of BASIC is underway in Oxfordshire with results expected in late 2002. See Gardner and Sylva (1999).

Outcome Evaluation (Trondheim and Tromsø, Norway – BASIC vs. BASIC + Dinosaur School vs. Wait-List Control Group): **Participants:** Families that have children (4-8 year olds) with clinically significant symptoms of conduct and/or oppositional defiant disorder. **Design:** Pre-post-follow up (at 12 and 36 months) with random assignment to condition: (Target N=252 families; BASIC n=72 families; BASIC + Dinosaur School n=72 families; and wait-list control group n=108 families). **Measures:** Parent Report: Child behavior (e.g., CBCL), social competence, emotional state; parental behavior (e.g., Child Rearing Disagreement; Parental Practices Interview, Life Experience Survey) and parental distress (e.g., Beck Depression Inventory), school involvement (e.g., Involve Parent Questionnaire), temperament (e.g., Brief Anger-Aggression Questionnaire). Teacher Report: Child behavior and social competence (e.g., PBQ; TRF), teacher links to home environment. Child Report: Competence (e.g. Problem-Solving Test WALLY) and emotional state. Observation: Parent-child interaction at home (e.g., DPICS-R) and in clinic; peer interaction at clinic (e.g., Peer Interaction Dyadic Relationship Q-set); Clinical diagnosis, DSM-IV. **Results:** The expected completion date is in 2003. See Mørch, et al. (2001).

Materials:
Webster-Stratton, C. (1992). *The Incredible Years: A trouble-shooting guide for parents of children aged 3-8.* Toronto, Canada: Umbrella Press.
Webster-Stratton, C. (1992). *The parents and children videotape series: Programs 1-10.* Seattle, WA: Seth Enterprises.

Further Reading:
Mørch, W-T., Clifford, G., Rypdal, P., Larsson, B., Fossum, S., & Drugli, M. B. (2001). *Treatment of oppositional defiant and conduct disorders in 4-8 year old children, using "The Incredible Years" parents and children series.* Symposium presented at the Society for Prevention Research. Washington, D.C.
Patterson, J., Barlow, J., Stewart-Brown, S., Mockford, C., Klimes, I., & Pyper, C., (2002). *Improving mental health among children and their parents through parenting programmes in general practice: A randomised controlled trial.* Submitted for publication.
Scott, S. (1999). *Parent training groups for childhood conduct disorder.* Symposium presented at the National Centre for Child and Adolescent Psychiatry's Conference on Interventions in Conduct Disorders: New Directions. Oslo, Norway.
Scott, S. (1998). Aggressive behaviour in childhood. *British Medical Journal, 316,* 202-206.
Scott, S. (1998). Intensive interventions to improve parenting. *Archives of Diseases in Childhood, 79,* 90-93.
Scott, S., Spender, Q., Doolan, M., Jacobs, B., & Aspland, H. (2001). Multicentre controlled trial of parenting groups for childhood antisocial behaviour in clinical practice. *British Medical Journal, 323,* 194-197.
Taylor, T., Schmidt, F., Pepler, D., & Hodgins, C. (1998). A comparison of eclectic treatment with Webster-Stratton's parents and children series in a children's mental health center: A randomized controlled trial. *Behavior Therapy, 29,* 221-240.
Webster-Stratton, C. (1981). Modification of mothers' behaviors and attitudes through a videotape modeling group discussion program. *Behavior Therapy, 12,* 634-642.
Webster-Stratton, C. (1982). The long term effects of a videotape modeling parent-training program: comparison of immediate and 1 year follow-up results. *Behavior Therapy, 13,* 702-714.
Webster-Stratton, C. (1984). Randomized trial of two parent-training programs for families with conduct-disordered children. *Journal of Consulting and Clinical Psychology, 52,* 666-678.

Webster-Stratton, C. (1990a). Long term follow-up of families with young conduct problem children: From preschool to grade school. *Journal of Clinical Child Psychology, 19,* 144-149.

Webster-Stratton, C. (1990b). Enhancing the effectiveness of self-administered videotape parent training for families with conduct-problem children. *Journal of Abnormal Child Psychology, 18* (5), 479-492.

Webster-Stratton, C. (1992). Individually administered videotape parent training: Who benefits? *Cognitive Therapy and Research, 16* (1), 31-35.

Webster-Stratton, C. (1994). Advancing videotape parent training: A comparison study. *Journal of Consulting and Clinical Psychology, 62*(3), 583-593.

Webster-Stratton, C. (1998). Preventing conduct problems in Head Start children: Strengthening parenting competencies. *Journal of Consulting and Clinical Psychology, 66,* 715-730.

Webster-Stratton, C. (1998). Parent training with low-income families: Promoting parental engagement through a collaborative approach. In J. R. Lutzker (Ed.), *Handbook of child abuse research and treatment* (pp. 183-210). New York: Plenum Press.

Webster-Stratton, C., & Hammond, M. (1997). Treating children with early-onset conduct problems: A comparison of child and parent training interventions. *Journal of Consulting and Clinical Psychology, 65,* 93-109.

Webster-Stratton, C., Hollinsworth, T., and Kolpacoff, M. (1989). The Long Term Effectiveness and Clinical Significance of Three Cost Effective Training Programs for Families with Conduct Problem Children. *Journal of Consulting and Clinical Psychology, 57,* 550-553.

Program Classification: Trans-Atlantic Family Therapy

Program Title: Multi-Systemic Therapy (MST)

Developmental Period: Adolescence

Amount of Protection/Risk: Selective/Indicated

Where was the Program Conducted? United States, Canada, Norway

Stated Theoretical Basis: Social Ecology (Bronfenbrenner)

Who Implemented the Program? Master's level therapists; Ph.D. level clinical supervisors; administrative staff; researchers

Program Description: MST is designed for young people who are at risk for persistent involvement in the justice system and their families. Interventionists, families, and youth work together to develop and tailor multi-sectoral prevention services based on the family's identified risks/strengths. Based on the family's needs interventionists provide mental health services (including addiction and marriage counseling, individualized therapy, strategic, structural, behavioral, and cognitive-behavioral family therapies) and advocacy for social/medical services. Parents are often trained in positive parenting practices (non-coercive behavioral management/monitoring of youth behavior, peer associations, and academic/vocational efforts, communication, problem solving, and conflict resolution skills). Youth also are able to receive direct services from the interventionist (socio-cognitive skills training, anger management). Most of the intervention activities are provided in the home as a means to overcome traditional barriers to service provision. **Program Duration:** Contact is individualized with at least three to five months of active intervention activities (average of 60 intervention contact hours). The MST approach was developed in the 1970's and has undergone comprehensive evaluations on at least four occasions. **Program Languages:** English and Norwegian. **Notes:** This program is listed as a model intervention on the Blue Prints Web site: http://www.colorado.edu/cspv/blueprints . Estimated costs are US$ 4,500 per youngster.

Outcome Evaluation (Simpsonville, South Carolina): **Participants:** Adolescents that have had contact with the juvenile justice system. **Design:** Pre-post testing with two and four year follow up. Random assignment to condition (MST, n=43; Regular Public Services = control group, n=41). **Measures:** Quality of family interactions (parent self report); Parent reported youth behavior problems; youth report and registry information (arrests; types of offenses). **Results:** MST families showed immediate increases in family cohesion relative to the control group. MST youth had lowered reoffending rates, self reported crime, and parent reported violence towards peers versus the control group. At two and four year follow up, registry information confirmed that lowered recidivism rates for MST youth were maintained relative to the control group.

Outcome Evaluation (Columbia, Missouri): **Participants:** Adolescents that have had contact with the juvenile justice system. Design: Pre-post testing with four year follow up. Random assignment to condition (MST, n=92; Individual Therapy IT, n=84). **Measures:** Quality of family interactions (observational tasks); parent mental health (clinic interviews); youth report and registry information (arrests; types of offenses). **Results:** Those participants that completed MST showed short and long-term gains (up to four years) in risk/protective factors (increased cohesion in family interactions; parent mental health) and behavior (lowered reoffending rates in general; lower violent and substance related crimes in particular). These gains were made relative to MST dropouts, IT completers, IT dropouts, and those who refused participation in either program (n=24).

Outcome Evaluation (Ontario, Canada): **Participants:** Youth who are predicted at high risk for future criminal conduct using the Risk/Need Assessment (RNA, Hoge, Andrews, & Leschied). **Design:** Pre-post testing with one, two and three year follow-up. Random assignment to condition: MST, estimated n=400; control group, estimated n= 400. **Measures:** Process measures of family functioning, social skills, cognitive orientation toward antisocial behavior, and general well-being as measured by the Standard Client Information system (parent, family & household, youth and teacher report); Beliefs and attitudes scale (youth self-report); Self-Report of Youth Behavior; FACES-II (parent and youth); Social skills rating system (youth, parent and teacher); Parental Supervision Index; time spent in custody or adult prison; MST adherence. **Results:** In progress: Site selection took place in 1996 with training beginning in 1997. As of March 1998 four trial sites were fully operational (London, Mississauga, Ottawa, Simcoe Co.) with a goal of reaching 400 participants by the end of the project.

Outcome Evaluation (Oslo, Akershus, Telemark, Vest-Agder, & Rogaland, Norway): **Participants:** Adolescents (12-17 year olds) who have been referred from the Child Welfare Services for delinquency and substance use. **Design:** Pre-post testing with one year post intervention follow up. Random assignment to condition: MST estimated n=60 families; Traditional Services estimated n=40 families (Interventions as usual range from treatment centers, out of home placement, to other family and individual therapies). **Measures:** Parent report: Teen behavior and social competence, quality of family interactions and social support; Teacher Report: Teen behavior and social competence. Youth Report: Behavior and social competence, substance use, quality of family interactions. Registry/Therapist Report: Academic achievement, removal from home, delinquency, arrests—types of offenses, substance use, mental health status (Clinical diagnosis, DSM-IV conduct disorder). **Results:** The evaluation is slated for completion in 2003.

Materials:
Henggeler, S.W., Schoenwald, S. K., Borduin, C. M., Rowland, M. D., Cunningham, P. B. (1998). *Multisystemic treatment of antisocial behavior in children and adolescents.* New York: Guilford.

Ogden, T. (2001). *Multisystemic treatment of antisocial behavior in children and adolescents* [Norwegian: Multisystemisk behandling av atferdsproblemer blant barn og unge" og er gitt ut på Kommuneforlaget]. Center for Research in Clinical Psychology, Institute of Psychology, University of Oslo, Oslo, Norway.

Further Reading:
Borduin, C. M. (1999). Multisystemic treatment of criminality and violence in adolescents. *Journal of the Academy of Child and Adolescent Psychiatry, 38*(3), 242-249.

Borduin, C. M., Mann, B. J., Cone, L. T., Henggeler, S. W., & et al., (1995). Multisystemic treatment of serious juvenile offenders: Long-term prevention of criminality and violence. *Journal of Consulting and Clinical Psychology, 63*(4): 569-578.

Henggeler, S. W., Cunningham, P. B., Pickrel, S. G., Schoenwald, S. K., & Brondino, M. J. (1996). Multisystemic therapy: An effective violence prevention approach for serious juvenile offenders. *Journal of Adolescence, 19,* 47-61.

Henggeler, S. W., Melton, G. B., & Smith, L. A. (1992). Family preservation using multisystemic therapy: An effective alternative to incarcerating serious juvenile offenders. *Journal of Consulting and Clinical Psychology, 60*(6), 953-961.

Henggeler, S. W., Melton, G. B., Smith, L. A., Schoenwald, S. K., & Hanley, H. (1993). Family preservation using multisystemic treatment: Long-term follow-up to a clinical trial with serious juvenile offenders. *Journal of Child and Family Studies, 2*(4), 283-293.

Leschied, A.W. & Cunningham, A. (1998). Alternatives to custody for high-risk young offenders: Application of the Multisystemic approach in Canada. *European Journal on Criminal Policy and Research, 6,* 545-560.

Leschied, A.W. & Cunningham, A. (1999). Clinical trials of Multisystemic Therapy in Ontario: Rationale and current status of a community-based alternative for high-risk young offenders. *Forum on Corrections Research, 11*(2): 25-29.

Leschied, A.W. & Cunningham, A. (in press). A review of the use of custody in Canada's young offender system and the development of a community-based program for high-risk young offenders. In A. M. van Kalmthout, H-J. Albrecht and J. Junger-Tas (Eds.), *Community sanctions, measures and execution modalities in Europe, the USA and Canada.* Kluwer Publishing, Dordrecht, The Netherlands.

Ogden, T. (2001). *Updating the Norwegian MST Clinical Trial.* Center for Research in Clinical Psychology, Institute of Psychology, University of Oslo, Norway.

Program Classification: European School-based Education-Skills Promotion

Program Title: Class 2000 [5]

Developmental Period: Childhood

Amount of Protection/Risk: Universal

Where was the Program Conducted? Germany

Stated Theoretical Basis: Behavioral principles and life skills approaches

Who Implemented the Program? Teachers; trained health workers

Program Description: This intervention is aimed at altering behavior through the formation of positive health beliefs and attitudes. Program efforts are focused on strengthening participants' view of themselves and their bodies. Life skills training involves the practice of social resistance skills in the context of alcohol and other drug use in daily life contexts. The standard teacher-student training sessions are supplemented by up to three training sessions provided by health workers that have been trained to implement Class 2000 program activities. Parents, health workers, sponsors, and the school environment itself should be coordinated to support program activities and goals. **Program Duration:** Class 2000 is conducted throughout primary school (Grade 1 to 4). Class 2000 is an ongoing project that began in 1991. **Program Language:** German. **Notes:** This program has been widely implemented throughout Germany with more than 130,000 children participating in 2002 to 2003. Almost one thousand health workers have been trained in the intervention protocol. Class 2000 has received the European Commission's Health Promotion Award (2000). More information on this program can be found in the Exchange on Drug Demand Reduction Action (EDDRA) Information System www.emcdda.org/databases/ databases_eddra.shtml.

Outcome Evaluation: **Participants:** Primary school children (6 to 10 year-olds). **Design:** Pre-post testing between the first and fourth grades with an intervention (n=1,919) and comparison (n= 1,570) condition. **Measures:** Surveys to children, parents, and teachers. **Results:** At the end of the first grade no difference between pupils was found. Approximately 10% of the children reported experiences with cigarettes both in the intervention and comparison groups. At the end of the fourth grade, those in the comparison group reported significantly more experience with smoking (32%) relative to youth in the intervention condition (25.2%). Further, the proportion of pupils who regularly smoked cigarettes was (1.5%) amongst Class 2000 students and (3.0%) in the comparison group.

Further Reading/Materials:
Bölcskei, P.L., Hörmann, A., Hollederer, A., Jordan, S., & Fenzel, H. (1997). Suchtprävention an Schulen: Besondere Aspekte des Nikotinabusus. *Prävention und Rehabilitation, 2,* 82-88.
European Commission (2000). *2nd European health promotion awards: Selected actions.* Brussels, Belgium: European Commission.
Hollederer, A. & Bölcskei, P. L. (2001). Einsatz von Präventionsfachleuten im Grundschulprogramm Klasse2000 – Kooperativer Unterricht im Programm Klasse2000. *Gesundheitsweisen, 63,* 619 – 624.
Kraus, D., Duprée, T. & Bölcskei, P. L. (2002). Erfahrungen mit dem Klasse2000-Programm. Ergebnisse einer Lehrerbefragung. *Prävention, 25,* 44–47.
Kraus, D., Duprée, Th., Bölcskei, P. L. (2003): Eltern als Partner in der schulischen Gesundheitsförderung und Suchtvorbeugung. Eine empirische Studie am Beispiel Klasse2000. *Gesundheitswesen, 64,* 371–377.

Program Classification: American School-based Education-Skills Promotion

Program Title: Project SNAPP (Skills and Knowledge for AIDS and Pregnancy Prevention)

Developmental Period: Early Adolescence

Amount of Protection/Risk: Selective

Where was the Program Conducted? United States- Los Angeles, California

Stated Theoretical Basis: Social Learning Theory, Health Belief Model

Who Implemented the Program? Trained peer educators

Program Description: Project SNAPP was intended to prevent HIV infection and unintended pregnancy by delaying onset of intercourse and increase use of condoms. Trained peer educators who were either HIV-positive or single teenage mothers delivered the intervention to the selected classrooms. The eight-session, focus group driven curriculum was facilitated through the use of games, role-plays, large and small group activities, and guided discussion. The first three sessions focused on myths, risks, consequences, and social influences on sexual behavior. The fourth session asked students to anonymously decide whether they would have intercourse and if so would they use a condom. This lesson was intended to dispel the idea that everyone was "doing it". Afterward, students identified barriers to abstaining and ways to overcome them. The next three sessions focused on skill building to help them carry out their decisions. The final session focused on providing information about the medical and psychosocial resources that are available for teens and teaching students to give knowledge to friends. **Program Duration:** Eight sessions over two weeks. **Program Language:** English.

Outcome Evaluation: **Design:** Pre, post, follow up with random assignment to intervention or curriculum as usual control. **Measures:** Bi-lingual (English or Spanish) youth report: Sexual behaviors (frequency of sexual intercourse, number of partners, use of condoms and other contraception), general knowledge and attitudes concerning sex. **Results:** There was an immediate and lasting impact on knowledge in the intervention group compared to the control group. Only two of the belief items, willingness to be friends an HIV-positive person and that friends believed people should use condoms, showed lasting but insignificant effects. No statistically significant changes were found for sexual and contraceptive behaviors. **Notes:** Among suggestions for improvement were to add more sessions, and to address additional risk and protective factors that affect teen sexual behavior, like social norms and having an older romantic partner. Another conclusion was that very charismatic peer leaders in this study may not have been the most ideal intervention leaders (Kirby, personal communication, 2003).

Further Reading/Materials:
Kirby, D., (2000). School-based interventions to prevent unprotected sex and HIV among adolescents. In J. L., Peterson, & R. J., DiClemente (Eds.), *Handbook of HIV prevention. AIDS prevention and mental health* (pp. 83-101). New York: Kluwer Academic/Plenum Publishers.
Kirby, D., Korpi, M., Adivi, C., & Weissman, J. (1997). An impact evaluation of Project SNAPP: An AIDS and pregnancy prevention middle school program. *AIDS Education and Prevention, 9*, Supplement A, 44-61.

Program Classification: Cross National School-based Education-Skills Promotion

Program Title: World Health Organization (WHO) Collaborative Study on Alcohol Education and Young People

Developmental Period: Adolescence

Amount of Protection/Risk: Universal/Selective

Where was the Program Conducted? Norway, Australia, Chile, Swaziland

Stated Theoretical Basis: Social Learning Theory (Bandura, 1986), Psychosocial theories of teen behavior (Perry & Murray, 1985; Perry & Jessor, 1985); Problem Behavior Theory (Jessor & Jessor, 1977)

Who Implemented the Program? Peer leaders, teachers, researchers

Program Description: The WHO Collaborative Study on Alcohol Education and Young People used a 5-lesson school-based alcohol prevention curriculum administered by students (trained peer leaders, training was for 4-12 hours) or teachers (training was for 2-10 hours). Intervention components centered on general drug education, normative education, resistance skill training, and an invitation to make a public commitment to abstain from alcohol until one is older. The strategies used to promote change included: Games, modeling, reinforcement, didactic and interactive lessons/discussions on a small group (peer-led condition) and classroom basis (teacher-led condition). **Program Duration:** Two months (1987). **Program Languages:** English, Norwegian, Spanish, Swazi.

Outcome Evaluation: **Participants:** Lower secondary school students (average age across countries ranged from 13 to 16 years old). **Design:** Random assignment of participating schools to one of two intervention conditions [Peer (n=10) or Teacher (n=9) program administration] or a control (n=6) condition. Pre-post test N=2,536 (Australia n=828, Chile n=195, Norway n=1,306, Swaziland n=207). Six and 12-month follow-ups were conducted in Australia and Norway. **Measures:** Youth report: Alcohol use, alcohol related knowledge and beliefs, resistance skills, friends' alcohol use. **Results:** *Findings Across Countries:* The following results were found irregardless of students' reported drinking experience at pre-testing-- Youngsters in the peer-administered program reported significantly less alcohol use than youth in the teacher-led program and control schools. Alcohol related attitudes showed improvement in both the peer and teacher-led conditions relative to the control condition. Findings for pre-test nondrinkers--Students in the peer-led intervention showed greater alcohol related knowledge at the posttest relative to youth in the control schools. Peer-led youngsters estimated that fewer of their friends were drinking at the post test relative youth in the teacher and control conditions. Results for pre-test drinkers--Pupils in the teacher-led program showed greater alcohol related knowledge at the posttest relative to youth in the control schools. At post-testing, peer-led youth estimated less drinking among their friends in comparison to youth in the teacher administered program. *Findings by Country:* Some intervention gains varied by country, however, one or more positive results were found in each country. More specifically, intervention related reductions in self reported alcohol use were found in all countries except for Australia; positive changes in alcohol related knowledge were shown in Australia and Chile; positive attitude changes were recorded in Chile; positive skills changes were found in Australia, students' perception of their friends' drinking was reduced in all countries except Swaziland. *Overall Conclusions:* The intervention curriculum seemed to function well with drinkers and non-drinkers. Further, the peer-administered program out performed the teacher-led program on the majority of the tested indices of change. This is the case whether one looks at data from all of the countries combined or separately. Positive changes in alcohol related knowledge and attitudes, views of friends' alcohol use were found to be related to reductions in alcohol use (this result was found via regression analysis). Researchers commented that there were not an adequate number of schools in each country to conduct an outcome evaluation with the school as the analytic unit (or as the subject). Some results varied by according to gender, however, positive results were found for both males and females. **Notes:** Students' full names were not known. Thus, the pupils pre and post test survey responses were matched on the teen's gender, school, birth day and month, first name, teacher, student number, and family characteristics (N=2,536 youngsters were matched using this criteria). [See Perry et al., 1989]

Further Reading/Materials:
Perry, C. L., Grant, M., Ernberg, G., Florenzano, R. U., Langdon, M. C., Myeni, A. D., Waahlberg, R., Berg, S., Andersson, K., Fisher, K. J., Blaze-Temple, D., Cross, D., Saunders, B., Jacobs, D. R., & Schmid, T. (1989). WHO collaborative study on alcohol education and young people: Outcomes of a four-country pilot study. *The International Journal of the Addictions, 24*, 1145-1171.

Program Classification: Trans-Atlantic Whole School Change

Program Title: Olweus Bullying Prevention Program

Developmental Period: Childhood/Early Adolescence

Stated Theoretical Basis: Development/Social/Ecological psychology; Social Learning Theories; Parenting models (Baumrind, 1967).

Amount of Protection/Risk: Universal/Selected

Where was the Program Conducted? Norway, United States. Partial replications have been conducted in England (Smith & Sharp, 1994) and Germany (Hanewinkel & Knaack, 1997a; 1997b; Lösel & Bliesener, 1999).

Who Implemented the Program? School staff; researchers; program coordinators

Program Description: The Olweus Bullying Prevention Program (OBPP) is designed to promote a safe school environment through a systematic restructuring school life in ways that limit pupils' chances to engage in bullying and obstruct rewards students may gain via bullying. OBPP program activities at the school-wide level involve awareness raising and survey activities aimed at bringing the issue of bullying to the attention of school staff, students, and parents. A Bullying Prevention Coordinating Committee is created, new policies on the supervision of students in areas where bullying frequently occurs are formulated, policies that specify the actions that should be taken in cases where bullying are established. At the classroom level, teachers and students have periodic class meetings in which they work on creating rules against bullying. Rules regularly center on debunking lassie faire attitudes about bullying, providing aid to students in need, and being socially inclusive of others. Examples of activities that regularly take place in these meetings include classroom exercises related to clarifying what bullying is and what its consequences are (role playing, written work, break out sessions for small group work within the classroom). At the individual student level, when bullying takes place meetings with identified bullies and victims are carried out. Victims receive social and emotional support and students involved in bullying are exposed to some form of non-punitive consequences and clarification of what is expected from students in terms of appropriate behavior. Parents are involved in this process and informed about the bullying. At all levels of intervention, consistent and non-punitive consequences for bullying behaviors and reinforcement for prosocial/empathic behaviors are encouraged. Program modifications: In addition to the core program, the trial in South Carolina trial included: Student made news programs, school-wide anti bullying rules, teacher newsletter, local media promotion, community participation in Bully-Free Days, and the transfer of program concepts to church related activities, and the use of teacher and resource guides. In the latest version of the OBPP conducted in Norway has added a series of regular meetings between teachers, program staff and the school psychologist in order to bolster program implementation. **Program Duration:** The first trial in Norway lasted for two and a half years (1983-1985). The South Carolina (U.S.A.) trial lasted for two years (1995-1997). **Program Languages:** Norwegian, English, German. **Notes:** A software package is available to help school staff summarize and analyze information provided by the Olweus Bully/Victim Questionnaire. Estimated program costs are the salary of an on-site program coordinator, measurement package $U.S. 200.00, program materials per teacher/staff member $U.S. 65.00, Bullying educational video $U.S. 69.95. In the coming years, it is the goal of the Norwegian government to have OBPP implemented in all schools. OBPP was selected as a model Blue Print program. OBPP is the only non-North American program to be selected and is currently undergoing field testing in multiple sites across the United States.

Outcome Evaluation (Bergen, Norway): **Participants:** Primary/lower secondary school children aged 11-14 at program start (n=2,500; 42 schools, 112 classes). **Design:** Quasi-experimental: Expanded age cohort design [comparisons between youngsters who are in the same grade and approximately the same age, (i.e., adjacent cohorts) but comparison data is taken from different points in time depending on whether or not pupils in that grade have been exposed to the intervention]. Pre and multiple posttests [at 8 months (n=1,500 to 2,100) and 20 months (n=1,000 to 1,400)]. **Measures:** Youth report: Anonymous reports of victimization due to bullying, bullying others and types of bullying (Olweus Bully/Victim Questionnaire-Extended version). Peer and Teacher report: Level of bullying and victimization in the class. **Results:** The level of bullying and victimization was significantly lower after students were exposed to eight and 20 months of program activities (ranging from 50%-70%) depending on the cohort group and dimension of bullying and victimization measured. There were also significant reductions in the number of new cases of bullying. Peer ratings of bullying/victimization problems within the class were also significantly lower after both 8 and 20 months of intervention exposure. Students exposed to the intervention also felt a greater affinity towards school and reported improvements in the class environment. **Notes:** A dosage-response relationship was also found in that those classes that more fully implemented the intervention showed greater intervention-related benefits.

Outcome Evaluation (South Carolina, U.S.A.): **Participants:** Rural and mostly African American primary and secondary school children who experience socio-economic disadvantage (in the 4th to 6th grades at program start; pre-testing n=6,388; first post-test n=6,263). **Design:** Quasi-experimental with an intervention (n=11) and wait-listed matched comparison (n=28) schools. Seven comparison schools implemented OBPP in the second year of program activities. Pre and multiple posttests (at 7 and 19 months). **Measures:** Youth report: Olweus Bully/Victim Questionnaire, Bergen Questionnaire on Antisocial Behavior. **Results:** Students in the intervention schools reported less engagement (approx. 25%) in bullying behavior after 7 months of program activities relative to an increase in comparison schools. Intervention school students also did not escalate their involvement in several anti-social behaviors relative to an increase among comparison school students.

Outcome Evaluation (The New Bergen Project Against Bullying): **Participants:** Upper primary and lower secondary school children aged 11-13 at program start. **Design:** Quasi-experimental: Expanded age cohort and comparison group designs (n=14 intervention schools; 16 comparison schools). Age cohort comparisons: pretest n=5,200 children; posttest n=3,200. Longitudinal comparisons were made for 6th and 7th grade students (n=1,800). Pre and post testing over a one-year period (1997-1998), with six months of program exposure. **Measure:** Youth report: Olweus Bully/Victim Questionnaire. **Results:** Age cohort comparisons, across grade levels, indicated a 22.9% reduction in bullying others and a 28.4% decline in reports of victimization in intervention schools with a 1.6% increase of reported bullying and 5.5% reduction in victimization evidenced in comparison schools. Longitudinal analyses showed a 37.5% reduction in bullying others and a 32.4% decline in reports of victimization in intervention schools with a 81.6% increase of reported bullying and 7.6% decline in victimization reported at comparison schools.

Materials:
Department for Education (1994). *Bullying: Don't suffer in silence. An anti-bullying pack for schools.* London: HMSO.
Olweus, D. (1993). *Bullying at school: What we know and what we can do.* Malden, MA: Blackwell.
Olweus, D. (1996). *Bullying: The U.S. Video.* Columbia, SC: South Carolina Educational Television Marketing Department.
Olweus, D. (1996). *Olweus Core Program Against Bullying and Antisocial Behavior: A teacher handbook.* Bergen, Norway: University of Bergen.

Further Reading:
Hanewinkel, R. & Knaack, R. (1997a). Prävention van aggression und gewalt an schulen. Ergebnisse einer Interventionsstudie. In H. G. Holtapples, W. Heitmeyer, W. Melzer, & K. J. Tillman (Eds.), *Schulische Gewaltforschung. Stand und perspektiven* (pp. 299-313). Weinheim: Juventa.
Hanewinkel, R. & Knaack, R. (1997b). Mobbing: Eine Fragebogenstudie zum Ausmaß von aggression und Gewalt an Schulen. *Empirische Pädagogik, 11*, 403-422.
Melton, G. B., Limber, S. P., Cunningham, P., Osgood, D. W., Chambers, J., Flerx, V., Henggeler, S., & Nation, M. (1998). *Violence among rural youth. Final report to the Office of Juvenile Justice and Delinquency Prevention.* Washington DC, OJJDP.
Olweus, D. (1978). *Aggression in the schools: Bullies and whipping boys.* Washington, DC: Hemisphere.
Olweus, D., Limber, S. & Mihalic, S.F. (1999). *Blueprints for Violence Prevention, Book Nine: Bullying Prevention Program.* Boulder, CO: Center for the Study and Prevention of Violence.
Olweus, D. (1999). Norway. In P. K. Smith, Y. Morita, J. Junger-Tas, D. Olweus, R. Catalano, & P. Slee (Eds.), *The nature of school bullying: A cross-national perspective* (pp. 28-48). London: Routledge.
Olweus, D. (2001). Peer harassment. A critical analysis and some important issues. In J. Juvonen & S. Graham (Eds.), *Peer harassment in school* (pp. 3-20). New York: Guilford.
Solberg, M. & Olweus, D. (in press). Prevalence estimation of school bullying with the Olweus/Bully Victim Questionnaire. *Aggressive Behavior.*
Smith, P. K. & Sharp, S. (Eds.). (1994). *School bullying: Insights and perspectives.* London, England: Routledge.

Program Classification: Trans-Atlantic Whole School Change

Program Title: Promoting Alternative Thinking Strategies (PATHS)

Developmental Period: Childhood

Amount of Protection/Risk: Universal/Selective/Indicated

Where was the Program Conducted? United States; United Kingdom, The Netherlands, Belgium

Stated Theoretical Basis: Affective-Behavioral-Cognitive-Dynamic Model of Development; Eco-Behavioral Systems Model; Neurobiological theories of vertical control and horizontal communication; Psychodynamic education (Greenberg & Kusché, 1993; Kusché, 1984); Theories of emotional competence (Goleman, 1995; Mayer & Salovey, 1997)

Who Implemented the Program? Teachers, school staff, researchers

Program Description: PATHS is a comprehensive and mostly teacher-implemented intervention that focuses on the promotion of social and emotional competence among primary school students. This intervention has fifteen years of program development behind it and has successfully undergone four program evaluations. PATHS is unique in that it has been tested with children who do and do not have special needs (e.g., hearing impairment, disruptiveness, learning disability). Specifically, PATHS lessons work with children through a number of interactive techniques (e.g., feeling faces, doing turtle, giving compliments, role play, control signals poster, PATHS child for the day) to facilitate students' ability to self regulate and gain greater insight into their emotions and the emotions of others. Children engage in exercises to promote a variety of skills that are involved with emotional adeptness and relating to others. Another set of intervention activities center on social cognitive problem solving skills and supporting the generalization of classroom based lessons to everyday life. Bolstering the child's self esteem is also a regular theme that cuts across content areas. **Program Duration:** Curriculum materials (131 lessons) can be used over a five-year period during primary school. Tests of the PATHS program have largely been conducted after at least one year of weekly lessons. In the United Kingdom trial, intervention activities spanned one year with sessions ranging in length from 30 minutes for fours times a week to 60-minute bi-weekly sessions. **Program Languages:** Dutch, English, French, Hebrew, and Spanish. **Notes:** Estimated costs for the complete program materials are $U.S. 640.00. All costs combined (e.g., curriculum, training, hiring support personnel) breaks down to $US 15.00-$45.00 per student.

Outcome Evaluation (United States)[6]: **Participants:** Primary school children, mean age of eight at program start (N=286). **Design:** Experimental with random assignment to an intervention (Pre-post testing: n=130 {83 in regular and 47 in special needs classes}) and control condition (Pre-post testing: n=156 {109 in regular and 47 in special needs classes}). Pre to post testing with one and two year follow-ups. **Measures:** Teacher report: Child's emotional and behavioral adjustment (CBCL-TRF). Child report: Emotional competence and insight (Kusché Affective Interview Revised). **Results:** Intervention children in both regular and special education classes showed significant pre to post test improvements in self reported indices of emotional competence and insight as well as confidence in managing emotional states. Teacher ratings of emotional and behavioral adjustment also showed pre to post test improvement. All changes were demonstrated relative to control group children (Greenburg, Kusché, Cook, & Quamma, 1995). Later follow ups indicated that children in regular and special needs classes maintained intervention gains in emotional competence and behavioral adjustment according to self and teacher reports (Weissberg & Greenberg, 1998). **Notes:** This study used a 60-lesson version of the curriculum with an emphasis on self-control, emotions, and problem solving. An earlier test of PATHS showed that positive change in emotional and cognitive competence among intervention children was related to improved behavioral adjustment (Greenberg & Kusché, 1993).

Outcome Evaluation (United Kingdom): **Participants:** Deaf children (approximately nine years of age on average). **Design:** Quasi-experimental with an intervention school (n= 24 children) and two wait list comparison schools and hearing impaired units (31 children). Children in the intervention condition were pre and post tested (at 9 and 12 months post baseline). Intervention activities were carried out over the course of one year. Intervention children were followed up nine months after PATHS activities ended (21 months post baseline). The wait-list group followed the same testing sequence but did not receive PATHS until the program was completed in the intervention school (12 months later). The wait-list group was evaluated after taking part in PATHS lessons for nine months (21 months after the first pre test assessment). **Measures:** Parent/Teacher report: Child's emotional competence and associated behavior/adjustment (Emotion Checklist; Kusché Emotional Inventories; Meadow and Kendall Social Emotional Adjustment Inventory; Strengths and Difficulties Questionnaire); child's ability to communicate. Child performance: Literacy (Edinburgh Reading Test); Lack of self-control (WISC III Maze subtest); Self-perception (drawings); Youth report: Self-perception. **Results:** The intervention group showed immediate improvements on indices of emotional competence and adjustment versus the wait-list comparison group. At follow up, these gains were maintained for the intervention group on indices of emotional competence but not on the adjustment measures. The wait-list control group after receiving PATHS showed program related benefits (e.g., emotional competence).

Outcome Evaluation (the Netherlands): **Participants:** Hearing impaired children (10-11 year olds) in four schools. **Design:** Intervention group only with pre-post testing (N=33 children). No control or comparison group. **Measures:** Parent/Teacher interviews: Child's emotional competence and behavior/adjustment. **Results:** Intervention children evidenced significant behavior improvement, social-emotional competence, and problem solving according to parent and teacher ratings. Teachers also noted positive attitudinal changes in the children's view of their tasks, independence, and self-control. **Notes:** Researchers commented that there was considerable variation in the teachers' use of the PATHS curriculum. PATHS (called PAD 'Programma Alternatieve Denkstrategieën in Dutch) has been integrated into the curriculum of the test schools since 1989. To date, a stronger empirical test of PAD is in the planning stage.

Further Reading/Materials:

Conduct Problems Prevention Research Group. (1999). Initial impact of the fast track prevention trial for conduct problems: II. Classroom effects. *Journal of Consulting and Clinical Psychology, 67*, 648-657.

Greenberg, M. T. & Kusché, C. A. (1993). *Promoting social and emotional development in deaf children: The PATHS project.* Seattle, WA: University of Washington Press.

Greenberg, M. T. & Kusché, C. A. (1998). Preventive interventions for school-age deaf children: The PATHS curriculum. *Journal of Deaf Studies and Deaf Education, 3*, 49-63.

Greenburg, M.T., Kusché, C.A., Cook, E.T., & Quamma, J.P. (1995). Promoting emotional competence in school-aged children: The effects of the PATHS curriculum. *Developmental Research and Psychopathology, 7*, 117-136.

Greenberg, M.T., Kusché, C. & Mihalic, S.F. (1998). *Blueprints for Violence Prevention, Book Ten: Promoting Alternative Thinking Strategies (PATHS).* Boulder, CO: Center for the Study and Prevention of Violence.

Gregory, S. & Hindley, P. (1996). Annotation: Communication strategies for deaf children. *Journal of Child Psychology and Psychiatry and Allied Disciplines,* 37(8), 895-905.

Hindley P. A. & Reed, H. (1999) Promoting Alternative Thinking Strategies (PATHS): Mental Health Promotion with Deaf Children in School. In: S., Decker, S., Kirby, A. Greenwood, & D. Moore (Eds.), *Taking Children seriously: Applications of counseling and Therapy in Education.* London Cassell.

Joha, D., Luit, H. & Vermeer, A. (1999). *Samen op PAD. Evaluatie van het Programma Alternatieve Denkstrategieën in het Nederlandse onderwijs aan dove kinderen.* Doetinchem: Graviant Educatieve Uitgaven.

Kusché, C. A. & Greenberg, M. T. (1994) *The PATHS Curriculum.* Seattle, WA: Developmental Research and Programs.

Kusché, C. A, & Greenberg, M. T. (1998) Integrating emotions and thinking in the classroom. *THINK, 9,* 32-34.

Program Classification: North American Cross Context Program [Family + School]

Program Title: Fast Track

Developmental Period: Childhood

Amount of Protection/Risk: Universal/Indicated

Where was the Program Conducted? United States – Durham, North Carolina; Nashville, Tennessee; Central Pennsylvania; Seattle, Washington

Stated Theoretical Basis: Unified prevention model (CPPRG, 1999a); Ecobehavioral systems Model (1999b); Developmental theory based on a risk and protective factors model of antisocial behavior (e.g., early identification is possible; risk is additive; transactional views of the individual and environment), life course-persistent offender models of antisocial behavior (Moffitt, 1993); Coercion theory (Patterson, et al., 1992), separate program components are drawn from relevant theory and previous research

Who Implemented the Program? Teachers, parents, lower risk classmates, paraprofessionals in education and counseling, researchers

Program Description: The Fast Track (FT) is a multiple component and context intervention (school plus home) with a primary aim of preventing future antisocial behavior in a group of youngsters identified as being at risk for serious and chronic antisocial behavior. FT focuses on the promotion of diversity of individual skills and competencies as well as family and school related risk and protective factors. FT has an explicit two pronged intervention approach with coordinated universal and selective intervention actions. Universal activities are directed at all children within the intervention schools, including at risk youth. The primary action here is the implementation of the teacher administered PATHS curriculum. In the FT trial, an average of 48 PATHS sessions were administered to first graders. FT PATHS was adapted for use in regular education classrooms and focused on the promotion of emotional-social competence and prosocial behavior (see the PATHS summary for more program details). In addition to FT PATHS, teachers were trained in behaviorally based classroom and child management techniques. Selective intervention activities are directed at children who were identified in kindergarten as being at risk for later antisocial behavior. A substantial amount of programming is also extended to the identified child's parents. A number of selective intervention components are delivered through a series of enrichment sessions. These sessions take place in the school building during after-school hours. For parents, training and rehearsal of effective and noncoercive parenting practices, communication, and parent support of the child's academic life are emphasized (c.f. Forehand & McMahon, 1981; Webster-Stratton, 1989; Hawkins, et al., 1988). Youth participate in 'child only' sessions designed to promote social and emotional competence as well as strengthen basic literacy skills through individual tutoring. Parents and children come back together to observe and practice together the skills-knowledge covered in the parent and child break out training sessions. Trained intervention staff facilitate the enrichment sessions. The intervention staff also conducts regular home visits and phone calls to reinforce the gains made in the enrichment sessions and to provide individualized training in parenting and general life coping skills (c.f., Wasik, Bryant, & Lyons, 1990). During the school day, at risk children take part in weekly supervised play with a more socially adept classmate, receive additional academic tutoring (c.f., Wallach & Wallach, 1976), and participate with their peers in the classroom based PATHS curriculum. Over the course of this ten year intervention, selective program components are designed to wax and wane in intensity. The identified youth's successful adaptation to major life transitions, such as entry into primary and secondary school are thought to be bolstered through exposure to intensive programming during and when possible just before the transition. FT also assumes a cumulative strategy by carrying out intervention activities during the intervening non-transitional years but at a lower level of intensity. **Program Duration:** FT activities span the childhood to middle adolescent period (6.5 -16.5 years old; Grades 1 to 10) with plans for longitudinal follow up. The intervention phase of FT began in 1991 and is still on going. **Program Language:** English.

Outcome Evaluation (Year 1 Results: Indicated Sample): **Participants:** At risk kindergarten children (N=891) their parents, and teachers. These children come from predominately African or European American families living in either a rural or urban community with low to middle incomes. **Design:** Experimental with pre with annual post testing. All kindergarten children (6.5 year olds) within four geographic regions were tested for their risk of engaging in later antisocial behavior (via parent and teacher ratings). Families with children who were assigned a high level of risk (in the top 10% of the surveyed sample) were recruited to take part in a longitudinal study of child adjustment. Over the course of three years, three successive cohorts or groups of at risk youngsters were identified and entered the study. Primary schools (N=54) with at risk catchment areas (based on local rates of delinquency) in the four regions were matched (number of students served, percentage of students who experience socio-economic disadvantage, ethnic composition of students, levels of student achievement) into pairs and then randomly assigned to either an experimental intervention or control condition. The high risk child's assignment to condition was determined by whether or not the youngster entered a primary school that was designated to be an experimental (n=445 selected youngsters) or control (n=446 selected youth) school. **Measures:** School records: Academic performance and amount of special education instruction. Blind observer ratings of the target child: Social competence/prosocial and problem behavior at school (Multi-Option Observation System for Experimental Studies). Blind observer ratings of target child and parent: Quality of parent-child relations, parenting practices (Parent-Child Interaction Task—Behavioral Coding System, Coder Impressions Inventory). Teacher report: Child social competence (Social Health Profile), child behavior problems in school and classroom performance (CBCL-Teacher Report Form, Teacher Observation of Classroom Adaptation-Revised, Teacher Ratings of Child Behavior Change), parent involvement with the child's academic life (Parent-Teacher Involvement Questionnaire-Teacher). Peer assessment of target child: Social competence, popularity, behavior problems at school. Parent report: Child social competence (Social Competence Scale-Parent Form), child behavior problems (CBCL, Parent Daily Report, Ratings of Child Behavior Change), parenting practices (The Parent Questionnaire, Parent Practices Scale), quality of family interactions (Developmental History), change in parental beliefs and practices (Rating of Parent Change), parent involvement with the child's academic life (Parent-Teacher Involvement Questionnaire-Parent), satisfaction with intervention experience (Parent Satisfaction Questionnaire). Youth report: Social and emotional competence (The Emotional Recognition Questionnaire, Interview of Emotional Experience, Social Problem-Solving Measure, Home Inventory with Child), reading skills (Woodcock-Johnson Psycho-Educational Battery, Diagnostic Reading Scales). **Results:** *Pre-Post Test Change (All cohorts/Full Sample):* Intervention related benefits were found for children in the experimental condition in terms of child's emotional competence, social problem solving and reactions (lessened aggressive retaliation) to hypothetical dilemmas. Pre to post change in favor of parents in the experimental group was evidenced in parent reactions to hypothetical childrearing situations (less endorsement of physical punishment) and greater teacher rated involvement of parents in the child's academic life. All positive changes for the experimental condition were demonstrated relative to the appropriate reference groups (child, parent, or teacher) in the control condition. *Pre-Post Test Change (Two Out of Three Cohorts/Partial Sample):* Intervention related benefits in observer rated parent-child interactions (warmth/positive involvement, appropriate/consistent discipline) were found in favor of experimental versus control families. *Cross Sectional Comparisons towards the End of First Grade (Full Sample):* After the first year of program activities, intervention children had better grades in the language arts, were observed to have more prosocial interactions with peers, and were judged by their peers to be more prosocial and popular. Further analyses showed that boys in the intervention condition had less special education instruction than boys in the comparison condition. Intervention children at the North Carolina (Durham) location were observed at school as accepting authority better than children in the Durham control group. *Cross Sectional Comparisons towards the End of the First Grade (Partial Sample):* Intervention parents noted a significant amount of change in their own parenting practices and in the problem behavior of their children relative to control parent ratings. Teachers in the experimental condition also reported changes in the target child's classroom behavior and performance relative to teacher ratings of control children. Finally, intervention children at the Durham site had better literacy skills than children in the Durham control group (CPPRG, 1999a).

Outcome Evaluation (Year 1 Results: Universal Sample – Fast Track PATHS): **Participants:** First grade students (N=6,715) in regular education classrooms (Intervention n=198 classrooms; Control n=180 classrooms). High risk children were not included in this program evaluation. **Design:** Experimental with pre with one year post testing. Random assignment of matched schools to an experimental intervention or control condition. Over the course of three years, three successive cohorts or groups of youngsters participated in this study. **Measures:** Non-Blind observer ratings of teacher instruction: Treatment fidelity. Blind observer ratings of classroom environment: Unruliness, attention and interest in tasks, prosocial behavior, social and emotional competence (Computer Assisted Rating Program, Classroom Rating Form). Teacher report: Child social competence (Social Health Profile), Teacher Observation of Classroom Adaptation-Revised, Teacher Ratings of Child Behavior Change). Peer assessment of classmates: Social competence, popularity, behavior problems in the classroom. **Results:** *Pre-Post Test Change (Teacher Report):* Control group teachers found their students to be increasingly unruly over the course of the first grade. Intervention youth also showed increased conduct problems but the increase was greater for the control group. Intervention related benefits were also found for teacher ratings of peer liking among classmates, relative to control teacher ratings. The quality of instruction (e.g., teacher adeptness at teaching/modeling PATHS, proactive classroom management) did relate to positive change in teacher ratings of pupil authority acceptance. *Cross Sectional Comparisons towards the End of First Grade (Peer and Observer reports):* Intervention children rated fewer of their classmates as aggressive and hyperactive/disorderly relative to child ratings in the control group. Blind observer ratings indicated that intervention classrooms had a more positive environment (e.g., on task behavior, emotional competence, compliance, levels of interest) than control classrooms. The amount and quality of instruction did relate to positive change in classroom environment. Teachers' willingness to take instruction from intervention staff predicted decreased peer ratings of classmates' hyperactivity /disorderliness (CPPRG, 1999a).

Further Reading/Materials:

Bierman, K.L., & the Conduct Problems Prevention Research Group. (1997). Implementing a comprehensive program for the prevention of conduct problems in rural communities: The FAST Track Experience. *American Journal of Community Psychology, 25*, 493-514.

Conduct Problems Prevention Research Group. (1999a). Initial impact of the Fast Track Prevention Trial for Conduct Problems: I. The high-risk sample. *Journal of Consulting and Clinical Psychology, 67*, 631-647.

Conduct Problems Prevention Research Group. (1999b). Initial impact of the Fast Track Prevention Trial for Conduct Problems: II. Classroom effects. *Journal of Consulting and Clinical Psychology, 67*, 648-657.

Conduct Problems Prevention Research Group. (in press). Evaluation of the first three years of the Fast Track Prevention Trial with Children at High Risk for Adolescent Conduct Problems. *Journal of Abnormal Child Psychology.*

Greenberg, M.L., Lengua, L.S., Coie, J., Pinderhughes, E.E., & The Conduct Problems Prevention Research Group. (in press). Predicting developmental outcomes at school entry using a multiple-risk model: Four American communities. *Developmental Psychology.*

McMahon, R.J., & The Conduct Problems Prevention Research Group. (in press). The prevention of conduct problems using targeted and universal interventions: The Fast Track Program. In D. Offord (Ed.), *Prevention of conduct disorder.* New York: Cambridge.

Program Classification: North American Cross Context Program [Family + School]

Program Title: Seattle Social Development Project[7]

Developmental Period: Childhood

Amount of Protection/Risk: Universal

Where was the Program Conducted? United States - Seattle, Washington

Stated Theoretical Basis: Social Development Model

Who Implemented the Program? Professional intervention staff conducted teacher training and parent training; teachers and a study consultant implemented classroom curricula with students

Program Description: The Seattle Social Development Project is a long-term program that included multiple interventions for teachers, students, and parents in an effort to prevent school failure, drug use and delinquency among children from high-crime neighborhoods. The teacher intervention consisted of training teachers in the use of proactive classroom management, interactive teaching, and cooperative learning (see Hawkins et al, 1999, pg. 227 for details). The student intervention consisted of child social and emotional skill development in the first and sixth grades. The first-grade program was based on a cognitive and social kills training curriculum, "Interpersonal Cognitive Problem Solving" (Shure & Spivack, 1980; Shure & Spivack, 1982), which teaches children the skills to identify a problem, generate alternative solutions, and choose and implement the chosen solution. During grade six, a study consultant provided students with training in skills to recognize and resist social influences to engage in problem behaviors (i.e., refusal skills) and to develop positive alternatives to stay out of trouble while maintaining friendships. The parent intervention included child behavior management skills, "Catch 'Em Being Good" (Hawkins, et al, 1987), academic support skills, "How to Help Your Child Succeed in School", now called "Preparing for School Success" (Hawkins & Catalano, 2003), and skills to reduce risks for drug use, "Preparing for the Drug Free Years", now called "Guiding Good Choices" (Hawkins & Kosterman, personal communication, 2003; See Hawkins & Catalano, 2003). **Program Duration:** Beginning in 1981, the intervention was initiated among a group of first-grade students in 8 public schools. These students, and a randomized control group were followed prospectively to 1985, when these children entered fifth grade. At that point, the study was expanded to include fifth-grade students in 10 additional schools. Schools were assigned non-randomly to conditions in the fall of 1985, and thereafter all fifth-grade students in each school participated in the same interventions through the sixth grade (Hawkins & Kosterman, personal communication, 2003). **Program Language:** English.

Outcome Evaluation: **Participants:** Children from high-crime neighborhoods. **Design:** Pre-post test with follow-up into adulthood (i.e., ten data collection waves from ages 10-24). Random and non random assignment to one of four groups: The full-intervention group received the interventions from grades one through six. The late-intervention group received the intervention during grades five and six only. The "parent-training only" group was offered only the "Preparing for the Drug Free Years" curriculum during grades five and six. The control group received no intervention. **Measures:** Teacher/Parent/ Youth Reports: social developmental constructs (e.g., perceived opportunities, skills, perceived reinforcements, bonding to school, parents, peers, etc.) and related risk and protective factors. Registry Data: school and court records. **Results:** Teachers in the treatment group utilized the intervention teaching strategies significantly more than comparison teachers. Short-term intervention related benefits have been demonstrated at various follow ups, including: less aggressiveness and antisocial behavior among males, and less self-destructiveness among females at the end of second grade (Hawkins, Von Cleve, & Catalano, 1991); less initiation of alcohol use and delinquency, better family management and family bonding, and better school bonding by the start of fifth grade (Hawkins et al., 1992); less initiation of cigarette use and more classroom participation and school bonding among low-income girls, and improved social skills, school bonding and school grades among low-income boys at the end of sixth grade (O'Donnell, Hawkins, Catalano, Abbott, & Day, 1995); and improved achievement test scores overall across grades five and six (Abbott et al., 1998). All program benefits were found relative to students in the comparison condition. Long-term follow up indicated that at the ages of 16 and 18 school bonding was significantly higher in the full intervention group. At age 18, the full intervention group reported less lifetime violence, less lifetime sexual activity, less heavy alcohol use, less school misbehavior, and improved school achievement (Hawkins, Catalano, Kosterman, Abbott, & Hill, 1999). Analyses of sexual behavior at age 21 found that the full intervention group had significantly fewer sexual partners by age 21, significantly fewer pregnancies and births to females by age 21, significantly increased condom use at "last intercourse" among single adults, and significant reductions in the prevalence of sexually transmitted disease among African Americans by age 21 Intervention related benefits were found relative to students in the comparison condition (Hawkins & Kosterman, personal communication, 2003; See Lonczak, Abbott, Hawkins, Kosterman, & Catalano, 2002).

Further Reading/Materials:

Abbott, R. D., O'Donnell, J., Hawkins, J. D., Hill, K. G., Kosterman, R., & Catalano, R. F. (1998). Changing teaching practices to promote achievement and bonding to school. *American Journal of Orthopsychiatry, 68*(4), 542-552.

Catalano, R. F., & Hawkins, J. D. (1996). The social development model: A theory of antisocial behavior. In J. D. Hawkins (Ed.), *Delinquency and Crime: Current theories* (pp. 149-197). New York: Cambridge University Press.

Hawkins, J. D., & Catalano, R. F. (2003). *Guiding Good Choices.* South Dearfield, MA: Channing Bete Company.

Hawkins, J. D., & Catalano, R. F. (2003). *Preparing for School Success.* South Dearfield, MA: Channing Bete Company.

Hawkins, J. D., Catalano, R. F., Kosterman, R., Abbott, R., & Hill, K. G. (1999). Preventing adolescent health-risk behaviors by strengthening protection during childhood. *Archives of Pediatric & Adolescent Medicine, 153,* 226-234.

Hawkins, J. D., Catalano, R. F., Morrison, D. M., O'Donnell, J., Abbott, R. D., & Day, L. E. (1992). The Seattle Social Development Project: Effects of the first four years on protective factors and problem behaviors. In J. McCord & R. E. Tremblay (Eds.), *Preventing antisocial behavior: Interventions from birth through adolescence* (pp. 139-161). New York: Guilford Press.

Hawkins, J. D., Doueck, H. J., & Lishner, D. M. (1988). Changing teaching practices in mainstream classrooms to improve bonding and behavior of low achievers. *American Educational Research Journal, 25*(1), 31-50.

Hawkins, J. D., Guo, J., Hill, K., Battin-Pearson, S., & Abbott, R. (in press). Long term effects of the Seattle Social Development intervention on school bonding trajectories. In J. Maggs & J. Schulenberg (Eds.), *Applied Developmental Science: Special issue: Prevention as Altering the Course of Development.*

Hawkins, J. D., Von Cleve, E., & Catalano, R. F., Jr. (1991). Reducing early childhood aggression: results of a primary prevention program. *Journal of the American Academy of Child and Adolescent Psychiatry, 30*(2), 208-217.

Lonczak, H. S., Abbott, R. D., Hawkins, J. D., Kosterman, R., & Catalano, R. F. (2002). Effects of the Seattle Social Development Project on sexual behavior, pregnancy, birth, and STD outcomes by age 21. *Archives of Pediatrics and Adolescent Medicine, 156*(4), 438-447.

O'Donnell. J., Hawkins, J. D., Catalano, R. F., Abbott, R. D., & Day, L. E. (1995). Preventing School Failure, drug use, and delinquency among low-income children: Long-term intervention in elementary schools. *American Journal of Orthopsychiatry, 65*(1), 87-100.

Program Classification: American Community Program

Program Title: Communities Mobilizing for Change on Alcohol (CMCA)

Developmental Period: Adolescence/Early Adulthood

Amount of Protection/Risk: Universal

Where was the Program Conducted? United States- Minnesota and Wisconsin

Stated Theoretical Basis: Learning (Skinner, 1953), cognitive and social learning (Bandura, 1977), problem behavior (Jessor, 1977), stage (Kandel, 1975), economic (Becker & Murphy, 1988), symbolic interactionism (Cooley, 1962; Mead, 1934), social control (Clinard & Meier, 1989), anomie (Merton, 1968), availability (Bruun, et al., 1975; Holder, 1987), community mobilization (Boyte, 1989; Minkler, 1990) theories – See Wagenaar & Perry (1994) for details.

Who Implemented the Program? Researchers, program organizers, community residents, public officials, law enforcement personnel, alcohol merchants and salespersons, school staff, teen confederates

Program Description: This prevention program focused on mobilizing community residents to initiate and maintain environmental change within the community. Systemic changes in policy and practices that have been found to encourage youth alcohol use were targeted for intervention.
Tolerant attitudes towards underage drinking were also addressed. In each intervention community, a local resident was employed on a part-time basis to lead community mobilization efforts by: 1) looking into the community's intervention desires and capabilities, 2) forming a broad based planning group, 3) laying out concrete intervention actions and a schedule of implementation, 4) mustering community support for program initiatives, 5) taking and upholding action, and 6) seeking to document actions and intervention results. In each community different types of intervention actions were taken. Some commonly implemented activities included: Designated drinking areas at community events, compliance checks, greater enforcement of existing laws/policy, restrictions on beer kegs on university premises, responsible beverage service training. **Program Duration:** Two and a half years (1992-1995). **Program Language:** English.

Outcome Evaluation: **Design:** Interrupted time-series and randomized intervention trial. Communities were matched (N=15) by state, population, proximity to colleges/universities, pre-test shopping trial performance and then randomly assigned to condition: Intervention (n=7) and control (n=8). **Nested sub-designs/measures:** Nested cohort design (pre-post testing with one birth cohort of high school students [Pre-test: n=5,885 9th graders; Post-test: n=3,694 12th graders]), nested cross sectional designs: Comparison of 12th graders in 1992 [n=4,506] versus 1995 [n=4,487]) and late adolescent phone surveys in 1992 [n=3,095] and 1995 [n=1,721]. Surveys of high school students and late adolescents indexed: Attitudes towards alcohol use, perceptions of alcohol availability and adherence to existing laws and policies e.g., consumption, binge drinking, distributing alcohol to others, purchases of alcohol. Nested cohort/cross sectional design: Shopping trials of on and off premise establishments in 1992 [n=1,004] and 1995 [n=1,112]. Alcohol availability and law/policy adherence e.g., was identification asked for; demographics of salesperson, success/failure rate for purchases were measured. Nested cohort/cross sectional design: Alcohol merchant surveys in 1992 [n=502] and 1995 [n=556]. Alcohol-related policy and training practices, beliefs regarding sales of alcohol to youth, attitudes towards existing laws/policies were assessed. Time series analysis of registry data was conducted for data from 1987-1995 (6 years pre-intervention period; 3 years across the intervention period). The number of youth involved in alcohol-related injuries and disorderly conduct arrests were analyzed. **Results:** An aggregate score that combined shopping trial and merchant survey information indicated that those establishments in the intervention communities that sold alcohol for use on the premise e.g., restaurants, pubs, etc. showed a significant change relative to the control communities (d=1.18). Aggregate survey responses from 18-20 year old youth living in the intervention versus control communities in 1992 and 1995 (d=.76) also showed significant change. Older adolescents in the intervention communities also evidenced a 17% decline in providing alcohol to younger peers relative to 18-

20 year olds residing in the control communities. Driving while under the influence (DUI) arrests for 18-20 year olds in the intervention communities showed a consistent decline during the pre-intervention (1987-1992) and intervention periods (1993-1995). Eighteen to twenty year olds in the control communities showed a decline during the pre-intervention period (1987-1992) with a marked increase in DUI arrests during the intervention period (1993-1995). **Notes:** There was a series of marginally significant findings (p=.06 or .07) in the following areas: Shopping trials (ID checking in on premise sites, confederate purchase rates), 18-20 year old surveys (attempted purchase rate, troubles accessing alcohol from commercial sources, alcohol use). As a part of the process evaluation records of community contacts, media coverage, community attitudes and organizational structure, mobilization and intervention activities, challenges encountered were recorded. This evaluation found that 141 community residents actively participated in the community planning groups and over 2000 residents took part in the intervention activities.

Further Reading/Materials:
Wagenaar, A. C., Gehan, J. P., Jones-Webb, R., Wolfson, M., Toomey, T. L., Forster, J. L., Murray, D. M. (1999). Communities Mobilizing for Change on Alcohol: Lessons and results from a 15-community randomized trial. *Journal of Community Psychology, 27*(3): 315-326.
Wagenaar, A. C., Murray, D. M., Gehan, J. P., Wolfson, M., Forster, J. L., Toomey, T. L., Perry, C. L., & Jones-Webb, R. (2000). Communities Mobilizing for Change on Alcohol: Outcomes from a randomized community trials. *Journal of Studies on Alcohol, 61*, 85-94.
Wagenaar, A. C., Murray, D. M., & Toomey, T. L. (2000). Communities Mobilizing for Change on Alcohol (CMCA): Effects of a randomized trial on arrests and traffic crashes. *Addiction, 95*, 209-217.

Program Classification: American Cross Context Programs [School + Community]

Program Title: Minnesota Heart Health Program and the Class of 1989 Study

Developmental Period: Childhood/Adolescence

Amount of Protection/Risk: Universal

Where was the Program Conducted? United States- Fargo and West Fargo, North Dakota; Moorhead, Minnesota; Sioux Fall, South Dakota

Stated Theoretical Basis: Social Learning Theory (Bandura, 1986), Problem Behavior Theory (Jessor et al., 1984)

Who Implemented the Program? Youth, teachers, community residents, researchers

Program Description: The Minnesota Heart Health Program (MHHP) was community-wide intervention aimed at the prevention of cardiovascular disease. The program included intervention activities that focused on nutrition, physical activity, smoking and alcohol use. Community-wide intervention strategies included the promotion of nutritional labeling of foods sold at restaurants and grocery stores, cardiovascular disease screening, and several forms of mass media education campaigns. As a part of this larger intervention, the Class of 1989 Study documented changes in youngsters who took part in a school-based health promotion intervention. The goal of the youth component was to influence early dietary and risk taking patterns. The interventions used youth and teacher administered, skills-based nutrition education programs. School-based programs that dealt with diet and/or exercise were entitled Hearty Heart, the Lunch Bag Program, Slice of Life, Health Olympics, FM250, and the Heart Health Screening Center. Curriculum that dealt with alcohol and tobacco prevention included the Minnesota Smoking Prevention Program, Amazing Alternatives and Shifting Gears. These interventions sought to increase knowledge, booster the youngster's sense of self efficacy, and the foster social resistance skills development. **Program Duration:** MHHP took place over a 13 year period (1980 to 1993). The Class of 1989 Study lasted for six years (1983 to 1989), with intervention actions taking place for 5 years (1983-1987). **Program Language:** English.

Outcome Evaluation (Youth Component): **Participants:** European American middle class upper primary and secondary school students (6th – 12th graders). **Design:** Quasi-experimental: Intervention and matched comparison communities. The results described here are for two of the six MHHP communities. Youth data was collected in one intervention and one comparison community (Pre-testing: N=2,376). Pre testing with multiple posttests: Intervention and comparison youth were sixth graders at the program start and were evaluated annually through 1989. **Measures:** Youth report: Smoking, alcohol use, diet, exercise, health/lifestyle knowledge and beliefs. Youth physiological tests: Saliva thiocynate analysis. **Results:** Throughout the study and by its end, indices indicative of reduced smoking behavior favored the intervention youth relative to comparison youth (in 12th grade 15% of intervention versus 24% of comparison community youth reported smoking). Significant intervention related improvements in alcohol consumption levels among intervention versus comparison condition youth were found, but the intensity of these benefits faded in later adolescence (10th -12th grades). **Notes:** There were a number of positive changes in terms of health behaviors: The making and knowledge of healthier food choices, and favorable views on the importance of exercise. What youth reported eating at the moment (i.e., current food choice) was more predictive of what they would eat in the future relative to simply having an understanding which foods are healthy, thus leading the authors of the study to conclude that behavior change in diet should be a central target for future intervention work. One of the community-wide strategies used in MHHP, the 'Quit and Win' smoking cessation contest, has been tested in Finland and Sweden (e.g., Korhonen, Sun, Korhonen, Uutela, & Puska, 1997; Tillgren, 1995; Tillgren, Eriksson, Guldbrandsson, & Spiik, 2000). Strategies such as direct mail, media and one on one campaign promotion, how to quit information guides, smoking cessation phone-in hot lines, and contest give-a-ways are typically used in 'Quit and Win' contests. Cessation rates after 12 months for women in the Swedish and Finish studies ranged from 11.5% to 14.3%. In MHHP, adult cessation rates ranged from 21%-24% after six to eight months (Lando, Pechacek, & Fruetel, 1994). Youth in the Class of 1989 Study participated in the Quit & Win contests by encouraging adults to sign up to quit smoking.

Further Reading/Materials:
Kelder, S. H., Perry, C. L., & Klepp, K. (1993). Community-wide youth exercise promotion: Long-term outcomes of the Minnesota Heart Health Program and the Class of 1989 Study. *Journal of School Health, 63*(5), 218-223.

Kelder, S. H., Perry, C. L., Klepp, K-I., & Lytle, L. L. (1994). Longitudinal tracking of adolescent smoking, physical activity, and food choice behaviors. *American Journal of Public Health, 84,* 1121-1126.

Kelder, S. H., Perry, C. L., Lytle, L. A., & Klepp, K. (1995). Community-wide youth nutrition education: Long-term outcomes of the Minnesota Heart Health Program. *Health Education Research: Theory and Practice, 10*(2), 119-131.

Korhonen, T., Sun, S., Korhonen, H. J. Uutela, A., & Puska, P. (1997). Evaluation of a national quit and win contest: Determinants for successful quitting. *Preventive Medicine, 26,* 556-564.

Lando, H. A., Pechacek, T. F., & Fruetel, J. (1994). The Minnesota Heart Health Program Community Quit and Win contests. *American Journal of Health Promotion, 9,* 85-87.

Lando, H. A., Pechacek, T. F., Pirie, P. L., Murray, D. M., et al., (1995). Changes in adult cigarette smoking in the Minnesota Heart Health Program. *American Journal of Public Health, 85,* 201-208.

Luepker, R. V. & Perry, C. L. (1991). The Minnesota Heart Health Program: Education for youth and parents. *Annals of the New York Academy of Sciences, 623,* 314-321.

Lytle, L. A., Kelder, S. H., Perry, C. L., Klepp, K-I. (1995). Covariance of adolescent health behaviors: The Class of 1989 study. *Health Education Research, 10,* 133-146.

Nothwehr, F., Lando, H. A., & Bobo, J-K. (1995). Alcohol and tobacco use in the Minnesota Heart Health Program. *Addictive Behaviors, 20,* 463-470.

Perry, C. L., Klepp, K-I., & Sillers, C. (1989). Community-wide strategies for cardiovascular health: The Minnesota Heart Health Program youth program. *Health Education Research, 4,* 87-101.

Perry, C. L., Kelder, S. H., Murray, D. M., & Klepp, K-I. (1992). Community-wide smoking prevention: long-term outcomes of the Minnesota Heart Health Program. *American Journal of Public Health, 82,* 1210-1216.

Prokhorov, A. V., Perry, C. L., Kelder, S. H., Klepp, K-I. (1993). Lifestyle values of adolescents: Results from Minnesota Heart Health Youth Program. *Adolescence, 28,* 637-647.

Tillgren, P., Eriksson, L., Guldbrandsson, K., & Spiik, M. (2000). Impact of direct mail as a method to recruit smoking mothers into a "quit and win" contest. *Journal of Health Communication, 5,* 293-303.

Tillgren, P. (1995). 'Quit and win' contests in tobacco cessation: Theoretical framework and practices from a community-based intervention in the Stockholm Cancer Prevention Program (SCPP). Doctoral dissertation. Department of International Health and Social Medicine, Unit of Social Medicine, Karolinska Institute, Sundbyberg, Sweden.

Program Classification: American Cross Context Programs [Family + School + Community]

Program Title: Midwestern Prevention Program [also called Project STAR (Students Taught Awareness and Resistance) and I-STAR (Indiana STAR)]

Developmental Period: Adolescence

Amount of Protection/Risk: Universal

Where was the Program Conducted? United States - Kansas City, Kansas; Kansas City, Missouri, Indianapolis, Indiana

Stated Theoretical Basis: Integrative transactional theory (Pentz, 1999), social influence models, social learning theory, social Competence skill training; Health Behavior Theories

Program Description: The Midwestern Prevention Project (MPP) is a multiple component and context intervention designed to alter early drug use patterns among youth entering into secondary school. The first test of the intervention was conducted in Kansas City (Kansas and Missouri, Project STAR) with a subsequent replication carried out in Indianapolis (Indiana, I-

STAR). The evaluation designs and program implementation of Project STAR and I-STAR are not identical. These trials do, however, share common intervention goals and content. Commonalities include the phasing in of a series of core intervention actions: 1) anti-drug and intervention relevant media campaigns ran over the entire intervention period {a combination of paid advertising and coverage garnered through media advocacy techniques}, 2) peer and teacher implemented anti-drug knowledge and skills training {normative education, resistance and problem solving skills, public abstinence commitments} with corresponding parent-teen take home activities in the first intervention year with subsequent booster activities taking place during the following academic year, 3) the second and third intervention years are focused on parent education/training {ATOD knowledge/skills training including a focus on parent-teen communication} through bi-annual events that are organized by school based planning teams (a school principal, parents and peer leaders) and take home parent-teen activities, 4) community mobilization efforts and the targeting of public policy change that is in line with the MPP's goals is initiated in the third through fifth intervention years. In Project STAR, those people residing in the control and comparison communities experienced the community mobilization and public policy intervention components but did not receive any of the school or parent targeted program activities. **Program Duration:** Project STAR (at the Kansas City site) was conducted for five years (1984-1989). I-STAR also had a five year intervention period (1987-1992). **Program Language:** English.

Outcome Evaluation (Project STAR – 1984-1987)[8]: **Participants:** Predominately European American upper primary and secondary school students. **Design:** Eight out of 42 schools were randomly assigned to an intervention (n=4) or control (n=4) condition. Pre-testing with yearly follow ups of a single cohort of youth to the program's end (five years, 1984-1989). Published accounts of the cohort study have described evaluation results up to 1987 (1984-1987; N=1,105). After three and half years of program activities, the majority of intervention components were in place with the exception of community coalition and public policy initiatives. Coalitions were in the process of organizing at this point. **Measures:** Youth report: Personal, peer, and parent ATOD use, risk factors related to ATOD use. Youth physiological testing: Smoking behaviors as indexed by CO levels (Mini CO Indicator). Parent report: ATOD use and ATOD risk factors. **Results:** Normative increasing in alcohol, tobacco, and marijuana use were noted, however, intervention youth evidenced a slower progression of drug involvement (for tobacco and marijuana use) relative to the rate of involvement shown among teens in the control condition. Intervention related gains were not found alcohol consumption[9]. An interaction between intervention and grade was noted on tobacco smoking and alcohol consumption indices with the seventh grade implementation showing greater benefits. See Johnson, et al., 1990 for more details. **Notes:** Training and materials for approximately 20 teachers, 20 parents, and 1,000 teens is estimated to be $US 175,000 for a three year intervention period.

Outcome Evaluation (I-STAR subgroup analysis): **Participants:** Predominately European American upper primary and secondary school students. **Design:** Schools (n=57) with a given school district (n=12) were randomly assigned to an intervention (n=32) or control (n=25) condition. Pre and multiple post tests (at 6 months, 1.5 years, 2.5 years, and 3.5 years after baseline measurement). One-third of the total number of students participating in the study (intervention + control) was assessed at pre-testing (N=3,412; Intervention n = 1,904; Control n=1,508). This cohort of teens was then followed over time. This evaluation is only for those teens who reported cigarette (n=400; Intervention n=212; Control n=188), alcohol (n=613; Intervention n=323; Control n=290), or marijuana (n=60; intervention n=22; control n=38) consumption before intervention activities were initiated. **Measures:** Youth report: Personal and shared (peers, family) ATOD use, personal and shared (peers, family) attitudes and beliefs regarding ATOD. **Results:** Program related benefits were shown for cigarette users at the six month post testing. This intervention gain was demonstrated relative to baseline cigarette users in the control condition. For alcohol users in the intervention group reductions were found for alcohol consumption at the six month and year and a half post tests. Once again, this change was demonstrated relative to the use reported by baseline alcohol users in the control group. Analyses that took into account the pattern of change across all measurement points (through the multiple post tests) indicated that cigarette, alcohol, and marijuana users in the intervention condition showed a significant decline in their respective drugs of choice (i.e., baseline cigarette users showed a decline in later cigarette smoking, etc.). See Chou, et al., 1998 for more details.

Further Reading/Materials:

Chou, C., Montgomery, S., Pentz, M. A., Rohrbach, L. A., Johnson, C. A., Flay, B., & MacKinnon, D. P. (1998). Effects of a community-based prevention program on decreasing drug use in high-risk adolescents. *American Journal of Public Health, 88*(6), 944-948.

Johnson, C. A., Pentz, M. A., Weber, M. D., Dwyer, J. H., Baer, N., MacKinnon, D. P., Hansen, W. B. & Flay, B. R. (1990). Relative effectiveness of comprehensive community programming for drug abuse prevention with high-risk and low-risk adolescents. *Journal of Consulting and Clinical Psychology, 58*(4), 447-456.

Pentz, M. A., Mihalic, S. F., & Grotpeter, J. K. (1997). The Midwestern Prevention Project. In D. S. Elliot (Ed.), *Blueprints for Violence Prevention.* Boulder, CO: Center for the Study and Prevention of Violence, Institute of Behavioral Science, University of Colorado.

Program Classification: European Cross Context Programs [Family + School + Community]

Program Title: Prevention and Management of Drug Abuse in Poland

Developmental Period: Adolescence

Amount of Protection/Risk: Universal/Secondary/Indicated

Where was the Program Conducted? Poland

Who Implemented the Program? Project Teams (of community officials and stakeholders); Project staff and coordinators; researchers (Institute of Psychiatry and Neurology, Warsaw)

Program Description: Odlot consisted of four main areas of activity: 1) Community-wide sensitivity raising on the topic of drug use/abuse through the distribution of promotional materials and a children's poster contest (and the later public display of posters) on drug abuse, 2) increasing opportunities for youngsters to participate in organized leisure activities, 3) individual counseling and workshops with parents who have and have not been affected by family alcohol misuse/addiction, 4) advocacy for and treatment of substance addicted adults, 5) training of teachers, journalists, community leaders including inter-agency training, teens (N=20) on drug prevention and treatment. The activity most directly concerned with children and adolescents was the leisure opportunity component. Funds and organizational support were provided to existing youth clubs within the intervention communities. Clubs that were defunct due to a lack of funds were reopened and new clubs (e.g., a railway station club, theater groups) were created either in neighborhoods or schools, based on local demands. Seventy club activity leaders were employed on a part time basis (20-40 hours per month) during the intervention year. Leaders were encouraged to redesign activities to accommodate a larger more diverse group of youth (e.g., non elite athletes, artists, and musicians). Schools and clubs were open for extended hours, over holidays, and were promoted in school through a series of special events (e.g., parties, concerts, etc.). **Program Duration:** One year (1994-1995). **Program Languages:** Polish, reports in English.

Outcome Evaluation: **Participants:** Intervention Community 1: Students aged 14-15; Intervention Community 2: Students aged 14-15 and 17-18; Comparison Community: Students aged 14-15 and 17-18. **Design:** Quasi-experimental: Pre-post testing. **Measures:** Youth reports: Leisure time, alcohol and other drug use, drug attitudes. Registry Information: Juvenile delinquency (crimes committed; number of youth making use of local sobering-up stations. **Results:** *Community 1 vs. the Comparison Community:* At the end of the intervention, 250 students (approximately 50% of available population) participated in Odlot sponsored leisure activities. Students surveyed in the intervention community reported a rate of 86% after school activity involvement. Intervention youth showed a pre to post test increase in prosocial home activities (doing homework, helping parents) relative to a decrease in comparison youth. The number of intervention youngsters reporting one-year abstinence from all drugs including alcohol also increased relative to a decrease in the comparison group. Registry information on juvenile delinquency was not kept in this community. *Community 2 vs. the Comparison Community:* At the program's conclusion, 3,000 local children and teens (30% of the available population) participated in Odlot related leisure activities. Those 14-15 year old students surveyed in the intervention community reported a rate of 70% after school activity involvement. Activity rates for 17-18 year old students were not reported. Registry information on juvenile crime and use of sobering up stations showed a pattern of differences in favor of the intervention community versus the comparison community. At the height of the project's implementation, the number of juvenile crimes and the number of youngsters using sobering up stations in the comparison community was twice that of the intervention community. 14-15 year old results: Intervention condition pupils showed an increase in prosocial home activities (doing homework, reading books) relative to a decrease in comparison youngsters. Intervention youth also showed a decrease in the taking of sedatives (during the last 12 months) relative to an increase in the comparison condition. 17-18 year old results: Intervention students showed a decline in the number of hours spent on watching TV relative to an increase among comparison youth. Intervention youth also evidenced a stable rate of drinking of wine and vodka (during the last 30 days) relative to a significant increase among comparison teens. **Notes:** A more precise estimate of how many surveyed children participated in Odlot sponsored activities was not reported. Matching or post-hoc statistical control of possible differences between the comparison and intervention communities was not reported.

Materials:
Moskalewicz, J. & Wolniewicz-Grzelak, B. (Eds.). (1996). *Pakiet Prewencyjny: Program Zapobiegania Narkomanii 'Odlot'*. Warszawa: Instytut Psychiatrii i Neurologii.

Further Reading:
Bronowski, P. & Gabrysiak, J. (1999). Community-based drug prevention in Poland. *Drugs: education, prevention and policy, 6*(3), 337-342.
Moskalewicz, J. (1995). Implementation of a drug prevention programme in local communities affected by high unemployment. *Eurosocial Report, 53*, 43-52. European Centre for Social Welfare Policy and Research.
Moskalewicz, J., Okulicz-Kozaryn, K., Ostaszewski, K., Sierosławski, J., Świątkiewicz, G., (1998). Doswiadczenia srodowiskowego programu zapobiegania narkomanii 'Odlot'. *Przeglad Psychologiczny, 3/4*, 133-143.

Moskalewicz, J., Sierosławski, J., Świątkiewicz, G., Zamecki, K., & Zieliński, A. (1999). *Prevention and management of drug abuse in Poland: Summary of final report.* Warsaw, Poland: Institute of Psychiatry and Neurology.

Moskalewicz J. & Świątkiewicz, G. (2000). Malczyce, Poland: A multifaceted community action project in Eastern Europe in a time of rapid economic change. *Substance Use and Misuse, 35*(1-2), 189-202.

Moskalewicz, J. & Wolniewicz-Grzelak, B. (Eds.). (1996). *Pakiet Prewencyjny: Program Zapobiegania Narkomanii 'Odlot'.* Warszawa: Instytut Psychiatrii i Neurologii.

Ostaszewski, K. (1998). Promotion of evaluation as a strategy towards an effective substance prevention. *European Addiction Research, 4/3,* 128-133.

Ostaszewski, K., Bobrowski, K., Borucka, A., Okulicz-Kozaryn, K., & Pisarska, A. (2000). Evaluating innovative drug-prevention programmes: Lessons learned. In *Evaluation – a key tool for improving drug prevention* (pp. 75-85). EMCDDA Scientific Monograph Series No 5, Office for Publications of the European Commission.

World Health Organization. (1992). *Programme of activities in Central and Eastern Europe for the prevention of drug abuse and concomitant HIV transmission: Report on the planning meeting.* Copenhagen, Denmark: WHO Regional Office for Europe.

Program Classification: American Cross Context Programs [Family + School + Community]

Program Title: Project Northland

Developmental Period: Early Adolescence

Amount of Protection/Risk: Universal

Where was the Program Conducted? United States - Northeast Minnesota

Stated Theoretical Basis: Health promotion and drug prevention model (Perry & Jessor, 1985), social influence model

Who Implemented the Program: Youth, teachers/school staff, community residents

Program Description: Project Northland (PN) was a multiple component and context intervention aimed at influencing early adolescent drug use. Intervention actions included educational events (Slick Tracy Family Fun Nights, Amazing Alternatives Kick off Night), newsletters (Northland Notes for Parents), and home based activity booklets (Slick Tracy Home Team Program, Amazing Alternatives! Home Program). These activities were largely aimed at the provision of accurate information about alcohol, tobacco, and other drugs (ATOD) as well as giving parents and teens a forum in which they could talk about drugs. Other intervention actions dealt with school based curricular activities, drug free leisure opportunities, and community mobilization. The Amazing Alternatives! (AA) curriculum was implemented by elected student peer leaders. AA was designed to correct student misperceptions about the prevalence of teen alcohol use as well as promote problem solving and social resistance skills. The Power Lines curriculum extended the community mobilization concept to youth by providing teens with training in social action techniques (e.g., interviewing local decision makers, purveyors of alcohol, etc.) and an opportunity to make suggestions about the way the community should proceed in its alcohol prevention efforts. Groups of youth were further brought into intervention process through peer decision making/planning groups. Through a program entitled The Exciting and Entertaining Northland Students (T.E.E.N.S.) peer leaders (n=73) were trained in organizational, finance, information gathering, and promotional techniques. Students who took part in T.E.E.N.S. groups (n=166) at each intervention school were subsequently given the task of planning and implementing a series of drug-free events for fellow students. Adult volunteers (n=33) from the local area provided support for T.E.E.N.S. activities. An adult community coalition was also formed to address the problem of teen access to alcohol in the community. The targets for change in this case were the passage of more restrictive laws and ordinances in support of compulsory responsible beverage service training, garnering material rewards from local businesses to reinforce youth who make a public commitment to ATOD abstinence, and alcohol merchant education programs. **Program Duration:** Three years of intervention activities (1991-1994). **Program Language:** English.

Outcome Evaluation: **Participants:** Predominately European American upper primary and secondary school students living in rural communities. One cohort group (the Class of 1998). **Design:** Pre and multiple posting (1991 N=2,351; 1992 N=2,191; 1993 N=2,060; 1994 N=1,901). Twenty combined school-districts and respective communities were matched in terms of population and then randomly assigned to either an intervention (n=10) or a control (n=10) condition. Control school districts carried on with their preexisting drug prevention programming (e.g., Project DARE or QUEST). Intervention districts phased out preexisting drug prevention programs over the course of the study. **Measures:** Youth report: ATOD use, personal and peer attitudes and beliefs on ATOD, refusal skills, the quality of parent—teen communication, views on the accessibility of alcohol in the community, and participation in T.E.E.N.S. activities. **Results:** A pre-test difference between intervention and control youth was noted with greater alcohol consumption among intervention teens. Analyses that controlled for pre-test differences found that by the study's end intervention related benefits (treatment versus control condition) accrued on multiple indices of alcohol consumption, beliefs regarding the utility of alcohol, and parent-teen communication. Particular benefits were found for those teens in the intervention condition that were not alcohol users at the start of the intervention (relative to nonusers in control school districts). In this case, pre to final post test intervention related benefits were found for peer influences, self efficacy, alcohol, tobacco, and marijuana use. Particular benefits in terms of reduced alcohol use were also documented for those teens in the intervention condition that directly took part in T.E.E.N.S planning groups (n=166) relative to other intervention youth who simply attended T.E.E.N.S. activities (n=335) or did not participate in these activities at all (n=527). See Komro, et al., (1996) for details. **Notes:** At baseline, surveys/interviews of the Class of 1998 parents, alcohol vendors, and community leaders were conducted. A pre-test shopping trial or purchase attempts also took place. According to a principal investigator on the study, post test results on purchase attempts showed significant reductions in the intervention communities (Perry, personal communication, 2003). During the intervention period eight restrictive/responsible alcohol policy changes were recorded in three out of the ten intervention communities. No other environmental changes were noted. At all measurement points, youth perception of alcohol access in the community did not show a significant difference between conditions (intervention versus control) although there were indications that commercial access was significantly reduced.

Further Reading/Materials:
Komro, K. A., Perry, C. L., Murray, D. M., Veblen-Mortenson, S., Williams, C. L., & Anstine,
    P. S. (1996). Peer-planned social activities for preventing alcohol use among young
    adolescents. *Journal of School Health, 66,* 9, 328-334.
Komro, K. A., Perry, C. L., Williams, C. L., Stigler, M. H., Farbakhsh, K., Veblen-Mortenson,
    S. (2001). How did Project Northland reduce alcohol use among adolescents?
    Analysis of mediating variables. *Health Education Research, 16,* 59-70.

Perry, C. L., Williams, C. L., Forster, J. L., Wolfson, M., & et al., (1993). Background, conceptualization and design of a community-wide research program on adolescent alcohol use: Project Northland. *Health Education Research, 8*, 125-136.

Perry, C. L., Williams, C. L., Komro, K. A., Veblen-Mortenson, S., Forster, J. L., Bernstein-Lachter, R., Pratt, L. K., Dudovitz, B., Munson, K. A., Farbakhsh, K., Finnegan, J., & McGovern, P. (2000). Project Northland high school interventions: Community action to reduce adolescent alcohol use. *Health Education and Behavior, 27*, 29-49.

Perry, C. L., Williams, C. L., Veblen-Mortenson, S., Toomey, T. L. Komro, K., Anstine, P. S., McGovern, P. G., Finnegan, J. R., Forster, J. L., Wagenaar, A. C., & Wolfson, M. (1996). Project Northland: Outcomes of a communitywide alcohol use prevention program during early adolescence. *American Journal of Public Health, 86*, 7, 956-965.

Rissel, C., Finnegan, J., Wolfson, M., & Perry, C. (1995). Factors which explain amount of participation in rural adolescent alcohol use prevention task forces. *American Journal of Health Promotion, 9*, 169-171.

Wagenaar, A. C. & Perry, C. L. (1994). Community strategies for the reduction of youth drinking: Theory and application. *Journal of Research on Adolescence, 4*, 319-345.

Williams, C. L. & Perry, C. L. (1998). Lessons from project Northland: Preventing alcohol problems during adolescence. *Alcohol Health and Research World, 22*, 107-116.

Williams, C. L., Perry, C. L., Dudovitz, B. Veblen-Mortenson, S., & et al., (1995). A home-based prevention program for sixth-grade alcohol use: Results from project Northland. *Journal of Primary Prevention, 16*, 125-147.

Chapter Endnotes

---

[1] In addition to the authors, Karol Kumpfer made a significant contribution to the content of this program summary.

[2] SFP has been evaluated on multiple occasions. The evaluations described here represent a sampling.

[3] As of 1998, FFT was tested a total of 13 times with experimental (e.g., Alexander & Parsons, 1973; Klein, Alexander, & Parsons, 1977; Hansson, 2000) and quasi-experimental designs (e.g., Barton et al., 1985; Gordon, et al., 1988; Gordon, Graves, & Arbuthnot, 1995). The evaluation described gives an overall representation of those evaluations. Researchers note that across evaluations FFT is 25-60% more successful than conventional approaches (or no intervention) in reducing reoffending and other institutional placements. Follow up studies have spanned up to 5-6 years post intervention (e.g. Gordon, Graves, & Arbuthnot, 1995). Positive results have also been noted for siblings up to 3 years after the intervention.

[4] Programs in the Incredible Years Series have been evaluated on multiple occasions. The evaluations described here represent a sampling of those evaluations.

[5] Due to language limitations, primary sources were not used. Program developers helped to create this summary.

[6] To date, PATHS has been tested on four occasions in the United States, including the PATHS/Fast Track trial. This study is representative in that other evaluations have also shown the same overall pattern of positive results. Also see the Fast Track Program for more details.

[7] In addition to the authors, David Hawkins and Rick Kosterman made significant contributions to the content of this program summary.

[8] The utility of Project STAR has been examined in a number of ways. This summary describes the results for intervention with the randomly assigned school sample (n=8 schools). While other evaluations with combined experimental/quasi-experimental or solely quasi-experimental samples represent important tests of the program, we have chosen to highlight this rigorous examination of Project STAR's utility. Quasi-experimental outcome evaluation results tend to parallel the positive intervention related gains shown for the experimental subsample (see reviews of the program by Catalano, et al., 1999; Flay, 2000).

[9] Project STAR quasi-experimental samples and I-STAR have shown intervention related benefits in terms of reduced alcohol use (e.g., Chou, et al., 1998; Pentz, Dwyer, et al., 1989)

Chapter 10
Web Resources

Prevention-Promotion Supporting Institutions and Agencies

American Psychological Association's The Prevention Connection: Promoting strength resilience and health in children, adolescents and adults
http://www.oslc.org/spr/home.html

Canadian Center on Substance Abuse
http://www.ccsa.ca/

Carnegie Corporation
http://www.carnegie.org/

Centers for Disease Control and Prevention (United States)
http://www.cdc.gov/

Drugscope (United Kingdom)
http://www.drugscope.org.uk/goodpractice/home.asp

EUROCARE
http://www.eurocare.org/

European Monitoring Centre for Drugs and Drug Addition
http://www.emcdda.org

Global Drug Prevention Network – LINKS
http://www.gdpn.org/gdpn/links/links.htm

Global Youth Network (United Nations Office on Drugs and Crime)
http://www.unodc.org/youthnet/

Institute of Alcohol Studies (United Kingdom)
http://www.ias.org.uk/

John D. and Catherine T. MacArthur Foundation
http://www.macfdn.org/

National Board for Youth Affairs (Sweden)
http://www.ungdomsstyrelsen.se

National Board of Health and Welfare (Sweden)
http://www.sos.se/sosmenye.htm

National Board of Institutional Care (Sweden)
http://www.stat-inst.se/

National Criminal Justice Reference Service (United States)
http://www.ncjrs.org/

National Institute of Child Health and Human Development (United States)
http://www.nichd.nih.gov/

National Institute of Mental Health (United States)
http://www.nimh.nih.gov/home.cfm

National Institute of Public Health (Sweden)
http://www.fhi.se/

National Institute on Alcohol Abuse and Alcoholism (United States)
http://www.niaaa.nih.gov/

National Institute on Drug Abuse (United States)
http://www.nida.nih.gov/

National Science Foundation
http://www.nsf.gov/

Nordic Counsel for Alcohol and Drug Research
http://www.kaapeli.fi/nad/

Office of Disease Prevention and Health Promotion (United States)
http://odphp.osophs.dhhs.gov/

Pew Charitable Trusts
http://www.pewtrusts.com/

Prevention Net
http://www.preventionnet.com/files/presites.cfm

Prevnet (European)
http://www.prevnet.net/

Robert Wood Johnson Foundation
http://www.rwjf.org/index.jsp

Substance Abuse and Mental Health Services Administration (United States)
http://www.samhsa.gov/

Swedish Council for Information on Alcohol and Other Drugs
http://www.can.se/

The European Commission – Youth
http://europa.eu.int/comm/youth/index_en.html

The National Council for Crime Prevention (Sweden)
http://www.bra.se/web/english/

Trust for the Study of Adolescence (United Kingdom)
http://www.tsa.uk.com

United Nations Children's Fund UNICEF
http://www.unicef.org/

U.S. Department of Education
http://www.ed.gov/

U.S. Department of Health and Human Services
http://www.hhs.gov/

World Health Organization
http://www.who.int/en/

Sources for Prevention-Promotion Related Statistics

10th Special Report to the U.S. Congress on Alcohol and Health
http://www.niaaa.nih.gov/publications/10report/intro.pdf

America's Children: Key National Indicators of Well Being, 2002
http://childstats.gov/americaschildren/

Behavioral Risk Factor Surveillance System (United States)
http://www.cdc.gov/brfss/

Bureau of Justice Statistics (United States)
http://www.ojp.usdoj.gov/bjs/

Eurostat (Europe)
http://europa.eu.int/comm/eurostat/

FedStats (United States)
http://www.fedstats.gov

KIDS COUNT - from the Annie E. Casey Foundation
http://www.aecf.org/kidscount/

Monitoring the Future (United States)
http://monitoringthefuture.org/

National Center for Educational Statistics (United States)
http://nces.ed.gov/

National Center for Health Statistics (United States)
http://www.cdc.gov/nchs/

Office of Applied Studies (SAMHSA) (United States)
http://www.drugabusestatistics.samhsa.gov/

Youth Risk Behavior Surveillance System (United States)
http://www.cdc.gov/nccdphp/dash/yrbs/index.htm

Prevention-Promotion Related Professional Organizations

American Psychological Association
www.apa.org/

American Public Health Association
www.apha.org/

Society for Prevention Research and the Early Career Preventionist Network
http://www.preventionresearch.org/

The Kettil Bruun Society for Social and Epidemiological Research on Alcohol
http://www.arg.org/kbs/

Lists of Model Programs

Blueprints for Violence Prevention
http://www.colorado.edu/cspv/blueprints/

CDC's Program Compendium (United States)
http://www.cdc.gov/hiv/pubs/HIVcompendium/HIVcompendium.pdf

CSAP's Prevention Pathways – Programs (United States)
http://preventionpathways.samhsa.gov/programs.htm

Exchange on Drug Demand Reduction Action Information System (Europe)
www.emcdda.org/databases/ databases_eddra.shtml

U.S. Department of Health and Human Services and SAMHSA's National Clearinghouse for Alcohol & Drug Information
http://www.health.org/features/youth/

References

Abbey, A., Oliansky, D., Stilianos, K., Hohlstein, L. A., & Kaczynski, R. (1990). Substance abuse prevention for second graders: Are they too young to benefit? *Journal of Applied Developmental Psychology, 11*(2), 149-162.

Aber, J. L., Jones, S. M., Brown, J. L., Chaudry, N., & Samples, F. (1998). Resolving conflict creatively: Evaluating the developmental effects of a school-based violence prevention program in neighborhood and classroom context. *Development and Psychopathology, 10*, 187-213.

Adlaf, E. M. & Ivis, F. J. (1996). Structure and relations: The influence of familial factors on adolescent substance use and delinquency. *Journal of Child and Adolescent Substance Abuse, 5*, 1-19.

Adler, P. A., & Adler, P. (1998). *Peer power: Preadolescent culture and identity.* New Brunswick, NJ: Rutgers University Press.

Ahlgren, A. & Merrick, S. (1984). *Evaluation of the effects of the Project Charlie curriculum in public schools of Richfield and Edina, Minnesota.* Edina, Minnesota: Storefront/Youth Action.

Ainsworth, M. D. S. (1989). Attachments beyond infancy. *American Psychologist, 44*, 709-716.

Ainsworth, M. D. S., Blehar, M. C., Waters, E., & Wall, S. (1978). *Patterns of attachment.* Hillsdale, NJ: Erlbaum.

Ajzen, I. & Fishbein, M. (1980). *Understanding attitudes and predicting social behavior.* Englewood Cliffs, NJ: Prentice-Hall.

Albee, G. W. & Gullotta, T. P. (Eds.). (1997). *Primary prevention works* (Vol. 6). Thousand Oaks, CA: Sage.

Alcohol Epidemiology Program (2001, October, 16). Model ordinances to reduce the supply of alcohol to youth under age 21. Retrieved from http://www.epi.umn.edu/alcohol/local/ordinanc.html

Alexander Jr., R., & Curtis, C. M. (1995). A critical review of strategies to reduce school violence. *Social Work in Education, 17*, 73-82.

Alexander, J., Barton, C., Gordon, D., Grotpeter, J., Hansson, K., Harrison, R., et al. (1998). *Blueprints for Violence Prevention, Book Three: Functional Family Therapy.* Boulder, CO: Center for the Study and Prevention of Violence.

Alexander, J. F. & Parsons, B.V. (1973). Short-term behavioral intervention with delinquent families: Impact on family process and recidivism. *Journal of Abnormal Psychology, 81*, 219-225.

Alexander, J. F., Sexton, T. L., & Robbins, M. S. (2000). The developmental status of family therapy in family psychology intervention science. In H. Liddle, D. Santisteban, R. Leavant, & J. Bray (Eds.), *Family psychology intervention science* (pp. 17-40). Washington, DC: American Psychological Association.

Alexander, J. F., Pugh, C., Parsons, B. V., & Sexton, T. L. (2000). Functional family therapy. In D. S. Elliott (Ed.). *Blueprints for Violence Prevention, Book Three* (2nd ed.). Boulder, CO: Center for the Study and Prevention of Violence.

Allamani, A. (1997). Community alcohol action: experiences in Europe. *Alcologia, 9*(1), 17-21.

Allen, J. P., Kuperminc, G., Philliber, S., & Herre, K. (1994). Programmatic prevention of adolescent problem behaviors: The role of autonomy, relatedness, and volunteer service in the Teen Outreach Program. *American Journal of Community Psychology, 22*, 617-638.

Allen, J. P., Philliber, S., Herrling, S., & Kuperminc, G. P. (1997). Preventing teen pregnancy and academic failure: Experimental evaluation of a developmentally based approach. *Child Development, 68,* 729-742.

Allen, J. P., Philliber, S., & Hoggson, N. (1990). School-based prevention of teenage pregnancy and school dropout: Process evaluation of the national replication of the Teen Outreach Program. *American Journal of Community Psychology, 8,* 505-524.

Allensworth, D. D. (1993). Health education: State of the art. *Journal of School Health, 63,* 14-20.

Allison, K. W., Crawford, I., Leone, P. E., Trickett, E., Perez-Febles, A., Burton, L. M., & Le Blanc, R. (1999). Adolescent substance use: Preliminary examinations of school and neighborhood context. *American Journal of Community Psychology, 27,* 111-141.

Alstead, M., Campsmith, M., Halley, C. S., Hartfield, K., Goldbaum, G., & Wood, R. W. (1999). Developing, implementing, and evaluating a condom promotion program targeting sexually active adolescents. *AIDS Education & Prevention, 11,* 497-512.

Altman, D. G., Rasenick-Douss, L., Foster, V., & Tye, J. B. (1991). Sustained effects of an educational program to reduce sales of cigarettes to minors. *American Journal of Public Health, 81*(7), 891-892.

Ambtman, R., Madak, P., Koss, D., & Strople, M. J. (1990). Evaluation of a comprehensive elementary school curriculum-based drug education program. *Journal of Drug Education, 20,* 199-225.

Ammerman, R. T. & Hersen, M. (Eds.). (1997). *Handbook of prevention and treatment with children and adolescents: Intervention in the real world context.* New York: John Wiley & Sons.

Andréasson, S., (2001, May-June). *Community Based Prevention of Alcohol and Drug Problems: The STAD Project.* Symposium presented at the Society for Prevention Research, Washington, D.C.

Andréasson, S., Lindewald, B., & Rehnman, C. (2000). Over-serving patrons in licensed premises in Stockholm. *Addiction, 95,* 359-363.

Archie-Booker, D. E., Cervero, R. M., & Langone, C. A. (1999). The politics of planning culturally relevant AIDS prevention education for African-American women. *Adult Education Quarterly, 49,* 163-175.

Arday, D. R., Klevens, R. M., Nelson, D. E., Huang, P., Giovino, G. A., & Mowery, P. (1997). Predictors of tobacco sales to minors. *Preventive Medicine, 26*(1), 8-13.

Arnett, J. J. (2001). *Adolescence and emerging adulthood: A cultural approach.* Upper Saddle River, NJ: Prentice Hall.

Aronen, E. (1993). The effect of family counseling on the mental health of 10-11-year-old children in low-and-high-risk families: A longitudinal approach. *Journal of Child Psychology and Psychiatry and Allied Disciplines, 34(2),* 155-165.

Arora, C. M. (1994). Is there any point in trying to reduce bullying in secondary schools? A two year follow-up of a whole-school anti-bullying policy in one school. *Educational Psychology in Practice, 10,* 155-162.

Arreaga-Mayer, C., Terry, B. J., & Greenwood, C. R. (1998). Classwide peer tutoring. In K. Topping & S. Ehly (Eds.), *Peer-assisted learning.* (pp. 105-119). Mahwah, NJ, US: Lawrence Erlbaum Associates, Inc.

Arthur, M. W., Ayers, C. D., Graham, K. A., & Hawkins, J. D. (in press). Mobilizing communities to reduce risks for drug abuse: A comparison of two strategies. In W. J. Bukoski & Z. Sloboda (Eds.), *Handbook of drug abuse theory, science and practice.* New York: Plenum.

Asher, S. R. & Parker, J. G. (1989). Significance of peer relationship problems in childhood. In B. H. Schneider & A. Grazia (Eds.), *Social competence in perspective* (pp. 5-23). Dordrecht, Netherlands: Kluwer.

Ashery, R. S. Robertson, E. B. & Kumpfer, K. L. (1998) (Eds.). *Drug abuse prevention through family interventions*. NIDA Research Monograph, 177 [NIH Publication No. 97-4135]. Rockville, MD: National Institute on Drug Abuse, Division of Epidemiology and Prevention Research.

Astor, R. A., Meyer, H. A., & Behre, W. J. (1999). Unowned places and times: Maps and interviews about violence in high schools. *American Educational Research Journal, 36*, 3-42.

Attar, B. K., Guerra, N. G., & Tolan, P. H. (1994). Neighborhood disadvantage, stressful life events, and adjustment in urban elementary-school children. *Journal of Clinical Child Psychology, 23*(4), 391-400.

Au, C. P. & Watkins, D. (1997). Towards a causal model of learned helplessness for Hong Kong adolescents. *Educational Studies, 23*, 377-391.

Bagley, C. & Pritchard, C. (1998). The reduction of problem behaviours and school exclusion in at-risk youth: An experimental study of school social work with cost-benefit analyses. *Child and Family Social Work, 3*, 219-226.

Bailey, D. B. (2001). Evaluating parent involvement and family support in early intervention and preschool programs. *Journal of Early Intervention, 24*(1), 1-14.

Baldwin, J. A. (1999). Conducting drug abuse prevention research in partnership with Native American communities: Meeting challenges through collaborative approaches. *Drugs & Society, 14*(1-2), 77-92.

Bandura, A. (1977). *Social learning theory*. Englewood Cliffs, NJ: Prentice Hall.

Bangert-Drowns, R. L. (1988). The effects of school-based substance abuse education: A meta-analysis. *Journal of Drug Education, 18*, 243-264.

Bank, L., Marlowe, J. H., Reid, J. B., Patterson, G. R., & Weinrott, M. R. (1991). A comparative evaluation of parent–training interventions for families of chronic delinquents. *Journal of Abnormal Child Psychology, 19*, 15-33.

Barber, B. R. (2000, September). *Can information technology save democracy from globalization?* Paper presented at the President's millennium seminars, The George Washington University, Washington, DC.

Barker, W. (1992). Health visiting: Action research in a controlled environment. *International Journal of Nursing Studies, 29*(3), 251-259.

Barker, W., & Anderson, R. (1988). *The Child Development Programme: an evaluation of process and outcomes*. Early Childhood Development Unit, Department of Social Work, University of Bristol.

Barker, W., Anderson, R., & Chalmers, C. (1992). *Child protection: the impact of the Child Development Programme – Evaluation Document 14*. Early Childhood Development Unit, Department of Social Work, University of Bristol.

Barnard, K. E., Magyary, D., Sumner, G., Booth, C. L., Mitchell, S. K., & Spieker, S. (1988). Prevention of parenting alterations for women with low social support. *Psychiatry: Journal for the Study of Interpersonal Processes, 51*(3), 248-253.

Barry, F. D. (1994). A neighborhood-based approach: What is it? In G. B. Melton & F. D. Barry (Eds.), *Protecting children from abuse and neglect* (pp. 14-39). New York: Guilford Press.

Bartell, R. (1995). Changing the role of school psychologists: School-family partnership. *Canadian Journal of School Psychology, 11*, 133-137.

Barton, C., Alexander, J. F., Waldron, H., Turner, C. W., & Warburton, J. (1985). Generalizing treatment effects of Functional Family Therapy: Three replications. *American Journal of Family Therapy, 13*, 16–26.

Baumrind, D. (1971). Current patterns of parental authority. *Developmental Psychology Monograph, 4*, 1-103.

Beauboeuf, T. (Ed.). (1995).Violence and youth [Special issue]. *Harvard Educational Review, 65*.

Beauvais, F. & Oetting, E. R. (1986). Drug use in an alternative high school. *Journal of Drug Education, 16,* 43-50.

Beeker, C., Guenther-Grey, C., & Raj, A. (1998). Community empowerment paradigm drift and the primary prevention of HIV/AIDS. *Social Science & Medicine, 46*(7), 831-842.

Beelmann, A., Pfingsten, U., & Lösel, F. (1994). Effect of training social competence in children: A meta analysis of recent evaluation studies. *Journal of Clinical Child Psychology, 23,* 260-271.

Bekman, S. (1998). *A fair chance. An evaluation of the Mother Child Education Program. Mother Child Education Foundation.* Publication 13, Yapim Matbaasi.

Beland, K. R. (1996). A school wide approach to violence prevention. In R. L. Hampton, P. Jenkins, & T. P. Gullotta (Eds.), *Preventing violence in America. Issues in children's and families' lives, 4,* (pp. 209-231). Thousand Oaks, CA: Sage.

Bell, S. K., Coleman, J. K., Anderson, A., Whelan, J. P., & Wilder, C. (2000). The effectiveness of peer mediation in a low-SES rural elementary school. *Psychology in the Schools, 37,* 505-516.

Belsky, J. (1993). Etiology of child maltreatment: A developmental-ecological analysis. *Psychological Bulletin, 114,* 413-434.

Benard, B. (1997). *Turning it around for all youth: From risk to resilience.* Report No. EDO-UD-07-7. Office of Educational Research and Improvement, Washington, DC.

Berlin, L. J., Brooks-Gunn, J., & Aber, J. L. (2001). Promoting early childhood development through comprehensive community initiatives. *Children's Services: Social Policy, Research, and Practice, 4*(1), 1-24.

Berlin, L. J., O'Neal, C. R., & Brooks-Gunn, J. (1998). What makes early intervention programs work? The program, its participants, and their interaction. *Zero to Three, February/March,* 4-15.

Berndt, T. J. (1982). The features and effects of friendship in early adolescence. *Child Development, 53,* 1447-1460.

Bierman, K. L., Greenberg, M. T., & Conduct Problems Prevention Research Group. (1996). Social skills training in the Fast Track Program. In R. DeV. Peters & R. J. McMahon (Eds.), *Preventing childhood disorders, substance abuse, and delinquency* (pp. 65-89). Thousand Oaks, CA: Sage

Bierman, K. L., Miller, C. L., & Stabb, S.D. (1987). Improving the social behavior and peer acceptance of rejected boys: Effects of social skill training with instructions and prohibitions. *Journal of Consulting and Clinical Psychology, 55*(2), 194-200.

Biglan, A., & Ary, D. V. (1985). Methodological issues in research on smoking prevention. US Department of Health and Human Services.

Biglan, A., Ary, D., Koehn, V., Levings, D., Smith, S., Wright, Z., James, L., & Henderson, J. (1996). Mobilizing positive reinforcement in communities to reduce youth access to tobacco. *American Journal of Community Psychology, 24*(5), 625-638.

Biglan, A., Metzler, C. W., Fowler, R. C., Gunn, B., Taylor, T. K., Rusby, J., & Irvine, B. (1997). Improving childrearing in America's communities. In P. A. Lamal (Ed.), *Cultural contingencies: Behavior analytic perspectives on cultural practices* (pp. 185-213). Westport, CT: Praeger Publishers/Greenwood Publishing Group.

Biglan, A. & Taylor, T. K. (2000). Why have we been more successful in reducing tobacco use than violent crime? *American Journal of Community Psychology, 28*(3), 269-302.

Bingenheimer, J. B., Repetto, P. B., Zimmerman, M. A., & Kelly, J. G. (2003). A brief history and analysis of health promotion. In T. Gullotta & M. Bloom (Series Ed.) & T. Gullotta & M. Bloom (Vol. Ed.), *The encyclopedia of primary prevention and health promotion: Foundations Volume* (pp. 15-26). New York: Kluwer Academic/Plenum.

Black, D. R., Tobler, N. S., & Sciacca, J. P. (1998). Peer helping/involvement: An efficacious way to meet the challenge of reducing alcohol, tobacco, and other drug use among youth? *Journal of School Health, 68,* 87-93.

Black, M. M., Nair, P., Kight, C., Wachtel, R., Roby, P., & Schuler, M. (1994). Parenting and early development among children of drug-abusing women: Effects of home intervention. *Pediatrics, 94*(4), 440-448.

Blair, C. (2002). School readiness: Integrating cognition and emotion in a neurobiological conceptualization of children's functioning at school entry. *American Psychologist, 57(2),* 111-127.

Bloom, M. (1996). *Primary prevention practices.* Thousand Oaks, CA: Sage.

Bloom, M. (2000). The uses of theory in primary prevention practice: Evolving thoughts on sports and after-school activities as influences of social competency. In S. J. Danish & T. P. Gullotta (Eds.), *Developing competent youth and strong communities through after-school programming* (pp. 17-66). Washington, DC: CWLA.

Bloom, M. & Gullotta, T. (2003). Evolving definitions of primary prevention. In T. Gullotta & M. Bloom (Series Ed.) & T. Gullotta & M. Bloom (Vol. Ed.), *The encyclopedia of primary prevention and health promotion: Foundations Volume* (pp. 9-15). New York: Kluwer Academic/Plenum.

Blum, D. J., & Jones, L. A. (1993). Academic growth group and mentoring program for potential dropouts. *School Counselor, 40,* 207-217.

Bölcskei, P.L., Hörmann, A., Hollederer, A., Jordan, S., & Fenzel, H. (1997). Suchtprävention an Schulen: Besondere Aspekte des Nikotinabusus. *Prävention und Rehabilitation, 2,* 82-88.

Booth, A. & Crouter, A. C. (2001). (Eds.), *Does it take a village?: Community effects on children adolescents, and families.* Mahwah, NJ: Lawrence Erlbaum Associates.

Borduin, C. M. (1999). Multisystemic treatment of criminality and violence in adolescents. *Journal of the Academy of Child and Adolescent Psychiatry, 38*(3), 242-249.

Borduin, C. M., Heiblum, N., Jones, M. R., & Grabe, S. A. (2000). Community-based treatments of serious antisocial behavior in adolescents. In W. E. Martin & J. L. Swartz-Kulstad (Eds.), *Person-environment psychology and mental health: Assessment and intervention* (pp. 113-141). Mahwah, NJ: Lawrence Erlbaum.

Borduin, C. M., Mann, B. J., Cone, L. T., Henggeler, S. W., & Fucci, B. R., Blaske, D. M., Williams, R. A. (1995). Multisystemic treatment of serious juvenile offenders: Long-term prevention of criminality and violence. *Journal of Consulting and Clinical Psychology, 63*(4): 569-578.

Bosworth, K., Espelage, D., & DuBay, T. (1998). A computer-based violence prevention intervention for young adolescents: Pilot study. *Adolescence, 33,* 785-795.

Bosworth, K., Espelage, D., DuBay, T., Daytner, G., & Karageorge, K. (2000). Preliminary evaluation of a multimedia violence prevention program for adolescents. *American Journal of Health Behavior, 24,* 268-280.

Botvin, G. J., Baker, E., Dusenbury, L. D., Botvin, E. M., & Diaz, T. (1995). Long-term follow-up results of a randomized drug abuse prevention trial in a White middle-class population. *Journal of the American Medical Association, 273,* 1106-1112.

Botvin, G. J., Botvin, E. M., & Ruchlin, H. (1998). School-based approaches to drug abuse prevention: Evidence for effectiveness and suggestions for determining cost-effectiveness. In W. J. Bukoski & R. I. Evans (Eds.), *Cost benefit/cost-effectiveness research for drug abuse prevention: Implications for programming and policy* (NIDA Monograph 176, pp. 59-82). Rockville, MD: U.S. National Institute on Drug Abuse.

Botvin, G. J., Dusenbury, L., Baker, E., James-Ortiz, S., & Kerner, J. (1989). A skills training approach to smoking prevention among Hispanic youth. *Journal of Behavioral Medicine, 12,* 279-296.

Botvin, G. J., Griffin, K. W., Diaz, T., Scheier, L. M., Williams, C., & Epstein, J. (2000). A Preventing illicit drug use in adolescents: Long-term follow-up data from a randomized control trial of a school population. *Addictive Behaviors, 25,* 769-774.

Botvin, G. J., Schinke, S. P., Epstein, J. A., Diaz, T. & Botvin, E. M. (1995). Effectiveness of culturally-focused and generic skills training approaches to alcohol and drug abuse prevention among minority adolescents: Two-Year follow-up results. *Psychology of Addictive Behaviors, 9,* 183-194.

Bowlby, J. (1969). *Attachment and loss.* Volume I: Attachment. New York, NY: Basic Books, Inc.

Bowlby, J. (1973). *Attachment and loss* (Vol. 2. Separation, anxiety, and anger). New York: Basic Books.

Bowlby, J. (1982). *Attachment and loss* (Vol. 1. Attachment, 2nd Ed.). New York: Basic Books.

Boys and Girls Clubs of America. (2000). *2000 Year in Review Highlights.* Author.

Brandtstaedter, J. & Lerner, R. M. (Eds.). (1999). *Action & self-development: Theory and research through the life span.* Thousand Oaks, CA: Sage.

Bremberg, S. & Karlsson, A. (2001). *Hur kan förskolan förbättra barns psykiska hälsa?* Manuscript in preparation. Institutionen för Folkhälsovetenskap, Karolinska Institutet samt Samhällsmedicin, Stockholms Läns Landsting.

Broberg, A. G. (2000). A review of interventions in the parent-child relationship informed by attachment theory. *Acta Paediatr, 434* (Suppl, iii), 37-42.

Bronfenbrenner, U. (1979). *The ecology of human development: Experiments by nature and design.* Cambridge, MA: Harvard University Press.

Bronfenbrenner, U. (1986). Ecology of the family as a context for human development: Research perspectives. *Developmental Psychology, 22*(6), 723-742.

Bronfenbrenner, U. (1999). Environments in developmental perspective: Theoretical and operational models. In S. L. Friedman, T. D. Wachs, (Eds.), *Measuring environment across the life span: Emerging methods and concepts.* (pp. 3-28). Washington, DC: American Psychological Association.

Bronfenbrenner, U. (2000). Ecological theory. In A. Kazdin (Ed.), Encyclopedia of psychology. Washington, DC, & New York: American Psychological Association and Oxford University Press.

Brooks-Gunn, J. (1995). Children in families in communities: Risk and intervention in the Bronfenbrenner tradition. In P. Moen, G. H. Elder, K. Lüscher (1995). Examining lives in context: Perspectives on the ecology of human development (pp. 467-519). Washington, DC: American Psychological Association.

Brooks-Gunn, J., McCormick, M., Shapiro, S., Benasich, A., & Black, G. (1994). The effects of early education intervention on maternal employment, public assistance, and health insurance: The infant health and development program. *American Journal of Public Health, 84*(6), 924-931.

Brosnan, R. & Carr, A. (2000). Adolescent conduct problems. In A. Carr (Ed.), *What works with children and adolescents?: A critical review of psychological interventions with children, adolescents and their families* (pp. 131-154). Florence, KY: Routledge.

Brown, P. & Richman, H. A. (1997). Neighborhood effects and state and local policy. In J. Brooks-Gunn, G. J. Duncan, & J. L. Aber (Eds.), *Neighborhood poverty: Vol. 2 Policy implications in studying neighborhoods* (pp. 164-181). New York: Russell Sage Foundation.

Brown, T. L., Henggeler, S. W., Schoenwald, S. K., Brondino, M. J., & Pickrel, S. G. (1999). Multisystemic treatment of substance abusing and dependent juvenile delinquents: Effects on school attendance at posttreatment and 6-month follow-up. *Children's Services: Social Policy, Research, and Practice, 2*(2), 81-93.

Brunk, M. A., Henggeler, S. W., & Whelan, J. P. (1987). Comparison of multisystemic therapy and parent training in the brief treatment of child abuse and neglect. *Journal of Consulting and Clinical Psychology, 55*, 171-178.

Bruun, K., Edwards, G., Lumio, M., Mäkelä, K., Pan, L., Popham, R. E. et al. (1975). *Alcohol control policies in a public health perspective.* No. 25. Helsinki: Finland: Forssa – Finnish Foundation for Alcohol Studies.

Bruvold, W. H. (1993). A meta-analysis of adolescent smoking prevention programs. *American Journal of Public Health, 83,* 872-880.

Bry, B. H., Catalano, R. F., Kumpfer, K. L., Lochman, J. E., & Szapocznik, J. (1998). Scientific findings from family prevention intervention research. In R. S. Ashery, E. B. Robertson, E. B. & K. L. Kumpfer, (Eds.), *Drug abuse prevention through family interventions.* NIDA Research Monograph, 177 [NIH Publication No. 97-4135] (pp. 103-129). Rockville, MD: National Institute on Drug Abuse, Division of Epidemiology and Prevention Research.

Bryant, C. A., Forthofer, M. S., Brown, K. R. M., Landis, D. C., & McDermott, R. J. (2000). Community-based prevention marketing: The next steps in disseminating behavior change. *American Journal of Health Behavior, 24*(1), 61-68.

Bukowski, W. J. & Evans, R. I. (Eds.) (1998). Cost-benefit/cost-effectiveness research on drug abuse prevention: implications for programming and policy. *NIDA Research Monograph, 176* [NIH Publication No. 98-4021] Rockville, MD: National Institute on Drug Abuse, Division of Epidemiology and Prevention Research.

Bukowski, W. M., & Hoza, B. (1989). Popularity and friendship: Issues in theory, measurement, and outcome. In T. J. Berndt, & G. W. Ladd, (Eds), (1989). *Peer relationships in child development. Wiley series on personality processes* (pp. 15-45). New York: John Wiley & Sons.

Buysse, V., Wesley, P. & Skinner, D. (1999). Community development approaches for early intervention. *Topics in Early Childhood Special Education, 19*(4), 236-243.

Calabrese, R. L. & Adams, J. (1990). Alienation: A cause of juvenile delinquency. *Adolescence, 25,* 435-440.

Campbell, D. T. & Cook, T. D. (1979). *Quasi-experimentation: Design and analysis issues for field settings.* Boston: Houghton Mifflin.

Campbell, D. T., & Stanley, J. C. (1963). *Experimental and quasi-experimental designs for research.* Chicago: Rand McNally & Company.

Campbell, J. J., Lamb, M. E., & Hwang, C. P. (2000). Early child-care experiences and children's social competence between ½ and 15 years of age. *Applied Developmental Science, 4,* 166-175.

Caplan, M., Weissberg, R. P., Grober, J. S., Sivo, P. J., Grady K., & Jacoby, C. (1992). Social competence promotion with inner-city and suburban young adolescents: Effects on social adjustment and alcohol use. *Journal of Consulting and Clinical Psychology, 60,* 56-63.

Cardemil, E. V. (2002). Preventing paralysis in culture-based research: Negotiating obstacles. *Prevention and Treatment, 5,* np.

Cardenas, J. A., Montecel, M. R., Supik, J. D., & Harris, R. J. (1992). The Coca-Cola Valued Youth Program. Dropout prevention strategies for at-risk students. *Texas Researcher, 3,* 111-130.

Carlson, C. (1993). The family school link: Methodological issues in studies of family processes related to children's school competence. *School Psychology Quarterly, 8(4),* 264-276.

Carlson K.A., Hughes J.D., & Deebach F.M. (1996). Proof positive: A student assistance program evaluation. *Student Assistance Journal 8(4),* 14-18, 29.

Carter, R. B. & Vuong, T. K. (1997). Unity from diversity: Fostering cultural awareness. *Professional School Counseling, 1,* 47-49.

Carroll, K. M., Chang, G., Behr, H., Clinton, B., & Kosten, T. R. (1995). Improving treatment outcome in pregnant, methadone-maintained women: Results from a randomized clinical trial. *American Journal on Addictions, 4*(1), 56-59.

Catalano, R., Arthur, M., Hawkins, D., Berglund, L., & Olson, J. (1998). Comprehensive community- and school-based interventions to prevent antisocial behavior. In R. Loeber, D. Farrington (Eds.), *Serious and violent juvenile offenders: Risk factors and successful interventions* (pp. 248-283). Thousand Oaks, CA: Sage Publications, Inc.

Catalano, R. F., Berglund, M. L., Ryan, J. A. M., Lonczak, H., & Hawkins, J. D. (1999). *Positive youth development in the United States: Research findings on evaluations of positive youth development programs.* Washington, DC: U. S. Department of Health and Human Services.

Catalano, R. F., Gainey, R. R., Fleming, C. B., Haggerty, K. P., & Johnson, N. O. (1999). An experimental intervention with families of substance abusers: One-year follow-up of the Focus on Families project. *Addiction, 94*(2), 241-255.

Catalano, R. F. & Hawkins, J. D. (1996). The social development model: A theory of antisocial behavior. In J. D. Hawkins (Ed.), *Delinquency and crime: Current theories* (pp. 149-197). New York: Cambridge University Press.

Catalano, R. F., Hawkins, J. D., Berglund, L., Pollard, J. A., & Arthur, M. W. (2002). Prevention science and positive youth development: Competitive or cooperative frameworks? *Journal of Adolescent Health, 31*, 230-239.

Cates, W., Jr. & Berman, S. M. (1999). Prevention of sexually transmitted diseases other than human immunodeficiency virus. In A. J. Goreczny & M. Hersen (Eds.), *Handbook of pediatric and adolescent health psychology* (pp. 361-370). Needham Heights, MA: Allyn & Bacon.

Celano, M. & Kaslow, N. J. (2000). Culturally competent family interventions: Review and case illustrations. *American Journal of Family Therapy, 28(3)*, 217-228.

Center, Y., Wheldall, K., Freeman, L., Outhred, L., & McNaught, M. (1995). An evaluation of reading recovery. *Reading Research Quarterly, 30*, 240-263.

Center for the Study and Prevention of Violence. (2000, June 6). CASASTART. Retrieved from http://www.colorado.edu/cspv/blueprints/promise/CAR.htm

Centers for Disease Control and Prevention (1994). Guidelines for school health programs to prevent tobacco use and addiction. *Morbidity and Mortality Weekly Report, 43*, (No. RR-2). U.S. Department of Health and Human Services, Washington, DC: Author.

Centers for Disease Control and Prevention (1998). Youth risk behavior surveillance – United States, 1997. *Morbidity and Mortality Weekly Report, 47*, (No. SS-3). U.S. Department of Health and Human Services, Washington, DC: Author.

Centers for Disease Control and Prevention (1999, November). *Compendium of HIV prevention interventions with evidence of effectiveness.* HIV/AIDS Prevention Research Synthesis Project, Centers for Disease Control and Prevention, National Center for HIV, STD, and TB Prevention, Divisions of HIV/AIDS Prevention.

Centers for Disease Control and Prevention (2000). CDC surveillance summaries, MMWR 2000; 49 (No. SS-5).

Centre de Prévention des Toxicomanies. (1999). *European Conference on Community Based Addiction Prevention (CBAP). Community approaches in addiction prevention: Strategies and outcomes.* Luxembourg: Author.

Chamberlian, P. & Reid, J. B. (1998). Comparison of two community alternatives to incarceration for chronic juvenile offenders. *Journal of Consulting and Clinical Psychology, 66*, 624-633.

Channing Bete Company, Inc. (2003, June 26). Communities That Care® prevention planning system: Success stories. Retrieved from http://www.channing-bete.com/positiveyouth/ pages/CTC/CTC.html

Chapman, D. A. & Scott, K. G. (2001). The impact of maternal intergenerational risk factors on adverse developmental outcomes. *Developmental Review, 21*(3), 305-325.

Chou, C. P., Montgomery, S., Pentz, M. A., Rohrbach, L. A., Johnson, C.A., Flay, B. R., et al. (1998). Effects of a community-based prevention program in decreasing drug use in high-risk adolescents. *American Journal of Public Health, 88,* 944-948.

Church, R. (1976). *Education in the United States.* New York: Free Press.

Cicchetti, D. (1990). A historical perspective on the discipline of developmental psychopathology. In J. E. Rolf, A. S. Masten, D. Cicchetti, K. Nuechterlein, & S. Weintraub, (Eds.), *Risk and protective factors in the development of psychopathology* (pp. 2-28). New York: Cambridge University Press.

Cicchetti, D. & Aber, J. L. (1998). Contextualism and developmental psychopathology. *Development and Psychopathology, 10,* 137-141.

Cicchetti, D. & Lynch, M. (1993). Toward an ecological/transactional model of community violence and child maltreatment: Consequences for children's development. *Psychiatry, 56,* 96-118.

Cicchetti, D. & Rogosch, F. A. (1996). Equifinality and multifinality in developmental psychopathology. *Development & Psychopathology, 8,* 597-600.

Cicchetti, D. & Rogosch, F. A. (1999). Psychopathology as risk for adolescent substance use disorders: A developmental psychopathology perspective. *Journal of Clinical Child Psychology, 28,* 355-365.

Cicchetti, D. & Toth, S. L. (1998). The development of depression in children and adolescents. *American Psychologist, 53,* 221-241.

Clarke, R. V. (1995). Situational crime prevention. In M. Tonry & D. P. Farrington (Eds.), *Crime and justice: A review of research: Vol. 19: Building a safer society: Strategic approaches to crime prevention* (pp. 91-150). Chicago: University of Chicago Press.

Clay, M. M. (1979/1985). *The early detection of reading difficulties.* Auckland, New Zealand: Heinemann.

Clay, M.M. (1991). *Becoming Literate: The construction of inner control.* Heinemann Education. Auckland, New Zealand.

Clinton, H. R. (1997, April). *A very special event.* Keynote address at biennial meeting of the Society for Research on Child Development, Washington, DC.

Coben, J. H., Weiss, H. B., Mulvey, E. P., & Dearwater, S. R. (1994). A primer on school violence prevention. *Journal of School Health, 64,* 309-313.

Cohen, J. M. (1977). Sources of peer group homogeneity. *Sociology of Education, 50,* 227-241.

Cohen, P. A., Kulik, J. A., & Kulik, C.-L. C. (1982). Educational outcomes of tutoring: A meta-analysis of findings. *American Educational Research Journal, 19,* 237-248.

Cohen, M. A. (1998). The monetary value of saving a high-risk youth. *Journal of Quantitative Criminology, 14*(1), 5-33.

Coie, J. D. (1996). Prevention of violence and antisocial behavior. In R. DeV. Peters & R. J. McMahon (Eds.), *Preventing childhood disorders, substance abuse, and delinquency* (pp. 1-18). Thousand Oaks, CA: Sage.

Coie, J. D. & Krehbiel, G. (1984). Effects of academic tutoring on the social status of low-achieving, socially rejected children. *Child Development, 55,* 1465-1478.

Coie, J. D., Watt, N. F., West, S. G., Hawkins, J. D., Asarnow, J. R., Markman, H. J., Ramey, S. L., Shure, M. B., & Long, B. (1993). The science of prevention. A conceptual framework and some directions for a national research program. *American Psychologist, 48,* 1013-1022.

Coleman, J. C. & Hendry, L. B. (1999). *The nature of adolescence.* London: Routledge.

Collaborative for Academic, Social, and Emotional Learning (CASEL). (2003, March). *Safe and Sound: An education leader's guide to evidence-based social and emotional learning (SEL) programs.* Chicago, IL: Author.

Collins, J. L., Small, M. L., Kann, L., Pateman, B. C., Gold, R. S., & Kolbe. L. J. (1995). School health education. *Journal of School Health, 65,* 302-311.

Commissioner's Office of Research and Evaluation, Head Start Bureau, Administration on Children, Youth, and Families, and Department of Health and Human Services (2001, December-January). *Building their futures: How Early Head Start programs are enhancing the lives of infants and toddlers in low-income families: Summary report.* Washington, DC: U.S. Department of Health and Human Services.

Conduct Problems Prevention Research Group (1999a). Initial impact of the fast track prevention trial for conduct problems: I. The high-risk sample. *Journal of Consulting and Clinical Psychology, 67*(5), 631-647.

Conduct Problems Prevention Research Group (1999b). Initial impact of the fast track prevention trial for conduct problems: II. Classroom effects. *Journal of Consulting and Clinical Psychology, 67*(5), 648-657.

Conduct Problems Prevention Research Group. (in press). Evaluation of the first three years of the Fast Track Prevention Trial with Children at High Risk for Adolescent Conduct Problems. *Journal of Abnormal Child Psychology.*

Connell, D. B. & Turner, R. R. (1985). The impact of instructional experience and the effects of cumulative instruction. *Journal of School Health, 55,* 324-331.

Connell, D. B., Turner, R. R., & Mason, E. F. (1985). Summary of Findings of the School Health Education Evaluation: Health Promotion Effectiveness, Implementation, and Costs. *Journal of School Health, 55,* 316-21.

Cooper, P. (1993). Improving the behavior and academic performance of pupils through the curriculum. *Therapeutic Care & Education, 2,* 252-260.

Corcoran, J., Miller, P. O., & Bultman, L. (1997). Effectiveness of prevention programs for adolescent pregnancy: A meta-analysis. *Journal of Marriage and the Family, 59,* 551-567.

Costa, F. M., Jessor, R., & Turbin, M. S. (1999). Transition into adolescent problem drinking: The role of psychosocial risk and protective factors. Journal of Studies on Alcohol, 60 480-490.

Coulton, C. J., Korbin, J. E., Su, M., & Chow, J. (1995). Community level factors and child maltreatment rates. *Child Development, 66,* 1262-1276.

Cowen, E. L. (1994). The enhancement of psychological wellness: Challenges and opportunities. *American Journal of Community Psychology, 22,* 149-178.

Cowen, E. L. & Durlak, J. A. (2000). Social policy and prevention in mental health. *Development and Psychopathology, 12,* 815-834.

Cowen, E. L., & Lorion, R. P. (1976). Changing roles for the school mental health professional. *Journal of School Psychology, 14,* 131-138.

Crick, N. R. (1997). Engagement in gender normative versus nonnormative forms of aggression: Links to social-psychological adjustment. *Developmental Psychology, 33,* 610-617.

Crick, N. R. & Grotpeter, J. K. (1996). Children's treatment by peers: Victims of relational and overt aggression. *Development & Psychopathology, 8,* 367-380.

Csikszentmihalyi, M., Rathunde, K-R., Whalen, S., & Wong, M. (1993/1997). *Talented teenagers: The roots of success and failure.* New York: Cambridge University Press.

Cummings, E., Davies, P., & Campbell, S. (2000). *Developmental psychopathology and family process: Theory, research and clinical implications.* New York: The Guilford Press.

Cummings, K. M. (1999). Community-wide interventions for tobacco control. *Nicotine & Tobacco Research, 1,* S113-S116.

Cunningham, P. B. & Henggeler, S. W. (1999). Engaging multiproblem families in treatment: Lessons learned throughout the development of multisystemic therapy. *Family Process, 38*(3), 265-286.

Dalenius, L. & Romelsjö, A. (2000). *Tvåårig studie visar att tillgängligheten till folköl bland minderåriga minskat i Trångsund-Skogås* [Two-year study shows that accessibility to beer among underage youth decreased in Trångsund-Skogås]. Huddinge, Sweden: Centrum för Alkohol och Drogprevention (CADP) - Novum.

D'Andrade, R. (1990). Some propositions about the relations between culture and human cognition. In J. W. Stigler, R. A. Shweder, & G. Herdt (Eds.), *Cultural psychology: Essays on comparative human development* (pp. 66-129). Cambridge, England: Cambridge University

Danish, S. J. (1996). Interventions for enhancing adolescents' life skills. *Humanistic Psychologist, 24,* 365-381.

Davis, H. & Hester, P. (1996). *An independent evaluation of Parent Link: A parenting education programme.* London, England: Parentline Plus.

Davis, H. & Rushton, R. (1991). Counseling and supporting parents of children with developmental delay: A research evaluation. *Journal of Mental Deficiency Research, 35,* 89-112.

Davis, H. & Spurr, P. (1998). Parent Counseling: An evaluation of a community child mental health service. *Journal of Child Psychology and Psychiatry, 39*(3), 365-376.

Davis, N. J. (1999). *Resilience: Status of the research and research-based programs.* Washington, DC: Substance Abuse and Mental Health Services Administration, Center for Mental Health Services, Division of Program Development, Special Populations and Projects, Special Programs Development Branch.

Davis, R. C. & Lurigio, A. J. (1996). *Fighting back: Neighborhood antidrug strategies.* Thousand Oaks, CA: Sage.

Day, C., Davis, H., & Hind, R. (1998). The development of a community child and family mental health service. *Child: Care, Health and Development, 24*(6), 487-500.

Dennison, S. (2000). A win-win peer mentoring and tutoring program: A collaborative model. *Journal of Primary Prevention, 20,* 161-174.

Derzon, J. H. & Lipsey, M. W. (1999). What good predictors of marijuana use are good for: A synthesis of research. *School Psychology International, 20,* 69-85.

Dewey, J. (1916/1966). *Democracy and education: An introduction to the philosophy of education.* New York: The Free Press.

Dielman, T. E., Shope, J. T., Leech, S. L., & Butchart, A. T. (1989). Differential effectiveness of an elementary school-based alcohol misuse prevention program. *Journal of School Health,59*(6), 255-263.

Dielman, T. E. (1994). School-based research on the prevention of adolescent alcohol use and misuse: Methodological issues and advances. *Journal of Research on Adolescence, 4,* 271-293.

Dishion, T. J. & Andrews, D. W. (1995). Preventing escalation in problem behaviors with high-risk young adolescents: Immediate and 1-year outcomes. *Journal of Consulting and Clinical Psychology, 63,*(4) 538-548.

Dishion, T. J., Andrews, D. W., Kavanagh, K., & Soberman, L. H. (1996). Preventive interventions for high-risk youth: The Adolescent Transitions Program. In R. D. Peters & R. J. McMahon (Eds.), *Preventing childhood disorders, substance abuse, and delinquency* (pp. 184-214). Thousand Oaks, CA: Sage.

Dishion, T. J., Capaldi, D., Spracklen, K. M., & Li, F. (1995). Peer ecology of male adolescent drug use. *Development and Psychopathology, 7,* 803-824.

Dishion, T. J. & Kavanagh, K. (2000). A multilevel approach to family-centered prevention in schools: Process and outcome. *Addictive Behaviors, 25(6),* 899-911.

Dishion, T. J., McCord, J., & Poulin, F. (1999). When interventions harm: Peer groups and problem behavior. *American Psychologist, 54,* 755-764.

Dishion, T. J., Patterson, G. R. & Griesler, P. C. (1994). Peer adaptations in the development of antisocial behavior: A confluence model. In H. L. Rowell (Ed.), *Aggressive behavior: Current perspectives* (pp. 61-95). New York: Plenum Press.

Dishion, T. J., Patterson, G. R., Stoolmiller, M., & Skinner, M. (1991). Family, school, and behavioral antecedents to early adolescent involvement with antisocial peers. *Developmental Psychology, 27*, 172-180.

Domitrovich, C. E. & Greenberg, M. T. (2000). The study of implementation: Current findings from effective programs that prevent mental disorders in school-aged children. *Journal of Educational and Psychological Consultation, 11(2),* 193-221.

Drummond, D. C. & Fitzpatrick, G. (2000). Children of substance misusing parents. In P. Reder, M. McClure, & A. Jolley (Eds.), *Family matters: Interfaces between child and adult mental health* (pp. 135-149). London, England: Routledge.

Dryfoos, J. G. (1991). Adolescents at risk: A summation of work in the field: Programs and policies. *Journal of Adolescent Health, 12(8),* 630-637.

Dryfoos, J. G. (1994). *Full service schools: A revolution in health and social services for children, youth, and families.* San Francisco: Jossey-Bass.

Dryfoos, J. G. (1995). Full service schools: Revolution or fad? *Journal of Research on Adolescence, 5,* 147-172.

Dryfoos, J. G. (1999). The role of the school in children's out-of-school time. *The Future of Children, 9,* 117-134.

Duffy, J. (1990). *The sanitarians: A history of American public health.* Chicago: University of Illinois Press.

Dumas, J. E., Prinz, R. J., Smith, E. P., & Laughlin, J. (1999). The EARLY ALLIANCE prevention trial: An integrated set of interventions to promote competence and reduce risk for conduct disorder, substance abuse, and school failure. *Clinical Child and Family Psychology, 37,* 37-53.

Dumas, J. E., Rollock, D., Prinz, R. J., Hops, H., & Blechman, E. A. (1999). Cultural sensitivity: Problems and solutions in applied and preventive intervention. *Applied and Preventive Psychology, 8,* 175-196.

Durlak, J. A. (1997). *Successful prevention programs for children and adolescents.* New York: Plenum.

Durlak, J. A. (2000). How to evaluate a meta-analysis. In D. Drotar (Ed). *Handbook of research in pediatric and clinical child psychology: Practical strategies and methods. Issues in clinical child psychology* (pp. 395-407). Dordrecht, Netherlands: Kluwer Academic Publishers.

Durlak, J. A. (1998). Common risk and protective factors in successful prevention programs. *American Journal of Orthopsychiatry, 68(4),* 512-520.

Durlak, J. A. & Wells, A. M. (1997). Primary prevention mental health programs for children and adolescents: A meta-analytic review. *American Journal of Community Psychology, 25,* 115-152.

Durlak, J. A. & Wells, A. M. (1998). Evaluation of indicated prevention intervention (secondary prevention) mental health programs for children and adolescents. *American Journal of Community Psychology, 26,* 775-802.

Dusenbury, L. (2000). Family-based drug abuse prevention programs: A review. *The Journal of Primary Prevention, 20(4),* 337-353.

Dusenbury, L. & Falco, M. (1995). Eleven components of effective drug abuse prevention curricula. *Journal of School Health, 65,* 420-425.

Dusenbury, L., Falco, M., Lake, A., Brannigan, R., & Bosworth, K. (1997). Nine critical elements of promising violence prevention programs. *Journal of School Health, 67,* 409-414.

Eccles, J. & Appleton, J. A. (Eds.). (2002). *Community programs to promote youth development.* Washington, DC: National Academy Press.

Eckenrode, J. (2000). What works in nurse home visiting programs. In M. P. Kluger, G. Alexander, & P. A. Curtis (Eds.)., *What works in child welfare* (pp. 35-43). Washington, DC: Child Welfare League of America, Inc.

Edwards, R. W., Jumper-Thurman, P., Plested, B. A., Oetting, E. R., Swanson, L. (2000). Community readiness: Research to practice. *Journal of Community Psychology, 28*(3), 291-307.

Eggert, L. L., Thompson, E. A., Herting, J. R., & Nicholas, L. J. (1994). Preventing adolescent drug abuse and high school dropout through an intensive school-based social network development program. *American Journal of Health Promotion, 8,* 202-215.

Elder, G. H. (1998b). The life course as developmental theory. *Child Development, 69* (1), 1-12.

Elias, M. J., Gara, M. A., Schuyler, T. F., Branden-Muller, L. R., & Sayette, M. A. (1991). The promotion of social competence: Longitudinal study of a preventive school-based program. *American Journal of Orthopsychiatry, 61*(3), 409-417.

Elias, M. J., Gara, M. A., Ubriaco, M., Rothbaum, P. A., Clabby, J. F., Schuyler, T. (1986). Impact of a preventive social problem solving intervention on children's coping with middle-school stressors. *American Journal of Community Psychology, 14,* 259-275.

Elias, M. J., Zins, J. E., Weissberg, K. S., Greenberg, M. T., Haynes, N. M., Kessler, R., et al., (1997). *Promoting social and emotional learning: Guidelines for educators.* Alexandria, VA: Association for Supervision and Curriculum Development.

Elliott, S. N. & Gresham, F. M. (1993). Social skills interventions for children. *Behavior Modification, 17,* 287-313.

Ellis, J., Small-McGinley, J., & Hart, S. (1998). Mentor-supported literacy development in elementary schools. *Alberta Journal of Educational Research, 44,* 149-162.

Ellis, R. A. (1998). Filling the prevention gap: Multi-factor, multi-system, multi-level intervention. *Journal of Primary Prevention, 19*(1), 57-71.

Elmeland, K. (1999). The third wave of decentralisation and consequences for research. In S. Larsson & B. S. Hanson (Eds.), *Community based alcohol prevention in Europe – Research and evaluations* (pp. 117-121). Lund, Sweden: Studentlitteratur.

Emshoff, J. G. (1983). The diversion of delinquent youth: family-focused intervention. *Children and Youth Services Review, 5*(4), 343-356.

Ennett, S. T., Tobler, N. S., Ringwalt, C. L., & Flewelling, R. L. (1994). How effective is drug abuse resistance education? A meta-analysis of Project DARE outcome evaluations. *American Journal of Public Health, 84,* 1394- 1401.

Eronen, S. & Nurmi, J. E. (1999). Life events, predisposing cognitive strategies and well-being. *European Journal of Personality, 13,* 129-148.

Eslea, M. & Smith, P. K. (1998). The long-term effectiveness of anti-bullying work in primary schools. *Educational Research, 40,* 203-218.

Etz, K. E., Robertson, E. B. & Ashery, R. S. (1998). Drug abuse prevention through family-based interventions: future research. In R. S. Ashery, E. B. Robertson, E. B. & K. L. Kumpfer, (Eds.), *Drug abuse prevention through family interventions.* NIDA Research Monograph, 177 [NIH Publication No. 97-4135] (pp. 1-11). Rockville, MD: National Institute on Drug Abuse, Division of Epidemiology and Prevention Research.

European Commission (2000). *2nd European health promotion awards: Selected actions.* Brussels, Belgium: European Commission.

European Confederation of Youth Clubs (2003, February, 7). What is ECYC?. Retrieved from http://web.ukonline.co.uk/ecyc/ecyc_graphic_home_page.htm.

Evans, G. D., Rey, J., Hemphill, M. M., Perkins, D. F., Austin, W., & Racine, P. (2001). Academic – community collaboration: An ecology for early childhood violence prevention. *American Journal of Preventive Medicine, 20* (1S), 22-30.

Evans, I. M., Okifuji, A., & Thomas, A. D. (1995). Home-school partnerships: Involving families in the educational process. In I. M. Evans, T. Cicchelli, M. Cohen, & N. P. Shapiro (Eds.), *Staying in school: Partnerships for educational change. Children, youth & change: Sociocultural perspectives.* (pp. 23-40). Baltimore, MD: Paul H. Brookes Publishing Co.

Evans, R. I. (1998). A historical perspective on effective prevention. In W. J. Bukoski & R. I. Evans (Eds.), *Cost-benefit/cost-effectiveness research of drug abuse prevention: Implications for programming and policy* (NIDA Monograph 176, pp. 37-58). Rockville, MD: National Institute on Drug Abuse.

Everhart, K., & Wandersman, A. (2000). Applying comprehensive quality programming and empowerment evaluation to reduce implementation barriers. *Journal of Educational and Psychological Consultation, 11,* 177-191.

Evertson, C. M. (1985). Training teachers in classroom management: An experiment in secondary school classrooms. *Journal of Educational Research, 79,* 51-58.

Evertson, C. M., Emmer, E. T., Sanford, J. P., & Clements, B. S. (1983). Improving classroom management: An experiment in elementary school classrooms. *Elementary School Journal, 84,* 173-188.

Fantuzzo, J. W., King, J. A., & Heller, L. R. (1992). Effects of reciprocal peer tutoring on mathematics and school adjustment: A component analysis. *Journal of Educational Psychology, 84,* 331-339.

Farrell, A. D. & Meyer, A. L. (1997). The effectiveness of a school-based curriculum for reducing violence among urban sixth-grade students. *American Journal of Public Health, 87,* 979-984.

Farrell, A. D., Meyer, A. L., & White, K. S. (2001). Evaluation of Responding in Peaceful and Positive Ways (RIPP): A school-based prevention program for reducing violence among urban adolescents. *Journal of Community Psychology, 30*(4), 451-463.

Farrington, D. P. (1990). Implications of criminal career research for the prevention of offending. *Journal of Adolescence, 13,* 93-113.

Farrington, D. P. (1995). The challenge of teenage antisocial behavior. In M. Rutter (Ed.), *Psychosocial disturbances in young people: Challenges for prevention* (pp. 83-130). New York: Cambridge University Press.

Farrington, D. P. (1996). *Understanding and preventing youth crime.* York, United Kingdom: York Publishing Services Ltd.

Feindler, E. L., Marriott, S. A., & Iwata, M. (1984). Group anger control training for junior high school delinquents. *Cognitive Therapy and Research, 8,* 299-311.

Felner, R. D., Brand, S., Adan, A. M., Mullhall, P. F., Flowers, N., Sartain, B., & DuBois, D. L. (1993). Restructuring the ecology of the school as an approach to prevention during school transitions: Longitudinal follow-ups and extensions of the School Transitional Environment Project (STEP). *Prevention in Human Services, 10,* 103-136.

Felner, R. D., Ginter, M., & Primavera, J. (1982). Primary prevention during school transitions: Social support and environmental structure. *American Journal of Community Psychology, 10*(3), 277-290.

Fergusson, D. M. & Lynskey, M. T. (1998). Conduct problems in childhood and psychosocial outcomes in young adulthood: A prospective study. *Journal of Emotional & Behavioral Disorders, 6,* 2-18.

Ferrer-Wreder, L., Montgomery, M. J., & Lorente, C. C. (2003). Identity promotion, adolescence. In T. Gullotta & M. Bloom (Series Ed.) & G. R. Adams (Vol. Ed.), *The encyclopedia of primary prevention and health promotion: Adolescent Volume* (600-607). New York: Plenum.

File, N. & Kontos, S. (1992). Indirect service delivery through consultation: Review and implications for early intervention. *Journal of Early Intervention, 16,* 221-234.

Finn, J. D., Pannozzo, G. M., & Voelkl, K. E. (1995). Disruptive and inattentive-withdrawn behavior and achievement among fourth graders. *Elementary School Journal, 95,* 421-434.

Fischer, R. L. (1997). Evaluating the delivery of a teen pregnancy and parenting program across two settings. *Research on Social Work Practice, 7,* 350-369.

Fitzgerald, H. E., Mann, T., Cabrera, N., & Wong, M. M. (2003). Diversity in caregiving contexts. In I. B. Weiner (Series Ed.) & R. M. Lerner, M. A. Easterbrooks, & J. Mistry (Vol. Eds.), *Comprehensive handbook of psychology: Vol. 6. Developmental psychology* (pp. 135-167). New York: Wiley.

Flay, B. R. (2000). Approaches to substance use prevention utilizing school curriculum plus social environment change. *Addictive Behaviors, 25,* 861-885.

Fletcher, A. C., Elder, G. H., Jr., & Mekos, D. (1997). Family influences on adolescent involvement in community activities. In G. H. Elder, Jr. (Chair), *Adolescent involvement in community activities: antecedents, correlates, and outcomes.* Symposium conducted at the biennial meeting of the Society for Research in Child Development, Washington, D.C.

Florida State Department of Education. (1997). *School staff guide to risk and resiliency.* Document no. ED416264. Bureau of Instructional Support and Community Services, Division of Public Schools and Community Education, Florida Department of Education, Tallahassee, FL.

Flynn, B. S., Worden, J. K., Secker-Walker, R. H., Pirie, P. L., Badger, G. J., Carpenter, J. H. (1997). Long-term responses of higher and lower risk youths to smoking prevention interventions. Preventive Medicine, 26, 389-394.

Forehand, R. L. & McMahon, R. J. (1981). *Helping the noncompliant child: a clinician's guide to parent training.* London: Guildford Press.

Forgatch, M. S. & Martinez, C. R. (1999). Parent management training: A program linking basic research and practical application. *Tidsskrift for Norsk Psykologforening, 36*(10), 923-937.

Forgey, M. A., Schinke, S., & Cole, K. (1997). School-based interventions to prevent substance use among inner-city minority adolescents. In D. K. Wilson, J. R. Rodrigue, & W. C. Taylor (Eds.), *Health promoting and health compromising behaviors among minority adolescents. Application and practice in health psychology.* (pp. 251-267). Washington, DC: American Psychological Association.

Forster, M. & Tegenmark, T. (1998). *Lärare kan hjälpa bråkiga och utstötta barn.* FoU-report 1998:10. Stockholm, Sweden: Forsknings- och utvecklingsenheten.

Forster, J. L., Wolfson, M., Murray, D. M., Wagenaar, A. C., & Claxton, A. J. (1997). Perceived and measured availability of tobacco to youth in fourteen Minnesota communities: The TPOP study. *American Journal of Preventive Medicine, 13,* 167-174.

France, A. & Crow, I. (2003). *CTC – the story so far: An interim evaluation of Communities That Care.* York, England: Joseph Rowntree Foundation.

Franklin, C., Grant, D., Corcoran, J., Miller, P. O'Dell, & Bultman, L. (1997). Effectiveness of prevention programs for adolescent pregnancy: A meta-analysis. *Journal of Marriage and the Family, 59(3),* 551-567.

Freire, P. (1970/1983). *Pedagogy of the oppressed.* New York: Herder & Herder.

French, D. C., Conrad, J., & Turner, T. M. (1995). Adjustment of antisocial and nonantisocial rejected adolescents. *Development and Psychopathology, 7,* 857-874.

Freud, S. (1965). *New introductory lectures.* New York: Norton.

Friedman, S. L. & Wachs, T. D (Eds.). (1999). *Measuring environment across the life span.* Washington, DC: American Psychological Association.

Fritz, J. J., Miller-Heyl, J., Kreutzer, J. C., & MacPhee, D. (1995). Fostering personal teaching efficacy through staff development and classroom activities. *Journal of Educational Research, 88*, 200-208.

Fuchs, L. S., Fuchs, D., Phillips, N. B., Hamlett, C. L., & Karns, K. (1995). Acquisition and transfer effects of classwide peer-assisted learning strategies in mathematics for students with varying learning histories. *School Psychology Review, 24*, 604-620.

Fukuzawa, D. (2000). Re-creating recreation in the inner city: A youth development initiative in Detroit. In S. J. Danish & T. P. Gullotta (Eds.), *Developing competent youth and strong communities through after-school programming* (pp. 239-274). Washington, DC: CWLA.

Fuligni A. J. & Eccles, J. S. (1993). Perceived parent-child relationships and early adolescents' orientation toward peers. *Developmental Psychology, 29(4)*, 622-632.

Furlong, M., Morrison, G., & Pavelski, R. (2000). Trends in school psychology for the 21st century: Influences of school violence on professional change. *Psychology in the Schools, 37*, 81-90.

Gabriel, R. M. (2000). Methodological challenges in evaluating community partnerships & coalitions: Still crazy after all these years. *Journal of Community Psychology, 28*, 339-352.

Galaif, E. R., Chou, C. P., Sussman, S., & Dent, C. W. (1998). Depression, suicidal ideation, and substance use among continuation high school students. *Journal of Youth and Adolescence, 27*, 275-299.

Galbraith, J., Ricardo, I., Stanton, B., Black, M., Feigelman, S., & Kaljee, L. (1996). Challenges and rewards of involving community in research: An overview of the "Focus on Kids" HIV risk reduction program. *Health Education Quarterly, 23(3)*, 383-394.

Garbarino, J. & Ganzel, B. (2000). The human ecology of early risk. In J. P. Shonkoff & S. J., Meisels (Eds.), *Handbook of early childhood intervention* (pp. 76-93). New York: Cambridge University Press.

Garbarino, J., Kostelny, K., & Barry, F. (1998). Neighborhood-based programs. In P. K. Trickett & C. J. Schellenbach (Eds.), *Violence against children in the family and the community* (pp. 287-314). Washington, DC: American Psychological Association.

Gardner, H., Kornhaber, M., & Wake, W. (1996). *Intelligence: Multiple perspectives.* Fort Worth, TX: Harcourt Brace.

Garmezy, N. (1991). Resiliency and vulnerability to adverse developmental outcomes associated with poverty. *American Behavioral Scientist, 34*, 416-430.

Genaux, M., Morgan, D. P., & Friedman, S. G. (1995). Substance use and its prevention: A survey of classroom practices. *Behavioral Disorders, 20*, 279-289.

Gensheimer, L. K., Ayers, T. S., & Roosa, M. W. (1993). School-based preventive intervention for at-risk populations. *Evaluation and Program Planning, 16*, 159-167.

Gentry, D. B. & Benenson, W. A. (1993). School-to-home transfer of conflict management skills among school-age children. *Families in Society, 74*, 67-73.

George, T. P., & Hartmann, D. P. (1996). Friendship networks of unpopular, average, and popular children. *Child Development, 67*, 2301-2316.

Gerris, J. R. M., Van As, N. M. C., Wels, P. M. A., & Janssens, J. M. A. M. (1998). From parent education to family empowerment programs. In L. L'Abate (Ed.), *Family Psychopathology: The relational roots of dysfunctional behavior* (pp. 427-465). New York: The Guilford Press.

Gettinger, M. (1988). Methods of proactive classroom management. *School Psychology Review, 17*, 227-242.

Giele, J. Z., & Elder, G. H. (Eds.). (1998). *Methods of life course research: Qualitative and quantitative approaches.* Thousand Oaks, CA: Sage.

Gillmore, M. R., Morrison, D. M., Richey, C. A., Balassone, M. L., Gutierrez, L., & Farris, M. (1997). Effects of a skill-based intervention to encourage condom use among high-risk heterosexually active adolescents. *AIDS Education and Prevention, 9*, (Suppl. A), 22-43.

Glynn, T. J. (1989). Essential elements of school-based smoking prevention programs. *Journal of School Health, 59*, 181-188.

Glynn, T., Crooks, T., Bethune, N., Ballard, K., & Smith, J. (1989). *Reading Recovery in context.* Wellington, New Zealand: Department of Education.

Goldberg, M. E. Fishbein, M., & Middlestadt, S. E. (Eds.) (1997). *Social marketing: Theoretical and practical perspectives.* Mahwah, NJ: Lawrence Erlbaum Associates.

Goleman, D. (1997). *Känslans intelligens.* Stockholm: Wahlström & Widstrand.

Gomby, D. S., Culross, P. L., & Behrman, R. E. (1999). Home-visiting; recent program evaluations – Analysis and recommendations. *The Future of Children: Home Visiting: Recent Program Evaluations, 9*, 4-26.

Gordon, D. A., Arbuthnot, J., Gustafson, K. E., & McGreen, P. (1988). Home-based behavioral-systems family therapy with disadvantaged juvenile delinquents. *The American Journal of Family Therapy, 16*, 243–255.

Gordon, D. A. Graves, K., & Arbuthnot, J. (1995). The effect of functional family therapy for delinquents on adult criminal behavior. *Criminal Justice & Behavior, 22*, 60-73.

Gorman-Smith, D., Tolan, P. H., & Henry, D. (1999). The relation of community and family to risk among urban-poor adolescents. In P. Cohen, C. Slomkowski, & L. N. Robins (Eds.), *Historical Geographical Influence On Psychopathology* (pp. 349-367). Mahwah, NJ: Lawrence Erlbaum.

Gorman-Smith, D., Tolan, P. H., Loeber, R., & Henry, D. B. (1998). Relation of family problems to patterns of delinquent involvement among urban youth. *Journal of Abnormal Child Psychology, 26(5)*, 319-333.

Gottfredson, D. C. (1987). An evaluation of an organization development approach to reducing school disorder. *Evaluation Review, 11*, 739-763.

Gottfredson, D. (1997). School based crime prevention. In L. Sherman, D. Gottfredson, D. MacKenzie, J. Eck, P. Reuter, & S. Bushway (Eds.), *Preventing crime: What works, what doesn't, what's promising: A report to the United States Congress.* Washington, DC: U.S. Department of Justice.

Gottfredson, D. C., Gottfredson, G. D., & Hybl, L. G. (1993). Managing adolescent behavior: A multiyear, multischool study. *American Educational Research Journal, 30*, 179-215.

Gottfredson, M. R., & Hirschi, T. (1994). A general theory of adolescent problem behavior: Problems and prospects. In R. D. Ketterlinus & M. E. Lamb (Eds.), *Adolescent problem behaviors* (pp. 41-56). Thousand Oaks, CA: Sage.

Greenberg, M. T., Domitrovich, C., & Bumbarger, B. (1999). *Preventing mental disorders in school age children: A review of the effectiveness of prevention programs.* Prevention Research Center for the Promotion of Human Development, College of Human Development, The Pennsylvania State University, University Park, PA.

Greenberg, M. T., Domitrovich, C., & Bumbarger, B. (2001). The prevention of mental disorders in school-aged children: Current state of the field. *Prevention and Treatment, 4*, np.

Greenberg, M. T. & Kusché, C. A. (1998). Preventive interventions for school-age deaf children: The PATHS curriculum. *Journal of Deaf Studies and Deaf Education, 3*, 49-63.

Greenburg, M.T., Kusché, C.A., Cook, E.T., & Quamma, J.P. (1995). Promoting emotional competence in school-aged children: The effects of the PATHS curriculum. *Developmental Research and Psychopathology, 7*, 117-136.

Greenberg, M. T., Weissberg, R. P., O'Brien, M. U., Zins, J. E., Fredericks, L., Resnik, H., & et al., (2003). Enhancing school-based prevention and youth development through coordinated social, emotional, and academic learning. *American Psychologist, 58*(6-7), 466-474.

Greenwood, C. R. (1991). Classwide peer tutoring: Longitudinal effects on the reading, language, and mathematics achievement of at-risk students. *Journal of Reading, Writing, and Learning Disabilities International, 7,* 105-123.

Greenwood, C. R. (1996). The case for performance-based instructional models. *School Psychology Quarterly, 11,* 283-296.

Greenwood, C. R., Carta, J. J., & Hall, R. V. (1988). The use of peer tutoring strategies in classroom management and educational instruction. *School Psychology Review, 17,* 258-275.

Greenwood, C. R., Delquadri, J. C., & Hall, R. V. (1989). Longitudinal effects of classwide peer tutoring. *Journal of Educational Psychology, 81,* 371-383.

Greenwood, C. R., Terry, B., Arreaga-Mayer, C., & Finney, R. (1992). The classwide peer tutoring program: Implementation factors moderating students' achievement. *Journal of Applied Behavior Analysis, 25,* 101-116.

Greenwood, P. W. (1996). Responding to juvenile crime: Lessons learned. *Future of Children, 6*(3), 75-85.

Griffin, K. W., Botvin, G. J., Scheier, L. M., Diaz, T., & Miller, N. L. (2000). Parenting practices as predictors of substance use, delinquency, and aggression among urban minority youth: Moderating effects of family structure and gender. *Psychology of Addictive Behaviors, 14(2),* 174-184.

Grossman, D. C., Neckerman, J. J., Koepsell, T. D., Liu, P., Asher, K. N., Beland, K., Frey, K., & Rivara, F. P. (1997). Effectiveness of a violence prevention curriculum among children in elementary school: A randomized controlled trial. *Journal of the American Medical Association, 277,* 1605-1611.

Grube, J. W. (1997). Preventing sales of alcohol to minors: Results from a community trial. *Addiction, 92* (supplement), S251-S260.

Gruenewald, P. J. (1997). Analysis approaches to community evaluation. *Evaluation Review, 21,* 209-230.

Gual, A., & Diaz, R. (1999). *Alcoholism prevention in children of alcoholics. European Symposium on Community Action to Prevent Alcohol Problems.* Porto, Portugal.

Gullotta, C. F. & Plant, R. W. (2000). Promoting social competency through the arts. In S. J. Danish & T. P. Gullotta (Eds.), *Developing competent youth and strong communities through after-school programming* (pp. 173-182). Washington, DC: CWLA.

Gullotta, T. P. (1994). The what, who, why, where, when, and how of primary prevention. *Journal of Primary Prevention, 15,* 5-14.

Gullotta, T. P. & Bloom, M. (Series Ed.) (2003). *The encyclopedia of primary prevention and health promotion.* New York: Kluwer Academic/Plenum.

Hall, G. E. & Loucks, S. F. (1978, March). *Innovation configurations: Analyzing the adaptation of innovations.* Paper presented at the annual meeting of the American Educational Research Association, Toronto, Canada.

Hall, N. W. & Zigler, E. (1997). Drug-abuse prevention efforts for young children: A review and critique of existing programs. *American Journal of Orthopsychiatry, 67,* 134-143.

Halpern, R. (1999). After-school programs for low-income children: Promise and challenges. *The Future of Children, 9,* 81-95.

Hanewinkel, R. & Knaack, R. (1997a). Prävention van aggression und gewalt an schulen. Ergebnisse einer Interventionsstudie. In H. G. Holtapples, W. Heitmeyer, W. Melzer,

& K. J. Tillman (Eds.), *Schulische Gewaltforschung. Stand und perspektiven* (pp. 299-313). Weinheim: Juventa.

Hanewinkel, R. & Knaack, R. (1997b). Mobbing: Eine Fragebogenstudie zum Ausmaß von aggression und Gewalt an Schulen. *Empirische Pädagogik, 11*, 403-422.

Hanrahan, M. H., & Prinsen, B. (Eds.) (1997). *Community health, community care and community support.* Utrecht, The Netherlands: Netherlands Institute of Care and Welfare and the Dutch MIM Cooperative.

Hanrahan, M. H., & Prinsen, B. (Eds.) (1998). *Let's talk. Mothers Inform Mothers: A Dutch community-based early-childhood care and development support programme.* Utrecht, The Netherlands: Netherlands Institute of Care and Welfare and the Dutch MIM Cooperative.

Hansen, W. B. (1992). School-based substance abuse prevention: A review of the state of the art in curriculum 1980-1990. *Health Education Research, 7*, 403-430.

Hansen, W. B., Graham, J. W., Wolkenstein, H. B., & Rohrbach, L. A. (1991). Program integrity as a moderator of prevention program effectiveness: Results for fifth grade students in the adolescent alcohol prevention trial. *Journal of Studies on Alcohol, 52*, 568-579.

Hansson, K., Cederblad, M., & Höök, B. (2000). Funktionell familjeterapi -- en behandlingsmetod vid ungdomskriminalitet. *Socialvetenskaplig Tidskrift, 3*, 231-242.

Harachi, T. W., Ayers, C. D., Hawkins, J. D., Catalano, R. F., & Cushing, J. (1996). Empowering communities to prevent adolescent substance abuse: Results from a risk-and protection-focused community mobilization effort. *Journal of Primary Prevention, 16*(3), 233-254.

Hardwick, D. & Patychuk, D. (1999). Geographic mapping demonstrates the association between social inequality, teen births and STDs among youth. *Canadian Journal of Human Sexuality, 8*(2), 77-90.

Harmon, M. A. (1993). Reducing the risk of drug involvement among early adolescents: An evaluation of Drug Abuse Resistance Education (DARE). *Evaluation Review, 17*, 221-239.

Harrison, P. A., Fulkerson, & Park, E. (2000). The relative importance of social versus commercial sources in youth access to tobacco, alcohol, and other drugs. *Preventive Medicine, 31*, 39-48.

Hartup, W. W. (1983). Peer relations. In P. H. Mussen (Series Ed.) & E. M. Hetherington (Vol. Ed.), *Handbook of child psychology: Volume 4. Socialization, personality, and social development* (4th ed., pp. 103-196). New York: Wiley.

Hartup, W. W. (1996). The company they keep: Friendships and their developmental significance. *Child Development, 67*, 1-13.

Haveman, R. H. & Wolfe, B-S. (1994). Succeeding generations: On the effects of investments in children. New York: Russell Sage Foundation.

Hawkins, J. D. (1999). Preventing crime and violence through Communities that Care. *European Journal on Criminal Policy and Research, 7*, 443-458.

Hawkins, J. D., Arthur, M. W., & Olson, J. J. (1997). Community interventions to reduce risks and enhance protection against antisocial behavior. In D. M. Stoff, J. Breiling, & J. D. Maser (Eds.), *The handbook of antisocial behavior* (pp. 365-374). New York: John Wiley & Sons.

Hawkins, J. D., & Catalano, R. F. (2003). *Guiding Good Choices.* South Dearfield, MA: Channing Bete Company.

Hawkins, J. D., Catalano, R. F., & Associates. (1992). *Communities that care: Action for drug abuse prevention.* San Francisco: Jossey-Bass.

Hawkins, J. D., Catalano, R. F., Kosterman, R., Abbott, R., & Hill, K. G. (1999). Preventing adolescent health-risk behaviors by strengthening protection during childhood. *Archives of Pediatric & Adolescent Medicine, 153*, 226-234.

Hawkins, J. D., Catalano, R. F., & Miller, J. Y. (1992). Risk and protective factors for alcohol and other drug problems in adolescence and early adulthood: Implications for substance use prevention. *Psychological Bulletin, 112*, 64-105.

Hawkins, J. D., Catalano, R. F., Morrison, D. M., O'Donnell, J., Abbott, R. D., & Day, L. E. (1992). The Seattle Social Development Project: Effects of the first four years on protective factors and problem behaviors. In J. McCord & R. E. Tremblay (Eds.), *Preventing antisocial behavior: Interventions from birth through adolescence* (139-161). New York: Guilford.

Hawkins, J. D., Doueck, H. J., & Lishner, D. M. (1988). Changing teaching practices in mainstream classrooms to improve bonding and behavior of low achievers. *American Education Research Journal, 25*, 31-50.

Hawkins, J. D., Farrington, D. P., & Catalano, R. F. (1998). Reducing violence through the schools. In D. S. Elliot, B. A. Hamburg, & K. R. Williams (Eds.), *Violence in American schools* (pp. 188-216). New York: Cambridge University Press.

Hawkins, J. D., Herrenkohl, T., Farrington, D. P., Brewer, D., Catalano, R. F., & Harachi, T. W. (1998). A review of predictors of youth violence. In R. Loeber & D. P. Farrington (Eds.), *Serious and Violent Juvenile Offenders* (pp. 106-146). Thousand Oaks, CA: Sage.

Hawkins, J. D., Lishner, D. M., Jenson, J. M., & Catalano, R. F. (1987). Delinquents and drugs: What the evidence suggests about prevention and treatment programming. In B. S. Brown, & A. R. Mills (Eds.) *Youth at high risk for substance abuse* (pp. 81-131). Rockville, MD: U.S. National Institute on Drug Abuse.

Hawley, P. (1999). The ontogenesis of social dominance. *Developmental Review, 19*, 97-132.

Hazelrigg, M. D., Cooper, H. M., & Borduin, C. M. (1987). Evaluating the effectiveness of family therapies: An integrative review and analysis. *Psychological Bulletin, 101*(3), 428-442.

Heins, H. C., Nance, N. W., & Ferguson, J. E. (1987). Social support in improving perinatal outcomes: The resource mothers program. *Obstetrical Gynecology, 70*, 263-266.

Heller, K. W., Fredrick, L. D., Best, S., Dykes, M. K., & Cohen, E. T. (2000). Specialized health care procedures in the schools: Training and service delivery. *Exceptional Children, 66*, 173-186.

Heller, L. R., & Fantuzzo, J. W. (1993). Reciprocal peer tutoring and parent partnership: Does parent involvement make a difference? *School Psychology Review, 22*, 517-534.

Henggeler, S. W. (1999). Multisystemic therapy: An overview of clinical procedures, outcomes, and policy implications. *Child Psychology and Psychiatry Review, 4*, 2-10.

Henggeler, S., Cunningham, P., Pickrel, S., Schoenwald, S., & Brondino, M. (1996). Multisystemic therapy: An effective violence prevention approach for serious juvenile offenders. *Journal of Adolescence, 19*, 47-61.

Henggeler, S. W., Melton, G. B., & Smith, L. A. (1992). Family preservation using multisystemic therapy: An effective alternative to incarcerating serious juvenile offenders. *Journal of Consulting and Clinical Psychology, 60*(6), 953-961.

Henggeler, S. W., Melton, G. B., Smith, L. A., Schoenwald, S. K., & Hanley, H. (1993). Family preservation using multisystemic treatment: Long-term follow-up to a clinical trial with serious juvenile offenders. *Journal of Child and Family Studies, 2*(4), 283-293.

Henggeler, Schoenwald, S. K., Borduin, C. M., Rowland, M. D., & Cunningham, P. B. (1998). *Multisystemic treatment of antisocial behavior in youth.* New York: Guilford.

Herrenkohl, T. I., Maguin, E., Hill, K. G., Hawkins, J. D., Abbott, R. D., Catalano, R. F. (2000). Developmental risk factors for youth violence. *Journal of Adolescent Health, 26*, 176-186.

Heyl-Miller, J., MacPhee, D., & Fritz, J. J. (1998). DARE to be you: A family-support, early prevention program. *Journal of Primary Prevention, 18*, (3) 257-285.

Hibbs, E. D., & Jensen, P. S. (Eds.) (1996). *Psychosocial treatments for child and adolescent disorders: Empirically based strategies for clinical practice.* Washington, DC: American Psychological Association.

Hindley P. A. & Reed, H. (1999) Promoting Alternative Thinking Strategies (PATHS): Mental Health Promotion with Deaf Children in School. In S. Decker, S. Kirby, A. Greenwood, & D. Moore (Eds.), *Taking Children seriously: Applications of counseling and Therapy in Education* (pp. 113-132). London: Cassell.

Hirschi, T. (1969). *Causes of delinquency.* Berkeley: University of California Press.

Holder, H. (1997). Can individually directed interventions reduce population-level alcohol-involved problems? *Addition, 92*(1), 5-7.

Holder, H. (1998). *Alcohol and the community: A systems approach to prevention.* Cambridge, UK: Cambridge University Press.

Holder, H. D. (2000). Community prevention of alcohol problems. *Addictive Behaviors, 25,* 843-859.

Holder, H. D. (2001). Prevention of alcohol problems in the 21st century: Challenges and opportunities. *The American Journal on Addictions, 10,* 1-15.

Holder, H. D., Gruenewald, P. J., Ponicki, W. R., Treno, A. J., Grube, J. W., Saltz, R. F., et al., (2000). Effect of community-based interventions on high-risk drinking and alcohol-related injuries. *JAMA: Journal of the American Medical Association, 284,* 2341-2347.

Holder, H. & Reynolds, R. I. (1997). Application of local policy to prevent alcohol problems: experiences from a community trial. *Addiction, 92* (supplement), S285-S292.

Holder, H. D., Saltz, R. F., Gruebe, J. W., Treno, A. J., Reynolds, R. I., Voas, R. B., & Gruenewald, P. J. (1997). Summing up: Lessons from a comprehensive community prevention trial. *Addiction, 92* (supplement), S293-S301.

Holder, H. D., & Treno, A. J. (1997). Media advocacy in community prevention: news as a means to advance policy change. *Addiction, 92* (supplement 2), S189-S199.

Holder, H. & Wagenaar, A. C. (1994). Mandated server training and reduced alcohol-involved traffic crashes: A time series analysis of the Oregon experience. *Accident Analysis and Prevention, 26,* 89-97.

Hollederer, A. & Bölcskei, P.L. (1999). Gesundheitsförderung als Gemeinschaftsaufgabe von Schule und Gesundheitsfachleuten. *Prävention,* 22-25.

Hollederer, A. & Bölcskei, P.L. (2000). Von der Pädagogik des erhobenen Zeigefingers zur schulischen Gesundheitsförderung. *PÄD Forum, 6,* 238-245.

Holmila, M. (1995). Community action on alcohol: Experiences of the Lahti Project in Finland. *Health Promotion International,10,* 283-291.

Holmila, M. (Ed.). (1997). *Community prevention of alcohol problems.* London: MacMillan Press.

Holmila, M. (1999). Community-based prevention of alcohol problems: a case study from Lahti, and its lessons for future prevention research in Finland. In S. Larsson & B. S. Hanson (Eds.), *Community based alcohol prevention in Europe – Research and evaluations* (pp. 141-151). Lund, Sweden: Studentlitteratur.

Holmila, M. (2000). The Finnish case: Community prevention in a time of rapid change in national and international trade. *Substance Use and Misuse, 35,* 111-123.

Hosman, C. M. H. (1992). Primary prevention of mental disorders and mental health promotion in Europe: Developments and possibilities for innovation. In G. W. Albee, L. A. Bond, T. V. Cook Monsey, (1992). *Improving children's lives: Global perspectives on prevention. Primary prevention of psychopathology,* Vol. 14 (pp. 151-166). Thousand Oaks, CA: Sage.

Hosman, C. M. H. & Clayton, R. (2001). Prevention and health promotion on the international scene: The need for a more effective and comprehensive approach: Erratum. *Addictive-Behaviors, 26*(1), 151.

Howard, M. & McCabe, J. A. (1992). An information and skills approach for younger teens: Postponing Sexual Involvement program. In B. C. Miller, J. J. Card, R. L. Paikoff, & J. L. Peterson (Eds.), *Preventing adolescent pregnancy: Model programs and evaluations* (pp. 83-109). Thousand Oaks, CA: Sage.

Hudley, C., & Graham, S. (1993). An attributional intervention to reduce peer-directed aggression among African-American boys. *Child Development, 64,* 124-138.

Huey, S. J. & Henggeler, S. W. (2001). Effective community-based interventions for antisocial and delinquent adolescents. In J. N. Hughes, A. M. La Greca, et al. (Eds.), Handbook of psychological services for children and adolescents (pp. 301-322). London: Oxford University Press.

Huey, S. J., Henggeler, S. W., Brondino, M. J., & Pickrel, S. G. (2000). Mechanisms of change in multisystemic therapy: Reducing delinquent behavior through therapist adherence and improved family and peer functioning. Journal of Consulting and Clinical Psychology, 68(3), 451-467.

Huizinga, D., Loeber, R., Thornberry, T. P., & Cothern, L. (2000, November). Co-occurrence of delinquency and other problem behaviors. *OJJDP Juvenile Justice Bulletin* [NCJ 182211]. Washington, DC: U.S. Department of Justice, Office of Justice Programs, Office of Juvenile Justice and Delinquency Prevention.

Hurry, J., Lloyd, C., & McGurk, H. (2000). Long-term effects of drugs education in primary school. *Addiction Research, 8,* 183-202.

Hurry, J. & McGurk, H. (1997). An evaluation of a primary prevention programme for schools. *Addiction Research 5,* 23-38.

Huxley, P. H., & Warner, M. B. (1993). Primary prevention of parenting dysfunction in high-risk cases. *American Journal of Orthopsychiatry, 63*(4), 582-588.

Ince, D., Beumer, M., Jonkman, H., & Pannebakker, M. (2001). *Veelbelovend en effectief overzicht van preventieve projecten en programma's in de domeienen Gezin, School, Jeugd, Wijk eerste editie CtC gids.* Utrecht: The Netherlands: Netherlands Institute for Care and Welfare (NIZW).

Irvine, A-B., Biglan, A., Smolkowski, K., Metzler, C. W., & Ary, D. V. (1999). The effectiveness of a parenting skills program for parents of middle school students in small communities. *Journal of Consulting and Clinical Psychology, 67*(6), 811-825.

Jacobson, S. W. & Frye, K. F. (1991). Effect of maternal social support on attachment: Experimental evidence. *Child Development, 62*(3), 572-582.

Jarlbro G. (1998:17). *Verksamheten vid landets ungdomsmottagningar.* Stockholm, Sweden: Folkhälsoinsititutet.

Jason, L., Billows, W., Schnopp-Wyatt, D., & King, C. (1996). Reducing the illegal sales of cigarettes to minors: Analysis of alternative enforcement schedules. *Journal of Applied Behavior Analysis, 29,* 333-344.

Jason, L. A., Ji, P. Y., Anes, M. D., & Birkhead, S. H. (1991). Active enforcement of cigarette control laws in the prevention of cigarette sales to minors. *Journal of the American Medical Association, 266,* 3159-3161.

Jemmott, J. B., III (1996). Social psychological influences on HIV risk behavior among African American youth. In S. Oskamp, & S. C. Thompson (Eds.), *Understanding and preventing HIV risk behavior: Safer sex and drug use. The Claremont Symposium on Applied Social Psychology.* (pp. 131-156).

Jemmott, J. B., III, & Jemmott. L. S. (2000). HIV behavioral interventions for adolescents in community settings. In J. L. Peterson, & R. J. DiClemente (Eds.), *Handbook of HIV prevention. AIDS prevention and mental health.* (pp. 103-127). New York: Kluwer Academic/Plenum.

Jemmott, J. B., Jemmott, L. S., & Fong, G. T. (1992). Reductions in HIV risk-associated sexual behaviors among Black male adolescents: Effects of an AIDS prevention intervention. *American Journal of Public* Health, 82, 372-377.

Jenson, J. M. & Howard, M. O. (1999). Hallucinogen use among juvenile probationers: Prevalence and characteristics. *Criminal Justice & Behavior, 26*, 357-372.

Jessor, R. (1998). *New perspectives on adolescent risk behavior.* New York: Cambridge University Press.

Jessor, R., & Jessor, S. L. (1977). *Problem behavior and psychosocial development: A longitudinal study of youth.* New York: Academic Press.

Joffee, J. M. (1982). Approaches to prevention of adverse developmental consequences of genetic and prenatal factors. In L. A. Bond & J. M. Joffee (Eds.), *Facilitating infant and early childhood development* (pp. 121-157). Hanover, NH: University Press of New England.

Joha, D., Luit, H., & Vermeer, A. (1999). *Samen op PAD. Evaluatie van het Programma Alternatieve Denkstrategieën in het Nederlandse onderwijs aan dove kinderen.* Doetinchem: Graviant Educatieve Uitgaven.

Johansson, P., Drott-Englén, G., Hansson, K., & Benderix, Y. (2002). *Funktionell familjeterapi i barnpsykiatrisk praxis: resultat av en samarbetsmodell vid behandling av ungdomskriminalitet utanför universitetsforskningen.* Manuscript submitted for publication.

Johnson, Z., Howell, F., & Molloy, B. (1993). Community mothers programme: Randomised controlled trial of nonprofessional intervention in parenting. *British Medical Journal, 306*(29), 1449-1452.

Johnson, D. W. & Johnson, R. T. (1996). Conflict resolution and peer mediation programs in elementary and secondary schools. *Review of Educational Research, 66*, 459-506.

Johnson, C. A., Pentz, M. A., Weber, M. D., Dwyer, J. H., Baer, N., MacKinnon, D. P., Hansen, W. B. & Flay, B. R. (1990). Relative effectiveness of comprehensive community programming for drug abuse prevention with high-risk and low-risk adolescents. *Journal of Consulting and Clinical Psychology, 58*(4), 447-456.

Johnson, K., Strader, T., Berbaum, M., Bryant, D., Bucholtz, G., Collins, D., & Noe, T. (1996). Reducing alcohol and other drug use by strengthening community, family, and youth resiliency: An evaluation of the Creating Lasting Connections Program. *Journal of Adolescent Research, 11*, 36-67.

Johnson, D. L. & Walker, T. (1987). Primary prevention of behavior problems in Mexican-American children. *American Journal of Community Psychology, 15*(4), 375-385.

Jones, M. B. & Offord, D. R. (1986). Participation and sibship size in a skill-development program: A research note. *Journal of Child Psychology and Psychiatry, 27*, 109-116.

Jones, M. B. & Offord, D. R. (1989).Reduction of antisocial behavior in poor children by nonschool skill-development. *Journal of Child Psychology and Psychiatry and Allied Disciplines, 30*(5), 737-750.

Juby, H. & Farrington, D. P. (2001). Disentangling the link between disrupted families and delinquency. *British Journal of Criminology, 41*(1), 22-40.

Julnes, G. J., Konefal, M., Pindur, W., & Kim, P. (1994). Community-based perinatal care for disadvantaged adolescents: Evaluation of the resource mothers program. *Journal of Community Health, 19*(1), 41-53.

Kagitcibasi, C. (1995). Is psychology relevant to global human development issues? Experience from Turkey. *American Psychologist, 50*, 293-300.

Kamerman, S. B. (2000). Early childhood intervention policies: An international perspective. In J. P. Shonkoff & S. J. Meisels (Eds.), *Handbook of early childhood intervention* (2nd Ed.), (pp. 613-629). New York: Cambridge University Press.

Kandel, D. B. (1973). Adolescent marihuana use: Role of parents and peers. *Science, 181*(4104), 1067-1070.

Kandel, D. B. (1978). Homophily, selection, and socialization in adolescent friendships. *American Journal of Sociology, 84*(2), 427-436.

Kandel, D. B. (1985). On processes of peer influences in adolescent drug use: A developmental perspective. *Advances in Alcohol and Substance Abuse, 4*, 139-163.

Kandel, D. B. (Ed.). (2002). *Stages and pathways of drug involvement: Examining the gateway hypothesis.* New York: Cambridge University Press.

Karoly, L. A., Greenwood, P. W., Everingham, S. S., Houbé, J., Kilburn, M. R., Rydell, C. P., Sanders, M., & Chiesa, J. (1998). *Investing in our children: What we know and don't know about the costs and benefits of early childhood interventions.* Santa Monica, CA: RAND.

Kaufman, N. H. & Rizzini, I (Eds.). (2002). *Globalization and children: Exploring Potentials for Enhancing Opportunities in the Lives of Children and Youth.* New York: Kluwer Academic/Plenum Publishers.

Kazdin, A. E. (1998). Psychosocial treatments for conduct disorder in children. In P. E. Nathan & J. M. Gorman (Eds.), *A guide to treatments that work* (pp. 65-89). London: Oxford University Press.

Kazdin, A. E. (1999). Current (lack of) status of theory in child and adolescent psychotherapy research. *Journal of Clinical Child Psychology, 28*, 533-543.

Keay, K. D., Woodruff, S. I., Wildey, M. B., & Kenny, E. M. (1993). Effect of a retailer intervention on cigarette sales to minors in San Diego County, CA. *Tobacco Control, 2*(2), 145-151.

Kelder, S. H., Perry, C. L., & Klepp, K. (1993). Community-wide youth exercise promotion: Long-term outcomes of the Minnesota Heart Health Program and the Class of 1989 Study. *Journal of School Health, 63*(5), 218-223.

Kelder, S. H., Perry, C. L., Lytle, L. A., & Klepp, K. (1995). Community-wide youth nutrition education: Long-term outcomes of the Minnesota Heart Health Program. *Health Education Research: Theory and Practice, 10*(2), 119-131.

Kellam, S. G., Rebok, G. W., Ialongo, N. & Mayer, L. S. (1994). The course and malleability of aggressive behavior from early first grade into middle school: results of a developmental epidemiologically-based prevention trial. *Journal of Child Psychiatry, 35*, 259-281.

Kellam, S. G., Werthamer-Larsson, L., Dolan, L. J., Brown, C. H., Mayer, L. S., Rebok, G. W., Anthony, J. C., Laudolff, J., & Edelsohn, G. (1991). Developmental epidemiologically based preventative trials: Baseline modeling of early target behaviors and depressive symptoms. *American Journal of Community Psychology, 19*, 563-584.

Keller, H. R. & Tapasak, R. C. (1997). Classroom management. In A. P. Goldstein, P. Arnold, & J. C. Conoley (Eds.), *School violence intervention: A practical handbook.* (pp. 107-126).

Kendall-Tackett, K. A., & Eckenroade, J. (1996). The effects of neglect on academic achievement and disciplinary problems: A developmental perspective. *Child Abuse & Neglect, 20.* 161-169.

Kerr, M., Stattin, H., Biesecker, G., & Ferrer-Wreder, L. (2003). Relationships with Parents and Peers in Adolescence. In I. B. Weiner (Series Ed.) & R. M. Lerner, M. A. Easterbrooks, & J. Mistry (Vol. Eds.), *Comprehensive handbook of psychology: Vol. 6. Developmental psychology* (pp. 395-419). New York: Wiley.

Kim, N., Stanton, B., Li, X., Dickersin, K., & Galbraith, J. (1997). Effectiveness of the 40 adolescent AIDS risk reduction interventions: A quantitative review. *Journal of Adolescent Health, 20*, 204-215.

Kimber, B. & Sandell, R. (2001). Primary prevention of psychological ill-health among children and adolescents through social emotional learning in school. *Nordisk Psykologi, 53*, 256-261.

Kirby, D. (1997). *No easy answers: Research findings on programs to reduce teen pregnancy.* Washington DC: The National Campaign to Prevent Teen Pregnancy.

Kirby, D. (2000). School-based interventions to prevent unprotected sex and HIV among adolescents. In J. L. Peterson & R. J. DiClemente (eds.), *Handbook of HIV prevention. AIDS prevention and mental health* (pp. 83-101). New York: Kluwer Academic/Plenum.

Kirby, D., Barth, R.P., Leland, N., & Fetro, J.V. (1991). *Family Planning Perspectives, 23*(6), 253 -263.

Kirby, D., Korpi, M., Adivi, C., & Weissman, J. (1997). An impact evaluation of Project SNAPP: An AIDS and pregnancy prevention middle school program. *AIDS Education and Prevention, 9* (Supplement A), 44-61.

Kirby, D., Korpi, M., Barth, R., & Cagampang, H. (1995). Evaluation of Education Now and Babies Later (ENABL). *Final Report: Berkeley: Univ. of California, School of Social Welfare.*

Kirby, D. & Waszak, C. (1992). School-based clinics. In B. C. Miller, J. J. Card, R. L. Paikoff, & J. L. Peterson (Eds.), *Preventing adolescent pregnancy: Model programs and evaluations* (pp. 185-219). Thousand Oaks, CA: Sage.

Klein, N. C., Alexander, J. F., & Parsons, B. V. (1977). Impact of family systems intervention on recidivism and sibling delinquency: A model of primary prevention and program evaluation. *Journal of Consulting and Clinical Psychology, 45*, 469–474.

Klepp, K. I., Tell, G. S., & Vellar, O. D. (1993). Ten-year follow-up of the Oslo Youth Study Smoking Prevention Program. *Preventive Medicine, 22*, 453-462.

Klitzner, M., Fisher, D.A., Stewart, K., & Gilbert, S. (1992). *Substance Abuse: Early Intervention for Adolescents.* Princeton, NJ: The Robert Wood Johnson Foundation.

Knapp, P. A. & Deluty, R. H. (1989). Relative effectiveness of two behavioral parent training programs. *Journal of Consulting and Clinical Psychology, 18*, 314-322.

Kok, G., van den Borne, B., & Mullen, P. D. (1997). Effectiveness of health education and health promotion: Meta-analyses of effect studies and determinants of effectiveness. *Patient Education and Counseling, 30,*19-27.

Kolbe, L. J., Collins, J., & Cortese, P. (1997). Building the capacity for schools to improve the health of the nation: A call for assistance from psychologists. *American Psychologist, 52*, 256-265.

Komro, K. A., Perry, C. L., Murray, D. M., Veblen-Mortenson, S., Williams, C. L., & Anstine, P. S. (1996). Peer-planned social activities for preventing alcohol use among young adolescents. *Journal of School Health, 66*(9), 328-334.

Koo, H. P., Dunteman, G. H., George, C., Green, Y., & Vincent, M. (1994). Reducing adolescent pregnancy through a school-and community-based intervention: Denmark, South Carolina, revisited. *Family Planning Perspectives, 26*, 206-217.

Koutakis, N., Ferrer-Wreder, L., & Stattin, H. (2001). *Örebro Prevention Project.* Presented at the Society for Prevention Research, Washington, DC.

Kraemer, H. C., & Thiemann, S. (1987). *How many subjects? Statistical power analysis in research.* Newbury Park: Sage Publications.

Kronick, R. F., (Ed.). (2000). Human services and the full service school: The need for collaboration. Springfield, IL: Charles C. Thomas Publisher.

Kumpfer, K. L., Alexander, J. F., McDonald, L., & Olds, D. L. (1998). Family-focused substance abuse prevention: what has been learned from other fields. In R. S. Ashery, E. B. Robertson, E. B. & K. L. Kumpfer, (Eds.), *Drug abuse prevention through family interventions.* NIDA Research Monograph, 177 [NIH Publication No. 97-4135] (pp. 78-102). Rockville, MD: National Institute on Drug Abuse, Division of Epidemiology and Prevention Research.

Kumpfer, K. L. & Alvarado, R. (1998, November). Effective family strengthening interventions. *OJJDP Juvenile Justice Bulletin* [NCJ 171121]. Washington, DC: U.S. Department of Justice, Office of Justice Programs, Office of Juvenile Justice and Delinquency Prevention.

Kumpfer, K. L. & DeMarsh, J. P. (1985). Prevention of chemical dependency in children of alcohol and drug abusers. *NIDA Notes, 5,* 2-3.

Kumpfer, K. L., Molgaard, V., & Spoth, R. (1996). The Strengthening Families Program for the prevention of delinquency and drug use. In R. D. Peters & R. J. McMahon (Eds.), *Preventing childhood disorders, substance abuse, and delinquency* (pp. 241-267). Thousand Oaks, CA: Sage.

Lagerberg, D. (2000). Secondary prevention in child health: effects of psychological intervention, particularly home visitation, on children's development and other outcome variables. *Acta Paediatr, 434* (Suppl, iii), 43-52.

Lahey, B. B., Waldman, I. D., & McBurnett, K. (1999). Annotation: The development of antisocial behavior: An integrative causal model. *Journal of Child Psychology and Psychiatry and Allied Disciplines, 40,* 669-682.

Lally, J. R., Mangione, P. L., & Honig, A. S. (1988). The Syracuse University Family Development Research Program: Long-range impact on an early intervention with low-income children and their families. In D. R. Powell (Ed.), *Parent education as early childhood intervention: Emerging directions in theory, research and practice. Annual advances in applied developmental psychology, Vol. 3.* (pp. 79-104). Westport, CT: Ablex Publishing.

Lally, J. R., Mangione, P. L., Honig, A. S., & Wittner, D. S. (1988). More pride, less delinquency: Findings from the ten-year follow-up study of the Syracuse University Family Development Research Program. *Zero to Three, 8*(4), 13-18.

Lambert, S. F. & Black, M. M. (2001). Comprehensive Community Initiatives: Expanded roles for developmental scientists. *Children's Services: Social Policy, Research, and Practice, 4*(1), 25-29.

Landrine, H., Klonoff, E. A., Campbell, R., & Reina-Patton, A. (2000). Sociocultural variables in youth access to tobacco: Replication 5 years later. *Preventive Medicine: An International Journal Devoted to Practice & Theory, 30,* 433-437.

Lattimore, C. B., Mihalic, S. F., Grotpeter, J. K., & Taggart, R. (1998). *Blueprints for violence prevention, book four: The Quantum Opportunities Program.* Boulder, CO: Center for the Study and Prevention of Violence.

LeDoux, J. (1998). Fear and the brain: Where have we been, and where are we going? *Biological Psychiatry, 44,* 1229-1238.

Lee, B. J. & Goerge, R. M. (1999). Poverty, early childbearing, and child maltreatment: A multinomial analysis. *Children and Youth Services Review, 21,* 755-780.

Leffert, N., Benson, P., Scales, P., Sharma, A., Drake, D., Blyth, D. (1998). Developmental assets: Measurement and prediction of risk behaviors among adolescents. *Applied Developmental Science, 2,* 209-230.

Leifman, H. (1995). Alcohol and primary prevention in Scotland and Sweden: A comparative study. *Nordisk Alkoholtidskrift, 12* (English Supplement), 31-60.

Leigh, B. C. (1999). Peril, chance, adventure: Concepts of risk, alcohol use and risky sexual behavior in young adults. *Addiction, 94,* 371-383.

Lepinski, S. (1984). *Drug usage by adolescents, 8th, 10th, and 12th grade survey: Edina and Richfield Minnesota.* Unpublished report. Washburn Child Guidance Center.

Lerner, R. M., Anderson, P. M., Balsano, A. B., Dowling, E. M., & Bobek, D. L. (2003). Applied developmental science of positive human development. In I. B. Weiner (Series Ed.) & R. M. Lerner, M. A. Easterbrooks, & J. Mistry (Vol. Eds.), *Comprehensive handbook of psychology: Vol. 6. Developmental psychology* (pp. 535-558). New York: Wiley.

Lerner, R. M., & Busch-Rossnagel, N. A. (1981). Individuals as producers of their development: Conceptual and empirical bases. In R. M. Lerner & M. A. Busch-Rossnagel (Eds.) _Individuals as producers of their development: A life span perspective (pp. 1-36). New York: Academic Press.

Lerner, R. M., Ostrom, C. W., & Freel, M. A. (1995). Promoting positive youth and community development through outreach scholarship: Comments on Zeldin and Peterson. *Journal of Adolescent Research, 10*(4), 486-502.

Leschied, A.W. & Cunningham, A. (1998). Alternatives to custody for high-risk young offenders: Application of the Multisystemic approach in Canada. *European Journal on Criminal Policy and Research, 6*, 545-560.

Leschied, A.W. & Cunningham, A. (1999). Clinical trials of Multisystemic Therapy in Ontario: Rationale and current status of a community-based alternative for high-risk young offenders. *Forum on Corrections Research, 11*(2): 25-29.

Leschied, A.W. & Cunningham, A. (in press). A review of the use of custody in Canada's young offender system and the development of a community-based program for high-risk young offenders. In A. M. van Kalmthout, H-J. Albrecht and J. Junger-Tas (Eds.), *Community sanctions, measures and execution modalities in Europe, the USA and Canada.* Kluwer Publishing, Dordrecht, The Netherlands.

Leventhal, T. & Brooks-Gunn, J. (2000). The neighborhoods they live in: The effects of neighborhood residence upon child and adolescent outcomes. *Psychological Bulletin, 126*, 309-337.

Lewis, C., Battistich, V., & Schaps, E. (1990). School-based primary prevention: What is an effective program? *New Directions for Child Development, 50*, 35-59.

Limber, S. P. & Nation, M. A. (1998). Violence within the neighborhood and community. In P. K. Trickett & C. J. Schellenbach (Eds.), *Violence against children in the family and the community* (pp. 171-193). Washington, DC: American Psychological Association.

Lipsey, M. W. (1992). The effect of treatment on juvenile delinquents: Results from meta-analysis. In F. Loesel, D. Bender, & T. Bliesener (Eds.), *Psychology and law: International perspectives* (pp. 131-143). Oxford, England: Walter De Gruyter.

Lipsey, M. W. (1995). What do we learn from 400 research studies on the effectiveness of treatment with juvenile delinquents? In J. McGuire (Ed.), *What Works: Reducing Reoffending—Guidelines from Research and Practice* (pp. 63-78). New York: Wiley.

Lipsey, M. W. (1998). Effective intervention for serious juvenile offenders: A synthesis of research. In R. Loeber, D. P. Farrington (Eds.), *Serious & violent juvenile offenders: Risk factors and successful interventions* (pp. 313-345). Thousand Oaks, CA: Sage Publications, Inc.

Lipsey, M. W. & Cordray, D. S. (2000). Evaluation methods for social intervention. *Annual Review of Psychology, 51*, 345-375.

Lipsey, M. & Derzon, J. H. (1998). Predictors of violent or serious delinquency in adolescence and early adulthood: A synthesis of longitudinal research. In R. Loeber & D. P. Farrington (Eds.). *Serious & violent juvenile offenders: Risk factors and successful interventions* (p. 86-105). Thousand Oaks, CA: Sage.

Lipsey, M. W. & Wilson, D. B. (1993). The efficacy of psychological, educational, and behavioral treatment. Confirmation from meta-analysis. *American Psychologist, 48*, 1181-1209.

Lipsey, M. W. & Wilson, D. B. (2001). *Practical meta-analysis.* Thousand Oaks, CA: Sage.

Lochman, J. E. (1992). Cognitive-behavioral intervention with aggressive boys: Three-year follow-up and preventive effects. *Journal of Consulting and Clinical Psychology, 60*, 426-432.

Lochman, J. E., Burch, P. R., Curry, J. F., & Lampron, L. B. (1984). Treatment and generalization effects of cognitive-behavioral and goal-setting interventions with aggressive boys. *Journal of Consulting & Clinical Psychology, 52*, 915-916.

Lochman, J. E., Lampron, L., Gemmer, T., & Harris, S. (1986). Anger coping intervention with aggressive children: A guide to implementation in school settings. In P. Keller & S. Heyman (Eds.), *Innovations in clinical practice: A source book* (Vol. 6, pp. 339-356). Sarasota, FL: Professional Resources Exchange.

Lochman, J. E. & Lenhart, L. A. (1993). Anger coping intervention for aggressive children: Conceptual models and outcome effects. *Clinical Psychology Review, 13*(8), 785-805.

Lochman, J. E. & van den Steenhoven, A. (2002). Family-based approaches to substance abuse prevention. *The Journal of Primary Prevention, 23*(1), 49-114.

Loeber, R. & Farrington, D. P. (1998a). *Serious & violent juvenile offenders: Risk factors and successful interventions.* Thousand Oaks, CA: Sage.

Loeber, R. & Farrington, D. P. (1998b). Never too early, never, too late: Risk factors and successful interventions for serious and violent juvenile offenders. *Studies on Crime and Crime Prevention, 7,* 7-30.

Loeber, R., Farrington, D. P., Stouthamer-Loeber, M., & Van Kammen, W. B. (1998). *Antisocial behavior and mental health problems: Explanatory factors in childhood and adolescence.* Mahwah, NJ: Lawrence Erlbaum.

Loeber, R. & Stouthamer-Loeber, M. (1998). Development of juvenile aggression and violence: Some common misconceptions and controversies. *American Psychologist, 53,* 242-259.

Loeber, R. & Wikström, P. O. (1993). Individual pathways to crime in different types of neighborhood. In D. P. Farrington, R. J. Sampson, & P. O. Wikström (Eds.), *Integrating individual and ecological aspects of crime* (pp. 169-204). Stockholm: National Council for Crime Prevention.

Lonczak, H. S., Abbott, R. D., Hawkins, J. D., Kosterman, R., & Catalano, R. F. (2002). Effects of the Seattle Social Development Project on sexual behavior, pregnancy, birth, and STD outcomes by age 21. *Archives of Pediatrics and Adolescent Medicine, 156*(4), 438-447.

Lopez, S. J., Edwards, L. M., Ito, A., Pedrotti, J. T., & Rusmussen, H. N. (2002). Culture counts: Examinations of recent applications of the Penn Resiliency Program or, toward a rubric for examining cultural appropriateness of prevention programming. *Prevention and Treatment, 5,* np.

LoSciuto, L. Freeman, M. A., Harrington, E., Altman, F., & Lanphear, A. (1997). An outcome evaluation of the Woodrock Youth Development Project. *Journal of Early Adolescence, 17*(1), 51-66.

LoSciuto, L., Hilbert, S.M., Fox, M., Porcellini, L., & Lanphear, A. (1999). A two-year evaluation of the Woodrock Youth Development Project. *Journal of Early Adolescence, 19*(4), 488-507.

LoSciuto, L., Rajala, A. K., Townsend, T. N., & Taylor, A. S. (1996). An outcome evaluation of Across Ages: An intergenerational mentoring approach to drug prevention. *Journal of Adolescent Research, 11*(1), 116-129.

Lösel, F. & Bliesener, T. (1999). Germany. In P. K. Smith, Y. Morita, J. Junger-Tas, D. Olweus, R. Catalano, & P. Slee (Eds.), *The nature of school bullying: A cross-national perspective* (pp. 224-249). London: Routledge.

Loveland-Cherry, C. J., Ross, L. T., & Kaufman, S. R. (1999). Effects of a home-based family intervention on adolescent alcohol use and misuse. *Journal of Studies on Alcohol, Supp 13,* 94-102.

Luepker, R. V. & Perry, C. L. (1991). The Minnesota Heart Health Program: Education for youth and parents. *Annals of the New York Academy of Sciences, 623,* 314-321.

Luthar, S. S. (1993). Annotation: Methodological and conceptual issues in research on childhood resilience. *Journal of Child Psychology and Psychiatry, 34,* 441-454.

Luthar, S. S. & Cicchetti, D. (2000). The construct of resilience: Implications for interventions and social policies. *Development of Psychopathology, 12*, 857-885.

Lynch, M. & Cicchetti, D. (1998). An ecological-transactional analysis of children and contexts: The longitudinal interplay among child maltreatment, community violence, and children's symptomatology. *Development and Psychopathology, 10*, 235-257.

MacLeod, J. & Nelson, G. (2000). Programs for the promotion of family wellness and the prevention of child maltreatment: A meta-analytic review. *Child Abuse & Neglect, 24*, 1127-1149.

Magnusson, D. & Stattin, H. (1998). Person-context interaction theories. In W. Damon & R. M. Lerner (Eds.)., *Handbook of Child Psychology* (Vol. 1, pp. 685-759). New York: Wiley.

Maheady, L., Sacca, M. K., & Harper, G. F. (1987). Classwide student tutoring teams: The effects of peer-mediated instruction on the academic performance of secondary mainstreamed students. *Journal of Special Education, 21*, 107-121.

Mahoney, J. L., & Magnusson, D. (1998). *Parent community engagement and the persistence of anti-social behavior: Patterns, parenting, and prevention.* Manuscript submitted for publication.

Mahoney, J. L., & Stattin, H. (2000). Leisure activities and adolescent anti-social behavior: The role of structure and social context. *Journal of Adolescence, 23*, 113-127.

Mahoney, J. L., Stattin, H., & Magnusson, D. (in press). Youth leisure activity participation and individual adjustment: The Swedish youth recreation center. *International Journal of Behavioral Development.*

Main, D. S., Iverson, D. C., McGloin, J., Banspach, S. W., Collins, J. L., Rugg, D. L., et al. (1994). Preventing HIV infection among adolescents: Evaluation of a school-based education program. *Preventive Medicine, 23*, 409-417.

Manley, M. W., Pierce, J. P., Gilpin, E. A., Rosbrook, B., Berry, C., & Wun L. M. (1997a). Impact of the American Stop Smoking Intervention Study on cigarette consumption. Tobacco Control, 6 (Suppl 2), S12-S16.

Manley, M., Lynn, W., Payne Epps, R., Grande, D., Glynn, T., & Shopland, D. (1997b). The American Stop Smoking Intervention Study for cancer prevention: an overview. Tobacco Control, 6 (Suppl 2), S5-S11.

Marcenko, M. O. & Spence, M. (1994). Home visitation services for at-risk pregnant and postpartum women: A randomized trial. *American Journal of Orthopsychiatry, 64*, 468-478.

Marcus, R. F. (1996). The friendships of delinquents. *Adolescence, 31*, 145-158.

Masten, A. S. & Coatsworth, J. D. (1998). The development of competence in favorable and unfavorable environments: Lessons from research on successful children. *American Psychologist, 53*, 205-220.

Masten, A. S., & Curtis, W. J. (2000). Integrating competence and psychopathology: Pathways toward a comprehensive science of adaptation in development. *Development & Psychopathology, 12*, 529-550.

Masten, A. S., Hubbard, J. J., Gest, S. D., Tellegen, A., Garmezy, N. & Ramirez, M. (1999). Competence in the context of adversity: Pathways to resilience and maladaptation from childhood to late adolescence. *Development and Psychopathology, 11*, 143-169.

Mattis, J. S. (2002). Grappling with culture, class, and context in cross-cultural research and intervention. *Prevention and Treatment, 5*, np.

Mattsson, U. & Romelsjö, A. (1999). *Tillgänglighet till folköl och tobak i livsmedelsaffärer och kiosker i Trångsund och Skogås 1998* [Accessibility to beer and tobacco in convenience stores/kiosks in Trångsund and Skogås]. Huddinge, Sweden: Centrum för Alkohol och Drogprevention (CADP) - Novum.

Matza, D. (1969). *Becoming delinquent.* Englewood Cliffs, NJ: Prentice-Hall.

Maurana, C. A. & Clark, M. A. (2000). The Health Action Fund: A community-based approach to enhancing health. *Journal of Health Communication, 5*(3), 243-254.

Mayer, G. R., Butterworth, T. W., Nafpaktitis, M., & Sulzer-Azaroff, B. (1983). Preventing school vandalism and improving discipline: A three-year study. *Journal of Applied Behavior Analysis, 16,* 355-369.

McCain, A. P. & Kelley, M. L. (1994). Improving classroom performance in underachieving preadolescents: The additive effects of response cost to a school-home note system. *Child & Family Behavior Therapy, 16,* 27-41.

McCall, R. B., Green, B. L., Strauss, M. S., & Groark, C. J. (1998). Issues in community-based research and program evaluation. In W. Damon (Series Ed.) & I. E. Sigel & K. A. Renninger (Vol. Eds.), *Handbook of child psychology: Vol. 5. Child psychology in practice* (5th ed, pp. 955-997). New York: John Wiley.

McCord, J. (1978). A thirty-year follow-up of treatment effects. *American Psychologist, 33,* 284-289.

McCormick, A., McKernan, M. M., Wilson, M., McKinney, L., Paikoff, R., Bell, C., Baptiste, D., Coleman, D., Gillming, G., Madison, S., & Scott, R. (2000). Involving families in an urban HIV preventive intervention: How community collaboration addresses barriers to participation. *AIDS Education & Prevention, 12*(4), 299-307.

McCurdy, K. (2000). What works in nonmedical home visiting: Healthy Families America. In M. P. Kluger, G. Alexander, & P. A. Curtis, P. A. (Eds.), *What works in child welfare* (pp. 45-55). Washington, DC: Child Welfare League of America, Inc.

McElhaney, S. J. & Effley, K. M. (1999). Community-based approaches to violence prevention.In T. P. Gullotta & S. J. McElhaney (Eds.), *Violence in homes and communities: Prevention intervention and treatment* (pp. 269-299). Thousand Oaks, CA: Sage.

McLaughlin, T. F., & Vacha, E . (1992). School programs for at-risk children and youth: A review. *Education and Treatment of Children, 15,* 255-267.

Mead, M. (1928/1955/1961). *Coming of Age in Samoa.* New York: Morrow Quill Paperbacks.

Melton, G. B. (1997). Why don't the knuckleheads use common sense? In S. W. Henggeler, & A. B. Santos (Eds.). *Innovative approaches for difficult-to-treat populations* (pp. 351-370). Washington, DC: American Psychiatric Press, Inc.

Melton, G. B., Limber, S. P., Cunningham, P., Osgood, D. W., Chambers, J., Flerx, V., et al. (1998). *Violence among rural youth. Final report to the Office of Juvenile Justice and Delinquency Prevention.* Washington DC, OJJDP.

Metzler, C. W., Biglan, A., Noell, J., Ary, D. V., & Ochs, L. (2000). A randomized controlled trial of a behavioral intervention to reduce high-risk sexual behavior among adolescents in STD clinics. *Behavior Therapy, 31*(1), 27-54.

Meyer, A., Miller, S., & Herman, M. (1993). Balancing the priorities of evaluation with the priorities of the setting: A focus on positive youth development programs in school settings. *Journal of Primary Prevention, 14,* 95-113.

Meyer, A-L., Farrell, A. D., Northup, W-B., Kung, E. M., & Plybon, L. (2000). Promoting nonviolence in early adolescence: Responding in peaceful and positive ways. New York: Kluwer Academic/Plenum Publishers.

Meyer, L. A. (1984). Long-term effects of the Direct Instruction Project Follow Through. *The Elementary School Journal, 84,* 380-394.

Milburn, K. (1995). A critical review of peer education with young people with special reference to sexual health. *Health & Education Research, 10,* 407-420.

Millar, A. B. & Gruenewald, P. J. (1997). Use of spatial models for community program evaluation of changes in alcohol outlet distribution. *Addiction, 92* (supplement), S273-S283.

Miller, B. C. & Paikoff, R. L. (1992). Comparing adolescent pregnancy prevention programs: Methods and results. In B. C. Miller, J. J. Card, R. L., Paikoff, & J. L. Peterson (Eds.), *Preventing adolescent pregnancy: Model programs and evaluations* (pp. 265-284). Newbury Park, CA: Sage.

Minuchin, S. (1974). *Families & family therapy*. Oxford, England: Harvard University Press.

Mistry, J. & Saraswathi, T. S. (2003). The cultural context of child development. In I. B. Weiner (Series Ed.) & R. M. Lerner, M. A. Easterbrooks, & J. Mistry (Vol. Eds.), *Comprehensive handbook of psychology: Vol. 6. Developmental psychology* (pp. 267-291). New York: Wiley.

Mortimer, J. T. & Larson, R. W. (Eds). (2002). *The changing adolescent experience: Societal trends and the transition to adulthood*. New York: Cambridge University Press.

Mørch, W-T., Clifford, G., Rypdal, P., Larsson, B., Fossum, S., & Drugli, M. B. (2001). *Treatment of oppositional defiant and conduct disorders in 4-8 year old children, using "The Incredible Years" parents and children series*. Symposium presented at the Society for Prevention Research. Washington, D.C.

Mørch, W-T. (2003). *Early intervention to help children affected by behavioral disturbances (CD & ODD)*. Symposium presented at the Society for Prevention Research. Washington, D.C.

Moore, M. & Wade, B. (1998). Reading and Comprehension: A Longitudinal Study of Ex-Reading Recovery Students. *Educational Studies, 24*(2), 195-203.

Morehouse, E. R. (1984). *A Study of Westchester County's Student Assistance Program: Participants' Alcohol and Drug Abuse Prior to and after Counseling during the School Year 1982-1983*. Unpublished report.

Morgan, D., Grant, K. A., Gage, H. D., Mach, R. H., Kaplan, J. R., Prioleau, O., et al. (2002). Social dominance in monkeys: dopamine D_2 receptors and cocaine self-administration. *Nature, 5*(2), 169-174.

Moskalewicz, J., Sierosławski, J., Świątkiewicz, G., Zamecki, K., & Zieliński, A. (1999). *Prevention and management of drug abuse in Poland: Summary of final report*. Warsaw, Poland: Institute of Psychiatry and Neurology.

Mounts, N. S. & Steinberg, L. (1995). An ecological analysis of peer influence on adolescent grade point average and drug use. *Developmental Psychology, 31*, 915-922.

Mrazek, P. J., & Haggerty, R. J. (Eds.). (1994). *Reducing risks for mental disorders: Frontiers for preventive intervention research*. Washington, DC: National Academy Press.

Mullen, B., Muellerleile, P., & Bryant, B. (2001). Cumulative meta-analysis: A consideration of indicators of sufficiency and stability. *Personality and Social Psychology Bulletin, 27*, 1450-1462.

Murray, D. M., Clark, M. H., & Wagenaar, A. C. (2000). Intraclass correlations from a community-based alcohol prevention study: The effect of repeat observations on the same communities. *Journal of Studies on Alcohol, 61*, 881-890.

Muscott, H. S. (2000). A review and analysis of service-learning programs involving students with emotional/behavioral disorders. *Education and Treatment of Children, 23*(3), 346-368.

Muscott, H. S. & O'Brien, S. T. (1999). Teaching character education to students with behavioral and learning disabilities through mentoring relationships. *Education and Treatment of children, 22*, 373-390.

Musick, J., & Stott, F. (2000). Paraprofessionals revisited and reconsidered. In J. P. Shonkoff, & S. J. Meisels (Eds.), *Handbook of early childhood intervention, 2nd ed* (pp. 439-453). New York: Cambridge University Press.

Nash, J. K. & Bowen, G. L. (1999). Perceived crime and informal social control in the neighborhood as a context for adolescent behavior: A risk and resilience perspective. *Social Work Research, 23, 171-185*.

Nelson, G., Amio, J. L., Prilleltensky, I., & Nickels, P. (2000). Partnerships for implementing school and community prevention programs. *Journal of Educational and Psychological Consultation, 11*, 121-145.

Nelson, J. R. (1996). Designing school to meet the needs of students who exhibit disruptive behavior problems. *Journal of Emotional & Behavioral Disorders, 4*, 147-161.

Newcomb, M. D., Maddahian, E., Skager, R., & Bentler, P. M. (1987). Substance abuse and psychosocial risk factors among teenagers: Associations with sex, age, ethnicity, and type of school. *American Journal of Drug and Alcohol Abuse, 13*, 413-433.

NICHD Early Child Care Research Network. (2000). Characteristics and quality of child care for toddlers and preschoolers. *Applied Developmental Science, 4*, 116-135.

Nichols, S. L. (1999). Gay, lesbian, and bisexual youth: Understanding diversity and promoting tolerance in schools. *Elementary School Journal, 99*, 505-519.

Nicholson, H. J. & Postrado, L. T. (1992). A comprehensive age-phased approach: Girls Incorporated. In B. C. Miller, J. J. Card, R. L., Paikoff, & J. L. Peterson (Eds.), *Preventing adolescent pregnancy: Model programs and evaluations* (pp. 110-138). Newbury Park, CA: Sage.

Nitz, K. (1999). Adolescent pregnancy prevention: A review of interventions and programs. *Clinical Psychology Review, 19*, 457-471.

Norström, T. (1995). Prevention strategies and alcohol policy. *Addiction, 90*, 515-524.

Nothwehr, F., Lando, H. A., & Bobo, J-K. (1995). Alcohol and tobacco use in the Minnesota Heart Health Program. *Addictive Behaviors, 20*, 463-470.

Nurmi, J. E. (1993a). Adolescent development in an age-graded context: The role of personal beliefs, goals, and strategies in the tackling of developmental tasks and standards. *International Journal of Behavioral Development, 16*, 169-189

Nurmi, J. E. (1993b). Self-handicapping and a failure-trap strategy: A cognitive approach to problem behaviour and delinquency. *Psychiatria Fennica, 24*, 75-85.

Nurmi, J. E., Berzonsky, M. D., Tammi, K., & Kinney, A. (1997). Identity processing orientation, cognitive and behavioural strategies and well-being. *International Journal of Behavioral Development, 21*, 555-570.

Nurmi, J. E., Salmela-Aro, A. K., & Haavisto, T. (1995). The strategy and attribution questionnaire: Psychometric properties. *European Journal of Psychological Assessment. 11*, 108-121

Nurmi, J. E., Salmela-Aro, A. K., & Ruotsalainen, H. (1994). Cognitive and attributional strategies among unemployed young adults: A case of the failure-trap strategy. *European Journal of Personality, 8*, 135-148.

Nye, C. L., Zucker, R. A., & Fitzgerald, H. E. (1995). Early intervention in the path to alcohol problems through conduct problems: Treatment involvement and child behavior change. *Journal of Consulting and Clinical Psychology, 63*, 831-840.

Nye, C. L., Zucker, R. A., & Fitzgerald, H. E. (1999). Early family-based intervention in the path to alcohol problems: Rationale and relationship between treatment process characteristics and child and parenting outcomes. *Journal of Studies on Alcohol, 13*, 10-21.

Oden, S. & Asher, S. R. (1977). Coaching children in social skills for friendship making. *Child Development, 48*, 495-506.

O'Donnell. J., Hawkins, J. D., Catalano, R. F., Abbott, R. D., & Day, L. E. (1995). Preventing school failure, drug use, and delinquency among low-income children: Long-term intervention in elementary schools. *American Journal of Orthopsychiatry, 65*(1), 87-100.

O'Donnell, L., Stueve, A., San Doval, A., Duran, R., Atnafou, R., Haber, D., et al. (1999). Violence prevention and young adolescents' participation in community youth service. *Journal of Adolescent Health, 24*, 28-37.

O'Farrell, T. J. & Feehan, M. (1999). Alcoholism treatment and the family: Do family and individual treatments for alcoholic adults have preventive effects for children? *Journal of Studies on Alcohol, 13(Suppl)*, 125-129.

Ogden, T. (2000). *Parent Management Training: Evaluation of treatment effectiveness.* Center for Research in Clinical Psychology, Institute of Psychology, University of Oslo, Norway.

Ogden, T. (2001). *Updating the Norwegian MST Clinical Trial.* Center for Research in Clinical Psychology, Institute of Psychology, University of Oslo, Norway.

Okabayashi, H. (1996). Intervention for school bullying: Observing American schools. *Psychologia: An International Journal of Psychology in the Orient, 39*, 163-178.

Oldenburg, B. (2002). Preventing chronic disease and improving health: Broadening the scope of behavioral medicine research and practice. *International Journal of Behavioral Medicine, 9*(1), 1-16.

Olds, D. L. (1997). The prenatal/early infancy project: Fifteen years later. In G. W. Albee & T. P. Gullotta (Eds.), *Primary prevention works* (pp. 41-67). Thousand Oaks, CA: Sage.

Olds, D. L. (2002). Prenatal and infancy home visiting by nurses: From randomized trials to community replication. *Prevention Science, 3*(3), 153-172.

Olds, D. L. & Henderson, C. R. (1994). Does prenatal and infancy home visitation have enduring effects on qualities of parental caregiving and child health at 25 to 50 months of life? *Pediatrics, 93*(1), 89-99.

Olds, D. L., Henderson, C. R., Birmingham, M., Chamberlin, R., & Tatelbaum, R. (1983). *Final report: Prenatal/Early Infancy Project. Final report to Maternal and Child Health and Crippled Children's Services Research Grants Program*, Bureau of Community Health Services, HSA, PHS, DHHS, Grant No. MCJ-36040307.

Olds, D. L., Henderson, C. R., Cole, R., Eckenrode, J., Kitzman, H., Luckey, D., Pettitt, L., Sidora, K., Morris, P., & Powers, J. (1998). Long-term effects of nurse home visitation on children's criminal and antisocial behavior: 15 year follow-up of a randomized control trial. *Journal of the American Medical Association, 280*, 1238-1244.

Olds, D. L., Henderson, C. R., Phelps, C., Kitzman, H., & Hanks, C. (1993). Effect of prenatal and infancy nurse home visitation on government spending. *Medical Care, 31*, 155-174.

Olds, D. L., Henderson, C. R., Tatelbaum, R., & Chamberlin, R. (1988). Improving the life-course development of socially disadvantaged mothers: A randomized trial of nurse home visitation. *American Journal of Public Health, 78*, 1436-1445.

Olds, D. L. & Kitzman, H. (1993). Review of research on home visiting for pregnant women and parents of young children. *Future of Children, 3*(3), 53-92.

Olds, D., Robinson, J., Song, N., Little, C., & Hill, P. (1999). *Reducing risks for mental disorders during the first five years of life: A review of preventive interventions.* Manuscript submitted to the Center for Mental Health Services (CMHS).

Olweus, D. (1993). Bully/victim problems among schoolchildren: Long-term consequences and an effective intervention program. In S. Hodgins (Ed). *Mental disorder and crime* (pp. 317-349). Thousand Oaks, CA: Sage.

Olweus, D. (1994). Annotation: Bullying at school: Basic facts and effects of a school based intervention program. *Journal of Child Psychology and Psychiatry and Allied Disciplines, 35*, 1171-1190.

Olweus, D. (1997). Bully/victim problems in school: Facts and intervention. *European Journal of Psychology of Education, 12*, 495-510.

Olweus, D., & Alsaker, F. D. (1994). Assessing change in a cohort-longitudinal study with hierarchical data. In D. Magnusson, L. R. Bergman, G. Rudinger, & B. Toerestad (Eds.), *Problems and methods in longitudinal research: Stability and change.*

European Network on Longitudinal Studies on Individual Development, 5 (pp. 107-132). New York: Cambridge University Press.

Olweus, D., Limber, S. & Mihalic, S. F. (1999). *Blueprints for Violence Prevention, Book Nine: Bullying Prevention Program.* Boulder, CO: Center for the Study and Prevention of Violence.

Ondersma, S. J., Simpson, S. M., Brestan, E. V., & Ward, M (2000). Prenatal drug exposure and social policy: The search for an appropriate response. *Child Maltreatment: Journal of the American Professional Society on the Abuse of Children, 5,* 93-108.

Orpinus, P., Kelder, S., Frankowski, R., Murray, N., Zhang, Q., & McAlister, A. (2000). Outcome evaluation of a multi-component violence-prevention program for middle schools: The Students for Peace project. *Health Education Research, 15,* 45-58.

Ortega, R. & Lera, M. J. (2000). The Seville Anti-Bullying in School Project. *Aggressive Behavior, 26,* 113-123.

Ostrom, C. W., Lerner, R. M., & Freel, M. A. (1995). Building the capacity of youth and families through university-community collaborations: The Development-In-Context Evaluation (DICE) Model. *Journal of Adolescent Research, 10*(4), 427-448.

Ostrow, D. G., & Kalichman, S. (2000). Methodological issues in HIV behavioral interventions. In J. L. Peterson, R. J. DiClemente, (Eds.). *Handbook of HIV prevention. AIDS prevention and mental health.* (pp. 67-80).

Paikoff, R. L., McCormick, A., & Sagrestano, L. M. (2000). Adolescent sexuality. In L. Szuchman & F. Muscarella (Eds.), *Psychological perspectives on human sexuality* (pp. 416-439). New York: Wiley.

Paine-Andrews, A., Fawcett, S. B., Richter, K. P., Berkley, J. Y., Williams, E. L., & Lopez, C. M. (1996). Community coalitions to prevent adolescent substance abuse: The case of the "Project Freedom" Replication Initiative. *Journal of Prevention & Intervention in the Community, 14*(1-2), 81-99.

Park, J., Kosterman, R. Hawkins, J. D., Haggerty, K. P., Duncan, T. E. Duncan, S. C., & Spoth, R. (2000). Effects of the "Preparing for the Drug Free Years" curriculum on growth in alcohol use and risk for alcohol use in early adolescence. *Prevention Science, 1,* 125-138.

Parsons, B. V. & Alexander, J. F. (1973). Short-term family intervention: A therapy outcome study. *Journal of Consulting and Clinical Psychology, 41,* 195-201.

Patterson, G. R. (1982). *Coercive family process.* Eugene, OR: Castalia.

Patterson, G. R. (1992). Developmental changes in antisocial behavior. In R. DeV. Peters, R. J. McMahon, & V. L. Quinsey (Eds.), *Aggression and violence throughout the lifespan* (pp. 52-82). Newbury Park, CA: Sage.

Patterson, G. & Forgatch, M. (1987). Parents and adolescents living together: Part 1. *The basics.* Eugene, OR: Castalia.

Patterson, G. R., & Narrett, C. M. (1990). The development of a reliable and valid treatment program for aggressive young children. *International Journal of Mental Health, 19,* 19-26.

Patterson, G. R., Dishion, T. J. & Chamberlain, P. (1993). Outcomes and methodological issues relating to treatment of antisocial children. In T. R. Giles (Ed.) *Handbook of effective psychotherapy.* Plenum behavior therapy series (pp. 43-88). New York: Plenum.

Patterson, G. R., Reid, J. B., & Dishion, T. J. (1992). *Antisocial boys: A social interactional approach, Volume 4.* Eugene, OR: Castalia Publishing Company.

Patterson, J., Barlow, J., Stewart-Brown, S., Mockford, C., Klimes, I., & Pyper, C., (2002). *Improving mental health among children and their parents through parenting programmes in general practice: A randomised controlled trial.* Submitted for publication.

Pekurinen, M. & Valtonen, H. (1987). Price, policy and consumption of tobacco: The Finnish experience. *Social Science Medicine, 25*(8), 875-881.

Pentz, M. A. (2000). Institutionalizing community-based prevention through policy change. *Journal of Community Psychology, 28*, 257-270.

Pentz, M. A., Bonnie, R. J., & Shopland, D. S. (1996). Integrating supply and demand reduction strategies for drug abuse prevention. *American Behavioral Scientist, 39*, 897-910.

Pentz, M. A., Dwyer, J. H., MacKinnon, D. P., Flay, B., Hansen, W. B., Wang, E. Y. I., & Johnson, C. A. (1989). A multi-community trial for primary prevention of adolescent drug abuse. *Journal of the American Medical Association, 261*, 3259-3266.

Pentz, M. A., Trebow, E. A., Hansen, W. B., MacKinnon, D. P., Dwyer, J. H., Flay, B. R., Daniels, S., Cormack, C., & Johnson, C. A. (1990). Effects of program implementation on adolescent drug use behavior: The Midwestern Prevention Project (MPP). *Evaluation Review, 14*, 264-289.

Pepler, D. J., Craig, W. M., Ziegler, S. & Charach, A. (1994). An evaluation of an anti-bullying intervention in Toronto schools. *Canadian Journal of Community Mental Health, 13*, 95-110.

Perhats, C., Oh, K., Levy, S. R., Flay, B. R., & McFall, S. (1996). Role differences in gatekeeper perceptions of school-based drug and sexuality education programs: A cross-sectional survey. *Health Education Research, 11*, 11-27.

Perrino, T., Coatsworth, J. D., Briones, E., Pantin, H., & Szapocznik, J. (2001). Initial engagement in parent-centered preventive interventions: A family systems perspective. *Journal of Primary Prevention, 22*, 21-44.

Perry, C. L. (1999). *Creating health behavior change: How to develop community-wide programs for youth.* Thousand Oaks, CA: Sage.

Perry, C. L. & Grant, M. (1991). A cross-cultural pilot study on alcohol education and young people. *Rapp. Trimest. Statist. Sanit. Mond., 44*, 70-73.

Perry, C. L., Grant, M., Ernberg, G., Florenzano, R. U., Langdon, M. C., Myeni, A. D., et al. (1989). WHO collaborative study on alcohol education and young people: Outcomes of a four-country pilot study. *The International Journal of the Addictions, 24*, 1145-1171.

Perry, C. L., Kelder, S., Murray, D. M., & Klepp, K. (1992). Community-wide smoking prevention: Long-term outcomes of the Minnesota Heart Health Program and the Class of 1989 Study. *American Journal of Public Health, 82*, 1210-1216.

Perry, C. L., Klepp, K-I., & Sillers, C. (1989). Community-wide strategies for cardiovascular health: The Minnesota Heart Health Program youth program. *Health Education Research, 4*, 87-101.

Perry, C. L., Williams, C. L., Forster, J. L., Wolfson, M., Wagenaar, A. C., Finnegan, J.R., et al. (1993). Background, conceptualization and design of a community-wide research program on adolescent alcohol use: Project Northland. *Health Education Research, 8*, 125-136.

Perry, C. L., Williams, C. L., Komro, K. A., Veblen-Mortenson, S., Forster, J. L., Bernstein-Lachter, R., et al. (2000). Project Northland high school interventions: Community action to reduce adolescent alcohol use. *Health Education and Behavior, 27*, 29-49.

Perry, C. L., Williams, C. L., Veblen-Mortenson, S., Toomey, T. L. Komro, K., Anstine, P. S., et al. (1996). Project Northland: Outcomes of a communitywide alcohol use prevention program during early adolescence. *American Journal of Public Health, 86*, 7, 956-965.

Peterson, G. W. (1995). The need for common principles in prevention programs for children, adolescents, and families. *Journal of Adolescent Research, 10*(4), 470-485.

Peterson, J. L. & DiClemente, R. J. (Eds.). (2000). *Handbook of HIV prevention.* New York: Kluwer Academic/Plenum.

Pettit, G. S. (1997). The developmental course of violence and aggression: Mechanisms of family and peer influence. *The Psychiatric Clinics of North America, 20*, 283-299.

Posavac, E. J., Kattapong, K. R., & Dew, D. E. (1999). Peer-based interventions to influence health related-behaviors and attitudes: A meta-analysis. *Psychological Reports, 85,* 1179-1194.

Petitpas, A. J. & Champagne, D. E. (2000). Sports and social competence. In S. J. Danish & T. P. Gullotta (Eds.), *Developing competent youth and strong communities through after-school programming* (pp. 115-138). Washington, DC: CWLA.

Philip, K. & Hendry, L. B. (2000). Making sense of mentoring or mentoring making sense? Reflections on the mentoring process by adult mentors with young people. *Journal of Community & Applied Social Psychology, 10,* 211-223.

Piaget, J. (1932/1965). *The moral judgment of the child.* Oxford, England: Harcourt, Brace.

Pickrel, S. G. & Henggeler, S. W. (1996). Multisystemic therapy for adolescent substance abuse and dependence. *Child & Adolescent Psychiatric Clinics of North America, 5,* 201-211.

Piquero, A. & Tibbetts, S. (1999). The impact of pre/perinatal disturbances and disadvantaged familial environment in predicting criminal offending. *Studies on Crime and Crime Prevention, 8,* 52-70.

Plested, B., Smithman, D. M., Jumper-Thurman, P., Oetting, E. R., & Edwards, R. W. (1999). Readiness for drug use prevention in rural minority communities. *Substance Use & Misuse, 34*(4-5), 521-544.

Posavac, E. J., Kattapong, K. R., & Dew, D. E. Jr. (1999). Peer-based interventions to influence health-related behaviors and attitudes: A meta-analysis. *Psychological Reports, 85,* 1179-1194.

Poulin, F., Dishion, T. J., & Burraston, B. (in press). Long-term iatrogenic effects associated with aggregating high-risk adolescents in preventive interventions. *Applied Developmental Science.*

Poulin, F., Dishion, T. J., & Haas, E. (1999). The peer influence paradox: Friendship quality and deviancy training within male adolescent friendships. *Merrill-Palmer Quarterly, 45,* 42-61.

Preski, S. & Shelton, D. (2001). The role of contextual, child, and parent factors in predicting criminal outcomes in adolescence. *Issues In Mental Health Nursing, 22,* 197-205.

Prinz, R. J., Blechman, E. A., & Dumas, J. E. (1994). An evaluation of peer coping-skills training for childhood aggression. *Journal of Clinical Child Psychology, 23,* 193-203.

Prinz, R. J., Smith, E. P, Dumas, J. E., Laughlin, J. E., White, D., & Barron, R. (2001). Recruitment and retention of participants in prevention trials involving family-based interventions. *American Journal of Preventive Medicine, 20,* 31-37.

Pritchard, C. (2001). *A family-teacher-social work alliance to reduce truancy and delinquency – the Dorset Healthy Alliance Project.* London, United Kingdom: Home Office, RDS Communications Development Unit.

Pritchard, C. (1998). *A family, teacher, and social work alliance to reduce truancy and delinquency. A report to the Programme Development Unit.* London, United Kingdom: Home Office, RDS Communications Development Unit.

Preusser, D. F. & Williams, A. F. (1992). Sales of alcohol to underage purchasers in three New York counties and Washington, DC. *Journal of Public Health Policy, 13,* 306-317.

Prokhorov, A. V., Perry, C. L., Kelder, S. H., & Klepp, K-I. (1993). Lifestyle values of adolescents: Results from Minnesota Heart Health Youth Program. *Adolescence, 28,* 637-647.

Puska, P. & Uutela, A. (2001). Community intervention in cardiovascular health promotion: North Karelia, 1972-1999. In N. Schneiderman, M. A. Speers, J. M. Silva, H. Tomes, & J. H. Gentry (Eds.), *Integrating behavioral and social sciences with public health* (pp. 73-96). Washington, DC: American Psychological Association.

Puska, P., Vartiainen, E., Pallonen, U., Salonen, J. T., Poyhia, P., Koskela, K., et al. (1982). The North Karelia Youth Project: evaluation of two years' intervention on health behaviour and CVD risk factors among 13- to 15-yearold children. *Prevention Medicine, 11,* 550-570.

Puura, K., Davis, H., Papadopoulou, K., Tsiantis, J., Ispanovic-Radojkovic, V., Rudic, N., et al. (2002). The European Early Promotion Project: A new primary health care service to promote children' mental health. *Infant Mental Health Journal, 23*(6), 606-624.

Quinn, J. (1999). Where need meets opportunity: Youth development programs for early teens. *The Future of Children, 9,* 96-116.

Quinn, M. M., Kavale, K. A., Mathur, S. R., Rutherform, R. B., & Forness, S. R. (1999). A meta-analysis of social skill interventions for students with emotional or behavioral disorders. *Journal of Emotional and Behavioral Disorders, 7,* 54-64.

Raine, A., Brennan, P., Farrington, D. P., & Mednick, S. A. (Eds.). (1997). *Biosocial bases of violence.* New York: Plenum.

Ramey, C. T., Campbell, F. A. (1987). The Carolina Abecedarian Project: An educational experiment concerning human malleability. In J. J. Gallagher & C. T. Ramey (Eds.), *The malleability of children* (pp. 127-140). Baltimore, MD: Brookes.

Ramey, C. T., Bryant, D. M., Wasik, B. H., Sparling, J. J., Fendt, K. H., LaVange, L. M. (1992). Infant Health and Development Program for low birth weight, premature infants: Program elements, family participation, and child intelligence. *Pediatrics, 3,* 454-465.

Randall, J., Swenson, C. C., & Henggeler, S. W. (1999). Neighborhood solutions for neighborhood problems: An empirically based violence prevention collaboration. *Health Education & Behavior, 26*(6), 806-820.

Raywid, M. A. (1994). Alternative schools: The state of the art. *Educational Leadership, 52,* 26-31.

Redmond, C., Spoth, R., Shin, C., & Lepper, H. (1999). Modeling long-term parent outcomes of two universal family focused preventive interventions: One-year follow-up results. *Journal of Consulting and Clinical Psychology, 67*(6), 975-984.

Redondo, S., Sánchez-Meca, J., & Garrido, V. (1999). The influence of treatment programmes on the recidivism of juvenile and adult offenders: An European meta-analytic review. *Psychology Crime and Law, 5,* 251-278.

Reid, J. B., & Eddy, J. M. (1997). The prevention of antisocial behavior: Some considerations in the search for effective interventions. In D. M. Stoff, J. Breiling, & J. D. Maser (Eds.), *The handbook of antisocial behavior* (pp. 343-356). New York: John Wiley & Sons.

Reiss, D., Neiderhiser, J. M., Hetherington, E. M., & Plomin, R. (2000). *The relationship code: Deciphering genetic and social influences on adolescent development.* Cambridge, MA: Harvard University Press.

Reppucci, N. D., Woolard, J. L., & Fried, C. S. (1999). Social, community, and preventive interventions. *Annual Review of Psychology, 50,* 387-418.

Resnicow, K., Cohn, L., Reinhardt, J., Cross, D., Futterman, R., Kirschner, E., Wynder, E. L., Allegrante, J. P. (1992). A three-year evaluation of the Know Your Body Program in inner-city schoolchildren. *Health Education Quarterly, 19,* 463-480.

Resnicow, K., Soler, R., Braithwaite, R. L., Ahluwalia, J. S., & Butler, J. (2000). Cultural sensitivity in substance use prevention. *Journal of Community Psychology, 28,* 271-290.

Reynolds, R. I., Holder, H. D. & Gruenewald, P. J. (1997). Community prevention and alcohol retail access. *Addiction, 92* (supplement), S261-S272.

Reynolds, A., & Temple, J. A. (1998). Extended early childhood intervention and school achievement: Age thirteen findings from the Chicago Longitudinal Study. *Child Development, 69,* 231-246.

Rhodes, T., Lilly, R., Fernandez, C., Giorgino, E., Kemmesis, U. E., Ossebaard, H. C., Lalam, N., Faasen, I., & Spannow, K. E. (1997). *Risk factors associated with drug use: The importance of 'risk environment'*. Lisbon, Portugal: European Monitoring Centre for Drugs and Drug Addiction.

Riksen-Walraven, M. J., Meij, J-T., Hubbard, F. O., & Zevalkink, J. (1996). Intervention in lower-class Surinam-Dutch families: Effects on mothers and infants. *International Journal of Behavioral Development, 19*(4), 739-756.

Robinson, L. A., Klesges, R. C., & Zbikowski, S. M. (1998). Gender and ethnic differences in youth adolescents' sources of cigarettes. *Tobacco Control, 7*, 353-359.

Roditti, M. G. (2000). What works in child care. In M. P. Kluger, G. Alexander & P. A. Curtis (Eds.), *What works in child welfare* (pp. 285-292). Washington, DC: CWLA.

Rogers, M., & Peoples-Sheps, M. D. (1995). Translating research into MCH service: Comparison of a pilot project with a large-scale resource. *Public Health Reports, 110*(5), 563-570.

Rohrbach, L. A., D'Onofrio, C. N., Backer, T. E., & Montgomery, S. B. (1996). Diffusion of school-based substance abuse prevention programs. *American Behavioral Scientist, 39*, 919-934.

Roker, D. & Coleman, J. (1998). 'Parenting teenagers' programmes: A UK perspective. *Children & Society, 12*, 359-372.

Roland, E. (2000). Bullying in school: Three national innovations in Norwegian schools in 15 years. *Aggressive Behavior, 26*, 135-143.

Romelsjö, A. (1987). Decline in alcohol-related in-patient care and mortality in Stockholm County. *British Journal of Addiction, 82*, 653-663.

Romelsjö, A. (1998). *Evaluation of the adoption and implementation of alcohol and drug policy and prevention programs in the 24 districts in Stockholm: Application to the Council for Social Research and to the National Public Health Institute for program support*. Huddinge, Sweden: Centrum för Alkohol och Drogprevention (CADP) - Novum.

Romelsjö A., Andren, A., & Borg, S. (1993). Design, implementation, and evaluation of a community action program for prevention of alcohol-related problems in Stockholm City: initial experiences. In T. K. Greenfield & R. Zimmerman (Eds.), *CSAP Prevention Monograph - 14. Experiences with community action projects: new research in the prevention of alcohol and other drug problems* (pp. 130-137). Rockville MD: Center for Substance Abuse Prevention.

Romelsjö, A. & Haeggman, U. (2000). *Plan för evaluering av Stockholm stads Alkohol Preventiva Program (ESAPP)*. Huddinge, Sweden: Centrum för Alkohol och Drogprevention (CADP) - Novum.

Romualdi, V. & Sandoval, J. (1995). Comprehensive school-linked services: Implications for school psychologists. *Psychology in the Schools, 32*, 306-317.

Roosa, M. W., Dumka, L. E., Gonzales, N. A., & Knight, G. P. (2002). Cultural/ethnic issues and the prevention scientist in the 21st century. *Prevention and Treatment, 5*, np.

Rosenthal, R. & Rosnow, R. L. (1991). *Essentials of behavioral research: Methods and data analysis* (2nd ed.). New York: McGraw-Hill

Roski, J., Perry, C. L., McGovern, P. G., Williams, C. L. Farbakhsh, K., & Veblen-Mortenson, S. (1997). School and community influences on adolescent alcohol and drug use. *Health Education Research, 12*, 255-266.

Ross, D. M. (1996). *Childhood bullying and teasing: What school personnel, other professionals, and parents can do*. New York: Routledge.

Ross, J. G., Einhaus, K. E., Hohenemser, L. K., Greene, B. Z., Kann, L., & Gold, R. S. (1995). School health policies prohibiting tobacco use, alcohol and other drug use, and violence. *Journal of School Health, 65*, 333-338.

Ross, J. G., Saavedra, P. J., Shur, G. H., Winters, F., & Felner, R. D. (1992). The effectiveness of an after-school program for primary grade latchkey children on precursors of substance use. *Journal of Community Psychology, Special Issue*, 22-38.

Roth, J., Brooks-Gunn, J., Murray, L., & Foster, W. (1998). Promoting healthy adolescents: Synthesis of youth development program evaluations. *Journal of Research on Adolescence, 8,* 423-459.

Rowe, K. J. (1989). *100 schools project. Summary report of second stage results.* Melbourne, Australia: Ministry of Education, School Programs Division.

Rutter, M. (1987). Psychosocial resilience and protective mechanisms. *American Journal of Orthopsychiatry, 57*(3), 316-331.

Rutter, M. (1989). Pathways from childhood to adult life. *Journal of Child Psychology and Psychiatry, 30,* 23-51.

Rutter, M. (2000). Resilience reconsidered: Conceptual considerations, empirical findings, and policy implications. In J. P. Shonkoff & S. J. Meisels (Eds.), *Handbook of early childhood intervention* (pp. 651-682). New York: Cambridge University Press.

St. Lawrence, J. S., Brasfield, T. L., Jefferson, K. W., Alleyne, E., O'Bannon, R. E., & Shirley, A. (1995). Cognitive-behavioral intervention to reduce African-American adolescents' risk for HIV infection. *Journal of Consulting and Clinical Psychology, 63,* 221-237.

St. Pierre, T. L., Kaltreider, D. L., Mark, M. M., & Aikin, K. J. (1992). Drug prevention in a community setting: A longitudinal study of the relative effectiveness of a three-year primary prevention program in Boys & Girls Clubs across the nation. American *Journal of Community Psychology, 20,* 673-706.

St. Pierre, T. L., Mark, M. M., Kaltreider, D. L., & Aikin, K. J. (1997). Involving parents of high-risk youth in drug prevention: A three-year longitudinal study in Boys & Girls Clubs. American *Journal of Early Adolescence, 17,* 21-50.

St. Pierre, T. L. Mark, M. M., Kaltreider, D. L., & Campbell, B. (2001). Boys & Girls Clubs and school collaborations: A longitudinal study of a multicomponent substance abuse prevention program for high-risk elementary school children. *Journal of Community Psychology, 29,* 87-106.

Sattler, J. M. (1992). Assessment of children's intelligence. In C. E. Walker & M. C. Roberts (Eds.), *Handbook of clinical child psychology* (pp. 85-100). Oxford, England: John Wiley & Sons.

Salovey, P. & Mayer, J. D. (1990). Emotional intelligence. *Imagination, Cognition and Personality, 9,* 185-211.

Salovey, P. & Sluyter, D. J. (Eds.). (1997). *Emotional development and emotional intelligence: Educational implications.* New York: Basic Books.

Saltz, R. F. & Stanghetta, P. (1997). A community-wide Responsible Beverage Service program in three communities: early findings. *Addiction, 92* (supplement 2), S237-S249.

Sameroff, A. & Chandler, M. J. (1975). Reproductive risk and the continuum of caretaking casualty. In F. D. Horowitz (Ed.), *Review of child development research, Vol. 4* (pp. 187-244). Chicago: University of Chicago Press.

Sameroff, A. J. & Fiese, B. H. (2000). Transactional regulation: The developmental ecology of early intervention. In J. P. Shonkoff & S. J. Meisels (Eds.), *Handbook of early childhood intervention* (pp. 135-159). New York: Cambridge University Press.

Samples, F. & Aber, L. (1998). Evaluations of school-based violence prevention programs. In D. S. Elliott, B. A. Hamburg (Eds.), *Violence in American schools: A new perspective* (pp. 217-252). New York: Cambridge University Press.

Sanders, M. R. (2000). Community-based parenting and family support interventions and the prevention of drug abuse. *Addictive Behaviors, 25*(6), 929-942.

Schinke, S. P. (1994). Prevention science and practice: An agenda for action. *Journal of Primary Prevention, 15,* 45-57.

Schinke, S. P., Botvin, G. J., Trimble, J. E. Orlandi, M. A., Gilchrist, L. D., & Locklear, V. S. (1988). Preventing substance abuse among American-Indian adolescents: A bicultural competence skills approach. *Journal of Counseling Psychology, 35*, 87-90.

Schinke, S. P., Brounstein, P., & Gardner, S. (2002). *Science-based prevention programs and principles*. DHHS Pub. No. (SMA) 03-3764. Rockville, MD: Center for Substance Abuse Prevention, Substance Abuse and Mental Health Services Administration.

Schinke, S. P., Orlandi, M. A., & Cole, K. C. (1992). Boys & Girls Clubs in public housing developments: Prevention services for youth at risk. *Journal of Community Psychology, OSAP Special Issue*, 118-128.

Schmidt, H. G. & Moust, J. H. C. (2000). Factors affecting small-group tutorial learning: A review of research. In D. H. Evensen, H. Dorothy, & C. E. Hmelo (Eds.), Problem-based learning: A research perspective on learning interactions (pp. 19-51). Mahwah, NJ: Lawrence Erlbaum.

Schneider, B. H. (1992). Didactic methods for enhancing children's peer relations: A quantitative review. *Clinical Psychology Review, 12*(3), 363-382.

Schulenberg, J., Maggs, J. L., & Hurrelmann, K. (Eds.) (1997). *Health risks and developmental transitions during adolescence*. New York: Cambridge University Press.

Schulenberg, J., Wadsworth, K. N., O'Malley, P. M., Bachman, J. G., & Johnston, L. D. (1996). Adolescent risk factors for binge drinking during the transition to young adulthood: Variable- and pattern –centered approaches to change. *Developmental Psychology, 32*, 659-674.

Schweinhart, L., McNair, S., Barnes, H., & Larner, M. (1993). Observing young children in action to assess their development: The High/Scope Child Observation Record study. *Educational and Psychological Measurement, 53*(2), 445-455

Schweinhart, L. J., & Weikart, D. P. (1989). The High/Scope Perry Preschool study: Implications for early childhood care and education. Prevention in Human Services, 7, 109-132.

Scott, S. (in press). Parent training programmes. In M. Rutter & E. Talyor (Eds.), *Child and Adolescent Psychiatry*. Oxford: Blackwell Science.

Scott, S., Spender, Q., Doolan, M., Jacobs, B., & Aspland, H. (2001). Multicentre controlled trial of parenting groups for childhood antisocial behaviour in clinical practice. *British Medical Journal, 323*, 194-197.

Scott, S., Knapp, M., Henderson, J., & Maughan, B. (2001). Financial cost of social exclusion: Follow up study of antisocial children into adulthood. *British Medical Journal, 323*, 1-5.

Seidman, E., Yoshikawa, H., Roberts, A., Chesir-Teran, D., Allen, L., Friedman, J., et al. (1998). Structural and experimental neighborhood contexts, developmental stage, and antisocial behavior among urban adolescents in poverty. *Development and Psychopathology, 10*, 259-281.

Seidman, S. N., & Reider, R. O. (1994). A review of sexual behavior in the United States. *American Journal of Psychiatry, 151*, 330-341.

Seitz, V. (1996). Adolescent pregnancy and parenting. In E. F. Zigler, S. L. Kagan, & N. W. Hall (Eds.), Children, families, and government: Preparing for the twenty-first century (pp. 268-287). New York: Cambridge University Press.

Seitz, V., & Apfel, N. H. (1994). Effects of a school for pregnant students on the incidence of low-birthweight deliveries. *Child Development, 65*, 666-676.

Seitz, V., Rosenbaum, L. K., & Apfel, N. H. (1985). Effects of family support intervention: A ten-year follow-up. *Child Development, 56*(2), 376-391.

Serketich, W. J. & Dumas, J. E. (1996). The effectiveness of behavioral parent training to modify antisocial behavior in children: A meta-analysis. *Behavior Therapy, 27*, 171-186.

Shanahan, T. & Barr, R. (1995). Reading recovery: An independent evaluation of the effects of an early instructional intervention for at-risk learners. *Reading Research Quarterly, 30,* 958-996.

Shanahan, M. J., Mortimer, J. T., & Krueger, H. (2002). Adolescence and adult work in the twenty-first century. *Journal of Research on Adolescence, 12,* 99-120.

Sharma, A. & Griffin, T. (1999). *An evaluation of Project Charlie.* Edina, Minnesota: Storefront/Youth Action.

Sharp, S. (1996). Self-esteem, response style and victimization: Possible ways of preventing victimization through parenting and school based training programs. *School Psychology International, 17,* 347-357.

Sherman, L. W. Gottfredson, D. C., MacKenzie, D. L., Eck, J., Reuter, P., & Bushway, S. D. (1997). (Eds.), *Preventing crime: What works, what doesn't, what's promising: A report to the United States Congress.* Washington, DC: U.S. Department of Justice.

Sherman, L. W. Gottfredson, D. C., MacKenzie, D. L., Eck, J., Reuter, P., & Bushway, S. D. (1998). *Preventing crime: What works, what doesn't, what's promising.* Washington, DC: U.S. Department of Justice, Office of Justice Programs, NIJ Research in Brief (NCJ 171676).

Shweder, R. A., & Jensen, L. (1997, April). *Who sleeps by whom: What experts say, what anthropologists know.* Paper presented at Society for Research on Child Development, Washington, DC.

Shumow, L., Vandell, D. L., & Posner, J. (1998). Perceptions of danger: A psychological mediator of neighborhood demographic characteristics. *American Journal of Orthopsychiatry, 68,* 468-478.

Shure, M. B. (1997). Interpersonal cognitive problem solving: Primary prevention of early high-risk behaviors in the preschool and primary years. In G. W. Albee, & T. P. Gullotta, (Eds.), *Primary prevention works. Issues in children's and families' lives, 6,* (pp. 167-188). Thousand Oaks, CA, US: Sage Publications, Inc.

Shure, M. B. & Spivack, G. (1988). Interpersonal Cognitive Problem Solving. In R. H. Price, & E. L. Cowen, R. P. Lorion, & J. Ramos-McKay (Eds.), *Fourteen ounces of prevention: A casebook for practitioners.* (pp. 69-82). Washington, DC, US: American Psychological Association.

Silverman, M. M. (2003). Theories of primary prevention and health promotion. In T. Gullotta & M. Bloom (Series Ed.) & T. Gullotta & M. Bloom (Vol. Ed.), *The encyclopedia of primary prevention and health promotion: Foundations Volume* (pp. 27-42). New York: Kluwer Academic/Plenum.

Simeonsson, R. J. & Simeonsson, N. E. (1999). Designing community-based school health services for at-risk students. *Journal of Educational and Psychological Consultation, 10,* 215-228.

Skinner, C. H. & Smith, E. S. (1992). Issues surrounding the use of self-management interventions for increasing academic performance. *School Psychology Review, 21,* 202-210.

Slavin, R. E. (1995). Best evidence synthesis: An intelligent alternative to meta-analysis. *Journal of Clinical Epidemiology, 48,* 9-18.

Slavin, R. E., Karweit, N. L., & Wasik, B. A. (Eds.) (1994). *Preventing early school failure: Research, policy, and practice.* Needham Heights, MA: Allyn & Bacon.

Slavin, R. E., Karweit, N. L., Wasik, B. A., Madden, N. A., & Dolan, L. J. (1994). Success for All: A comprehensive approach to prevention and early intervention. In R. E. Slavin, N. L. Karwiet & B. A. Wasik (Eds.), *Preventing early school failure: Research, policy, and practice* (pp. 175-205). Needham Heights, MA: Allyn & Bacon.

Slavin, R. E. & Madden, N. A. (2001). *One million children: Success for All.* Thousand Oaks, CA, Corwin Press, Inc.

Sloboda, Z. & David, S. L. (1997). *Preventing drug use among children and adolescents: A research-based guide.* Washington, DC: National Institute on Drug Abuse.

Smith, P. K., Morita, Y., Junger-Tas, J., Olweus, D., Catalano, R., & Slee, P. (1999). *The nature of school bullying: A cross-national perspective.* London: Routledge.

Smith, D. W., Redican, K. J. & Olsen, L. K. (1992). The longevity of growing healthy: An analysis of the eight original sties implementing the School Health Curriculum Project. *Journal of School Health, 62(3),* 83-87.

Smith, P. K. & Sharp, S. (Eds.). (1994). *School bullying: Insights and perspectives.* London, England: Routledge.

Socialstyrelsen. (1996:7). *Hälsovård före, under och efter graviditet.* SoS rapport. Stockholm: Sweden: Author.

Sokol-Katz, J., Dunham, R., Zimmerman, R. (1997). Family structure versus parental attachment in controlling adolescent deviant behavior: A social control model. *Adolescence, 32(125),* 199-215.

Sosale, S., Finnegan, J. R., Schmid, L. Perry, C., & Wolfson, M. (1999). Adolescent alcohol use and the community health agenda: A study of leaders' perceptions in 28 small towns. *Health Education Research, 14(1),* 7-14.

SOU. (2000/01:20). Nationell Handlingsplan för att Förebygga Alkoholskador.

Spaccarelli, S., Cotler, S., & Penman, D. (1992). Problem-solving skills training as a supplement to behavioral parent training. *Cognitive Therapy & Research, 16,* 1-17.

Spaulding, J. & Balch, P. (1983). A brief history of primary prevention in the twentieth century: 1908 to 1980. *American Journal of Community Psychology, 11,* 59-80.

Spilton-Koretz, D. (1991). Prevention-centered science in mental health. *American Journal of Community Psychology, 19(4),* 453-459.

Spivack, G. & Shure, M. B. (1982). The cognition of social adjustment: Interpersonal cognitive problem-solving and thinking. In B. B. Lahey & A. E. Kazdin (Eds.), *Advances in clinical psychology* (Vol. 5, pp. 323-372). New York: Plenum.

Spivack, G., Platt, J. J., & Shure, M. B. (1976). *The problem-solving approach to adjustment.* San Francisco: Jossey-Bass.

Spoth, R., Reyes, M. L., Redmond, C., & Shin, C. (1999). Assessing a public health approach to delay onset and progression of adolescent substance use: Latent transition and log-linear analyses of longitudinal family preventive intervention outcomes. *Journal of Consulting and Clinical Psychology, 67(5),* 619-630.

Spoth, R., Redmond, C., & Lepper, H. (1999). Alcohol initiation outcomes of universal family-focused preventive interventions: One-and two-year follow-ups of a controlled study. *Journal of Studies on Alcohol, Suppl. 13,* 103-111.

Spoth, R., Redmond, C., & Shin, C. (1998). Direct and indirect latent-variable parenting outcomes of two universal family-focused preventive interventions: Extending a public health oriented research base. *Journal of Consulting and Clinical Psychology, 66(2),* 385-399.

Spooner, C. (1999). Causes and correlates of adolescent drug abuse and implications for treatment. *Drug and Alcohol Review, 18,* 453-475.

Sroufe, L. A. (1997). Psychopathology as an outcome of development. *Development and Psychopathology, 9,* 251-268.

Stanton, B., Li, X., Black, M., Feigleman, S., Ricardo, I., Galbraith, J., Kaljee,L., & Nesbitt, R. (1995). Development of a culturally theoretically and developmentally based survey instrument for assessing risk behaviors among African-American early adolescents. *AIDS Education Prevention, 7,* 160-177.

Stanton, B., Li, X., Ricardo, I., Galbraith, Feigleman, S., & Kaljee,L. (1996). A randomized effectiveness trial of an AIDS prevention program for low-income African-American youth. *Archives of Pediatric Adolescent Medicine, 150,* 363-372.

Stattin, H. (2000). *An integrated, community based prevention program for reducing the risk for advanced alcohol drinking among adolescents*. Manuscript in preparation. Center for Developmental Research, University of Örebro, Örebro, Sweden.

Stattin, H. & Kerr, M. (2000). Parental monitoring: A reinterpretation. *Child Development, 71*(4), 1072-1085.

Stearns, P. N. (2003, May 2). Expanding the agenda of cultural research. *The Chronicle of Higher Education*, p. B7-B9.

Steinhausen, H. (1995). Children of alcoholic parents: A review. *European Child & Adolescent Psychiatry, 4*, 419-432.

Sternberg, R. J. (1997). The triarchic theory of intelligence. In D. P. Flanagan, J. L. Genshaft, & P. L. Harrison (Eds.), *Contemporary intellectual assessment: Theories, tests, and issues* (pp. 92-104). New York: The Guilford Press.

Stevens, V., Van-Oost, P., & de-Bourdeaudhuij, I. (2000). The effects of an anti-bullying intervention programme on peers' attitudes and behaviour. *Journal of Adolescence, 23*, 21-34.

Stevens, V., De-Bourdeaudhuij, I., & Van-Oost, P. (2000). Bullying in Flemish schools: An evaluation of anti-bullying intervention in primary and secondary schools. *British Journal of Educational Psychology, 70*, 195-210.

Storefront/Youth Action (1987). *Project Charlie Manual*. Edina, Minnesota: Storefront/Youth Action.

Strauss, A., & Corbin, J. (1998). *Basics of qualitative research: Techniques and procedures for developing grounded theory*. Thousand Oaks, CA: Sage.

Substance Abuse and Mental Health Services Administration. (1996). Tobacco regulation for substance abuse prevention and treatment block grants: Final rule. *Federal Registry, 16* (13), 1492-1500.

Sulkunen, P. & Simpura, J. (1997). Alcohol policy, the state and the local community. In M. Holmila (Ed.), *Community prevention of alcohol problems* (pp. 23-40). London: MacMillan Press.

Super, C. M. & Harkness, S. (1986). Developmental niche: A conceptualization at the interface of child and culture. *International Journal of Behavioral Development, 9*, 545-569.

Super, C. M. & Harkness, S. (1999). The environment as culture in developmental research. In S. L. Friedman & T. D. Wachs (Eds.), *Measuring environment across the life span* (pp.279-323). Washington, DC: American Psychological Association.

Super, C. M. & Harkness, S. (2002). Culture structures the environment for development. *Human Development, 45*, 270-274.

Sussman, S., Dent C. W., & Galaif, E. R. (1997). The correlates of substance abuse and dependence among adolescents at high risk for drug abuse. *Journal of Substance Abuse, 9*, 241-255.

Sussman, S., Dent, C. W., Simon, T. R., & Stacy, A. W. (1995). Immediate impact of social influence-oriented substance abuse prevention curricula in traditional and continuation high schools. *Drugs & Society, 8*, 65-81.

Swedish National Board for Youth Affairs. (1997). *Young Sweden*. Stockholm, Sweden: Author.

Swedish Society for Youth Centers (FSUM). (1994). *Sweden's youth centers: Policy program and guide to start your own center*. Garnisonstryckeriet.

Swedish Society for Youth Centers (FSUM). (1997). *UM. Sveriges ungdomsmottagningars policyprogram och guide för nya ungdomsmottagningar* (3rd edition). Lund: Sweden: Rhams.

Swisher, J. D. (2000). Sustainability of prevention. *Addictive Behaviors, 25*(6), 965-973.

Sylva, K. & Hurry, J. (1995). *The effectiveness of Reading Recovery and phonological training for children with reading problems: Full report*. Report prepared for the School Curriculum Committee and Assessment Authority. London: SCAA.

Szapocznik, J. & Kurtines, W. (1989). *Break-throughs in family therapy with drug abusing and problem youth.* New York: Springer.

Szapocznik, J. & Williams, R. A. (2000). Brief Strategic Family Therapy: Twenty five years of interplay among theory, research, and practice in adolescent behavior problems and drug abuse. *Clinical Child and Family Psychology Review, 3*(2), 117-135.

Tableman, B. (2001). *Effective home visitation for very young children* (Best Practice Brief No. 17). East Lansing: Michigan State University, University Outreach Partnerships.

Tammi, T. & Peltoniemi, T. (1999). (Eds.). *Telematic drug and alcohol prevention: Guidelines and experiences from PREVNET EURO.* Helsinki, Finland: Painotalo Aurane, Forssa.

Tanner, D. (1972). *Secondary education.* New York: MacMillian.

Tattum, D. (1997). A whole-school response: From crisis management to prevention. *Irish Journal of Psychology, 18,* 221-232.

Taylor, A. S., LoSciuto, L., Fox, M., Hilbert, S. M., & Sonkowsky, M. (1999). The mentoring factor: Evaluation of the across ages' intergenerational approach to drug abuse prevention. *Child and Youth Services, 20,* 77-99.

Taylor, T.K., & Biglan, A. (1998). Behavioral family interventions for improving child-rearing: A review of the literature for clinicians and policy makers. *Clinical Child and Family Psychology Review, 1*(1), 41-60.

Taylor, T., Eddy, J. M., & Biglan, A. (1999). Interpersonal skills training to reduce aggressive and delinquent behavior: Limited evidence and the need for an evidence-based system of care. *Clinical Child and Family Psychology Review, 2,* 169-182.

Taylor, T., Schmidt, F., Pepler, D., & Hodgins, C., (1998). A comparison of eclectic treatment with Webster-Stratton's parents and children series in a children's mental health center: A randomized controlled trial. *Behavior Therapy, 29,* 221-240.

Tazeau, Y. N. (2003, June). *Mental health of elderly Latinos: The intersection of indigenous Latino healing systems and Western European psychiatric medicine.* Symposium presented at the Society for Prevention Research, Washington, DC.

Tebes, J. K., Kaufman, J. S., & Connell, C. M. (2003). The evaluation of prevention and health promotion programs. In T. Gullotta & M. Bloom (Series Ed.) & T. Gullotta & M. Bloom (Vol. Ed.), *The encyclopedia of primary prevention and health promotion: Foundations Volume* (pp. 42-61). New York: Kluwer Academic/Plenum.

Tell, G. S., Klepp, K. I., Vellar, O. D., & McAlister, A. L. (1984). Preventing the onset of cigarette smoking in Norwegian adolescents: The Oslo Youth Study. *Preventive Medicine, 13,* 256-275.

Terry, J. (1999). A community/school mentoring program for elementary students. *Professional School Counseling, 2,* 237-240.

Thayer, Y. V. (1996). The Virginia model: School to community intervention techniques to prevent violence. In A. M. Hoffman (Ed.), *Schools, violence, and society* (pp. 275-295). Wesport, CT: Praeger Publishers/Greenwood Publishing Group, Inc.

The Economist. (2003, June 14). *Dancing to a new tune: A survey of the Nordic region.* S1-16.

Thompson, R. A., Easterbrooks, M. A., & Padilla-Walker, L. M. (2003). Social and emotional development in infancy. In I. B. Weiner (Series Ed.) & R. M. Lerner, M. A. Easterbrooks, & J. Mistry (Vol. Eds.), *Comprehensive handbook of psychology: Vol. 6. Developmental psychology* (pp. 91-112). New York: Wiley.

Tierney, J. & Grossman, J. B. (2000). What works in promoting positive youth development: Mentoring. In M. P. Kluger, G. Alexander, P. A. Curtis (Eds.), *What works in child welfare* (pp. 323-328). Washington, DC: CWLA Press.

Tierney, J. Grossman, J. B., & Resch, N. L. (1995). *Making a difference: An impact study of Big Brothers/Big Sisters.* Philadelphia, PA: Public/Private Ventures.

Tobler, N. S. (1992). Drug prevention programs can work: Research findings. *Journal of Addictive Diseases, 11,* 1-28.

Tobler, N. S., Lessard, T., Marshall, D., Ochshorn, P., & Roona, M. (1999). Effectiveness of school-based drug prevention programs for marijuana use. *School Psychology International, 20*, 105-137.

Tobler, N. S., Roona, M. R., Ochshorn, P., Marshall, D. G., Streke, A. V., & Stackpole, K. M. (2000). School-based adolescent drug prevention programs: 1998 meta-analysis. *Journal of Primary Prevention, 20*(4): 275-336.

Tobler, N. S. & Stratton, H. H. (1997). Effectiveness of school-based drug prevention programs: A meta-analysis of the research. *Journal of Primary Prevention, 18,* 71-128.

Tolan, P. H. & Guerra, N. G. (1994). Prevention of delinquency: Current status and issues. *Applied and Preventive Psychology, 3*, 251-273.

Tolan, P. H., Quintana, E., Gorman-Smith, D. (1998). Prevention approaches for families. In L. L'Abate (Ed.), *Family psychopathology: The relational roots of dysfunctional behavior* (pp. 379-400). New York: Guilford Press.

Tompkins, N. O., Dino, G. A., Zedosky, L. K., Harman, M., & Shaler, G. (1999). A collaborative partnership to enhance school-based tobacco control policies in West Virginia. *American Journal of Preventive Medicine, 16*(3S), 29-34.

Tremblay, R. E., Masse, B., Perron, D., & LeBlanc, M. (1992). Early disruptive behavior, poor school achievement, delinquent behavior, and delinquent personality: Longitudinal analyses. *Journal of Consulting and Clinical Psychology, 60,* 64-72.

Tremblay, R. E., Pagani-Kurtz, L, Masse, L. C., Vitaro, F., & Pihl, R. O. (1995). A bimodal preventive intervention for disruptive kindergarten boys: Its impact through mid-adolescence. *Journal of Consulting and Clinical Psychology, 63*, 560-568.

Treno, A. J., & Holder, H. D. (1997). Community mobilization: evaluation of an environmental approach to local action. *Addiction, 92* (supplement 2), S173-S187.

Trickett, E. J. (2002). Context, culture, and collaboration in AIDS interventions: Ecological ideas for enhancing community impact. *Journal of Primary Prevention, 23*(2), 157-174.

Tsiantis, J., Dragonas, Th., Cox, A., Smith, M., Ispanovic, V., & Sampaio-Faria, J. (1996). Promotion of children's early psychosocial development through primary health care services. *Paediatric and Perinatal Epidemiology, 10*, 339-354.

Tubman, J. G., Vento-Soza, R., Barr, J. E., & Langer, L. M. (2002). Teachers' perceptions of tobacco use prevention education (TUPE) programs in Florida: Relations with perceived barriers and other contextual factors. *Journal of Child and Adolescent Substance Abuse, 11*(3), 63-88.

Tubman, J. G., Windle, M., & Windle, R. C. (1996). Cumulative sexual intercourse patterns among middle adolescents: Problem behavior precursors and concurrent health risk behaviors. *Journal of Adolescent Health, 18,* 182-191.

Turner, G. & Shepherd, J. (1999). A method in search of a theory: Peer education and health promotion. *Health Education Research, 14*, 235-247.

UNAIDS. (1998). Social marketing: An effective tool in the global response to HIV/AIDS. New York: Author.

United Nations. (1948). *Universal Declaration of Human Rights* (Resolution 217 A III). Office of the High Commissioner for Human Rights. Geneva, Switzerland.

U.S. Census Bureau (2001a, May, 7). *Participant statistical areas program. Census 2000 Statistical Areas Boundary Criteria.* Retrived from: http://www.census.gov/geo/www/psapage.html

U.S. Census Bureau (2001b, May, 7). *Geographic areas reference manual.* Retrived from: http://www.census.gov/geo/www/garm.html

U.S. Department of Health and Human Services. (1992). *Smoking and health in the Americas.* Atlanta, GA: Author. DHHS Publication No. (CDC) 92-8419.

U.S. Department of Health and Human Services. (1999). *Blending perspectives and building common ground: A report to Congress on substance abuse and child protection.* Washington, DC: U.S. Government Printing Office.

Utting, D. (Ed.), (1999). *A guide to promising approaches: Communities that Care.* London: Communities that Care.

van den Boom, D. C. (1994). The influence of temperament and mothering on attachment and exploration: An experimental manipulation of sensitive responsiveness among lower class mothers with irritable infants. *Child Development, 65,* 1449-1469.

van den Boom, D. C. (1995). Do first-year intervention effects endure? Follow-up during toddlerhood of a sample of Dutch irritable infants. *Child Development, 66,* 1798-1816.

van Ijzendoorn, M. H., Juffer, F., & Duyvesteyn, M. G. C. (1995). Breaking the intergenerational cycle of insecure attachment: A review of the effects of attachment-based interventions on maternal sensitivity and infant security. *Journal of Child Psychology and Psychiatry, 36,* 225-248.

van Ijzendoorn, M. H., Schuengel, C., & Bakermans-Kranenburg, M. J. (1999). Disorganized attachment in early childhood: Meta-analysis of precursors, concomitants, and sequelae. *Development and Psychopathology, 11,* 225-249.

Vartiainen, E., Paavola, M., McAlister, A., & Puska, P. (1998). Fifteen-year follow-up of smoking prevention effects in the North Karelia Youth Project. *American Journal of Public Health, 88,* 81-85.

Vartiainen, E., Pallonen, U., McAlister, A., Koskela, K., & Puska, P. (1986). Four-year follow-up results of the smoking prevention program in the North Karelia Youth Project. *Prevention Medicine, 15,* 692-698.

Vartiainen, E., Pallonen, U., McAlister, A., & Puska, P. (1990). Eight-year follow-up results of an adolescent smoking prevention program: the North Karelia Youth Project. *American Journal of Public Health, 80,* 78-79.

Vartiainen, E., Saukko, A., Paavola, M., & Vertio, H. (1996). No Smoking Class competitions in Finland: their value in delaying the onset of smoking in adolescence. *Health Promotion International, 11,* 189-192.

Vincent, M. L., Clearie, A. F., & Schluchter, M. D. (1987). Reducing adolescent pregnancy through school- and community-based education. *Journal of the American Medical Association, 257,* 3382-3386.

Volkow, N. D. (2003, June). *Prevention research: Progress in the field, gaps in the knowledge base and future research initiatives.* Symposium presented at the Society for Prevention Research, Washington, DC.

Vries, Hans P. de (2001). *Smoke Free Teams project.* Evaluatieverslag, GGD Noord-Kennemerland, Alkmaar, The Netherlands.

Wagenaar, A. C., Gehan, J. P., Jones-Webb, R., Toomey, T. L., Forster, J. L., Wolfson, M., & Murray, D. M. (1999). Communities Mobilizing for Change on Alcohol: Lessons and results from a 15-community randomized trial. *Journal of Community Psychology, 27,* 315-326.

Wagenaar, A. C., Murray, D. M., Gehan, J. P., Wolfson, M., Forster, J. L., Toomey, T. L., Perry, C. L., & Jones-Webb, R. (2000). Communities mobilizing for change on alcohol: Outcomes from a randomized community trials. *Journal of Studies on Alcohol, 61,* 85-94.

Wagenaar, A. C., Murray, D. M., & Toomey, T. L. (2000). Communities Mobilizing for Change on Alcohol (CMCA): Effects of a randomized trial on arrests and traffic crashes. *Addiction, 95,* 209-217.

Wagenaar, A. C., Murray, D. M., Wolfson, M., Forster, J. L., & Finnegan, J. R. (1994). Communities mobilizing for change on alcohol: Design of a randomized community trial. *Journal of Community Psychology, CSAP Special Issue,* 79-101.

Wagenaar, A. C. & Perry, C. L. (1994). Community strategies for the reduction of youth drinking: Theory and application. *Journal of Research on Adolescence, 4,* 319-345.

Wagenaar, A. C., Toomey, T. L., Murray, D. M., Short, B. J., Wolfson, M., & Jones-Webb, R. (1996). Sources of alcohol for underage drinkers. *Journal of Studies on Alcohol, 57,* 325-333.

Wagner, E. F., Dinklage, S.C., Cudworth, C., & Vyse, J. (1999). A preliminary evaluation of the effectiveness of a standardized student assistance program. *Substance Use & Misuse, 34,* 1571-1584.

Wagner, E. F., Kortlander, E., & Leon Morris, S. (2001). The Teen Intervention Project: A school-based intervention for adolescents with substance use problems. In E.F. Wagner & H. B. Waldron (Eds.), *Innovations in adolescent substance abuse interventions* (pp. 189-203). New York: Pergamon.

Wagner, E. F., Swenson, C. C., & Henggeler, S. W. (2000). Practical and methodological challenges in validating community-based interventions. *Children's Services: Social Policy, Research and Practice, 3,* 211-231.

Walker, S.A., & Avis, M. (1999). Common reasons why peer education fails. *Journal of Adolescence, 22,* 573-577.

Walker, H. M., Stiller, B., Severson, H. H., Feil, E. G., & Golly, A. (1998). First Step to Success: Intervening at the point of school entry to prevent antisocial behavior patterns. *Psychology in the Schools, 35,* 259-269.

Walsh, J. A. (1982). Prevention in mental health: Organizational and ideological perspectives. *Social Work, 27*(4), 298-301.

Wang, M. C., Haertel, G. D., & Walberg, H. J. (1997). *Fostering educational resilience in inner-city schools.* Publication Series No. 4, Document no. ED419856. Washington, DC: Office of Educational Research and Improvement.

Ward, C. M. (1998). Student discipline and alleviating criminal behavior in the inner city. *The Urban Review, 30,* 29-48.

Ward, S. (1999). An investigation into the effectiveness of an early intervention method for delayed language development in young children. *International Journal of Language and Communication Disorders, 34*(3), 243-264.

Wasik, B. A. & Karweit, N. L. (1994). Off to a good start: Effects of birth to three interventions on early school success. In R. E. Slavin, N. L. Karwiet & B. A. Wasik (Eds.), *Preventing early school failure: Research, Policy, and Practice* (pp.13-57). Needham Heights, MA: Allyn & Bacon.

Wasik, B. H., Bryant, D. M., & Lyons, C. M. (1990). Home visiting: Procedures for helping families. Thousand Oaks, CA, US: Sage Publications, Inc.

Wasserman, G. A., & Miller, L. S. (1998). The prevention of serious and violent juvenile offending. In R. Loeber, & D. Farrington (Eds.), *Serious & violent juvenile offenders: Risk factors and successful interventions* (pp. 197-247). Thousand Oaks, CA: Sage.

Waters, E. & Sroufe, L. A. (1983). Social competence as a developmental construct. *Developmental Review, 3,* 79-97.

Webster-Stratton, C. (1981). Modification of mothers' behaviors and attitudes through a videotape modeling group discussion program. *Behavior Therapy, 12,* 634-642.

Webster-Stratton, C. (1982). The long term effects of a videotape modeling parent-training program: comparison of immediate and 1 year follow-up results. *Behavior Therapy, 13,* 702-714.

Webster-Stratton, C. (1984). Randomized trial of two parent-training programs for families with conduct-disordered children. *Journal of Consulting and Clinical Psychology, 52,* 666-678.

Webster-Stratton, C. (1990a). Long term follow-up of families with young conduct problem children: From preschool to grade school. *Journal of Clinical Child Psychology, 19,* 144-149.

Webster-Stratton, C. (1990b). Enhancing the effectiveness of self-administered videotape parent training for families with conduct-problem children. *Journal of Abnormal Child Psychology, 18* (5), 479-492.

Webster-Stratton, C. (1992). Individually administered videotape parent training: Who benefits? *Cognitive Therapy and Research, 16* (1), 31-35.

Webster-Stratton, C. (1998a). *The Incredible Years: Parents, Teachers, and Children Training Series.* School of Nursing, University of Washington, Seattle, Washington, U.S.A.

Webster-Stratton, C. (1998b). Preventing conduct problems in Head Start children: Strengthening parenting competencies. *Journal of Consulting and Clinical Psychology, 66,* 715-730.

Webster-Stratton, C. (1998c). Parent training with low-income families: Promoting parental engagement through a collaborative approach. In J. R. Lutzker (Ed.), *Handbook of child abuse research and treatment* (pp. 183-210). New York: Plenum Press.

Webster-Stratton, C. (2001). Commentary: nipping conduct problems in the bud. *British Medical Journal, 323,* 7.

Webster-Stratton, C., & Hammond, M. (1997). Treating children with early-onset conduct problems: A comparison of child and parent training interventions. *Journal of Consulting and Clinical Psychology, 65*(1), 93-109.

Webster-Stratton, C., Hollinsworth, T., & Kolpacoff, M. (1989). The long-term effectiveness and clinical significance of three cost-effective training programs for families with conduct-problem children. *Journal of Consulting and Clinical Psychology, 57*(4), 550-553.

Webster-Stratton, C., Kolpacoff, M., & Hollinsworth, T. (1988). Self administered videotape therapy for families with conduct problem children: Comparison with two cost-effective treatments and a control group. *Journal of Consulting and Clinical Psychology, 56*(4), 558-566.

Webster-Stratton, C., Reid, M. J., & Hammond, M. (2001). Preventing conduct problems, promoting social competence: A parent and teacher training partnership in Head Start. *Journal of Community Psychology, 30*(3), 283-302.

Weikart, D. P. & Schweinhart, L. J. (1997). High/Scope Perry Preschool Program. In G. W. Albee & T. P. Gullotta (Eds.), *Primary prevention works* (pp. 146-166). Thousand Oaks, CA: Sage.

Weiss, C. H. (1998). Improving the use of evaluations: Whose job is it anyway? In A. J. Reynolds, & H. J. Walberg (Eds.), *Advances in educational productivity, Vol. 7: Evaluation research for educational productivity* (pp. 263-276). Stamford: JAI Press, Inc.

Weiss, S. J. & Seed, M. S-J. (2002). Precursors of mental health problems for low birth weight children: The salience of family environment during the first year of life. *Child Psychiatry and Human Development, 33*(1), 3-27.

Weissberg, R. P., Caplan, M., & Harwood, R. L. (1991). Promoting competent young people in competence-enhancing environments: A systems-based perspective on primary prevention. *Journal of Consulting and Clinical Psychology, 59,* 830-841.

Weissberg, R. P. & Greenberg, M. T. (1998). School and community competence-enhancement and prevention programs. In W. Damon (Series Ed.) & I. E. Sigel & K. A. Renninger (Vol. Eds.), *Handbook of child psychology: Vol. 5. Child psychology in practice* (5th ed, pp. 877-954). New York: John Wiley.

Weisz, J. R., Weiss, B., Han, S. S., Granger, D. A., Morton, T. (1995). Effects of psychotherapy with children and adolescents revisited: A meta-analysis of treatment outcome studies. *Psychological Bulletin, 117*(3), 450-468.

Werner, E. E. (2000). Protective factors and individual resilience. In J. P. Shonkoff & S. J. Meisels (Eds.), *Handbook of early childhood intervention* (pp. 115-132). New York: Cambridge University Press.

Westerman, M. A. & La Luz, E. J. (1995). Marital adjustment and children's academic achievement. *Merrill-Palmer Quarterly, 41,* 453-470.

White, D. & Pitts, M. (1998). Educating young people about drugs: A systematic review. *Addiction, 93,* 1475-1487.

Wiborg, G. & Hanewinkel, R. (2002). Effectiveness of the "Smokefree Class Competition" in delaying the onset of smoking in adolescence. *Preventive Medicine, 35*(3): 241-249.

Wikström, P.-O. H. (1995). Preventing city-center street crimes. *Crime and Justice, 19,* 429-468.

Wilson, S. J. & Lipsey, M. W. (2000a). *Effects of school violence prevention programs on aggressive and disruptive behavior: A meta-analysis of outcome evaluations.* Manuscript in preparation. Vanderbilt University, Nashville, Tennessee, U.S.A.

Wilson, S. J. & Lipsey, M. W. (2000b). Wilderness challenge programs for delinquent youth: a meta-analysis of outcome evaluations. *Evaluation and Program Planning, 23,* 1-12.

Wood, D. & O'Malley, C. (1996). Collaborative learning between peers. *Educational Psychology in Practice, 11*(4), 4-9.

Woolfenden, S. R., Williams, K., & Peat, J. (2003). Family and parenting interventions in children and adolescents with conduct disorder and delinquency aged 10-17 (Cochrane Review). In: *The Cochrane Library,* Issue 1, 2003. Oxford: Update Software.

Worden, J. K. (1999). Research in using mass media to prevent smoking. *Nicotine & Tobacco Research, 1,* S117-S121.

Worden, J. K., Flynn, B. S., Solomon, L. J., & Secker-Walker, R. H. (1996). Using mass media to prevent cigarette smoking among adolescent girls. *Health Education Quarterly, 23,* 453-468.

Worden, J. K., Flynn, B. S., Solomon, L. J., Secker-Walker, R. H., Badger, G. J., & Carpenter, J. F. (1996). Using mass media to prevent cigarette smoking among adolescent girls. *Health Education Quarterly, 23,* 453-468.

World Health Organization. (2000). *European alcohol action plan.* Copenhagen, Denmark: WHO Regional Office for Europe.

World Health Organization. (2001). *European Minister Conference: Young people and alcohol.* Stockholm, Sweden.

Yates, M. & Youniss, J. (Eds.), (1999). *Roots of civic identity: International perspectives on community service and activism in youth* (pp. 114-134). New York: Cambridge University Press.

Yoshikawa, H. (1994). Prevention as cumulative protection: Effects of early family support and education on chronic delinquency and its risks. *Psychological Bulletin, 115*(1), 28-54.

Young, S. (1998). The support group approach to bullying in schools. *Educational Psychology in Practice, 14,* 32-39.

Young Men's Christian Association. (2001). *YMCAs at a glance.* Author.

Youniss, J. (1994). Children's friendship and peer culture: Implications for theories of networks and support. In F. Nestmann & K. Hurrelmann (Eds.), *Social networks and social support in childhood and adolescence* (pp. 75-88). Oxford, England: Walter De Gruyter.

Youniss, J., & Smollar, J. (1989). Adolescents' interpersonal relationships in social context. In T. J. Berndt, G. W. Ladd (Eds.), *Peer relationships in child development. Wiley series on personality processes* (pp.300-316). New York: John Wiley & Sons.

Youniss, J., McLellan, J. A., Su, Y., & Yates, M. (1999). The role of community service in identity development: Normative, unconventional, and deviant orientations. *Journal of Adolescent Research, 14*(2), 248-261.

Youniss, J. & Yates, M (1997). *Community service and social responsibility in youth.* Chicago, IL: University of Chicago Press.

Youniss, J. & Yates, M. (1999). Youth service and moral-civic identity: A case for everyday morality. *Educational Psychology Review, 11*(4), 361-376.

Yung, B. R. & Hammond, W. R. (1998). Breaking the cycle: A culturally sensitive violence prevention program for African-American children and adolescents. In J. R. Lutzker (Ed.), *Handbook of child abuse research and treatment: Issues in clinical child psychology* (pp. 319-340). New York: Plenum Press.

Zabin, L. S. (1992). School-linked reproductive health services: The Johns Hopkins program. In B. C. Miller, J. J. Card, R. L. Paikoff, & J. L. Peterson (Eds.), *Preventing adolescent pregnancy: Model programs and evaluations* (pp. 156-184). Sage focus editions, Vol. 140. Thousand Oaks, CA: Sage Publications, Inc.

Zabin, L. S., Hirsch, M.B., Streett, R., Emerson, M.R., Smith, M., Hardy, J.B., & King, T.M. (1988). The Baltimore Pregnancy Prevention Program for Urban Teenagers. *Family Planning Perspectives, 20* (4), 182-187.

Zeldin, S. (1995). Community-university collaborations for youth development: From theory to practice. *Journal of Adolescent Research, 10*(4), 449-469.

Zoerink, D. A., Magafas, A. H., & Pawelko, K. A. (1997). Empowering youth at risk through community service. *Child and Youth Care Forum, 26*(2), 127-138.

Index

Note: Page numbers in boldface refer to terms defined in the Glossary.